SOCIAL POLICY REVIEW 32

Analysis and Debate
in Social Policy, 2020

Edited by
James Rees, Marco Pomati and Elke Heins

First published in Great Britain in 2020 by

Policy Press
University of Bristol
1-9 Old Park Hill
Bristol
BS2 8BB
UK
t: +44 (0)117 954 5940
pp-info@bristol.ac.uk
www.policypress.co.uk

British Library Cataloguing in Publication Data
A catalogue record for this book is available from the British Library.

ISBN 978-1-4473-4166-6 hardback
ISBN 978-1-4473-5559-5 paperback SPA members' edition (not on general release)
ISBN 978-1-4473-5560-1 ePdf

Cover design by Policy Press
Front cover image: Getty Images 686797325
Printed and bound in Great Britain by CPI Group (UK)
Ltd, Croydon, CR0 4YY
Policy Press uses environmentally responsible print partners

Contents

List of figures and tables   v
Notes on contributors   vii

Part I: Race, racism and social policy   1
James Rees

1   Race and social policy: challenges and obstacles   5
     Nasar Meer
2   'Race': the missing dimension in social policy higher education? 25
     Bankole Cole, Gary Craig and Nasreen Ali
3   Young people as cultural critics of the monocultural   51
     landscapes that fail them
     Rick Bowler and Amina Razak
4   Returnees: unwanted citizens or cherished countrymen   71
     Bozena Sojka and Maarja Saar

Part II: Social policy and young people   93
Elke Heins

5   The family welfare source and inequality in liberal welfare   97
     states: evidence from cohort studies
     Sarah Weakley
6   Economic hardship in young adulthood: a cause for concern   135
     or a matter of course while settling into the Swedish labour
     market?
     Anna Kahlmeter
7   Cultural education and the good citizen: a systematic analysis 163
     of a neoliberal communitarian policy trend
     Katherine Tonkiss, Malgorzata Wootton and Eleni Stamou
8   How geographical and ideological proximity impact   183
     community youth justice (in)accessibility in England
     and Wales
     Sarah Brooks-Wilson

Part III: Austerity   207
Marco Pomati

9   After a decade of austerity, does the UK have an income   211
        safety net worth its name?
        Donald Hirsch
10   A new page? The public library in austerity   227
        Emma Davidson
11   No way home: the challenges of exiting homelessness   249
        in austere times
        Christina Carmichael
12   'Everywhere and nowhere': interventions and services   271
        under austerity
        Stephen Crossley

Index   291

List of figures and tables

Figures

2.1	Comparison between BAME and 'White' student numbers at UK universities (2008–17) for all courses listed under 'Social Policy' (%)	32
2.2	Higher education participation by ethnic group and socio-economic status (2010–12)	34
2.3	Proportion of key stage 5 leavers at an HEI by detailed ethnicity (2015/16)	35
2.4	Non-continuation rates among UK-domiciled first degree students in English HEIs (2008–15)	37
6.1	State distribution across time by cluster	148
9.1	Changes in weekly minimum income entitlements since 1997 (in 2019 prices)	215
9.2	Supplementary Benefit/IS compared to average weekly earnings for a single person (1969–2019)	216
9.3	Safety-net benefits relative to MIS (2010–19)	219
9.4	Policy effects on the percentage of MIS covered by the safety net (2019)	222

Tables

2.1	Type of university offering some form of Social Policy course	28
2.2	Breakdown of students by ethnicity for all courses listed under 'Social Policy' in UK universities (2008–17)	31
2.3	UK BAME representation in *JSP*	45
2.4	UK BAME representation in *SPS*	45
2.5	UK BAME representation in *SPR*	45
2.6	UK BAME representation in *CSP*	45
2.7	BAME representation at annual SPA conferences	46
5.1	Key features of empirical models	105
5.2	Correlated random effects model of monthly wages (ln), BCS 1970 sample	106
5.3	Ordered logistic regression of gross household income (2012), BCS 1970 sample	108

5.4	Longitudinal ordered logit models of work intensity, BCS 1970 sample	110
5.5	Longitudinal ordered logit models of waged work intensity, NLSY 1997	112
5.6	Correlated random effects models of logged annual employment income, NLSY 1997	114
5.7	Longitudinal ordered logit models of poverty ratio, NLSY 1997	118
6.1	The SELMA model	141
6.2	Sample characteristics by degree of economic hardship in 2001 (row %)	144
6.3	Characteristics of labour market sequences by degree of economic hardship in 2001	146
6.4	Average marginal effects of economic hardship from multinomial logistic regression – low and high degree of social assistance receipt, compared to no receipt	149
6.5	Sensitivity analyses for multinomial logit model RRR estimates	150
6.A1	Sample characteristics by cluster of labour market establishment trajectory (row %)	158
6.A2	Multinomial logit model, predictions (RRR) of labour market establishment trajectory	162
8.1	A typology of children's institutional disengagement	185
10.1	Number of public libraries open more than ten hours per week (2008–18)	233
10.2	Number of staff and volunteers (2008–18)	235

Notes on contributors

Nasreen Ali is Reader at the University of Bedfordshire and her research focuses on taking an intersectional approach to looking at the way in which gender, ethnicity and health impact on how black, Asian and minority ethnic (BAME) groups experience health and illness. She is Editor in Chief for the *Journal of Diversity and Equality in Health and Care*.

Rick Bowler is Senior Lecturer at the University of Sunderland. Rick's work involves sharing time between teaching, research and outreach. His pedagogical interests focus on transformative approaches to critical youth-work practice. Rick has extensive community youth-work experience connecting therapeutic with sociocultural explanations of the lifeworlds of young people. His doctoral study focused on anti-racist youth-work practice in monocultural settings. He draws upon an intersectional Critical Race Theory lens to trouble the white standards that perpetuate British racism. Rick was chairperson of the Young Asian Voices youth project from its formation in 1996 until 2003.

Sarah Brooks-Wilson is Lecturer in Criminology in the Department of Social Policy, Sociology and Criminology at the University of Birmingham. Current research interests include the new mobilities paradigm, transport and youth justice, institutional accessibility, and the journey inequalities experienced by populations with complex needs. Sarah recently co-produced the service accessibility resource 'Shifting Journey Cards' with children in the justice system (for further details, see: www.accessing-services.com).

Christina Carmichael is a member of the School of Social Work at the University of East Anglia, where she is currently completing her doctorate. The central focus of her research is the lived experiences of single homeless people and professionals working in the homelessness sector in the context of the post-2010 austerity programme.

Bankole Cole is Reader in Criminology and Human Rights at the Helena Kennedy Centre for International Justice, Department of Law and Criminology, Sheffield Hallam University. He has taught 'race', crime and justice topics at Lincoln, Hull, York and Northumbria universities. His areas of specialism are policing, youth and criminal justice. His publications include: 'Young people, "race" and criminal justice' in Chattoo et al (eds) *Understanding 'race' and ethnicity* (Policy Press. 2019); *Racism in the North East* (with Craig, O'Neil and Antonopoloous) (Durham University, 2012); *Globalisation, citizenship and the War on Terror* (edited with M. Mullard) (Edward Elgar, 2007); and *Black and Asian offenders on probation* (with Calverley, Kaur, Lewis, Raynor, Sadeghi, Smith, Vanstone and Wardak) (Home Office, 2004).

Gary Craig is Emeritus Professor of Social Justice and Visiting Professor at the Law School, University of Newcastle upon Tyne. He has worked half his adult life in community-based organisations and half in academic settings, including five universities. His research interests are 'race' and ethnicity, migration, and modern slavery. Recent books include *The modern slavery agenda* (with others) (Policy Press, 2019) and *Global social justice* (Edward Elgar, 2020).

Stephen Crossley is Assistant Professor at Durham University. He completed his PhD from Durham University examining the UK government's Troubled Families Programme in August 2017. Prior to this, he worked on a regional child poverty project in the North-East, based in the Institute for Local Governance at Durham University. He has also worked in a variety of neighbourhood management and community development roles for local authorities and voluntary sector organisations across the North-East. His first book, *In their place: The imagined geographies of poverty*, was published by Pluto Press in 2017, and his second book, *Troublemakers: The construction of 'troubled families' as a social problem*, was published by Policy Press in 2018.

Emma Davidson is Leverhulme Early Career Senior Research Fellow at the University of Edinburgh and Co-director of the Centre for Research on Families and Relationships (CRFR). Her work is concerned with the relationship between macro-socio-economic structures and micro-personal experiences, and typically draws on qualitative methods that help understand people and their lives from their own vantage points. Emma's current study, 'A new page? Libraries, austerity and the shifting boundaries of civil society', is funded by the Leverhulme Trust and aims to explore the everyday social worlds of public libraries and the challenges they face under austerity.

Elke Heins is Senior Lecturer in Social Policy at the School of Social and Political Science, University of Edinburgh. Her research interests mainly focus on comparative and European social policy, as well as the politics of welfare in the UK. She has most recently co-edited *Social policy review 30* and *Social policy review 31* (with Catherine Needham and James Rees) (Policy Press, 2018, 2019).

Donald Hirsch is Professor of Social Policy and Director of the Centre for Research in Social Policy at Loughborough University. A former journalist and international policy consultant, he was poverty advisor to the Joseph Rowntree Foundation for the ten years prior to joining CRSP in 2008. He played a central role in establishing a Minimum Income Standard for the UK, CRSP's ongoing research programme showing what incomes households need for an acceptable standard of living as agreed by members of the public. He has written widely on the adequacy of the public welfare system and on poverty trends.

Anna Kahlmeter is a PhD candidate in Sociology at the Swedish Institute for Social Research (SOFI), Stockholm University. Her research interests primarily concern poverty, inequality of opportunity and processes of social exclusion, with a particular focus on youth. Her PhD project concerns issues of youth-to-adulthood transitions and stressful life events. She has previously published research on housing eviction issues. Prior to her doctoral studies, she had several years of experience as a social worker practising mostly with young adults with substance abuse and precarious housing conditions.

Nasar Meer is Professor of Race, Identity and Citizenship in the School of Social and Political Sciences at the University of Edinburgh. He is Editor in Chief of the journal *Identities: Global Studies in Culture and Power*. His publications include: *Islam and modernity* (4 vols) (ed, 2017); *Interculturalism and multiculturalism: Debating the dividing lines* (co-ed, 2016); *Citizenship, identity and the politics of multiculturalism* (2nd edn) (2015); *Racialization and religion* (ed, 2014); *Race and ethnicity* (2014); and *European multiculturalism(s)* (co-ed, 2012). In 2016, he was awarded the Royal Society of Edinburgh (RSE) Thomas Reid Medal for excellence in the social sciences, and in 2017, he was elected as a Fellow of the Academy of Social Sciences.

Marco Pomati is Lecturer at Cardiff University. His recent work focuses on the exploration and validation of policy-relevant living standards measures in Europe, the UK and Africa, and the relationship between low income and parenting practices in the UK.

Amina Razak is Research Associate at the University of Sunderland. Amina's research interests focus on gender, ethnicity and racism. Her doctoral thesis focused on masculinities and South Asian young men. Her study was specifically concerned with young 'South Asian', in particular, Bangladeshi and Pakistani, men, their new masculinities, and their experiences of racism. Amina has extensive experience in academic and public sector research, including researching domestic violence, forced marriage, BAME engagement and racism. Amina also currently works in the housing sector undertaking research, insight and engagement.

James Rees is Reader and Deputy Director of the Institute for Community Research and Development (ICRD) at the University of Wolverhampton. His research focuses on the third sector, public service delivery and reform, as well as leadership, governance and citizen involvement. He is co-editor of *Voluntary Sector Review* (Policy Press).

Maarja Saar works as a post-doctoral researcher at Södertörn University and as a Research Assistant at the University of Bristol. Her research mostly engages with various issues related to migration. She has approached the topic of migration from two main angles: from the welfare perspective; and from the perspective of reflexivity. Her current project focuses on the welfare strategies of migrant lone mothers.

Bozena Sojka is a Research Fellow at the Institute for Community Research and Development (ICRD) at the University of Wolverhampton, UK. Her research interests are in geographies of migration, social policy and governance analysis as a new approach to the interpretation of public policy in a wide range of institutional settings. Her current research focuses on the emotional health and well-being of children and young people seeking asylum support in Wolverhampton. Recently, she co-authored a book chapter with Emma Carmel on 'Social security and "management" of migration' in the third edition of *Understanding social security: Issues for policy and practice* (Policy Press, 2018).

Eleni Stamou is Research Fellow on the Cultural Heritage and Identities of Europe's Future (CHIEF) project at the University of

Aston, Birmingham. She is a sociologist of education with over ten years' experience in social and educational research. She has worked in the areas of youth identities and educational pathways, inclusion and the prevention of social exclusion, and the analysis of education policy in practice. Previously, she has held research posts at the University College London Institute of Education and the University of Oxford.

Katherine Tonkiss is Senior Lecturer in Sociology and Policy at Aston University. Her work is primarily concerned with critically interrogating the relationship between citizenship and national identity. Her current research examines post-national practices of community and resistance in migration rights struggles, and explores the intersection of national identity, belonging and diversity in the UK. Katherine's work has been funded by the Economic and Social Research Council (ESRC), the British Academy and, most recently, the European Commission.

Sarah Weakley is Research and Impact Officer at Policy Scotland at the University of Glasgow. Her research focuses on poverty and inequality, social security in the US and UK, and young people's transitions to adulthood.

Malgorzata Wootton is a PhD student at Aston University and Research Assistant on the Cultural Heritage and Identities of Europe's Future (CHIEF) project. She is currently working on a PhD thesis with the working title of 'Migration and national identity in transnational social spaces: comparative study between post-WW2 and post-Cold War migration from Poland to the UK'.

Part I
Race, racism and social policy

James Rees

The last decade has seen an unmistakable rise of new forms of (primarily) online activism driven by the social justice commitments of younger generations, facilitated by social media and new technologies, highlighting and tackling entrenched forms of inequality and discrimination. The rise of such broad-based movements as #BlackLivesMatter or #Metoo (from 2013 and 2017, respectively) has been augmented by more specific initiatives in relation to race and racism. Of particular note has been the Rhodes Must Fall campaign at the University of Oxford and elsewhere, as well as wider calls to decolonise university curricula (Why is My Curriculum White?), usually targeted at specific disciplinary areas; indeed, these have had echoes outside of academia, such as the recent Twitter campaign #CharitySoWhite. Of course, this cannot fail to have influenced particular academic disciplines and Social Policy is not alone in urgently needing to come to terms with this challenge. The Royal Historical Society established an inquiry into racial and ethnic inequalities in the teaching and practice of History in the UK, resulting in its landmark 'Race, ethnicity & equality report' in late 2018 (RHS, 2018). Although this wider context has undoubtedly influenced the Social Policy Association (SPA) in its thinking on the topic, a more direct challenge was the difficulty in establishing a diverse sub-panel in the lead-up to Research Excellence Framework 2021 (REF2021). There was a notable absence of black and minority ethnic (BAME) academics coming forward and being endorsed for panel membership, as well as a shortage of academics with a central focus on race and ethnicity. It was also recognised that race and ethnicity were relatively absent from conferences and journals, and that SPA membership does not exactly model ethnic and other forms of diversity. Thus, as the beginning of a response, in 2018, the SPA commissioned an independent audit of the position of 'race' and ethnicity in Social Policy. The resulting report recognises various areas where teaching and learning in Social Policy could be diversified, as well as the role of the SPA in supporting a higher profile for journal articles, research and curriculum development

1

(Craig et al, 2019). Of course, in many ways, this is only the start of the conversation.

An early step was that the 2019 SPA conference opened with a Plenary on 'Race, Racism and Social Policy', featuring lively debate between Claire Alexander, Gary Craig and Coretta Phillips, and stimulating interventions from the audience. To follow on from this debate, this year, the *Social policy review* (SPR) adopted three themes that emerged most strongly from the conference (of which race was pre-eminent), and used that to structure contributions both from the conference and from others who caught our eye within the discipline. In the first chapter of this section, Nasar Meer sets the scene by asking: what are the pressing racial inequalities in contemporary British society and to what extent is Social Policy as a discipline equipped to analyse and respond to these? He helpfully puts our other contributions in a wider context by providing an overview of some contemporary outcomes in the key areas of labour market participation, education and criminal justice, summarising some prevailing features and patterns, before going on to explore in more detail whether Social Policy as it is presently configured, focusing as it does on the concern with a redistributive notion of equality, is sufficiently well placed to grasp these. He develops a fascinating argument based on the observation of the need to fully incorporate an account of institutional racism and 'everyday bordering', as well as a critical understanding of the so-called 'progressives dilemma' set out by David Goodhart. He does not shy away from ending the chapter on a critical note by suggesting that the history of Social Policy as a disciplinary practice may stymie the kinds of foci that he thinks are needed. This analysis demands a recognition that mainstream Social Policy inquiry is parochial, but also that the object of inquiry is shaped by historical racism.

Next we come to an important contribution from Cole, Craig and Ali, the authors of the SPA race audit. The chapter distils the key analysis and messages from the report, and is an authoritative account and overview of the challenges facing the discipline. The report was tasked with looking at Social Policy in terms of student composition, staff composition, conference/journal content and curriculum content. Cole et al point out that Social Policy has treated debates on 'race' and racism as marginal for too long, as reflected in the relative absence of 'race' from the major Social Policy journals. The audit was based on a literature review, a survey of higher education institutions (HEIs) offering some form of Social Policy teaching and an analysis of published data sets in relation to student and staff characteristics.

Finally, the team also spoke to a number of key informant experts across the discipline. An important issue that has arisen is that the SPA has never made use of ethnic monitoring in membership applications, making it impossible to assess the representativeness or otherwise of its membership. As the authors conclude, the SPA clearly has some way to go to persuade Social Policy academics of the importance of confronting this challenge, and they suggest that this is unlikely to happen without what the authors refer to as a major cultural shift within HEIs and the discipline more broadly.

In their chapter, which stood out when presented as a paper at the 2019 SPA conference as directly addressing the concerns of 'race' and ethnicity, Bowler and Razak focus on the experience and views of young British Muslim women and their solutions to the limitations embedded in the monocultural mindsets organising the public spaces of their Sunderland cityscape. The narratives of the young 'Mackem'[1] women clearly identify how long-standing racialised ideas connecting whiteness as belonging, which were pervasive in the local monoculture, act as an impediment to solution-focused opportunities for a multi-vocal intercultural present. The authors draw on empirical data to foreground the voice of young women, offering a counter-narrative to dominant constructions of young British Asian Muslims whose experiences have been publicly articulated through the prism of continuing British racism and Islamophobia. The young women involved in the research articulated themselves as cultural critics of the dominant monocultural white imaginary of Britishness, nationhood and belonging. Their nuanced understanding of British identity illustrated an orientation of their life-world beyond the confines of monocultural imaginaries, offering hope for intercultural belonging.

The final chapter in Part I takes a somewhat different tack, in which Sojka and Saar look at the 'othering' of migrants within discourses of return migration – a reflection of the complex interplay between race, ethnicity and other aspects of identity, particularly in the fluid context of migration. In a context in which European Union (EU) policymakers are interested in the portability of social security and especially in mobile EU citizens' access to benefits in receiving countries, immigrants' access to welfare is highly politicised. The authors note that there is a significant body of academic literature regarding the political discourse surrounding migration and migrants' access to welfare. However, little is known about discourses on return migration and returnees' access to welfare in sending countries. The article fills this gap by analysing Polish and Estonian Social Policy experts' narratives on returnees and their access to welfare. In the chapter, the authors argue that the concept of othering in relation to welfare can help us to better understand national discourses around migration and return migration. Poland and Estonia have adopted vastly different attitudes towards return migrants: while Estonian policy experts stressed the positive nature of migration (migrants were seen as successful individuals), Polish narratives around migration are more negative, drawing attention to the 'social costs' of migration, such as broken families. The Polish experts interviewed by the authors thus questioned the potential belonging of return migrants, seeing them as a burden on the welfare state, while Estonian experts saw return migration as mostly positive and a sign of loyalty.

We are pleased to have been able to support this early stage of the conversation around 'race' and ethnicity within Social Policy, and we feel that there is much more to come. The Chair of the SPA is leading on the development of a BAME action plan to guide the SPA's next steps. The plan will be broken down into three main sections: what happens within the SPA; how we engage with schools, further education establishments and HEIs; and how we engage with research institutions.[2]

Notes

[1] 'Mackem' is the local colloquial term for a person from Sunderland or Wearside in the North-East of England.

[2] I am grateful to SPA Chair Steve Iafrati for providing me with background information about the SPA race audit.

References

Craig, G., Cole, B. and Ali, N. (2019) 'The missing dimension: where is 'race' in Social Policy teaching and learning?', Social Policy Association, www.social-policy.org.uk/uncategorized/the-missing-dimension-where-is-race-in-social-policy-teaching-and-learning/

RHS (Royal Historical Society) (2018) *Race, ethnicity & equality in UK History: A report and resource for change*, London: Royal Historical Society.

Race and social policy: challenges and obstacles

Nasar Meer

Introduction

Over 30 years ago, Williams (1987: 7) argued that 'mainstream Social Administration has largely marginalised the issue of "race", and ignored the racism institutionalized within the practice and provision of the welfare state'. Notwithstanding disciplinary distinctions between Social Administration and Social Policy, in so far as these distinctions remain, it is a complaint that would not look wholly out of place if it were directed at Social Policy today. Indeed, the recent Social Policy Association (SPA)-commissioned report *The missing dimension* (Craig et al, 2019) broadly concurred with the assessment of one Social Policy academic that, 'overall the picture was that "race" teaching within social policy courses was, as one lecturer put it "a drop in the ocean" and not regarded in any sense as mainstream features' (Craig et al, 2019: 17). This is not unique to Social Policy of course; as the Royal Historical Society's (RHS, 2018) *Race, ethnicity & equality in UK History: A report and resource for change* makes abundantly clear, and as Alexander (2016) has argued of Sociology too, racial inequality is an overlooked feature across a number of disciplinary homes in UK universities.

For Social Policy, it seems an especially unfortunate tendency when so much research beyond, as well as allied to, Social Policy disciplines documents a variety of gross ethnic and racial disparities across sectors typically deemed its terra firma. Indeed, while the report of the United Nations (UN) Special Rapporteur on Extreme Poverty and Human Rights resonated loudly with Social Policy scholars – not least the assessment that 'much of the glue that has held British society together since the Second World War has been deliberately removed and replaced with a harsh and uncaring ethos' (Alston, 2018: 1) – its sister report by the UN Special Rapporteur on Contemporary Forms of Racism, Racial

Discrimination, Xenophobia and Related Intolerance went largely unnoticed. The findings in the latter were no less damning, reporting that 'the United Kingdom has adopted sweeping austerity measures that have dramatically cut public sector funding and services and public benefits, including changes to tax policy that have consequences on access to welfare for racial and ethnic minority communities' (Achiume, 2018: 9). It continued:

> [T]he racially disparate impact of austerity measures adopted by the Government between 2010 and 2017 will result in a 5 per-cent loss in income for Black households, which is double the loss for White households. Similarly, cash losses as a result of tax, welfare and wage reforms will be the largest for Black households (about £1,600 on average) and the smallest for White households (about £950 on average). (Achiume, 2018: 9)

Drawing on a variety of openly available sources, including the 'Race disparity audit' (Cabinet Office, 2017: paras 2.9, 5.12–5.13), among the ethnic and racial inequalities that it highlighted was that across the UK, black and minority ethnic (BAME) households were 'twice as likely to be in persistent poverty as White households' (Achiume, 2018: 7). As somebody who participated in the 'Race disparity audit', and, in fact, convened an expert group on Scotland to feed into it, the findings confirmed our knowledge that very significant ethnic and racial disparities continue to feature across all key sectors of British society.

An overview restatement of these data might include how one quarter of black and Asian children, compared with one tenth of white children, are likely to be in persistent poverty,[1] and that the unemployment rate for Black-African and Black-Caribbean groups across the UK is more than twice the national average, while Pakistani and Bangladeshi groups have an unemployment rate of 10 per cent compared with 4 per cent for white groups.[2] This finding was previously recognised by the Equality and Human Rights Commission (EHRC, 2016), and confirmed a trend signalled in Trades Union Congress research that highlighted how 45 per cent of black 16–24 year olds were unemployed, which is over double the level of unemployment of their white counterparts. Meanwhile, BAME employees with degrees earned 23.1 per cent less on average than white workers with comparable education and training (TUC, 2012: 6). Moreover, as Bowyer et al. (2020) have recently shown, BAME young people are 47% more likely to be on a zero-hours contract, compared to their White peers.

In higher education, among Black-African and Black-Caribbean groups, just 6 per cent of school leavers attended a Russell Group university, as compared with 11 per cent of white school leavers. As for employment in the university sector, the Equality Challenge Unit's audit showed that nearly 70 per cent of UK professorships are held by white men, while just under 22 per cent are held by white women (ECU, 2016). Some 7.3 per cent of professors are BAME men, and just 1.9 per cent are BAME women. Among university senior managers, 67.5 per cent are white male, 28.3 per cent are white female, 3.3 per cent are BAME male and only 0.9 per cent are BAME female. Corresponding inquiry from Rollock (2019) documents the qualitative character of these discrepancies, and how 'the lack of fellow Black academics within universities, especially at senior levels, along with the challenges, delays, racism and passive bullying they have experienced, means that these respondents are attuned to the ways in which power, whiteness and racism operate in higher education institutions'.

Elsewhere, in housing, we know that Pakistani, Bangladeshi and black adults are more likely to live in substandard accommodation than white people (around 30 per cent compared with around 8 per cent, respectively). Indeed, as the Joseph Rowntree Foundation (JRF, 2017: 26) reported, over the past 20 years:

> working-age people in the White ethnic group have always had the lowest risk of poverty, with those from the Indian group having the second lowest. Those in the Bangladeshi and Pakistani groups have continuously had the highest and second highest poverty rates respectively, with the people in the Black, and Chinese and Other ethnic groups having similar rates.

Given the disproportionate impact of austerity measures on BAME groups already highlighted, and BAME women in particular, there is every reason to anticipate that this disparity has increased. This is corroborated by findings from the EHRC (2016: 27), in which the UN Rapporteur (Achiume, 2018: 7) stated that 'children from Pakistani or Bangladeshi households (28.6 per cent) and Black households (24.2 per cent) were more likely to live in substandard accommodation than those in White households (18.6 per cent)'. This is related to the status of homeownership reported in the 'Race disparity audit', which showed how in England in 2015–17, Black-African and Black-Caribbean households were the ethnic groups most likely to rent social housing (47 per cent and 45 per cent, respectively).[3]

The disparities that are found in the labour market, higher education and housing sectors reappear in areas such as formal and informal school exclusions and criminal justice, where in England, black children are nearly three times more likely to be permanently excluded than White-British pupils.[4] In the area of criminal justice meanwhile, rates of prosecution for Black-African and African-Caribbean people are three times higher than for white people – 18 per thousand of the population compared with six per thousand, respectively (EHRC, 2016), and the National Crime Intelligence DNA Database holds the records of 30 per cent of all black men in Britain, as compared to 10 per cent for white and Asian men; in short, they are three times more likely to have their DNA stored (Bennetto, 2012). Elsewhere, Muslims, who are about 4 per cent of the UK population, now make up about 16 per cent of the prison population (Sturge, 2019). Black people make up 3 per cent of the UK population but accounted for 12 per cent of the adult prison population and more than 20 per cent of children in custody in 2015/16 (Lammy, 2017: 3). Other racial and ethnic minority groups are also over-represented but to a lesser degree.

To be clear, what is being stated is not that all these disparities can be explained solely by a focus on race and ethnicity, but rather that: first, race and ethnicity cannot be ignored in any explanation of them; and, second, the discipline of Social Policy should have a greater investment in seeking to do so. This point is made at an interesting and challenging time for the topics of race and ethnicity in our universities in general, and the social and human sciences in particular. This is where the critical questions cluster. The 'Why is My Curriculum White' campaign brings this home to teaching and learning, and mobilises the argument that universities need to not only 'diversify' faculty and curricula, but also 'decolonise', before disciplinary inquiry might be reconstructed with racial equalities as core rather than peripheral concerns (Bhambra, Gebrial and Nisancioglu, 2018; Rhodes Must Fall, 2018; Elliott-Cooper, 2017). Whether this can be done in a discipline like Social Policy – where the 'historical and material understanding of the roots of racism were excluded by this idealist orientation of the discipline' (Williams, 1987: 8) – remains to be seen and will be taken up in the following discussion.

What this chapter does not therefore rehearse is what is done very well elsewhere in the SPA-commissioned 'The missing dimension'

(Craig et al, 2019) or the RHS's (2018) *Race, ethnicity & equality in UK History* (see also Chapter 2, this volume), both of which highlight issues such as institutional deficits and the degree 'attainment gap', something that is also discussed by scholars of higher education (for example, Bhopal and Rhamie, 2014) and recognised by Universities UK and the National Union on Students (UUK/NUS, 2019). Instead, I want to suggest three urgent normative dimensions that I consider Social Policy as uniquely positioned to address, as well as one obstacle that may prevent it from doing so. These are not the only concerns by any means, but, to my mind, they capture a breadth of broader considerations that should be much better included in mainstream Social Policy disciplinary inquiry.

Social Policy and institutional racism

It is 25 years since the racist murder of teenager Stephen Lawrence would eventually lead, after six years of campaigning, to a public inquiry deeming the UK's largest police authority guilty of institutional racism. Indeed, 2019 marked 20 years since the Macpherson Report (Macpherson, 1999) was published – a report that touches all the core concerns of Social Policy as a disciplinary pursuit. It is noteworthy how a concept from radically dissenting critique, in the form of Black Power activism, would give birth to a concept that would then become a common (though not uncontested) feature of public discourse across the UK and beyond. As Scott and Marshall (quoted in Murji, 2007: 844) observed:

> In a remarkable episode in the history of ideas the concept of 'institutional racism' emerged in the context of a radical political struggle and the Black Power movement in the United States in the 1960s and then traversed three decades, two continents and the social class structure to be adopted by a member of the British nobility.

While it may have penetrated the British nobility, it has arguably met more resistance in Social Policy analyses, even though its explanatory power is straightforward and no more radical than others concerned with registering inequality. In their book *Black power* (Carmichael and Hamilton, 1967: 4), Stokely Carmichael (who later changed his name to Kwame Ture) and the political scientist Charles Hamilton described it in the following terms:

Racism is both overt and covert. It takes two, closely related forms ... we call these individual racism and institutional racism.... The second type is less overt, far subtler, and less identifiable in terms of specific individuals committing these acts. But it is no less destructive of human life. The second type originates in the operation of established and respected forces in society, and thus receives far less condemnation than the first type.

Then much as now, a key issue relates to the role of what is deemed 'unwitting', and this is precisely how institutional racism came to be described in the inquiry into the London Metropolitan Police Service, the improper investigation of the racist murder of Stephen Lawrence and the attendant findings of institutional police racism. The investigating judge found ample evidence of this in the prevailing institutional practice, and so made a number of wide-ranging recommendations with a broad scope, which then had implications outside the police force in a manner that related to the public sector more broadly. Convention is the key here, to the extent that individual motives and objectives become much less relevant to sustaining and proliferating racialised outcomes.

Of course, Carmichael and Hamilton were writing during a period of civil rights, and the lack of progress across a number of sectors in society gave rise to a complimentary analysis with the emergence of Critical Race Theory (CRT). This foregrounded a concern with the historical, political and socio-economic position of racial minorities relative to white American society. In Britain today, and over 50 years after the Labour government's second Race Relations Act in 1968, it is not hard to see the virtue of this account, unless one explains the persistent racial and ethnic inequalities highlighted earlier as either a rational outcome or a reflection of BAME deficits.

On the contrary, if Social Policy analysis is to be serious about grasping these inequalities, I would maintain that issues of whiteness and majority racial preference are key. This means treating 'whiteness' not merely as a census category, but as a source of relative capital within our institutions. This is something central to CRT approaches, and specifically how these outcomes are contoured by questions of race and power. This is not intended as a benign description, and there is a need to recognise 'normalisation' here. In Delgado's (1995: xiv) classic text *Critical Race Theory: The cutting edge*, he presents racism as having formed 'an ingrained feature of our landscape, [where] it looks ordinary and natural to persons in the culture'. He continued:

Formal equal opportunity rules and laws that insist on treating Blacks and whites (for example) alike, can thus remedy only the more extreme and shocking sorts of injustice.... Formal equality can do little about the business-as-usual forms of racism that people of color confront every day and that account for much misery, alienation, and despair. (Delgado, 1995: xiv)

An under-recognised feature of this process among Social Policy scholars is the notion of a wider *social desensitisation* to racism, as signalled in Delgado's description of racism as 'business as usual'. A similar set of social processes are arguably characterised by other authors in their discussion of 'everyday racism' (Essed 1991) and the subjective negotiation of this. What is presently overlooked relates to how 'desensitisation', in turn, increases the thresholds for what constitutes 'real' racism. This is what Goldberg (2006: 339) gestures to as the phenomenology of 'race' disappearing 'into the seams of sociality, invisibly holding the social fabric together even as it tears apart'. While policies promoting anti-racism continue to exist in society, they become focused on addressing unambiguous forms of racism, which incrementally normalises what ought to be considered extreme. Therefore, running parallel to observations about desensitisation, CRT scholars have long been interested in the nature and function of so-called 'smokescreens'.

There are certainly conceptual and empirical gaps here, and the CRT literature struggles with the more ambivalent mechanics of racialisation, for much of the CRT literature works with a broad brush and is typically concerned with the ways in which racial justice has been embraced 'in terms that excluded radical and fundamental challenges to status quo institutional practices' (Crenshaw et al, 1995: xiv). CRT theorists have been enmeshed in these debates and commenced with the implications of these historical relationships, before advancing the more normative position that a failure to question and acknowledge the function of racism is synonymous with acting to maintain the marginalised position of racialised minorities (Preston and Chadderton, 2012). They were then, just as I am now, not complaining about individuals who may or may not have been racist. Instead, they argued that prevailing societal institutions had internalised and normalised a number of conventions that were not codified in a statute, but instead sanctioned by a prevailing cultural expectation that unduly disadvantaged racial minorities.[5]

Social Policy and everyday bordering

In addition to institutional racism, and amongst a prominent set of Social Policy issues around the racialisation of migration, the issue of everyday bordering must also be better registered as a core Social Policy concern. T.S. Eliot once commented that 'History has many cunning passages', and so it came to be for a number of the children who settled in Britain from the Caribbean between 1948 and 1973. Legally entitled to live here, these members of the 'Windrush generation' came to be denied citizenship in adulthood as successive UK Home Office 'hostile environment' approaches changed the criteria of their right to be in the country without taking their legitimate status into account. A key part of the story relies on what has come to be known as everyday bordering (Yuval-Davis et al, 2017). The pernicious yet overlooked features in Social Policy analysis are not solely the changing of entry criteria, however, but how successive UK governments have also sought to deploy everyday bordering measures to control and regulate the social, socio-economic and geographic mobility of migrants, and in ways that remain under-studied even though they span every Social Policy sector, from health to education, and criminal justice to social welfare (cf Jolly, 2019). Asylum seekers whose claims have been refused or refugees whose leave to remain has not been renewed are especially vulnerable to everyday bordering controls – and, of course, detention and deportation – in ways that both rely upon and reproduce racialised policies (Mayblin, 2017).

Of course, asylum is arguably the area of the border over which states bound by the 1951 Convention for Refugees have least control. Unlike the restrictive criteria states are able to place upon economic or familial immigration, entry criteria for displaced migrants are ostensibly rights-based, and therefore have less scope for direct restrictions. Although varying according to immigration status, these controls seek instead to: (1) restrict displaced migrants' day-to-day access to social services and amenities; (2) subject displaced migrants to enhanced scrutiny by service providers, employers and educators; and (3) create additional barriers to housing, education and employment. A key issue is that the responsibility for checking, carrying out and enforcing indirect immigration controls on displaced migrants has increasingly been 'outsourced' away from central government to public and private service providers. Examples include: private subcontractors enacting and enforcing immigration decisions through lock changes and evictions; local authorities administrating social housing access according to conservative interpretations of 'no recourse to public funds'; and employers, educators and social and private landlords being made responsible for compliance with immigration controls (Meer, Peace and Hill, 2019).

The Home Office has recruited service providers to carry out these activities through both the threat of punitive legal measures if they fail to comply, and incentivising cooperation. Combined, these are precisely the measures that sustained the 'hostile environment' directed at the Windrush Generation, and it worth registering that it has not gone unnoticed in the past. In an early analysis of race and social security provision from the race equality charity Runnymede Trust, Gordon (1986: 31) noted that 'All black claimants are at risk in that they may be assumed by staff to be immigrants and subject to immigration control and subject too, therefore, to questioning about their immigration status, their right to be in this country and their right to welfare benefits.' Unheeded, this observation is precisely what prevailed in the years to come. Equally, this is something that is also tied to the dynamic that has been termed 'welfare chauvinism' (Guentner et al, 2016), which pivots on a particular framing of social solidarity that is central to social welfare provision.

Social Policy and 'solidarities'

As it has been articulated in the UK, what is sometimes termed the 'progressive's dilemma' centres mostly on ethnic and racial minorities and the multicultural reality of British life. Perhaps most obviously, David Goodhart's (2004) article 'Too diverse?' and subsequent iterations maintained that compared with the immediate post-war social welfare consensus, 'the difference now in a developed country like Britain is that we not only live among stranger citizens but we must share with them'. Goodhart, a former editor-at-large of the centrist political magazine *Prospect*, then a director in the London-based think tanks Demos and Policy Exchange, has been very influential in arguing that ethnic and racial diversity undermines national solidarity and presents a threat to the social-democratic ideals of a welfare state. The key parts of this dilemma expressed in a number of places might be distilled in the following steps:

1. The basis on which you can extract large sums of money in tax and pay it out in benefits is that most people think that the recipients are people like themselves, facing difficulties that they themselves could face.

2. If values become more diverse, and if lifestyles become more differentiated, then it is more difficult to sustain the legitimacy of a universal risk-pooling welfare state. People ask, 'Why should I pay for them when they are doing things I wouldn't do?'

3. You can have a Swedish welfare state provided that you are a homogeneous society with intensely shared values. In the US, you have a very diverse, individualistic society where people feel fewer obligations to fellow citizens.

4. Progressives want diversity but they thereby undermine part of the moral consensus on which a large welfare state rests.

Of course, one feature of this formulation is how 'the US haunts this debate, as if its experience confirms some natural law that diversity erodes solidarity' (Banting and Kymlicka, 2006: 1). No less relevant is how Goodhart's thesis is not purely focused on social and value diversity per se, but, in contrast, precisely concerned with ethnic and racial diversity only. Indeed, it does, in fact, employ what others have observed as a type of 'banal majoritarianism' (Fenton and Mann, 2010), in which the 'we' are not remade over time to have in common a 'shared fate' (Williams, 2003), and is arguably part of a broader attempt to launder race and ethnicity from the making of the British working class.

I would make three observations here that I think have implications for 'the new progressive's dilemma' in Social Policy more broadly. First, it is a reading that relies on highly contestable empirical assumptions about past solidarity. Among others, Harris (2004: 5) argues that Britain has never experienced the levels of social solidarity measured in terms of 'shared values' that Goodhart's iteration of the 'progressive's dilemma' assumes. While there might have been less ethnic diversity upon the post-war creation of the UK welfare state, there was greater class and gender inequality, something compounded by fractured nationalism and strong localisms – precisely the historical diversity that is overlooked by Goodhart. As Parekh (2004: 7) puts it: 'even if all immigrants were to leave the country, deep diversity would remain and continue to pose challenges to a strong view of solidarity'. Deep diversity is not therefore the preserve of ethnic and migration-related difference, but part of the evolving story of a territorialised social formation. Indeed, as the late Bernard Crick (2004: 1–2) put it: 'the fallacy of the excluded middle is hard at work here: it is not either solidarity or loss of identity – our identity lies in our political sense of living with dual identities'.

Second, and as Parekh (2004) elaborates, the dilemma more broadly assumes that solidarity is a necessary precondition of redistribution, and insufficiently explores how solidarity comes into existence in the first place – and specifically confuses contingent connections for causality. For example, from a historical perspective, it could be argued that it was the movement of Commonwealth citizens to post-war Britain that facilitated the necessary reconstruction of Britain from which welfare was an outgrowth. In this respect, 'instead of treating diversity as an independent variable that affects the welfare state, we can invert the question to ask how the welfare state shapes diversity' (Smith, 2009: 837).

A more historically informed response may equally show how, in particular, white English working-class history has a long and productive relationship with ethnic and racial difference in a manner that forged the conditions for universal welfare. For example, in *Racism, class and the racialized outsider*, Virdee (2014: 164) makes visible the 'racialized minorities in socialist movements who played an instrumental role in trying to align struggles against racism with those against class exploitation'. Another, more social theory, way of addressing this is to think about race and class solidarities and the ways in which race became 'the modality in which class [was] lived, the medium through which class relations [were] experienced, the form in which it [was] appropriated and "fought through"' (Hall, 1980: 341). In this respect, we might argue that the kinds of cleavages that can erode the social solidarity required for the welfare state have little to do with immigration; 'rather, it depends primarily on the level of immigrant economic and political incorporation' (Myles and St-Arnaud, 2006: 353 cf Bhattacharyya, 2915).

Third, Goodhart's iteration of the 'progressive's dilemma' conflates ethnic diversity with immigration. Where a cornerstone of 'shared values' might be an attachment to or self-identification with Britishness (whatever this may entail), settled post-migrant minority ethnic groups are consistently found to have the same, if not greater, attitudinal affinity to British nationhood (Heath and Roberts, 2008: 14; Rheault, 2011; Wind-Cowie and Gregory, 2011: 41). Additionally, and by mapping the empirical terrain through the British Social Attitudes Survey (BSA) and British Election Studies (BES), Evans (2006: 173) forcefully argues that 'there is no evidence that negative attitudes toward minority rights provision have become more closely linked to the rejection of welfare'.

So, where does this leave us? Social Policy scholarship should treat the 'new progressive's dilemma' with critical caution; more precisely, if we are serious about grasping how and why solidarities are forged and broken over time, Social Policy scholarship should better try to delineate the three-way interaction between markets, states and race. This means not conceding the framing in advance to those who view the 'new progressive's dilemma' as a given social fact. This is not least the case because transnational forces (such as globalisation) and domestic forces (such as devolution) affect social welfare delivery in ways that have very little to do with shared identity.

We can observe an example of the former in the shift of onus from the state itself, which means that statutory social services are planned and administered by profit-seeking parties who are operating according to their own transnational imperatives. We see an example of the latter in the devolution of social care, which invites us to rethink the status of solidarity in devolved provisions where the national is a background feature. Finally, the 'new progressive's dilemma' is increasingly expressed as a reactionary hope against the revision that comes with remaking common membership, and seeks to restate a majoritarian 'we' through a sleight of hand. This will become especially charged in light of the 2019 UK general election, following which the Labour movement will directly and indirectly debate the relationship between race, class and the distribution of social welfare provision.

Provenance and revision

A final consideration is related to all that has previously been discussed, and returns us to the provenance of Social Policy as a discipline, as well as anticipating contemporary debates concerning the constitution of the populations that make up the focus of Social Policy analyses signalled earlier. It has to do with the possibilities of a Social Policy discipline that can, borrowing from Grosfoguel (2013: 75), acknowledge the provincialism of foundational epistemic structures before breaking with them to facilitate greater epistemic diversity:

> In the Westernized universities, the knowledge produced by other epistemologies, cosmologies, and world views arising from other world-regions with diverse time/space dimensions and characterized by different geopolitics and body-politics of knowledge are considered 'inferior' in relation to the 'superior' knowledge produced by the few Western men of five countries (i.e., England, France, Germany, Italy, and the USA) that compose the canon of thought in the Humanities and Social Sciences.

This may appear somewhat removed from the activity of Social Policy but I would argue that it is relevant in two ways. One is to point to a parochialism of *mainstream* Social Policy inquiry that simultaneously presumes itself to be universal, as neatly captured in the title of Esping-Andersen's (1990) influential account *The three worlds of welfare capitalism*. Without seeking to reduce this or other profoundly enlightening and nuanced Social Policy accounts of welfare provision, it is notable and somewhat astonishing how little has been written to register the emergence of such European welfare regimes in the context of European imperial assets and colonial resources. There is insufficient space to develop this point here, but for the purposes of this argument, merely registering the existing deficit is both pertinent and undeniable.

The second way in which the argument that Grosfoguel (2013) and others make is relevant for Social Policy disciplinary inquiry concerns the ways in which 'the constellation of imperialism with patriarchal capitalism also found its way into the demands of the working class for welfare reforms at the turn of the century' (Williams, 1987: 26). This is a recognition that racism featured centrally in the historical development of the welfare state, in ways which meant that 'the white skilled male working class in the 1920s gained from National Insurance, for example, whilst "aliens" and women were denied access. Jews, Irish, Black, women and the undeserving share a history of welfare being denied them or controlling them' (Williams, 1987: 11). Historians such as Holmes (1979) and Cohen (1985) have shown how this had both a *breadth* across social welfare arenas, and a historical *depth* that connected 19th-century racism to people as key as William Beveridge and Richard Titmuss: the former through his essays on 'Children's allowances and the race' (Beveridge, 1943); and the latter with his insistence that 'Western civilisation slowly evolved a higher way of life and it was our duty to help and guide the teeming millions of India and Africa to a more abundant life' (Titmuss, quoted in Jacobs, 1985: 9). This was the time 'when the welfare state was still "in the making", when post-war black immigration to Britain was hesitantly beginning, and when racism was first fully institutionalised in welfare provision' (Jacobs, 1985: 6). Yet, they are treated as vestiges of a bygone age without properly accounting for how they may have shaped, and continue to shape, the criteria of relevance for right and rewards. In light of this, and borrowing from Bhambra (2007: 873), an ambition for Social Policy scholarship should be to recognise and challenge entrenched conventions that protect 'core categories of analysis from any reconstruction of what such recognition would entail'. While one might point to surface-level reconstruction in

Social Policy, it is arguable and demonstrable that this has not hitherto penetrated the depths of our prevailing modes of thought and inquiry. This is a crucial point because there are and have been important examples of race scholarship in Social Policy, with that quoted earlier and elsewhere being indicative of this (cf Murji, 2017). However, what this scholarship has not hitherto become, or has been prevented from becoming, is something more than marginal in the identity of Social Policy as a disciplinary tradition.

Conclusions

This chapter has suggested three urgent normative dimensions for Social Policy analyses, and which Social Policy as a disciplinary tradition appears uniquely positioned to address, as well as one obstacle that may prevent it from doing so. These include, firstly, an incorporation of institutional racism as a part of the repertoire of social policy inquiry and analysis. Presently this remains a peripheral rather than a central concern, such that persistent racial and ethnic inequalities may be understood as a reflection of BAME deficits. Secondly, a recognition of everyday bordering that both relies on and reproduces racialized social policy across every sector of concern to the field. In this respect there is a reterritorializing of the state, the conventional unit of study in social policy, to everyday fields of social policy and yet the effects of this remain understudied. Thirdly, there is a need to be explicit about registering the way race narrates a current concern with solidarities, or at least to better delineation of the three-way interaction between markets, states and race. This is not a new discussion, but it has reappeared in a way that relies on a proxy language of the 'progressive's dilemma', something that launders a longer tradition about considering an interaction between race and class. These are not the only concerns by any means, but, to my mind, they capture a breadth of broader considerations that should be much better included if it Social Policy as a tradition of disciplinary inquiry is ever to move beyond surface-level reconstruction.

Notes

[1] See 'UK government ethnicity facts and figures, persistent low income', available at: www.ethnicity-facts-figures.service.gov.uk/work-pay-and-benefits/pay-and-income/low-income/latest

[2] See 'UK government ethnicity facts and figures, unemployment', available at: https://www.ethnicity-facts-figures.service.gov.uk/work-pay-and-benefits/unemployment-and-economic-inactivity/unemployment/latest

[3]   See 'UK government ethnicity facts and figures, housing', available at: https://www.ethnicity-facts-figures.service.gov.uk/housing/social-housing/renting-from-a-local-authority-or-housing-association-social-housing/latest

[4]   See 'UK government ethnicity facts and figures, pupil exclusions', available at: www.ethnicity-facts-figures.service.gov.uk/education-skills-and-training/absence-and-exclusions/pupil-exclusions/latest

[5]   What is true of social and policy outcomes is also a feature of social policy as a disciplinary tradition. It is striking, for example, that one of the leading social policy publications, the journal *Policy & Politics*, has not published one single paper on race, racism, race-equality, racial disadvantage etc in ten years. It is highly unlikely that this is a consciously engineered outcome, but instead a reflection of intellectual and research priorities which fail to register the significance of race as a policy concern.

References

Achiume, T. (2018) 'End of mission statement of the Special Rapporteur on Contemporary Forms of Racism, Racial Discrimination, Xenophobia and Related Intolerance at the conclusion of her mission to the United Kingdom of Great Britain and Northern Ireland', United Nations Human Rights, Office of the High Commissioner, www.ohchr.org/EN/NewsEvents/Pages/DisplayNews.aspx?NewsID=23073&LangID=E

Alexander, C. (2016) BSA plenary lecture with Anoop Nayak on 'Researching Race in and out of the Academy'. https://vimeo.com/176452879 (viewed 6 March 2020).

Alston, P. (2018) 'Report of the Special Rapporteur on Extreme Poverty and Human Rights on his visit to the United Kingdom of Great Britain and Northern Ireland', United Nations Human Rights, Office of the High Commissioner, https://undocs.org/A/HRC/41/39/Add.1

Banting, K. and Kymlicka, W. (eds) (2006) *Multiculturalism and the welfare state: Recognition and redistribution in contemporary democracies*, Oxford: Oxford University Press.

Bennetto, J. (2012) *Police and racism: What has been achieved 10 years after the Stephen Lawrence Inquiry report?*, London: EHRC.

Beveridge, W. (1943) *The pillars of security, and other war-time essays and addresses*, London: G. Allen & Unwin Ltd.

Bhambra, G. (2007) 'Sociology and postcolonialism: another "missing" revolution?', *Sociology*, 41(5): 871–84.

Bhambra, G., Gebrial, D. and Nisancioglu, K. (eds) (2018) *Decolonising the university*, London: Pluto Books.

Bhattacharyya, G. (2015) *Crisis, austerity, and everyday life: Living in a time of diminishing expectations*, Basingstoke: Palgrave.

Bhopal, K. and Rhamie, J. (2014) 'Initial teacher training: understanding "race", diversity and inclusion', *Race Ethnicity and Education*, 17(3): 304–25.

Bowyer, G., Henderson, M., White. D. and Wooley, S. (2020) *Race Inequality in the Workforce*. London: Carnegie UK Trust, UCL Centre for Longitudinal Studies and Operation Black Vote. https://cls.ucl.ac.uk/wp-content/uploads/2017/02/Race-Inequality-in-the-Workforce-Final.pdf

Cabinet Office (2017) 'Race disparity audit: summary findings from the ethnicity facts and figures website', www.ethnicity-facts-figures.service.gov.uk/static/race-disparity-audit-summary-findings.pdf

Carmichael, S. and Hamilton, C.V. (1967) *Black power: The politics of liberation in America*, New York, NY: Random House.

Cohen, S. (1985) 'Anti-Semitism, immigration controls and the welfare state', *Critical Social Policy*, 13(1): 75–92.

Craig, G., Cole, B. and Ali, N. (2019) 'The missing dimension: where is "race" in Social Policy teaching and learning', Social Policy Association, www.social-policy.org.uk/uncategorized/the-missing-dimension-where-is-race-in-social-policy-teaching-and-learning/

Crenshaw, K., Gotanda, K., Peller, G. and Thomas, K. (eds) (1995) *Critical Race Theory: The key writings that formed the movement*, New York, NY: New York Press.

Crick, B. (2004) 'But what about the Scots?', March, pp 1–2, www.nasarmeer.com/uploads/7/7/4/6/7746984/prospect_refs.pdf

Delgado, R. (ed) (1995) *Critical Race Theory: The cutting edge*, Philadelphia, PA: Temple University Press.

ECU (Equality Challenge Unit) (2016) 'Equality in higher education: statistical report 2016', www.ecu.ac.uk/publications/equality-in-higher-education-statistical-report-2016/

EHRC (Equality and Human Rights Commission) (2016) *Race report: Healing a divided Britain*, London: EHRC.

Elliott-Cooper, A. (2017) '"Free, decolonised education": a lesson from the South African student struggle', *Area*, 49: 332–4.

Esping-Andersen, G. (1990) *The three worlds of welfare capitalism*, Princeton, NJ: Princeton University Press.

Essed, P. (1991) *Understanding everyday racism: An interdisciplinary theory*, Amsterdam: University of Amsterdam.

Evans, G. (2006) 'Is multiculturalism eroding support for welfare state provision', in K. Banting and W. Kymlicka (eds) *Multiculturalism and the welfare state: Recognition and redistribution in contemporary democracies*, Oxford: Oxford University Press.

Fenton, S. and Mann, R. (2010) 'Introducing the majority to ethnicity: do they like what they see', in G. Calder, P. Cole and J. Seglow (eds) *Citizenship acquisition and national belonging*, Basingstoke: Palgrave.

Goldberg, T.G. (2006) 'Racial Europeanization', *Ethnic and Racial Studies*, 29(2): 332–64.

Goodhart, D. (2004) 'Too diverse?', *Prospect*, 20 February, www.prospectmagazine.co.uk/features/too-diverse-david-goodhart-multiculturalism-britain-immigration-globalisation

Gordon, P. (1986) 'Racism and social security', *Critical Social Policy*, 6(17): 23–40.

Grosfoguel, R. (2013) 'The structure of knowledge in Westernized universities: epistemic racism/sexism and the four genocides/epistemicides of the long 16th century,' *Human Architecture: Journal of the Sociology of Self-Knowledge*, 11(1): 73–90.

Guentner, S., Lukes, S., Stanton, R., Vollmer, B.A. and Wilding, J. (2016) 'Bordering practices in the UK welfare system', *Critical Social Policy*, 36(3): 391–411.

Hall, S. (1980) 'Essay on race, articulation and structured dominance', in UNESCO (ed) *Sociological theories: Race and colonialism*, Paris: UNESCO, pp 305–45.

Harris, N. (2004) 'Who needs homogeneity', *Prospect*, March, p 5, www.nasarmeer.com/uploads/7/7/4/6/7746984/prospect_refs.pdf

Heath, A. and Roberts, J. (2008) 'British identity, its sources and possible implications for civic attitudes and behaviour', research report for Lord Goldsmith's Citizenship Review.

Holmes, C. (1979) *Anti-Semitism in British Society, 1876–1939*, London: Edward Arnold.

Jacobs, S. (1985) 'Race, empire and the welfare state: council housing and racism', *Critical Social Policy*, 5(13): 6–28.

Jolly, A. (2019) 'From the Windrush Generation to the "Air Jamaica Generation": local authority support for families with no recourse to public funds', in: Heins, E., Rees, J. and Needham, C. (eds) *Social policy review 31: Analysis and debate in Social Policy*, Bristol: Policy Press, p 129.

JRF (Joseph Rowntree Foundation) (2017) *UK poverty 2017: A comprehensive analysis of poverty trends and figures*, London: JRF, www.jrf.org.uk/sites/default/files/jrf/files-research/uk_poverty_2017.pdf

Lammy, D. (2017) 'An independent review into the treatment of, and outcomes for, black, Asian and minority ethnic individuals in the criminal justice system', www.gov.uk/government/publications/lammy-review-final-report

Macpherson, W. (1999) *Macpherson inquiry into the matters arising from the death of Stephen Lawrence*, London: HMSO.

Mayblin, L. (2017) *Asylum after empire: Colonial legacies in the politics of asylum seeking*, London: Rowman and Littlefield International.

Meer, N., Peace, T. and Hill, E. (2019) 'Integration governance in Scotland: accommodation, regeneration and exclusion', University of Edinburgh, GLIMER Project.

Murji, K. (2007) 'Sociological entanglements: institutional racism and beyond', *Sociology*, 41(5): 843–55.

Murji, K. (2017) *Racism, policy and politics*. Bristol: Policy Press.

Myles, J. and St-Arnaud, S. (2006) 'Population diversity, multiculturalism, and the welfare state: should welfare state theory be revised', in K. Banting and W. Kymlicka (eds) *Multiculturalism and the welfare state: Recognition and redistribution in contemporary democracies*, Oxford: Oxford University Press.

Parekh, B. (2004) 'What are civilised rules?', *Prospect*, March, pp 7–8, www.nasarmeer.com/uploads/7/7/4/6/7746984/prospect_refs.pdf

Preston, J. and Chadderton, C. (2012) 'Rediscovering "race traitor": towards a Critical Race Theory informed public pedagogy', *Race, Ethnicity and Education*, 15(1): 85–100.

Rollock, N. (2019) *Staying Power The career experiences and strategies of UK Black female professors*. London: UCU.

Rheault, M. (2011) 'British Muslims feel, well, British', Gallup, 8 February, www.gallup.com/opinion/queue/173222/british-muslims-feel-british.aspx

Rhodes Must Fall (2018) *The struggle to decolonise the racist heart of empire*, London: Zed Books.

RHS (Royal Historical Society) (2018) *Race, ethnicity & equality in UK History: A report and resource for change*, London: Royal Historical Society.

Smith, M. (2009) 'Diversity and Canadian political development', *Canadian Journal of Political Science*, 42(4): 831–954.

Sturge, G. (2019) *UK prison population statistics*. House of Commons Library, https://researchbriefings.files.parliament.uk/documents/SN04334/SN04334.pdf

TUC (Trades Union Congress) (2012) 'Youth unemployment and ethnicity', www.tuc.org.uk/sites/default/files/BMEyouth unemployment.pdf

UUK/NUS (Universities UK and the National Union of Students) (2019) *Black, Asian and Minority Ethnic Student Attainment at UK Universities*. UUK/NUS: https://www.universitiesuk.ac.uk/policy-and-analysis/reports/Documents/2019/bame-student-attainment-uk-universities-closing-the-gap.pdf

Virdee, S. (2014) *Racism, class and the racialized outsider*, Basingstoke: Palgrave.

Williams, F. (1987) 'Racism and the discipline of Social Policy: a critique of welfare theory', *Critical Social Policy*, 7(20): 4–29.

Williams, M. (2003) 'Citizenship as identity, citizenship as shared fate, and the functions of multicultural education', in K. McDonough and W. Feinberg (eds) *Citizenship and education in liberal-democratic societies: Teaching for cosmopolitan values and collective identities*, Oxford: Oxford University Press.

Wind-Cowie, M. and Gregory, T. (2011) *A place for pride*, London: Demos.

Yuval-Davis, N., Wemyss, G. and Cassidy, K. (2017) 'Everyday bordering, belonging and the reorientation of British immigration legislation', *Sociology*, 52(2): 228–44.

2

'Race': the missing dimension in social policy higher education?

Bankole Cole, Gary Craig and Nasreen Ali

Introduction

The discipline of Social Policy within university teaching provision is closely linked to key questions addressed by public policy, particularly those concerned with the welfare of the population, such as poverty, gender and disability, as well as the well-established divisions of welfare, such as housing, health, education, the labour market, social assistance and social care. Over the past hundred years or so, the work of individual academics and researchers in the fields of Social Administration and Social Policy, and, more recently, the work of the Social Policy Association (SPA) and its predecessor the Social Administration Association, has been at the forefront of critiques of public welfare provision, seeking and often achieving significant improvements in aspects of welfare.

However, it has been noticeable that public policy has failed to address the issue of 'race', or, more precisely, racism, to any significant degree, despite the slow emergence of anti-discriminatory legislation since the 1960s (Craig, 2007). Furthermore, over the last ten years, the state, as legitimised by public comments by both major parliamentary parties, has steadily rendered invisible the dimension of 'race' within public policy, both directly and indirectly, through, for example, targeted cuts to equality machinery and public pronouncements that 'race' is no longer a key policy issue despite massive evidence to the contrary, including reports commissioned by the government itself (Craig, 2013; Craig and O'Neill, 2013). These signals were picked up by a range of organisations, including many local authorities, which set about reducing their commitment to anti-discriminatory practice and cutting services and funding targeted towards black, Asian and minority ethnic (BAME) populations (Craig, 2011). The failure to act on the findings of a long series of reports and some, albeit limited, academic literature (see later) detailing the ways in which members of BAME groups were disadvantaged is, in reality, a national and continuing scandal that is largely ignored in policy discussions (Chattoo et al, 2019).

More than ten years ago, Craig (2007: 610–11) commented: 'It is important to acknowledge that neglect of the issue of "race" is not confined to social policy as *political practice*; it is shared by the *academic discipline* of social policy.' It is still not uncommon for mainstream Social Policy texts to treat debates on 'race' and racism as marginal. This is striking considering that the Social Policy discipline is centrally concerned with issues of citizenship rights, welfare, equality, poverty alleviation and social engineering. This lacuna extends to the practice of social research, where many proposals, proposers, funders or commissioners still treat the dimension of ethnicity as too complex, too expensive or too marginal to be worthy of serious attention (Craig and Katbamna, 2004), and where it remains difficult to find groups of researchers, particularly minority ethnic researchers, and most of all minority ethnic researchers with permanent contracts and high-status roles, focused on issues of 'race' and ethnicity. Some of the reviews that I have examined or had returned to me for proposals for projects to be funded by significant research funders would have been risible were they not so serious in their failure to address the central issues of 'race'. One proposal submitted to the Economic and Social Research Council (ESRC) to look at the health needs of minority ethnic groups in rural areas generated a review that preferred to argue about the precise definitions of rurality than to think about the issues facing rural minority ethnic groups: of isolation, of difficulties in accessing services or of the failure of health organisations to provide culturally sensitive services. This failure of the Social Policy community also extends to Social Policy teaching and to the high-profile Social Policy journals: a review of the last five years' contents of *Social policy review* (*SPR*) and of *Policy and Politics*, the *British Journal of Social Work* and *Social Policy and Administration* shows a striking absence of the dimension of 'race' in their tables of contents. Until very recently, when a few articles have appeared in print, the only slightly honourable exception to this criticism was *Critical Social Policy* (CSP). In this unhelpful context, this chapter examines the question of how 'race' is currently placed within the teaching and learning of Social Policy in UK higher education institutions (HEIs).

The study

This chapter is based on the findings of an audit of Social Policy teaching and learning in UK HEIs, and of the dimension of 'race' and ethnicity within the Social Policy curriculum, student bodies and staffing. The audit was commissioned by the SPA and carried out from the autumn of 2018 through the spring of 2019 by the current authors. The brief was to explore the extent to which 'race' and ethnicity are appropriately placed dimensions within Social Policy and related curricula, or are significant factors in shaping access to courses or employment within Social Policy and other departments and schools offering some involvement in Social Policy and related subjects. The SPA commissioned the work in order to have independent research to inform the development of an action plan and its future work, both independently and with other parties. In line with the requirements of the call, the audit consisted of the following:

1. A brief contextual review of the presence of 'race' and ethnicity within the curricula of Social Policy courses or those courses with Social Policy named in their title. This was done by means of a questionnaire survey of all those 65 Higher Education Institutions (HEIs) in the UK identified as offering some form of Social Policy teaching.
2. A descriptive secondary analysis of Universities and Colleges Admissions Service (UCAS) and Higher Education Statistics Agency (HESA) data sets. This provided the proportion of domestic BAME students studying undergraduate and postgraduate Social Policy or related courses at UK HEIs.
3. The questionnaire survey also provided some information on BAME staffing in Social Policy that was then supplemented with statistics obtained from the literature review.
4. A literature review of BAME students' experiences of higher education in general and of Social Policy in particular.
5. One-to-one telephone interviews conducted with some experienced Social Policy academics ('experts') selected on the basis of their ability to provide the researchers with valuable additional information about the teaching of 'race' in Social Policy and other related academic issues.
6. Reflections on the ways in which 'race'/ethnicity has featured in the SPA's annual conferences and publications.

The survey

In order to understand how the issue of 'race' was dealt with within HEIs currently offering some form of Social Policy teaching, a questionnaire was sent to all HEIs identified as providing Social Policy courses. These courses ranged from occasional modules as part of degrees titled in some other way (typically Sociology or Criminology) through to single honours Social Policy degrees. From publicly available information, the SPA and our own research, we identified 65 UK HEIs where Social Policy was offered in some form. These were distributed in terms of the period of establishment into the indicative categories listed in Table 2.1.

The questionnaire included questions on the numbers of courses, the ethnicity of teaching staff by rank, student numbers and ethnicity, and arrangements in place for recruiting and supporting BAME students. The survey was first distributed by email to identified course leaders or, where that person was not clearly identifiable, to the appropriate head of department/school at the beginning of November 2018. Two reminders were sent in the following month, followed by a further reminder sent in the name of the SPA because of the low response rate. By mid-January 2019, when we decided to close the survey, 18 responses had been returned, of which two indicated that they would not be able to provide a response. The useable responses thus constituted 16 (24 per cent) of the HEIs surveyed.

The comments of those who gave nil returns, plus several other comments sent to us, implied that it was regarded as too much work to complete the survey due to the difficulties of retrieving the data from the relevant university administrative/student records departments. Most of those contacted simply did not reply. This was a very disappointing return by any standard, though it is not uncommon for national surveys to have low returns. The poor response could also have been the result of the time of year when the questionnaires were sent out and how long

Table 2.1: Type of university offering some form of Social Policy course

'Old' universities (that is, pre-20th century)	5 (1)
Civic universities (early 20th century)	15 (3)
'Robbins' universities (1960s)	6 (2)
Former polytechnics (1992 universities)	20 (4)
Others	19 (6)

Note: The first figure is the number of HEIs in each category; the second (in brackets) is the number of responses received in that category.

the course leaders/head of departments had to obtain the required data. The data provided by the usable returns are summarised in the following:

- *Numbers of courses offered with Social Policy content*: typically, these HEIs offered between two and four full courses, some of which were honours degrees; some HEIs specified the number of modules offered across a typical three-year undergraduate period. The number of these modules ranged from 12 to 65.
- *Senior teaching staff*: in terms of ethnicity, the proportion of senior teaching staff (that is, Senior Lecturer (SL) and above, including part-time and casual staff) of BAME origin was between 5 per cent and 25 per cent in five HEIs; in the remaining 11, there were no teaching staff of BAME ethnicities. Where there were BAME teaching staff, they were all full-time staff members. No HEI recorded employing BAME part-time or casual staff. The gender split indicated a slight majority of female staff teaching Social Policy in most HEIs.
- *Professors*: one HEI, with a medium-sized staff group, indicated that it had three full-time BAME professors in its staff group; no other HEI had any full-time BAME professors.
- *Junior teaching staff*: a few HEIs had substantial numbers of junior teaching staff, including, in one case, almost 40 teaching assistants in the Social Policy field. Several others had up to 20 but the number of junior teaching staff in the Social Policy field was typically around six. In relation to the junior staff identified, two HEIs had BAME staff, accounting for 4 per cent and 5 per cent of total junior teaching staff, respectively, with all being full-time staff. The remaining 14 HEIs had no BAME junior teaching staff at all.
- *Numbers of students taking Social Policy courses*: this showed considerable variation, largely accounted for by the mode of course. Five HEIs indicated that there were hundreds of students (one having 580) undertaking Social Policy courses or modules but the average for the remainder was around 20 students. Those HEIs with higher numbers taking Social Policy courses were generally situated in neighbourhoods where the local BAME population as a proportion of the population as a whole was significantly higher than the national picture. This may indicate that these universities recruited a significant number of locally based BAME students, though these figures have to be treated with caution: they may overstate the proportion of BAME students as some student records simply note ethnicity as 'non-white' regardless of national origin, thus including overseas students.

- *Special arrangements for recruiting BAME students or supporting them once recruited*: three HEIs indicated that they had special arrangements for recruiting BAME students. One, based on its own research with its students, talked about BAME ambassadors and peer support schemes, as well as addressing important BAME needs such as accommodation arrangements and catering on campus. A second referred to positive action measures without specifying what these were; a third indicated that it did particular work targeting BAME school students.

In summary, despite the very poor response rate, the survey very strongly suggests that in terms of both the numbers and the proportions of BAME students and teaching staff, BAME representation is very low within the Social Policy area. In general, the list of courses and modules reported to us does not indicate a particular emphasis on issues of 'race' and ethnicity, except in the very few cases where modules might be thought to address issues of particular relevance to BAME students, such as migration or citizenship, or where 'race' is implicit in module coverage, such as those addressing issues of inequality and disadvantage, alongside other forms of discrimination. The only exceptions to this pattern were two HEIs that offered optional modules in racism and xenophobia, and 'race' and racism, respectively.

What do published data say?

In addition to the survey, we undertook a secondary review of UCAS and HESA data sets in order to have a clearer picture of the ethnicities of BAME students studying undergraduate and postgraduate Social Policy courses, including those with Social Policy in the title, at UK HEIs. Undergraduate data were obtained from UCAS while postgraduate data were obtained from HESA. Postgraduate data from HESA were only available for the past six years and were obtained for the research team by the University of Bedfordshire via the Higher Education Interctive Dash Board Information (HEIDI Plus) business intelligence tool.

Ethnic group was recorded as declared by the applicant under 'White', 'Black' (including 'Black – Caribbean', 'Black – African', 'Black – Other Black background'), 'Asian' (including 'Asian – Indian', 'Asian – Pakistani', 'Asian – Bangladeshi', 'Asian – Chinese', 'Asian – Other Asian background'), 'Mixed' (including 'Mixed – White and Black Caribbean', 'Mixed – White and Black African', 'Mixed – White and Asian', 'Mixed – Other mixed background'), 'Other' and 'Unknown'. All data were rounded to the nearest five for data confidentiality purposes in line with UCAS/HESA policies. Subject categories were identified using the Joint Academic Coding System (JACS) codes. 'Social Policy' courses were listed under L4; all relevant courses were included using this categorisation. Table 2.2 shows the results of the analysis of undergraduate acceptances for all Social Policy-related courses in the UK by ethnicity between 2008 and 2017.

The data from Table 2.2 show that:

- Over a ten-year period, on average,76 per cent of Social Policy students were 'White' and 19 per cent were of BAME background (including 'Other' as part of the BAME group; 13 per cent if 'Other' is not included).
- Within BAME groups, 'Black' students were most likely to study Social Policy courses, followed by Asians.
- All ethnic groups followed a relatively stable pattern of course uptake in line with total course uptake across the period.

The results in terms of yearly percentages between BAME and 'White' students are shown in Figure 2.1.

Although these figures are interesting, they do not reflect the entire picture. The data did not include BAME students who applied to study Social Policy but declined an offer, as well as those who changed their minds and took other courses. It would have been useful to compare the Social Policy data with those of other disciplines. However, the

Table 2.2: Breakdown of students by ethnicity for all courses listed under 'Social Policy' in UK universities (2008–17)

Ethnicity	2008	2009	2010	2011	2012	2013	2014	2015	2016	2017
Asian	55	80	95	105	90	125	100	130	110	90
Black	75	95	120	205	145	160	135	175	170	135
Mixed	20	45	35	50	50	50	45	40	55	40
White	880	1,010	1,160	1,305	1,160	1,175	1,040	1,040	1,085	1,220
Other	10	5	10	5	5	5	10	35	25	30
Unknown	115	145	15	15	25	25	15	40	30	30
Total	**1,155**	**1,380**	**1,435**	**1,685**	**1,475**	**1,540**	**1,345**	**1,460**	**1,475**	**1,545**
BAME (%)	13	16	17	21	19	22	21	24	23	17
White (%)	76	73	81	77	79	76	77	71	74	79

Figure 2.1: Comparison between BAME and 'White' student numbers at UK universities (2008–17) for all courses listed under 'Social Policy' (%)

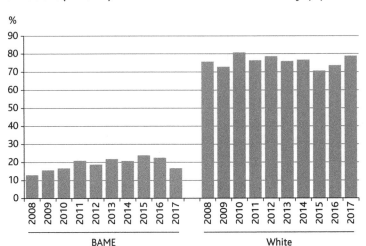

aim of this audit is not to compare Social Policy with other HEI disciplines, but to explain the disproportionately low numbers of BAME students taking Social Policy courses and the challenges that need to be addressed in order to tackle this problem. A key question is how can the disproportionately low numbers of BAME students on Social Policy courses be explained and how much of this situation can be explained by how Social Policy is taught in UK HEIs?

The literature review

The review of the literature was focused on three key issues, namely:

- the experiences of BAME students in UK HEIs in the areas of admissions, progression, retention and achievement;
- the impact of the teaching environment, content and teaching approaches on BAME students' choices and experiences of higher education; and
- BAME staff ratios in UK HEIs and the impact, if any, on the first two issues.

In all three areas, we found limited literature specifically related to Social Policy. Although it is essential that these issues are addressed within subject areas, studies show that this has been difficult with Social Policy. According to Senior (2012: 4), this was partly due to the fact that data and evidence from Social Policy departments have not been forthcoming. However, an in-depth analysis of BAME students' experiences in UK HEIs (Fielding et al, 2008) revealed that although there are variations by subject, none were statistically significant (cf Senior, 2012: 9). Senior (2012: 10) concluded that while Social Policy would benefit from researching within its own discipline for answers, it could also learn by examining the broader perspectives of others. This review provides much of the 'broader perspective', being fully aware of the fact that the variations between subjects and institutions are most likely negligible.

Admissions, retention and achievement of BAME students

Studies report that minority ethnic groups are, on average, more likely to gain admission into UK universities than their white UK counterparts (ECU, 2011). This is believed to be so even among groups who, until recently, were under-represented in higher education, such as those of Black Caribbean ethnic origin (Crawford and Greaves, 2015). This difference is also reflected in applicants' socio-economic backgrounds. BAME students from less advantaged backgrounds are more likely to attend HEIs than comparable white UK students, where the lowest socio-economic quintile group have participation rates more than ten percentage points lower than those of any other ethnic group. The National Education Opportunity Network reported that in 2019, more than half of UK HEIs had fewer than 5 per cent of white working-class students in their intakes. Some of the differences are more substantial. For example, Indian and Chinese pupils are, on average, twice as likely to go to university as their white UK counterparts (BIS, 2015; Crawford and Greaves, 2015) (see Figure 2.2).

These figures exist despite records of prior attainment that show pupils of black, Pakistani and Bangladeshi ethnic origin performing worse, on average, in national school tests and exams, and as more likely to have lower prior attainment points than their white peers (see also Department for Education, 2012; EHRC, 2015). The Department of Business, Innovation and Skills (BIS, 2015) report also showed that most minority ethnic groups are, on average, more likely to attend one of the 52 selective or 'high-tariff' institutions than their white UK counterparts, though the differences are smaller than those found in participation in other (post-1992) universities (see Figure 2.3).

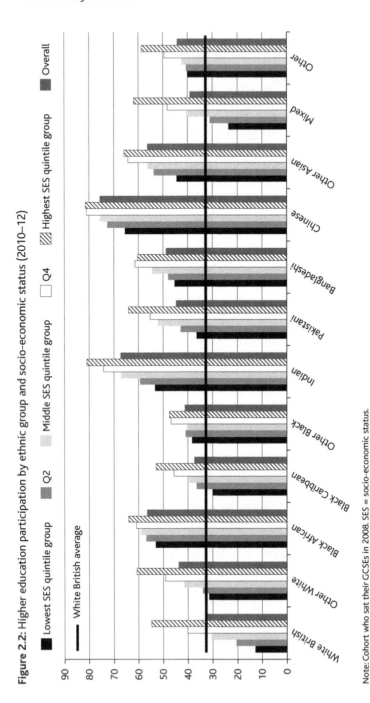

Figure 2.2: Higher education participation by ethnic group and socio-economic status (2010–12)

Note: Cohort who sat their GCSEs in 2008. SES = socio-economic status.

Source: Crawford and Greaves (2015) and Institute for Fiscal Studies, available at: http://www.ifs.org.uk/publications/8042

Figure 2.3: Proportion of key stage 5 leavers at an HEI by detailed ethnicity (2015/16)

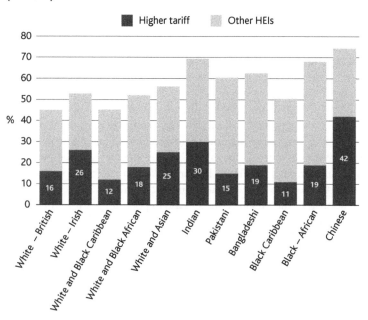

Source: Office for Students (no date: 3)

However, the BIS study acknowledged the findings from studies which have shown that minority ethnic groups are less likely to receive offers from allegedly 'prestigious' Russell Group UK universities than their equivalently qualified white UK counterparts (Boliver, 2013, 2015, 2016), but it argued that despite what appears like selective admissions on the part of these institutions, BAME admissions at these institutions were still, on average, higher than those of British white students. This contradicts UCAS figures (UCAS, 2015) showing that among young English applicants applying to higher-tariff providers, the offer rate to the 'White' ethnic group is higher than to the 'Asian', 'Black', 'Mixed' and 'Other' ethnic groups in every subject area. Runnymede's (2010) report confirms that in terms of actual size and numbers, most BAME students are more likely to attend post-1992 universities.

The reasons why more BAME young people might aspire to go to university compared to their white counterparts have been explained by several, mainly 'extra-academic', factors such as family pressures, which may also include parental choice of study area and future employment.

Location of university is another factor. BAME students predominantly attend universities in close proximity to the family home.[1] A 2012 survey showed that there were more black students at the University of East London than in the 'top' 20 UK HEIs combined (Elevation Networks Trust, 2012: 16). According to Chowdry et al (2013), evidence unsurprisingly showed that not all university degrees have equal economic value, that is, that the *type* of university that is attended makes a difference to a pupil's labour market outcomes. In the UK, the wage benefit from a degree varies markedly according to both the degree subject studied and the type of institution attended. Previous research has suggested that low socio-economic status students in the UK are concentrated in 'post-1992' universities and that degrees from these institutions attract lower labour market returns (cf Chowdry et al, 2013: 433; see also Higher Education Policy Institute, 2017). The issues mentioned in the previous studies raise important questions for Social Policy in terms of how the institution and perceived employability might have affected its BAME student intakes.

Official statistics also show that there are stark differences between ethnic groups in terms of retention and the degree class they achieve, with non-completion rates highest among Black Caribbean students and the lowest degree outcomes also occurring among black students (ECU, 2011), even after controlling for factors commonly known to affect academic performance, such as prior entry qualifications or points (Connor et al, 2003; Broecke and Nicholls, 2007; Richardson, 2015) (see Figure 2.4). These differences occur at institutions and on courses of all kinds, even in students taking courses by distance learning with the UK Open University (Richardson, 2009, 2015; Woodfield, 2014).

Several factors have been identified to explain this disparity, many relating to the fact that BAME students' experience of higher education is generally inferior to that of white students. Major factors that have been specifically identified include: discriminatory teaching, learning and assessment (TLA) practices; problems of segregation (for example, subtle exclusionary attitudes and behaviour on the part of teachers or other students); 'inadequate' course content and design; low teacher expectations; undervaluing or under-challenging BAME students; prejudiced attitudes associated with linguistic competence; discriminatory practices inherent in the learning environment; and inadequate student support mechanisms, including inadequate complaints mechanisms and the inadequate inclusion of BAME students in the composition of both informal advisory groups and formal governance committees (Richardson, 2010, 2015; Singh, 2011; Stevenson, 2012).

Figure 2.4: Non-continuation rates among UK-domiciled first degree students in English HEIs (2008–15)

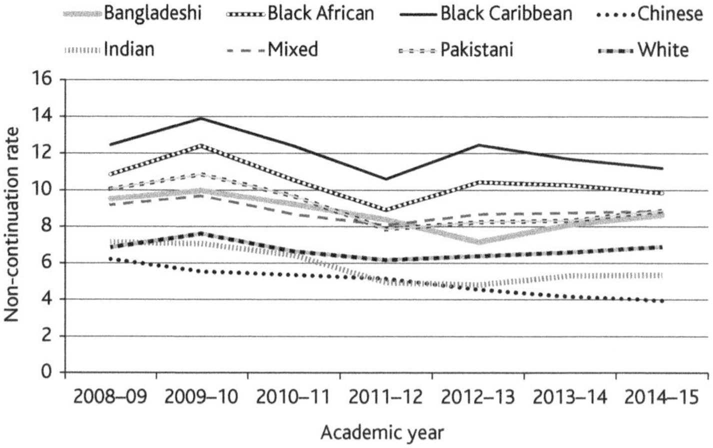

Source: Office for Students (no date: 4)

In relation to Social Policy in particular, the ECU (2011) report revealed that 12.6 per cent of black students and 8.9 per cent of Asian students chose to enrol onto Social Studies courses compared to 8.4 per cent of white students. According to Senior (2012), despite some of the earlier observations, given the fact that this subject area actually appears to attract more BAME students than white students, and in the face of evidence which suggests that an ongoing attainment gap exists between BAME and white students, it is essential that the issue of retention and attainment is addressed within the subject area. As indicated by Senior, data on the progression and retention of BAME students on Social Policy programmes in the UK are relatively very scarce. This means that issues of retention and performance that have been found to be problematic with BAME students are not currently addressed within Social Policy.

The teaching environment

Studies show how BAME students are marginalised on campus 'through the maintenance of white norms' (Crozier et al, 2016, cited in Woodfield, 2017: 234). In a comprehensive review of how 'race' and racism were presented by higher education researchers in the US, Harper (2012) noted how in several studies where the results showed that BAME students perceived and experienced campus racial climates differently than their white counterparts, few authors considered structural/institutional racism as a logical explanation for such differences. Harper (2012: 17) showed that studies on why BAME students disproportionately 'drop out' said:

> nothing about how constant interaction with white faculty, peers, and others whom minoritized students view as racist and the existence of racist environmental conditions in the residence halls could have engendered discomfort among minoritized students and consequently dissuaded their out-of-class engagement and might also have compelled them to take time off.

However, instead of viewing racial differences as by-products of institutionalised racism that requires systemic organisational change, these authors routinely suggested approaches that have little to do with investigating and responding to the realities of race on campus (Harper, 2012: 18). Harper noted that few authors actually discussed their findings in ways that engaged racism as a plausible explanation for racial differences or the negative experiences reported by 'minoritised' participants. Harper found that instead of calling these outcomes racist, researchers commonly used the following semantic substitutes to describe the campus environments that minoritised students, faculty and administrators often encountered: 'alienating', 'hostile', 'marginalizing', 'chilly', 'harmful', 'isolating', 'unfriendly', 'negative', 'antagonistic', 'unwelcoming', 'prejudicial', 'discriminatory', 'exclusionary' and 'unsupportive' (Harper, 2012: 20; see also Housee, 2018).

In the UK, the experience of racism by BAME students in UK HEIs is acknowledged (see EHRC, 2019) but the effects on BAME students' choices and performance are yet to be fully investigated. In a recent survey, UK university staff also dismissed the thought that their institutions might be racist while recognising that some colleagues might be. One lecturer went further and argued that the structures that UK universities operate 'are hangovers from a prior era; designed for rich white people, they're not designed to be conducive to the sort of cohorts that we have now' (cited in Stevenson, 2012: 9). In a survey involving BAME students in a UK HEI, Andall-Stanberry (2011: 9) found that students viewed teaching staff as ignorant of equality and diversity issues; as a result, staff have not been able to educate white students on how to develop a more balanced non-discriminatory view of their BAME peers. Many of the students in this survey said that they would strongly discourage others from attending their university unless there were changes made in how it treated BAME and international students (Andall-Stanberry, 2011: 10). Inadequate institutional awareness/understanding of the cultural differences and life experiences that impact significantly on BAME integration has been clearly identified as one key institutional barrier to BAME students' participation and achievement in UK HEIs. Some students surveyed were highly critical of institutions presenting an image of diversity in marketing materials, particularly on their websites, which turned out to be unrealistic, leading to a strong sense of 'deception' (Stevenson, 2012: 16).

Addressing 'race' issues in TLA

Stevenson's (2012) comprehensive report on black and minority ethnic student degree retention and attainment, which included surveys with university lecturers and BAME students in 11 UK HEIs, revealed that focusing on 'race' in HEI TLA strategies is not a straightforward issue. The report recommended various steps that ought to be taken, including: addressing institutional barriers; providing diverse approaches to TLA and support services (including 'safe spaces'); developing anti-racist skills among all staff, particularly personal tutors; strong central leadership; and the regular monitoring and evaluation of anti-racist strategies (Stevenson, 2012: 17–20; for similar suggestions specifically directed at Social Policy, see also Senior, 2012: 11–25). However, although the need to have inclusive TLA practices was acknowledged by most of the staff surveyed by Stevenson (2012), there was a general lack of knowledge of any type of teaching and learning strategies that should be directed specifically at BAME students or whether or not such an intervention would make a difference. In the interviews conducted with university lecturers and BAME students, Stevenson (2012: 15) found that both did not want BAME students to be singled out as a target group, as it 'smacked of inadvertent racism'.

There is no conclusive information on the nature and extent of the coverage of 'race' on all Social Policy courses taught in the UK's HEIs (other than our survey findings). Stevenson found substantial coverage of 'race' in only one of the 11 universities that she surveyed. However, there does appear to be an expectation that 'protected characteristics' (see Equality Act 2010), including 'race', will be covered on most topics as they are often the most vulnerable to welfare inequalities, political powerlessness and most forms of human suffering. There is no doubt that Social Policy as an academic subject has evolved significantly since it was first taught in 1921. However, this substantial progress has been mainly in terms of the subject matter or content, for example, significant developments have taken place in terms of the internationalisation of the curriculum, leading to new topics such as migration, human trafficking and modern slavery. As Irving and Young (2005) have argued, these developments have led to a teaching problem in terms of attempts to cover what is rapidly becoming a content overload at the expense of the development of transferable skills.

BAME staff ratios in UK HEIs

In 2016/17, there were 419,710 staff at UK HEIs, 49 per cent having an academic employment contract; 12 per cent were from other European Union (EU) countries, while 8 per cent were from outside the EU. In 2016/17, where sex and ethnicity were known, white males accounted for more than two thirds of academic professorial staff (Universities UK, 2018). Most of the studies on the experiences of BAME staff in UK's HEIs tend to agree that these staff are treated less favourably than their white counterparts. Surveys have shown that BAME staff are disproportionately in lower ranks, earn less than white counterparts, are more likely to have experienced discrimination, experience inferior pay and conditions, have their authority questioned, and face disproportionate levels of scrutiny and barriers to career development (see Leathwood et al, 2009). In terms of gender, there is very significant under-representation of BAME women in senior academic posts. Advance HE (formerly the Equality Challenge Unit [ECU]) reported in 2018 that of 4,735 female professors in UK HEIs, only 25 [0.5 per cent] were black and 55 were BAME. There are currently only seven BAME female professors of Social Policy or closely related subjects employed in UK HEIs.

The question has been raised as to whether increasing the numbers of BAME academics would have any significant effect on BAME students' enrolment, retention and achievements on courses. It has been suggested that BAME staff representation could be a contributing factor to the problem of BAME retention and performance as BAME staff would serve as role models for BAME students (see Runnymede, 2010; Singh, 2011; Senior, 2012). However, this view has been contested (Stevenson, 2012). There is no evidence on whether having BAME staff teaching 'race'-related topics (or teaching much more) on specific degrees will impact positively on BAME student enrolment and performance. More research is needed on why BAME students choose Social Policy as a degree course and whether having more focus on 'race', as well as having more BAME lecturers teach modules, would be advantageous to BAME students' admission, progression and completion rates on Social Policy courses.

The views of 'experts'

We identified 12 people who were geographically representative in terms of their location and had substantial experience in Social Policy teaching, who could together be regarded as an expert 'sounding board' for informing our investigations. Ten took part in short, structured telephone interviews to collect as much contextual information as possible from their own considerable collective experience. Two respondents were BAME academics. Questions asked covered: their knowledge of the literature; the key issues in relation to the coverage of 'race' in Social Policy teaching, including recruitment and enrolment; BAME involvement in courses and teaching; and learning more generally. In summary, the comments gleaned from the remaining ten respondents are summarised thematically as follows.

The 'whiteness' of Social Policy

As several respondents put it, Social Policy is "a white subject with a white colonial history and taught mainly by white people". One respondent stated that it is about the "dead white men of social policy". Another respondent suggested that Social Policy is increasingly focusing on welfare models but the notions of welfare underpinning this approach are very exclusive and do not focus strongly, if at all, on 'race', ethnicity and inequality. For example, 'race' topics are often covered in Social Policy modules but as subsidiary, not as mainstream. In several cases, lecturers coming new to some HEIs had devised new modules themselves on 'race' and related issues as there had been no full module on the subject previously. This implied that the teaching of 'race' was seen not as necessarily a departmental/school imperative, but as a particular interest of one lecturer.

However, some new subjects/disciplines have emerged that do not necessarily have Social Policy in their titles, but cover welfare topics that are also related to 'race', for example, Migration Studies or, more obliquely, Citizenship. In some cases, lecturers have been asked to make inputs on 'race' to courses other than Social Policy, and 'race' sometimes pops up in other core courses, such as Economics when, for example, the labour market is analysed. In some cases, Social Policy ended up being covered in other cognate courses such as Education, which means that its profile is nowhere near as high as it might be. Several suggested that they try to ensure that the dimension of 'race' is also discussed when dealing with overarching themes such as 'youth' or disability.

One lecturer offering a module on 'race' said that it attracted students from other core disciplines (such as Health or Politics) and excited considerable interest, but that some of the issues raised, such as slavery and colonialism, were experienced by students as shocking, which suggested that they had not been exposed to thinking in this area beforehand. Overall, the picture was that 'race' teaching within Social Policy courses was, as one lecturer put it, "a drop in the ocean", and is not regarded in any sense as a mainstream feature.

The lack of focus on 'race' in undergraduate courses was replicated in postgraduate taught courses, which is a finding emphasised by the results of our survey. In some cases, it was noted that white staff found themselves uncomfortable teaching 'race' to a mixed ethnic group and therefore avoided doing so. One respondent also noted that white people need to recognise the standpoint of BAME people, and if they are teaching 'race', they have to be absolutely sure about their own identity while doing so. Against this, multidimensional policy and political issues with high public profiles, such as Windrush and Grenfell, encouraged some staff to pick up these issues.

Low numbers of BAME students on Social Policy courses

In Northern Ireland in particular, but also in other areas of the UK, the low numbers of BAME students on Social Policy courses was said simply to reflect the demographics of the area. In Northern Ireland, for example, the students are predominantly Irish. This was the only strongly explicit reason given for low numbers of BAME people on Social Policy courses, though it was generally recognised that recruitment was a problematic area. In one university near London where there was relatively high BAME representation, the respondent there felt that the problem for them was not in recruitment – with many BAME students coming through non-traditional routes – but in attainment, in terms of degree class and in general marks, including resubmitted work. In another university, also set in a highly multicultural area, 80 per cent of students were local and 50–60 per cent were from BAME backgrounds.

Here, the pairing of Social Policy with Social Care and Sociology worked well for recruitment. In other HEIs, Social Policy seemed to be 'squeezed out' by a focus on Sociology, for example, with Social Policy seen as a minor element of a joint course or in bigger social science schools.

It was also felt that the route into employability is less clear for Social Policy than for Law or Nursing, for example, and that this affects recruitment. Another HEI undertook considerable outreach work into BAME communities, including work with churches and faith groups, and found that many BAME people believed themselves not to be able to work at the higher education level. They argued that while prospective BAME students may not 'choose' to do Social Policy, this can be addressed once students have been engaged with. This HEI used ex-students as role models. However, although recruitment was thus widely said to be problematic, most of the respondents had few suggestions, if any, on how the subject could be made attractive to BAME people. One respondent talked about employability and marketing but not specifically about how these can be targeted at BAME admissions. More widely, yet again, the issue of the alienation of BAME students from the curriculum was raised – that they are disengaged at some stage because it is not seen as relevant to their interests and experience. Some reported that BAME students failed to do as well on Social Policy courses as they had expected.

The SPA's profile in relation to 'race'

The SPA has never made use of ethnic monitoring in membership application forms and it is therefore not possible to identify whether its membership reflects the 15 per cent BAME proportion in the wider UK population.[2] We therefore turned to the public face of the SPA – its publications, conferences and strategic documents – to see to what extent the dimension of 'race' was reflected in them. Over the past few years, the two major public reports with which the SPA has been associated are *The current and future state of Social Policy teaching in UK HEIs* (Patrick et al, 2017 [2012])[3] and *Social Policy: Subject benchmark statement* (Quality Assurance Agency, 2016). The only salient point made in Patrick et al (2017 [2012]) about the position of 'race' within the curriculum came from one interviewee who observed that Social Policy was increasingly being concentrated within Russell Group universities (with their under-representation of BAME students), and that despite the rhetoric of its mission, Social Policy was not available to the most diverse range of potential students. This issue was not significantly addressed in the report's recommendations. The Quality Assurance Agency's (2016) *Subject benchmark* document refers to equality and diversity as important issues for discussion, as well as to the dimension of ethnicity in relation to social groups characterised by difference, but the terms 'race' and racism do not appear anywhere. We also undertook an analysis of material published in the SPA's two major journals (*Journal of Social Policy* [*JSP*] and *Social Policy and Society* [*SPS*]) and its annual review (*SPR*), as well as the profile of papers and keynote SPA conference speeches. These showed that over the past seven years, only 6–7 per cent of papers published in the *JSP*, the *SPS* and the *SPR* concerned issues of 'race' or were written by BAME authors.

Clearly, behind these data are several questions. For example, the *SPR* consists of chapters commissioned to reflect key current debates. It is perhaps surprising that 'race', with all the tensions and conflict associated with it in public policy (for example, about police behaviour in relation to minority groups, the exclusion of minority groups from education, housing ghettoisation and disadvantage in the labour market), has not been more strongly represented. As with papers submitted to the two journals of *JSP* and *SPS*, we do not know whether there has been a disproportionate number of papers addressing issues of 'race' and ethnicity that have been rejected for whatever reason. We also do not know (and given issues of both confidentiality and competitiveness within higher education publishing circles, we probably never will) whether many papers that might have appeared in the SPA's outputs have been directed to specialist journals (for example, the *Journal of Migration Studies* or *Ethnic and Racial Studies*) on the assumption that they would have a better fit or a more sympathetic review. We also analysed outputs of the comparable journal *CSP*, which argues that it takes a more radical stance and thus might address some of the gaps identified in relation to 'race' and ethnicity. *CSP* had a slightly larger proportion of relevant papers (see Tables 2.3–2.6). The most recent public SPA output is the series of short blogs marking 50 years since the SPA's founding. Only six had a strong or moderate focus on the dimension of ethnicity. Those submitting blogs were self-selecting.

In relation to conferences, again, no attempt has been made by the SPA at the ethnic monitoring of attendees, so proportions identified may be subject to slight inaccuracies (Table 2.7).

Although it might be regarded as inappropriate to talk about quotas for the representation of the issue of 'race', it is clear that the SPA's outputs (and, largely, the outputs of *CSP, the nearest comparatpor to the*

Table 2.3: UK BAME representation in *JSP*

Year	2014	2015	2016	2017	2018	Total 5 years	Annual average
Number of papers in volume	38	35	35	37	39	184	37
Number of papers with UK BAME topic	1	2	2	3	2	10	2
Number of BAME authors[a]	0	1	2	2	3	8	2

Note: [a] Only one author counted per paper even where multiple authorship.

Table 2.4: UK BAME representation in *SPS*

Year	2014	2015	2016	2017[b]	2018	Total 5 years	Annual average
Number of papers in volume	48	51	48	51	45	243	49
Number of papers with UK BAME topic	1	2	3	9	0	15	3
Number of BAME authors[a]	2	1	2	11	1	17	3

Notes: [a] Only one author counted per paper even where multiple authorship.
[b] Including a special themed issue on migration and labour markets.

Table 2.5: UK BAME representation in *SPR*

Year	2014	2015	2016	2017[b]	2018	Total 5 years	Annual average
Number of chapters in volume	14	12	13	12	13	64	13
Number of chapters with UK BAME topic	0	0	1	3	2	6	1
Number of BAME authors[a]	0	0	0	1	0	1	1

Notes: [a] Only one author counted per paper even where multiple authorship.
[b] Including one themed section on migrants.

Table 2.6: UK BAME representation in *CSP*

Year	2014	2015	2016	2017[b]	2018	Total 5 years	Annual average
Number of papers in volume	27	23	31	30	37	148	30
Number of papers with UK BAME topic	4	4	4	8	1	21	4
Number of BAME authors[a]	3	2	2	6	0	13	3

Notes: [a] Only one author counted per paper even where multiple authorship.
[b] Including a special issue on radicalisation and terrorism.

Table 2.7: BAME representation at annual SPA conferences

Year	2013 Sheffield	2014 Sheffield	2015 Ulster	2016 Belfast	2017 Durham	2018 York	Total 6 years	Annual average
Total number of papers	203	159	208	165	162	202	1,099	183
Number of plenaries	4	4	4	3	3	3	21	3
Number of plenaries with UK 'race'-related topics	0	0	0	0	0	0	0	0
Number of plenaries with BAME presenters	0	0	0	0	0	0	0	0
Number of papers with UK 'race'-related topics	9	6	4	5	0	3	27	4
Number of papers with UK BAME presenters	8	6	3	5	1	8	31	5
Number of papers with non-UK topics	36	42	23	38	38	45	216	36
Number of papers with non-UK presenters	41	46	21	34	36	47	226	38

SPA's house journals) nowhere near reflect the UK's demography. What they do reflect, however, is the wide-ranging ways (comprising the various elements and stages detailed earlier) in which both BAME authors and discussion of 'race' and racism (whether by BAME authors or others) remain marginal to Social Policy's published face.

Conclusion

It is clear from this analysis that the SPA has a considerable way to go to persuade Social Policy academics to take the issue of 'race' seriously. As one senior academic put it, "we are the problem, not the solution". Despite some hopeful initiatives, we argue that this task cannot be achieved from the current base of Social Policy teaching in higher education: the staff profile in most Social Policy departments is almost entirely white, providing little impetus for the development of courses that address issues of 'race', colonialism, slavery and the black experience of welfare; promotion for BAME staff is problematic; achievement levels for BAME students are generally poor in the absence of appropriate support; drop-out rates are higher than average; and the ingredients for a supportive environment for BAME students are usually missing. On the basis of our survey, most HEIs surveyed were disinterested in the audit at best. Responses were incomplete and we were often referred to university administrative sections for data on staffing and student numbers, which should have been a matter of core concern for teaching staff. Russell Group universities showed up particularly poorly. Few HEIs had any provisions in place to promote the recruitment of BAME applicants, or to provide support. Interestingly, in the few HEIs where there had been initiatives to address racism, these tended to be prompted by student action rather than from staff groups.

This all suggests that institutions and the academics within them that make and implement policy and practice have to take responsibility for the present situation and not, as some still do, try to shift responsibility onto BAME students and prospective students. To change this requires a major cultural shift within the organisation and the discipline, which the SPA has to lead. Our full report[4] provides an agenda for change, which, as noted, the SPA executive has enthusiastically taken up. We hope that this energy will drive change effectively in the interests of present and future students, as well as of the subject itself, which needs to be made much more relevant to a multicultural and diverse society in which 'race' currently features most strongly as a tool to oppress minority groups. The SPA's response commits it to a programme of action. However, we would argue that it is clearly not its problem alone. It cannot do this without the support of the wider Social Policy community; it is a problem facing every HEI and every Social Policy academic. Furthermore, this struggle can draw on concern beyond the Social Policy community. The British Sociological Association is conducting a similar enquiry and the Royal Historical Society has recently examined the teaching of 'race' in History departments, coming to parallel, dismal, conclusions.[5]

Acknowledgement

The authors acknowledge considerable research help from Irtiza Qureshi.

Notes

[1] This was identified as an issue in the early days of the Hull York Medical School, with a split campus, where Pakistani-British applicants were found to favour studying at York rather than at Hull because of the former' closer location to the city of origin (Bradford) of many of them.

[2] We understand that the SPA is now including ethnic monitoring in its membership procedures.

³ See: www.social-policy.org.uk/wordpress/wp-content/uploads/2014/05/
Teaching-Learning-Report2c-2017.pdf
⁴ See: www.social-policy.org.uk/uncategorized/the-missing-dimension-
where-is-race-in-social-policy-teaching-and-learning/
⁵ See: https://5hm1h4aktue2uejbs1hsqt31-wpengine.netdna-ssl.com/wp-
content/uploads/2018/10/RHS_race_report_EMBARGO_0001_18Oct.
pdf

References

Andall-Stanberry, M. (2011) '"Widening participation": retention, achievement, and support for BAME students', paper presented at the RANHLE Project conference, University of Seville, Spain, April, www.dsw.edu.pl/fileadmin/www-ranlhe/files/Andall-Stanberry.pdf

BIS (Department of Business, Innovation and Skills) (2015) *Socio-economic, ethnic and gender differences in HE participation*, BIS Research Paper No 186, London: BIS.

Boliver, V. (2013) 'How fair is access to more prestigious UK universities?', *British Journal of Sociology*, 64(2): 345–64.

Boliver, V. (2015) 'Lies, damned lies and statistics on widening access to Russell Group universities', *Radical Statistics*, 113: 29–38.

Boliver, V. (2016) 'Exploring ethnic inequalities in admission to Russell Group universities', *Sociology*, 50(2): 247–66.

Broecke, S. and Nicholls, T. (2007) *Ethnicity and degree attainment*, DfES Research Report RW92, London: Department for Education and Skills (DfES).

Chattoo, S., Atkin, K., Craig, G. and Flynn, R. (2019) *Understanding 'race' and ethnicity: Theory, history, policy, practice* (2nd edn), Bristol: Policy Press.

Chowdry, H., Crawford, C., Dearden, L., Goodman, A. and Vignoles, A. (2013) 'Widening participation in higher education: analysis using linked administrative data', *Journal of the Royal Statistical Society Series A*, 176(2): 431–57.

Connor, H., Tyers, C., Davis, S. and Tackey, N.D. (2003) *Minority ethnic students in higher education: Interim report, Institute for Employment Studies*, DfES Report RR448, London: Department for Education and Skills (DfES).

Craig, G. (2007) '"Cunning, unprincipled, loathsome": the racist tail wags the welfare dog', *Journal of Social Policy*, 36(4): 605–23.

Craig, G. (2011) 'Forward to the past: does the BAME third sector have a future?', *Voluntary Sector Review*, 2(3): 367–89.

Craig, G. (2013) 'Invisibilising "race" in public policy', *Critical Social Policy*, 33(4): 712–20.

Craig, G. and Katbamna, S. (2004) '"Race" and social policy research' in S. Becker and A. Bryman, (eds) *Understanding research for Social Policy and Practice*, Bristol: Policy Press: 158-164.

Craig, G. and O'Neill, M. (2013) 'It's time to move on from "race"?', in G.Ramia, K. Farnsworth and Z. Irving (eds), *Social policy review 25*, Sheffield: Social Policy Association: 93-112.

Crawford, C. and Greaves, E. (2015) *Ethnic minorities substantially more likely to go to university than their white British peers*, London: Institute for Fiscal Studies and ESRC, www.ifs.org.uk/publications/8042

Crozier, G., Burke, P.-J. and Archer, L. (2016) 'Peer relations in higher education: raced, classed and gendered constructions and Othering', *Whiteness and Education*, 1(1): 39–53.

Department for Education (2012) *A profile of pupil exclusions in England*, Education Standards Analysis and Research Division, Research Report DFE-RR190, London: Department for Education.

ECU (Equality Challenge Unit) (2011) *Equality in higher education: Statistical report 2011*, London: ECU.

EHRC (Equality and Human Rights Commission) (2015) *Is Britain fairer? The state of equality and human rights 2015*, London: EHRC.

EHRC (2019) *Tackling racial harassment: Universities challenged*, London: EHRC.

Elevation Networks Trust (2012) *Race to the top: The experience of black students in higher education*, London: The Bow Group.

Fielding, A., Charlton, C., Kounali, D. and Leckie, G. (2008) *Degree attainment, ethnicity and gender: Interactions and the modification of effects. A quantitative analysis*, York: Higher Education Academy.

Harper, S.R. (2012) 'Race without racism: how higher education researchers minimize racist institutional norms', *The Review of Higher Education*, 36(1, Supplement): 9–29.

Higher Education Policy Institute (2017) *Where next for widening participation and fair access? New insights from leading thinkers*, HEPI Report 98, London: HEPI.

Housee, S. (2018) *Speaking out against racism in the university space*, London: UCL Press.

Irving, Z. and Young, P. (2005) 'When less is more: the dominance of subject-content in the teaching of undergraduate Social Policy', *Social Policy & Society*, 4(1): 1–9.

Leathwood, C., Maylor, U. and Moreau, M. (2009) *The experience of black and minority ethnic staff working in higher education. Literature review*, London: Equality Challenge Unit.

Office for Students (no date) 'Topic briefing: black and minority ethnic (BME) students', pp 3–4, www.officeforstudents.org.uk/media/145556db-8183-40b8-b7af-741bf2b55d79/topic-briefing_bme-students.pdf

Patrick, R., Brown, K. and Drever, E. (2017 [2012]) *The current and future state of Social Policy teaching in UK HEIs*, Manchester: Social Policy Association.

Quality Assurance Agency (QAA) (2016) *Subject Benchmark Statement, Social Policy*, Gloucester: QAA.

Richardson, J.T.E. (2009) 'The role of ethnicity in the attainment and experiences of graduates in distance education', *Higher Education*, 58: 321–38.

Richardson, J.T.E. (2010) 'Conceptions of learning and approaches to studying among white and ethnic minority students in distance education', *British Journal of Educational Psychology*, 80: 535–56.

Richardson, J.T.E. (2015) 'The under-attainment of ethnic minority students in UK higher education: what we know and what we don't know', *Journal of Further and Higher Education*, 39(2): 278–91.

Runnymede (2010) *Ethnicity and participation in higher education*, London: Runnymede.

Senior, N. (2012) *Exploring the retention and attainment of black and minority ethnic (BAME) students on Social Policy pathways in higher education*, York: The Higher Education Academy.

Singh, G. (2011) *Black and minority ethnic (BAME) students' participation in higher education: Improving retention and success. A synthesis of research evidence*, York: Higher Education Academy.

Stevenson, J. (2012) *Black and minority ethnic student degree retention and attainment*, York: Higher Education Academy.

UCAS (Universities and Colleges Admissions Service) (2015) *Analysis note 2015/05*, 18 September, London: UCAS Analysis and Research, www.ucas.com

Universities UK (2018) *Higher education in facts and figures 2018*, London: Universities UK.

Woodfield, R. (2014) *Undergraduate retention and attainment across the disciplines*, York: Higher Education Academy.

Woodfield, R. (2017) 'Undergraduate students who are required to withdraw from university: the role of ethnicity', *British Educational Research Journal*, 43(2): 230–52.

3

Young people as cultural critics of the monocultural landscapes that fail them

Rick Bowler and Amina Razak

Introduction

> The so-called English ideal excluded most of the population
> from the identity with which they had been born. (Paxman,
> 1999: 177–8)

This chapter focuses on the experiences and views of British Muslim
young women and their solutions to the limitations embedded in the
monocultural mindsets organising the public spaces of their urban
landscape. The data come from a recent research project mapping the
needs of young people who are members of the Young Asian Voices
(YAV) youth project in Sunderland (Bowler and Razak, 2017). Their
narratives were conscious of place and identified how longstanding
racialised ideas connecting whiteness as belonging, pervasive in the local
monoculture,[1] act as an impediment to opportunities for a multi-vocal
intercultural present.[2]

In 2012, the British government introduced a policy to make the
social landscape of the nation a hostile environment. The hostile
environment policy took shape when Theresa May was Home
Secretary, under a secretive Home Office working group titled the
'Hostile Environment Working Group' (Elgot, 2018). Theresa May
was two years into her job as Home Secretary when she told *The
Telegraph* in 2012 that her aim 'was to create here in Britain a really
hostile environment for illegal migration' (Grierson, 2018). As Liberty
(2018: 5) have argued: 'The hostile environment is a sprawling web
of immigration controls embedded in the heart of our public services
and communities.'

This narration of the hostile environment and the 'new forms of
intersectional racist practices' arising from it (Yuval-Davis et al, 2018:

241) has been identified as contributing to the spikes in racial and religious hate crime arising from the Brexit referendum (Bowler, 2017). The argument here is that acts of racism and processes of racialisation emerge from and are woven into political, cultural and social formations dominant in society. A difficulty for the British-Asian Muslim Mackem[3] young women in Sunderland is the impact of the dominant political discourse that has posited the idea of Britain as a neoliberal post-racial state (Garner, 2016), despite racist violence becoming normalised (Fekete, 2019).

In contemporary Britain, some spaces operate as contexts described as super-diverse[4] (Vertovec, 2007; Wessendorf and Phillimore, 2018), while others have been experienced and named as monocultural 'failed spaces' (Thomas et al, 2018: 262).[5] The local city and its regional geography, which gave birth to YAV and where all the young women identified in this chapter were born, has been identified as predominantly a monocultural failed space (Saeed, 2007). In monocultural white settings, the complexity of 'race' and class intersecting as everyday realities in regions such as the North-East of England require a critical understanding (Sviensson, 2009; Khan and Shaheen, 2017; Snoussi and Mompelat, 2019).

Sunderland is a city located on the coast in the North-East of England with a population of 275,300, of which 95.9 per cent of people self-identify as white (Sunderland Census, 2019). The black, Asian and minority ethnic (BAME) population is less than 5 per cent, meaning that the city is slightly below the average for the North-East of England as a whole. Rushton (2017) identified the city as having one of the smallest proportions of British minority ethnic groups and recently arrived migrants anywhere in the North-East.

Sunderland is a place that has not yet recovered from large-scale rapid deindustrialisation and where opportunity structures for many people fit the description of precarious (Standing, 2016). Unemployment for BAME groups, and specifically BAME women, in Sunderland is more than double that of the white communities (Sunderland City Council, 2019) and the City 'has high levels of social and economic deprivation' (Sunderland Partnership, 2019: 34).

Sunderland also has a history of Far-Right political activity, as demonstrated by the British National Party gaining up to 14 per cent of the votes in local elections on 1 May 2003 (Teale, 2002–17, cited in Rushton, 2017: 8). Despite this targeting by Far-Right activists and their actions of 'hateful extremism', as described by Sara Khan, (2019), an overtly racist party has never won an election in Sunderland.

Therefore, the racial reality for BAME and white young people is one of a contested space where anti-racist activity and balanced media reporting are also visible and vocal in their city (Clark, 2019; Khan, S., 2019).

Mirroring research on Manchester, the monoculture dominant in the politics of a place like Sunderland and its cultural city aspiration diminishes the extent of racism's reach when it 'claims diversity as a celebration whilst ignoring difference in experience' (Harries, 2018: 23). It is the critical exposition of the lived experience of the young women in our study that so clearly illuminates the gap that exists between the desire for diversity and culture of the civic leaders of the city, and the lack of cognisance about the different experiences of young people in their realm.

Therefore, how lived experiences of 'race' play out in everyday encounters is likely to be an important factor when challenging monocultural norms within a city aspiring to become a vibrant intercultural hub (Sunderland Culture, 2018). The chapter illuminates the commonplace realities of a racialised and gendered violence that influence the lifeworld[6] of young people in Sunderland and the surrounding area (Bowler, 2006, 2013; Saeed, 2007; Nayak, 2017). How young people understand, collude with or challenge the tensions arising from their lived experience as they develop their literacies about the orientations of those experiences in places such as Sunderland should be of core concern to all with an interest in developing socially just social policy.

Contextual and conceptual landscapes

In the 1960s, racism was endemic in Britain, enacted by many white people in everyday settings and fuelled by leading members of the political elite (Holbourne et al, 2010). Paul (1997) identified the ideology underpinning policy development in that period as 'whitewashed' and 'racialising', enmeshing 'whiteness' with British national identity. In this post-colonial period, whiteness was the underpinning ideological core of British state policy about immigration, nationality and citizenship (Paul, 1997; Schwarz, 2011; Olusoga, 2019). Today, the context in which racism operates has changed, with Britain now having a strong legislative framework of racial equality and human rights (for example, the Equality Act 2010). Despite these progressive steps, racialised inequality and racist violence remain an everyday part of the British landscape (Chattoo et al, 2019).

Recent research for the UK Social Policy Association has identified the failings since the 1960s in British Public Policy to take seriously the issue of 'race' and, more specifically, racism (Craig et al, 2019). This history of failure leaves the racial reality of the colonial logic, where whiteness operated as the national identifier for Britishness, absent from critical public debate (Paul, 1997; Shwarz, 2011; Olusoga, 2019). As Hall (2000: 221) reminds us, 'Britishness [operates as a category] the empty signifier, the norm, against which "difference" (ethnicity) is measured.' The invisibilising of race (Craig, 2013) and the absence of anti-racism from public policy, while the government makes overt associations between migrants and hostility, creates a permissive public space for racialising discourses to flourish. These racialising discourses connect uncritical ideas about whiteness to national and local belonging within Britain, leaving white British people to feel that they experience unfairness in the allocation of public resources and entitlement (Garner, 2016).

Despite a legal duty (the Equality Act 2010), the absence of policies to address systemic racism (Craig, 2013) is a major concern for anti-racist educators in their attempt to help young people to articulate their concerns about everyday racist encounters. As Harries (2014: 1107) has identified: 'It is not easy to name racism in a context in which race is almost entirely denied.' The local places where everyday racism unfolds are connected to the national policies made by the government and narrated to the public through the racialised discursive practices of the mainstream media. This racialised cultural context establishes the framework for young people to understand their concerns and therefore orders the conduct of BAME and white majoritarian young people.

The absence of anti-racism in policy sets the tone of a racialised public discourse and this limits the ability of young people to develop anti-racist knowledge, which is a prerequisite to the foundation of a post-racial society. The hostile environment pursued as a publicly known social policy by the British government since 2012 has 'relied on notions of a fantasy citizenship' (Jones et al, 2017: 122). These fantasies are narrated through binaries where some white English people associate the logic of race with citizenship and nationhood, leaving them to uncritically believe and reproduce racist myths about BAME people, coded in current dominant discursive practices as migrants, asylum seekers and Muslims.

The cultural forces orienting the minoritised BAME and white majoritarian lifeworlds of young people necessitate illumination, exploration and interpretation. One aspect of the current context is narrated through anti-asylum, anti-immigrant and anti-Muslim prejudice (Lowles and Levene, 2019), underpinned by 'white governmentality' (Hesse, 1997). This sets out a narrow framing of Muslim identity (Hoque, 2015). In this landscape, the concerns arising from young people's experience is predetermined outside of a critical engagement with their lifeworlds.

Who lives where, how young people and their communities are mapped onto/into the landscape, and how this is historically known are all important frames for how people understand their present relationships. The contextual orienting of the critical eye of researchers and young people that exposes the monocultural setting of northern places such as Sunderland are made possible through a 'place-conscious education' (Gruenwald, 2003: 619), where 'bounded territorial space' (Anderson, 2006: 173) and 'zones of freedom' (Anderson, 2006: 170) are part of the conceptual lens.

As Gruenwald (2003: 639) identified in his considerations on the importance of place-conscious education: 'paying attention to the presence of public and private places can help raise consciousness about the political process that works to shape cultural space'. In relation to the racialised, gendered and class-based realities of the lifeworlds of BAME and majoritarian white young people in northern places such as Sunderland, the powerful forces where 'history and memory are locally constructed' (Rushton, 2017: 9) involve 'emotional legitimacy' (Anderson, 2006: 4). How these memories, histories and emotions unfold is not by itself totalising. An important contextual reality is the recognition that minoritised and majoritarian people can and do reject and resist the 'all-pervading anti-immigration rhetoric' (Jones et al, 2017: 131). As Gruenwald (2003) reminds us, places are made by, as well as mould, the lifeworlds of those who enter them.

The everyday experiences and support structures available to help young people to identify and critique their concerns (Bowler, 2013) are an important starting point for understanding how the young women in our research became cultural critics. A core finding in recent research critically examining neoliberal governmentality and the politics of immigration suggests that organisations working from a value base grounded in equality concerns and aspirations for social justice offer a safe social space to re-conceptualise different approaches to diversity and belonging (Jones et al, 2017).

These safe spaces outside of the immediate control of the standards set by a Britishness enmeshed in the racialisation of difference are the 'zones of freedom' identified by Anderson (2006: 170) that enable young people to develop their agency and resilience (Bowler, 2013; Ní Charraighe, 2019). The youth-work project that offered the young women such a safe social space had itself survived the decimation of youth services caused by the policy of austerity.

The survival of YAV has enabled the young people to co-create a safe anti-racist youth-work space. This anti-racist space enabled the young women to explore their ideas about the place of Sunderland and their marginalised and minoritised experiences as British-Asian Muslim Mackems (Bowler and Razak, 2019). Their identification as young people born and made in Sunderland offered new emergent meaning to the racialised interpretations 'whitewashing' national and local constructions of being British and being Mackem.

For the British-Asian Muslim Mackem young women their marginality created a space to assess the place that marked them as deficient, dangerous and not from here. In understanding their lived experience in the dominant monoculture of Sunderland, it is necessary to recognise that one reality of living in a society where 'race' is invisibilised and rarely interrogated critically is that BAME people 'occupy parallel discursive spheres' (Wright et al, 2010: 30). Seeing the absence of racial literacy in the dominant monoculture through the positioned space of marginality offered them a critical standpoint on the place that marked them as 'other' and 'outsiders' to their home city.

The young people who occupied the safe anti-racist spaces that the youth project provided shared with the authors their 'other ways of knowing' (Wright et al, 2010: 29). In this, the young women were demonstrating the importance of connecting their own struggles against exclusionary cultural spaces with the positive collective history of resistance to unjust authority (see, for example, Sivanandan, 1990; Ramamurthy, 2013). The young people spoke back to the 'everyday acts of white micro-denial, obfuscation and bad faith' (Yancy, 2018: 273).

The research case study

The first phase of the research was conducted over a period of 12 months in 2016 and 2017 in Sunderland. The authors met with the YAV project management committee and project leader to discuss the boundaries of ownership to the research and identified at this stage core concerns for the agency in relation to youth work with BAME young people in the city.

The research set out to generate data from young people that would map their needs, identify key risk factors, explore what services are available to meet those needs (from a young person/youth worker vantage point) and illuminate any risks/needs that were identified. The research was grounded in an anti-racist methodological frame (Twine and Warren, 2000; Dei and Johal, 2005), which enabled a critical understanding of the design when researching racism (Quraishi and Philburn, 2015).

The researchers acknowledged their responsibility to interpret the data in the contexts from which the participants' lifeworlds are positioned while enabling the participating young people to speak and define their own concerns (Bowler, 2013). In this, the responsibility of the researcher is to acknowledge that 'race' and racism are always relational to 'how we claim, occupy and defend spaces' (Dei and Johal, 2005: 3). The research was designed as participatory, with a focus on actions that would enable the YAV to learn from the empirical data.

The researchers undertook an in-depth interview with the YAV project manager, alongside a focus group with staff and volunteers. The background information from the project manager and youth workers offered the baseline data for a survey, where 99 out of a possible 200 questionnaires were returned. The findings from the survey were then used as a guide to explore, through a focus group, the needs and experiences of young women who were members of the YAV. The formal report from this phase was launched in February 2018 (Bowler and Razak, 2017).

The findings discussed in this chapter centre on the data from the focus group with young women. The young women were vocal from the outset and articulated themselves as cultural critics of the dominant ways in which they were identified in their everyday encounters with white people in their city. Their nuanced understanding of local and national identity illustrated an orientation of their lifeworlds beyond the confines of monocultural imaginaries. The articulation of their complex, nuanced identities, alongside their transnational and multilingual knowledge, offered hope for intercultural belonging.

Findings

The focus group involved 13 young women aged between 15 and 18 years old. The young women shared a collective desire to engage in open dialogue about their intercultural knowledge. This desire for dialogue was driven by belonging, not as 'the object of debate' (Ahmed, 2019: 67), but as consciously aware young women who embodied the complexities of being British, Asian, Muslim and Mackem.

The young women's agency and desire for activism and change chimed with long-standing recommendations from research that focuses upon intergenerational relationships, community cohesion and intercultural understandings (Thomas, 2011, 2012, 2016; Cantle and Thomas, 2014). This discussion around agency and activism occurred when talking about what else the YAV could offer them as young women when one of the young women instigated a discussion about sharing culture. These data emerged from the young women's willingness to engage in unexpected and transformational conversation, breaking free from the confines of researcher–researched transactions to explore and explain a more active youth-work approach that could amplify their intercultural vantage point about their city.

Cultural ignorance and racism

The young women discussed how they were often questioned by white people about culture and religion. This questioning was focused upon the markers of skin (biological racism) and dress (cultural racism). These are what Hall (2000: 223) identifies as constituting racism's 'two registers'. The following narratives identify how the young women experienced a regular questioning of them as different to the dominant norms of the place in which they were born and made:

YP1[7]:   'I work at the hospital and none of them knew about me, and I'm the only Asian, so they ask me a lot of questions. They are unaware of like … Islam or about our culture … in general.'

YP2:   'Yeh, same in my placement. They don't know like about Eid and Ramadan.'

YP1:   'Or why I am wearing a headscarf or something.'

The young women identify how some white peers and staff ask questions about culture, ethnicity, religion and nationality without understanding the complications in conflating categories. Those asking the young women appear absent of any acknowledgement that their questions, as well as the answers, are always positioned from somewhere:

YP3:   'Why do you wear that scarf around your head? Those questions: do you sleep with it? [A lot of laughter from the group.]'

YP2:	'They don't even know, like, about halal – like, the difference, yeh … and quite a lot of staff don't know either.… I was asked if I was Hindu or Bengali and then the question was, "What is Hinduism?" and "What is…?"'
YP4:	'You can be Bengali and Hindu.'
YP3:	'They think it is an ethnicity.'
YP2:	'And then there was questions on both of them and they had no knowledge of both.'
YP4:	'Religion sometimes gets like Ahhhh! [She makes a face of disgust.]'
YP5:	'Because they ask it rudely.'

Cultural ignorance was a theme that emerged and something that the young women found hard to grapple with. They identified the failure of their white peers to have basic cultural awareness and the questioning to be underpinned by ignorance, often inflected with rudeness. This rudeness and ignorance are one example of a racialising discourse, in part, because the ignorance is not only individual. The lack of knowledge is 'located' from 'somewhere' (Hall, 2000: 233). It is part of the monoculture of the city. The local monoculture is connected to a wider national discourse contaminated by xeno-racism (Fekete, 2001) but absent of a dialogue about it. The young women indicate this when they discuss the focused questioning about their headscarves, which are now one of the core objects for racist and religious hate incidents (Tell MAMA, 2019):

YP2:	'They kind of make you question yourself: "Why don't you wear a scarf?" I'm like….'
YP3:	'So, do you wear it all the time?'
YP4:	'Do your parents make you wear it? Do your parents pressure you?'
YP2:	'Why does she wear it? Why does she not?'
YP4:	'Are you trying to rebel against your religion?'
YP2:	'Why don't you? Does your mum not make you? I've seen girls around college that do and then you have to kind of answer, why? Where you really should cos in our religion, you should. You're kind of, like, "Yeh, you should but I don't." It kind of makes you feel bad.'

YP5: 'The first thing they say is, "I'm not trying to be racist", that puts you on guard, you'd be, like, "What are they going to say?"'

Cultural awareness of local landscape

The young women understood their complex nuanced identities and had developed a critical lens on the cultural messages about them that dominated the terrains of their everyday lives. They named the street, the parks, the schools, the college, shops and workplaces as 'containers' where ignorance, unsolicited questions and violating actions were/are directed to them by white colleagues, peers, teachers and strangers. These lived experiences are everyday racial realities in the communal and institutional spaces across the city. The threats of racism and Islamophobia affect how, when and where young people travel:

YP9: 'For example, when I'm in my Asian areas, I feel safer....'

YP10: 'Cos you're comfortable on your street but, like, say I went on your street [a predominantly white area where one of her peers lived], I would feel scared ... cos I know there's more chance of a guy walking past, or a girl, and making a racist comment.'

The young women we spoke to were acutely aware of the ignorance, ambivalence and hostility that they contend with, and they have developed coping strategies such as fending off racist and religiously ignorant comments with humour, refusing to take offence, or trying to educate the person. The young women also exhibited their own ambivalence to the contexts framing their lives. They were affirming of their developing consciousness as Muslim young women and they were attentive to challenging, through dialogue, the ignorance and hostility that they experienced from white people.

The young women identified hostility as an everyday experience. The young women shared their experiences of living with a critical eye upon safety in different places across the cityscape. The everydayness of their experiences of racism occurred at work, in education, in the street and when travelling between different areas. Unsurprisingly, our research found that the young people of the YAV are frequent victims of racism, with over 74 per cent of respondents reporting experiencing racism in the survey. Our focus group with the young women confirmed that racism is an all-too-regular occurrence and made it acutely clear that the racist Islamophobic hate crime narrated by them is seemingly gendered and related to their 'dress' as well as their skin:

YP11:   'Yeh, do you know, at work the other week, this old woman came in and she refused, she wouldn't let me serve her. She said she didn't want to be served by me.... I had my head scarf on ... as I was serving her she goes, "Don't touch my stuff."'

YP6:   'I was waiting for my brother to pick me up, just outside of college, some guy drives past and he shouts "Oi, you dirty Paki terrorist" and he drives past. And I'm like "OK! At least stop" [group laughter].'

However, it was highly concerning that, at times, the young women appeared to dismiss their lived experiences as something that 'just happens', and as something that they feel they have no choice but to accept. In this, they were influenced by the collective experience of their families and communities to believe that local civic leaders and the criminal justice system were inattentive to acting seriously about the hateful extremism (Khan, S, 2019) that they encountered.

For example, one of the very confident young women shared the following extract: "I was like at the bus stop. Right. And there was a boy with this bike. I don't know. Like our age. He grabbed on my scarf and tried to pull it" (YP6). We asked her if she had reported this hate crime and her response was: "No. I was, like, 'Oh, whatever. It just happened. I don't care anymore. Let me just go home and go to bed'" (YP6). This confident young woman who was one of the more vocal members in the group, who we did not think would hesitate to challenge or report hate crime, illuminated for us the felt reality that reporting these everyday hostile acts was understood to be pointless. She had come to believe this because it happens on such a regular occurrence and she had no faith that anything positive would come of reporting it. The YAV project manager informed us that the community-based reporting system for hate incidents in Sunderland had closed because of austerity (Clayton et al, 2016).

This feeling of hopelessness about the systems of crime and justice, and their failure to fulfil the duty to protect the public, was echoed by other young women in the group. One young woman talked about her father being attacked and not reporting it to the police: "They're [the police] not going to do anything." (YP10) A depressing aspect of hearing about this discrimination for this group of young women was that their stories were comparable to the experiences of daily racist abuse reported by their mothers, aunties and older sisters who the YAV undertook research with in 1998 (Bowler and Razak, 2019).

Solutions to the monocultural landscapes that fail them

The voices of the young women in our focus group offered a counter-narrative to dominant constructions of young British-Asian Muslims. They offered a nuanced vision of their citizenship and their identities were consciously grounded in organic multicultural possibility. Their resistant identities as cultural critics of a failing monocultural landscape challenged dominant misconceptions about young people while demonstrating ongoing vigilance and challenge to the white standards ordering local conduct.

The young women shared 'othering' experiences through intrusive questions from some white people:

YP2:	'We're quite educated I would say [laughter] … you live around, like, other [white] people but, like, they [white people] don't live around us.… I'd rather people be educated rather than have thoughts.'
YP13:	'Not in a racist way, but what can you say to, like, white people?'
YP4:	'I know.'
YP1:	'Not in a racist way [laughs].'
YP13:	'Not in a racist way. I'm not saying anything against anybody … there are some [ignorant] Muslims … its just, like … there's nothing, like, they [white people] wear that's different.'
Interviewer:	'So, do you mean you know more about white British culture than they know about your culture?'
YP13:	'Yeh, that's what I'm trying to say.'

The young women comprehend that the prevalence of a monocultural white landscape paves the way for how their white peers conduct themselves. They understood that their white peers were confined by the limits imposed on their cultural knowledge (Bowler and Razak, 2019). They resisted the racial logics woven into the white standards ordering the cultural knowledge of young people. They sought an intercultural dialogue to expose the workings of the monocultural imaginations so prevalent in their city: "We could be sharing knowledge cos there is more people that are unaware of what goes around and what's the culture like" (YP4).

The stories from the young women suggest that they could be at the forefront of creating their own futures. They have chosen to identify themselves as British, as Asian, as Muslim and as Mackem. They want to open dialogues intergenerationally, as well as across the borders of faith, culture and community.

Conclusions

> For Muslim women to thrive in our current climate, we need to start from a point at which the default, if we must have one, is inclusive and mindful of the many intersections that exist, not predicated on white males being the standard. (Bakkar, 2019: 47)

The young women talked about experiencing racial micro-aggressions in the school/college, work and community spaces that were part of their lives. The young women have been empowered through place-conscious dialogue in an anti-racist safe space to resist becoming 'the objects of debate' (Ahmed, 2019: 67).[8] They sought to create a multi-vocal dialogue to enable them to meet with and explore their intercultural knowledge with their white peers and the wider community about faith, culture, gender and the needs of young people. The young women engaged with a cultural critique through informal educational spaces that enabled them to explore and interrogate their experiences of 'othering' in a safe, consciously anti-racist environment. The author's reading of their cultural 'eye' suggested that they knew more about white British culture than their white counterparts did about them.

The British-Asian Muslim Mackem young women used the YAV as a space where they practised ideas of 'resistance, agency and affiliation' (Gruenwald, 2003: 631) to expose the normative, racialised and gendered assumptions embodied in much of the white monochromatic frame on daily display. The young women's ability to 'synthesise [their] Muslim-consciousness' (Meer, 2010: 204) to inform their complex and nuanced identity enabled them to challenge the imposed construction of them as 'a problem'. This also drove their activist agency to talk back, and to seek opportunities to talk with and to those who problematised them.

The researchers recognised the young women's conscious resistance to the unjust authority limiting their opportunity to explore in safety their racialised, cultural, faith, classed and gendered experiences as British-Asian Muslim Mackem young women. The contextual terrain orienting the lifeworlds of the young women in this chapter has been named as a geography of 'dual exclusion' (Hoque, 2015: 2). The patriarchal frame in each of the cultural terrains they occupied (Khan, M., 2019) meshed into the dominant whitewashed constructions marking their faith and ethnicity as deficient and/or dangerous.

Their counter-narrative set out to challenge the essentialist logic foundational to British anti-Muslim racism, which identifies British Muslim young people in places such as Sunderland as a threat or a problem. Their counter-narrative framed their identities as intercultural (Cantle, 2012). The monoculture dominant in the politics of a place like Sunderland and its cultural city aspiration create a dissonance between what is and what is aspired to be. This local conflict and the dominance of monoculture allow the hostile environment established by the government to become part of the everyday ethos influencing the lifeworlds of young people. It is the critical exposition of the lived experiences of the young women in our study that so clearly illuminates the chasm that exists between the white space that desires diversity and its lack of cognisance about the different lifeworlds in its realm.

The young women voiced their own concerns, identifying the importance of maintaining a focus on young people as democratic citizens whose sense of agency offers solutions to monocultural imaginaries. It is our contention that the YAV and its young people understand that progress towards a post-racial future is not possible unless all in our society 'confront the fact that this is a racial present' (Hirsch, 2018: 311). Their articulation spoke back against the hostility that they experienced as British Muslim young women. They were the convivial juxtaposed against the post-colonial melancholia (Gilroy, 2004) underpinning much of the Brexit-inspired hate-crime spike (Burnett, 2016; Bowler, 2017; Goodwin and Milazzo, 2017). They were alive to the possibilities of an intercultural Mackem identity while their racial realities exposed the monocultural imaginaries among many of their white peers and the cityscape that is their home.

The young women in our study identified their desire to resist racism and described their intention to educate for a better world. Given the challenges that they face in their everyday encounters with British racism, they articulated some local solutions to the deeper societal problems as racially literate locals. Their rich layering of their lifeworlds, given space to breathe in a youth-work setting attentive to context, is a positive challenge to the monocultural landscape that is failing them and failing their white peers.

Notes

1 The idea of monoculture and multiculture used throughout the chapter draws upon the work of Sibley (1998: 123), identifying how landscapes in Britain can be spatially and socially homogeneous (monocultural) or spatially and socially heterogeneous, where difference is more readily accepted and relationships across divides are convivial. Important to these ideas is how our social spaces are racialised, and how dominant and/or minoritised experiences are recognised and represented.

2 'Intercultural' is used throughout to identify how 'civil society institutions ... bring into play a multitude of diverse voices' (Gundara, 2000: 205) in order to enable the variety of identities and histories of a place to be known.

3 The young people interviewed were all born in Sunderland and offered a range of positive narratives about their relationship to their city and to their identities as young Sunderland people. The term 'Mackem' used by the young people is the colloquial expression used within the region to describe people who come from Sunderland (Rowley, 2013).

4 Super-diversity suggests that diverse populations in social spaces seek nuanced and complex means for accommodating difference. Identities are no longer bound by essentialist understandings of identity focused, for example, upon class, ethnicity, nationality, sexuality or gender.

5 Here, the failure denotes the absence of public policy to bring young people from different backgrounds together to build an anti-racist intercultural understanding focused upon their similarities as well as their differences.

6 The term 'lifeworld' takes into consideration how the world is interpreted by people. It begins by always setting in context the meaning making that individuals and groups have about their identity and place in the world.

7 YP denotes young person.

8 The YAV was established in 1996 as a response to the lack of 'safe-space' youth-work provision across the city for BAME young people (Bowler, 2006, 2018; Bowler and Razak, 2019).

References

Ahmed, A. (2019) 'The clothes of my faith', in M. Khan (ed) *It's not about the burqa: Muslim women on faith, feminism, sexuality and race*, London: Picador, pp 65–77.

Anderson, B. (2006) *Imagined communities*, London: Verso Press.

Bakkar, N. (2019) 'On the representation of Muslims: terms and conditions apply', in M. Khan (ed) *It's not about the burqa: Muslim women on faith, feminism, sexuality and race*, London: Picador, pp 45–63.

Bowler, R. (2006) *Countering racisms: Reflections from working with young people*, Belfast: Northern Ireland Youth Council, pp 17–19, www.community-relations.org.uk/sites/crc/files/media-files/09-CRED-RShaRdFutR.pdf

Bowler, R. (2013) 'The risky business of challenging risk: Youth work and young people through the lens of "race"', in J. Kearney and C. Donovan (eds) *Constructing risky identities: Consequences for policy and practice*, Basingstoke: Palgrave, pp 146–62.

Bowler, R. (2017) 'Whiteness, Britishness and the racist reality of Brexit', CASS Working Paper No. 2, University of Sunderland, UK.

Bowler, R. (2018) 'Critical youth and community work and its struggle with white standards', in G. Craig (ed) *Community development, race and ethnicity: Theory, practice and policy*, Bristol: Policy Press, pp 41–60.

Bowler, R. and Razak, A. (2017) 'Voicing the needs of YAV's young people Sunderland', project report, University of Sunderland, UK.

Bowler, R. and Razak, A. (2019) 'Continuities and change: some reflections on 21 years of anti-racist youth work', *Youth and Policy Journal*, May, www.youthandpolicy.org/articles/continuities-and-change-some-reflections-on-21-years-of-anti-racist-youth-work/

Burnett, J. (2016) *Racial violence and the Brexit state*, London: Institute of Race Relations, www.irr.org.uk/app/uploads/2016/11/Racial-violence-and-the-Brexit-state-final.pdf

Cantle, T. (2012) *Interculturalism: The new era of cohesion and diversity*, Basingstoke: Palgrave Macmillan.

Cantle, T. and Thomas, P. (2014) 'Taking the Think Project forward – the need for preventative anti-extremism educational work', project report, Think Project, Swansea, http://eprints.hud.ac.uk/19790/1/Think_project_report.pdf

Chattoo, S., Atkin, K., Craig, G. and Flynn, R. (eds) (2019) *Understanding 'race' and ethnicity: Theory, history, policy, practice* (2nd edn), Bristol: Policy Press.

Clark, K. (2019) 'Sunderland landmarks lit up for anti-racism message in the week that England players faced abuse in Bulgaria', *Sunderland Echo*, 18 October, www.sunderlandecho.com/news/people/sunderland-landmarks-lit-anti-racism-message-week-england-players-faced-abuse-bulgaria-816290

Clayton, J., Donovan, C. and Macdonald, S. (2016) 'A critical portrait of hate crime/incident reporting in North East England: the value of statistical data and the politics of recording in an age of austerity', Geoforum, 75: 64–74.

Craig, G. (2013) 'Invisibilising "race" in public policy', *Critical Social Policy*, 33(4): 712–20.

Craig, G., Cole, B., Ali, N. and Qureshi, I. (2019) *The missing dimension: Where is 'race' in Social Policy teaching and learning?*, London: The Social Policy Association, www.social-policy.org.uk/wordpress/wp-content/uploads/2019/06/BME-Audit-Final-Report.pdf

Dei, G.J.S. and Johal, S.G. (eds) (2005) *Critical issues in anti-racist research methodologies*, Oxford: Peter Lang.

Elgot, J. (2018) 'Teresa May's "hostile environment" at heart of Windrush scandal', *The Guardian*, 17 April, www.theguardian.com/uk-news/2018/apr/17/theresa-mays-hostile-environment-policy-at-heart-of-windrush-scandal

Fekete, L. (2001) 'The emergence of xeno racism', *Race and Class*, 43(2): 23–40.

Fekete, L. (2019) *Racist violence: It's become normalised*, London: Institute of Race Relations, www.irr.org.uk/news/racist-violence-its-become-normalised/

Garner, S. (2016) *The moral economy of whiteness: Four frames of racialising discourse*, London: Routledge.

Gilroy, P. (2004) *After empire: Multi culture or postcolonial melancholia*, London: Routledge.

Goodwin, M. and Milazzo, C. (2017) 'Taking back control? Investigating the role of immigration in the 2016 vote for Brexit', *The British Journal of Politics and International Relations*, 19(3): 450–64.

Grierson, J. (2018) 'Hostile environment: anatomy of a policy disaster', *The Guardian*, 27 August, www.theguardian.com/uk-news/2018/aug/27/hostile-environment-anatomy-of-a-policy-disaster

Gruenwald, D. (2003) 'Foundations of place: a multidisciplinary framework for place-conscious education', *American Educational Research Journal*, 40(3): 619–54.

Gundara, J.S. (2000) *Interculturalism, education and inclusion*, London: Paul Chapman Publishing.

Hall, S. (2000) 'Conclusion: the multi-cultural question' in B. Hesse (ed) *Un/settled multiculturalisms: Diaspora, entanglements, transruptions*, London: Zed Books, pp 209–41.

Harries, B. (2014) 'We need to talk about race', *Sociology*, 48(6): 1107–22.

Harries, B. (2018) *Talking race in young adulthood: Race and everyday life in contemporary Britain*, London: Routledge.

Hesse, B. (1997) 'White governmentality: urbanism, nationalism, racism', in S. Westwood and J. Williams (eds) *Imagining cities: Scripts, signs, memory*, London: Routledge, pp 86–103.

Hirsch, A. (2018) *BRIT(ish): On race, identity and belonging*, London: Penguin Random House.

Holbourne, Z., Bennett, W., Benoit, H., Rigg, M. and Begg, A. (2010) 'Growing up with racism in Britain', *Socialist Review*, October, www.socialistreview.org.uk/article.php?articlenumber=11405

Hoque, A. (2015) *British-Islamic identity: Third generation Bangladeshi's from East London*, London: Trentham Books.

Jones, H., Gunaratnum, Y., Bhattacharyya, G., Davies, W., Dhaliwal, S., Forkert, K., Jackson, E. and Saltus, R. (2017) *GO HOME? The politics of immigration discourse*, Manchester: Manchester University Press.

Khan, M. (2019) *It's not about the burqa: Muslim women on faith, feminism, sexuality and race*, London: Picador.

Khan, O. and Shaheen, F. (eds) (2017) *Minority report: Race and class in post-Brexit Britain*, London: Runnymede Trust, www.runnymedetrust. org/uploads/publications/pdfs/Race%20and%20Class%20Post-Brexit%20Perspectives%20report%20v5.pdf

Khan, S. (2019) 'Challenging hateful extremism', Commission for Countering Extremism, https://assets.publishing.service.gov.uk/government/uploads/system/uploads/attachment_data/file/836538/Challenging_Hateful_Extremism_report.pdf

Liberty (2018) *A guide to the hostile environment: The border controls dividing our communities – and how we can bring them down*, London: Liberty.

Lowles, N. and Levene, J. (2019) *State of hate 2019*, London: Hope not Hate Ltd.

Meer, N. (2010) *Citizenship, identity and the politics of multiculturalism: The rise of Muslim consciousness*, London: Palgrave Macmillan.

Nayak, A. (2017) 'Purging the nation: race, conviviality and embodied encounters in the lives of British Bangladeshi Muslim young women', *Transactions of the Institute of British Geographers*, Vol. 42 Issue 2: 289–302, https://doi.org/10.1111/tran.12168

Ní Charraighe, A. (2019) 'Re/membering resilience – a reflection of resilience and youth work', *Youth and Policy Journal*, April, www.youthandpolicy.org/articles/re-membering-resilience/

Olusoga, D. (2019) 'Windrush: archives show the long betrayal', *The Guardian*, 19 June, www.theguardian.com/uk-news/2019/jun/16/windrush -scandal-the-long-betrayal-archived-documents-david-olusoga

Paul, K. (1997) *Whitewashing Britain: Race and citizenship in the postwar era*, New York, NY: Cornell University.

Paxman, J. (1999) *The English: A portrait of a people*, London: Penguin Books.

Quraishi, M. and Philburn, R. (2015) *Researching racism*, London: Sage.

Ramamurthy, A. (2013) *Black star: Britain's Asian youth movements*, London: Pluto Press.

Rowley, T. (2013) 'Are you a Geordie, Mackem or Smoggie?', *Evening Chronicle*, 25 February, www.chroniclelive.co.uk/news/north-east-news/you-geordie-mackem-smoggie-1363415

Rushton, P. (2017) 'The myth and reality of Brexit city: Sunderland and the 2016 referendum', CASS Working Paper No.1, University of Sunderland, UK.

Saeed, A. (2007) 'Northern racism: a pilot study of racism in Sunderland', in C. Ehland (ed) *Thinking Northern: Textures of identity in the North of England*, Amsterdam and New York, NY: Rodopi Press: 163–89.

Schwarz, B. (2011) *The white man's world: Memories of empire*, Oxford: Oxford University Press.

Sibley, D. (1998) 'The racialisation of space in British cities', *Soundings*, 10: Windrush Echoes: 119–127.

Sivanandan, A. (1990) *Communities of resistance: Writings on black struggles for socialism*, London: Verso.

Snoussi, D. and Mompelat, L. (2019) *'We are ghosts': Race, class and institutional prejudice*, London: Runnymede Trust, www.runnymede trust.org/uploads/publications/We%20Are%20Ghosts.pdf

Standing, G. (2016) *The precariat: The new dangerous class*, London: Bloomsbury.

Sunderland Culture (2018) *Sunderland Celebrates Winning Place On City Of Culture Shortlist*, www.sunderlandculture.org.uk/sunderland-celebrates-winning-place-on-city-of-culture-shortlist/

Sunderland City Council (2019) 'Understanding inequalities and integration: the picture of Sunderland', www.sunderland.gov.uk/ media/21082/Understanding-inequalities-and-integration/pdf/ Understanding_inequalities_and_integration.pdf?m=63682811430 0370000

Sunderland Partnership (2019) 'Sunderland children and young people's mental health and wellbeing transformational plan 2015–2020', file://uni.ad.sunderland.ac.uk/Data/HOME$/os0rbo/Downloads/2018_07_CAMHS-PLAN-2018-19-refresh-JULY-18-FINAL.pdf

Sviensson, P.K. (ed) (2009) *Who cares about the white working class*, London: Runnymede Trust Publications, www.runnymedetrust.org/uploads/publications/pdfs/WhoCaresAboutTheWhiteWorkingClass-2009.pdf

Teale, A. (2002–17) 'Local election results 2002', Local Elections Archive Project, www.andrewteale.me.uk/leap/results/2002/56/

Tell MAMA (2019) *Normalised Hatred: Tell MAMA annual report 2018*, London: Faith Matters.

Thomas, P. (2011) *Youth, multiculturalism and community cohesion*, Basingstoke: Palgrave Macmillan.

Thomas, P. (2012) *Responding to the threat of violent extremism – Failing to prevent*, London: Bloomsbury Academic.

Thomas, P. (2016) 'Youth, terrorism and education: Britain's Prevent programme', *International Journal of Life-Long Education*, 35(2, special issue: 'Youth, social crisis and learning'): 171–87.

Thomas, P., Busher, J., Macklin, G., Rogerson, M. and Chrstmann, K. (2018) 'Hopes and fears: community cohesion and the "white working class" in one of the "failed spaces" of multiculturalism', *Sociology*, 52(2): 262–81.

Twine, W.F. and Warren, J.W. (eds) (2000) Racing research, researching race: Methodological dilemmas in critical race studies, London: New York University Press.

Vertovec, S. (2007) 'Super-diversity and its implications', *Ethnic and Racial Studies*, 30(6): 1024–54.

Wessendorf, S. and Phillimore, J. (2018) 'New migrants' social integration, embedding and emplacement in superdiverse contexts', *Sociology*, 52(2): 1–16.

Wright, C., Standen, P. and Paterl, T. (2010) *Black youth matters: Transitions from school to success*, London: Routledge.

Yancy, G. (2018) 'Afterword', in A. Johnson, R. Joseph-Salisbury and B. Kamunge (eds) *The fire now: Anti-racist scholarship in times of explicit racial violence*, London: Zed Books, pp 266–74.

Yuval-Davis, N., Wemyss, G. and Cassidy, K. (2018) 'Everyday bordering, belonging and the reorientation of British immigration legislation', *Sociology*, 52(2): 228–44.

4

Returnees: unwanted citizens or cherished countrymen

Bozena Sojka and Maarja Saar

Introduction

There is considerable interest among European Union (EU) policymakers in social security portability, especially in EU mobile citizens' access to benefits in receiving countries. Historically, the portability of social security rights was the strategy adopted to organise the social security of mobile workers between two social security schemes of sending and receiving countries (Avato et al, 2010). Further development of portability regulation was a response to the challenge that migration poses to welfare states, being designed to secure the social citizenship of migrant workers. Portability is defined as 'the ability of migrant workers to preserve, maintain, and transfer benefits from a social security programme from one country to another and between localities in a country (spatial portability), between jobs' (Taha et al, 2015: 98). The portability of social security rights in the EU for EU citizens is highly regulated; however, in short, social security benefits must be paid in whichever member state the EU citizen resides (Carmel et al, 2019a). In this context, immigrants' access to welfare is highly politicised and occupies a significant space in political and policy discourse on migration (Balch and Balabanova, 2016). One of the most dominant discourses on migrants' access to welfare is anti-immigrant discourse (Van Dijk, 2018), which often portrays immigrants as a burden on receiving countries (Richardson and Colombo, 2013; Bocskor, 2018), especially in the context of the welfare state and immigrants' access to social security rights. The modern othering and racialisation of the migrants is captured well in Barker's (1981, 2001) theory of new racism, which shows how neo-racial political discourse focuses on cultural and economic rather than physical difference. Also, today's racism is linked with classism, where 'poverty is the new Black' (Sivanandan, 2001: 3).

For example, migrant workers with irregular and low-paid employment are othered by the modern sate and often denied access to social security (Carmel and Sojka, 2018). Also, analysing discourses of the othering of returnees and their access to social welfare requires reflection on the roles of nationalism, culture, national identity and belonging as elements of today's 'xeno-racism' (Sivanandan, 2001, 2006). This article explores the othering of returnees in political and, in particular, policy discourses on returnees and their access to welfare in Poland and Estonia. This exploration allows us to look at the changing notion of belonging in relation to returnees' participation in welfare.

This article examines Polish and Estonian social policy experts' narratives on returnees and their access to welfare. We examine discourses on migration by drawing on in-depth qualitative interviews with 14 Polish and Estonian social policy and welfare experts. We use discourses as a way of understanding return migration and national attitudes towards return migration. Consequently, our analysis provides new insights into the discursive construction of an ideal returnee. Unlike much of the existing literature that explores returnees' perspectives on return, including their decision-making as regards their return, we explore policy experts' viewpoint on return migration. Although return migration has long been subject to various analyses, most of the literature focuses on who returns, when and why (Dustmann and Görlach, 2016). Our article contributes to the literature on return migration by exploring social policymakers' perspectives on returnees.

Welfare state and unwanted citizens

Welfare states are involved in the processes of othering as they privilege some social/economic/political groups and create hierarchies of conditional belonging and insiderness (Morris, 2002; Anderson, 2013; Carmel and Paul, 2013). At the centre of the concept of othering more generally lies the idea that each state defines itself via deciding 'what it is not' (Sibley, 1995). As such, othering serves the purpose of creating a common identity via the reinforcement of shared values, culture and so on, which are defined as superior to those of the opposed group. By default, othering simplifies both the self and the other by representing those categories through sharply opposed, polarised, binary extremes, such as good–bad, civilised–primitive and so on (Hall, 1997). Such ideas of the self and the other are especially prevalent in defining the nation, where the use of outside groups such as migrants has been relatively common (Brubaker, 2004; Anderson, 2006).

Most of the literature focusing on othering in the context of nation-states seems to assume the existence of one predominant other, for example, in the case of Estonia, this is ethnic Russians, while in the case of Germany, it is often Turkish immigrants. Petersoo (2007) has suggested widening the concept of the other and posits that each state has multiple others, such as negative and positive others, as well as internal and external others. She further argues that in its discourses of identity, the self is continuously negotiating several identities simultaneously. She therefore challenges Triandafyllidou (1998), who has suggested that even though each nation-state goes through multiple others throughout history, at any given time, there is only one significant other for each nation-state that affects the formation and transformation of its identity. Petersoo (2007) suggests that national identity formation should be seen as a complex interplay between the nation-state and various others.

What we find useful in Petersoo's (2007) approach is the notion of internal others. The suggestion that each nation-state can also identify an other within agrees with our findings from the interviews with Estonian and Polish welfare experts. Furthermore, we also consider the idea of multiple others useful as we suggest that in addition to looking at the ethnic dimension – which is where othering is usually used – one should also focus on other potential fields of othering. Hence, we argue that defining internal otherness solely based on ethnicity does not take into account the strong development of the welfare state during the last 50 years. Marshall (1963) has defined social citizenship as comprising civil, political and social rights. If we only focus on political citizenship, we can indeed define immigrants as the other; however, if we pay attention to more symbolic, as well as value-laden and welfare-related, aspects of citizenship (social rights), we can widen the concept of the other.

Selectivity over who is the other and who is not takes place within institutions, usually those of nation-states (Wieviorka, 2010). Those institutions then govern the state in ways that define the obligations, rights and entitlements of citizens. One of the central pillars of the welfare state governed by these very institutions is its social policies. It is important to look at the welfare state in the context of the development of idealised citizens as welfare states organise social groups, often by excluding individuals based on socio-economic characteristics and behaviours. Therefore, the welfare state decides who is unwanted and undesirable by privileging chosen groups who are perceived as belonging. This is organised through the regulation of social rights, which governs who is entitled and consequently who is not (Carmel et al, 2019a). Moreover, this perception, which is embedded in social policy, is used to advance dominant ideologies and expose the nature of nationhood favoured by policymakers; as such, it is present in the wider discourse on social security rights and nationhood. Therefore, it is important to look into social policy experts' perceptions of the other.

In today's Europe, the national level of social security management intervenes in the EU level. EU social coordination is complex and provides common rules to protect EU citizens' social security rights when moving within Europe. Like the conditionality of social security more generally, assumptions of inclusion, exclusion and stratification are embedded in EU social security coordination as well. The portability of social security rights is 'the ability to preserve, maintain, and transfer vested social security rights (or rights in the process of being vested), independent of profession, nationality, and country of residency' (Holzmann and Koettl, 2015: 390). Therefore, 'portability regulation' offers selective openness to particular migrants (Ferrera, 2005) and thus embeds contingent selectivity. Consequently, EU social security coordination also employs processes of othering by promoting and recording certain types of behaviour (Carmel et al, 2019a, 2019b).

Furthermore, since the social security benefits are to be paid by whichever member state the EU citizen resides in (Pennings, 2012), the topic has become increasingly politicised, with migrants facing accusations of welfare tourism (Ehata and Seeleib-Kaiser, 2017). However this politicisation has mostly been studied from the perspective of receiving countries and very little is known about the sending countries, even though migration is often temporary, especially in the EU context (White, 2014, 2017; Wahba, 2015).

There is a significant body of academic literature regarding the discourses of migration and return migration that focuses on migrants' narratives on return (Ní Laoire, 2008), or cultural identity and ethnic policies related to returnees (Kuscu-Bonnenfant, 2012). Additionally, Horváth (2008) has proposed the idea of migration cultures, suggesting that certain regions in Europe have developed cultures where migration is seen as a normal part of becoming an adult. However, there is a lack of consideration on the welfare state in the current idea of cultures of migration. Instead of migration cultures, we therefore focus on migration discourses and suggest that such discourses are strongly influenced by ideas of deserving and undeserving citizens. To explore the connections between ideology, the welfare state and discourses of migration, we now turn attention towards the development of national ideologies in Poland and Estonia.

Polish and Estonian welfare states

Cerami (2005) has criticised many scholars for assuming similar experiences across East and Central Europe, also stressing that the transitions during the 1990s were carried out dissimilarly across the region. These transitions were mostly linked with a shift from a planned to a market economy (Atas, 2018). Both Poland and Estonia were faced with the need to re-establish their nationhood. Even though Poland was officially not part of the Soviet Union, the 1990s were understood in Poland as a time for recovering sovereignty and the reconstitution of the independent state (Buzalka, 2008). However, unlike in Estonia, Polish independence also included negotiations over the role of the Catholic Church, which had held the dominant role under communism (Eberts, 1998; Ramet, 2017). Whereas a lot of Estonian politics during the 1990s was focused on distancing the state from Russia, which was perceived as the key enemy, Polish politics concentrated on trying to establish a balance between the Church and the state (Buzalka, 2008).

Estonian nationhood is said by many authors to have been constructed in opposition to their Soviet past (Vihalemm and Masso, 2003). From the perspective of social policy, the attempts of othering from Russia were perhaps of instrumental importance as Estonia chose to adapt the neoliberal ideology. Compared to other former socialist countries, Estonia is said to be the most neoliberal country in the 'East'. During the 1990s, self-sufficiency and entrepreneurship were encouraged as important values in Estonian society (Bohle and Greskovits, 2007). Kalmus and Vihalemm (2006) have also noted that people used self-sufficiency as a way to deal with abrupt changes and to protect themselves against feelings of insecurity and a lack of control. Even though Estonia has lately moved somewhat towards more social-democratic policy, its welfare regime can still be identified as neoliberal. Some examples of how neoliberalism is embedded into Estonian social policy are, for instance, low unemployment benefits that are also limited to only one year, as well as generally quite low child support (Aidukaite, 2004). One exception to such a low level of social support is parental leave, which is one of the most generous in Europe, being directly connected to the former salary of the individual and granted for one-and-a-half years. However, as the ceiling for maximal parental leave is extremely high, even this generous benefit can be seen as carrying some traces of neoliberal ideology.

While Estonian social policy can be described as more of a case of pure liberalism, the Polish case is a bit more difficult to pin down.

The Polish modern welfare system was created through the gradual privatisation of many areas of social life (Żuk and Żuk, 2018). Today, Polish social policy is described as a hybrid system that combines elements of the liberal, conservative and social-democratic welfare types (Perek-Białas and Racław, 2014). The social-democratic element is reflected in the attempt to cover all individuals; while the liberal element comes out, for instance, from the fact that in order to receive unemployment insurance, one had to earn at least the minimum salary. Such a mix of different welfare regimes could be indicative of other discords in society. According to Zubrzycki (2002), Poland is struggling between adapting either ethnic or civic nationhood, and has not decided on either. Whereas those in favour of strong Catholicism are clearly in favour of defining the Polish nation according to ethnic-religious lines, they were political outsiders for a long time as the elites promoted a legitimate counter-discourse, though this had little support in wider society (Zubrzycki, 2001). The interference of the Church in politics in Poland is especially visible in the case of family politics and the recent discussions around abortion. In terms of social welfare, as we demonstrate later, there is a strong belief in the family as of outmost importance. The differences in terms of the approach towards the family and community between Estonia and Poland were also illustrated by a European values survey, where Estonians clearly preferred values such as success and self-sufficiency, whereas Poles rooted for more communal values. For Poland, the family is at the core of the nation and welfare state, which reflects strong traditions of social Catholicism and its political expression in Christian democracy (Zuba, 2010). This is because Catholic social teaching emphasises communal living and the role of the family within the community. In turn, increasing people's self-sufficiency and the individualisation of civil society has become more and more important in Estonia, where individual self-realisation is one of the main objectives.

Our data

The material is drawn from data collected during the 'Mobile Welfare in a Transnational Europe: An Analysis of Portability Regimes of Social Security Rights' (TRANSWEL) research project[1] examining mobile EU citizens' access to social security rights in the EU. We interviewed 13 policy experts, officials from ministries, policy advisors and senior legal experts to gain insight into their interpretations, experiences and understandings of the EU regulation of social security rights of mobile EU citizens and its intersection with their national context. The selection criteria for participants was policy relevance, seniority and, of course, availability. It was decided to maintain the anonymity of all participants in order to encourage openness and a higher degree of trust between the participant and interviewer in each case. We asked experts about their reflections on the relationship between mobility and the regulation of social rights in their country, as well as their interpretation of the nature of the wider institutional, political and social context within which the relationship between mobility and the portability of social rights is framed. Participants were also asked about the characteristics and purposes of any reforms (recent or proposed). Our fieldwork was undertaken in Poland and Estonia from June to September 2016. We used instructions regarding the protocol for interviewing senior policy experts, as well as ethical requirements for the project regarding anonymity, the storage of data and informed consent. Although we asked the same questions of Polish and Estonian experts, we received very different answers.

Given the specificity of our policy domain, with its small number of specialist experts across the EU, and with regard to the contentious and, in some cases, politicised nature of the subject matter of the interviews, our participants' potential reputational vulnerability seemed both particularly important and, in some cases, possibly difficult to protect. Therefore, in order to avoid inadvertently revealing participants' identity through descriptions of their institutional role, we asked them to offer descriptions of their role in this policy field, and it is these that we use in our analysis.

All interviews were transcribed in Polish and Estonian, respectively, with transcription being a first step in qualitative data analysis as it involves ad hoc judgements and reflections on what have been transcribed. In other words, the transcribing process involved the close observation of data through repeated careful listening. Furthermore, transcriptions themselves are not free from interpretations of data as they include non-verbal communication, such as pauses, laughter, emotions and so on. The expert interviews were analysed using critical discourse analysis (Fairclough, 2013). The next section presents those very discourses.

Poland and its focus on the family

The interviews with Polish experts were characterised by their concern over Poland's future, especially what they perceived as a demographic crisis. In fact, according to one expert, dealing with the demographic crisis has been one of the priority areas for Polish welfare policy: "In recent years, one can see a strong focus on two issues in Polish welfare politics: improving the demographic situation (extension of maternity leave, the introduction of paternal leave, providing pre-school care for all the children); and to improving employment services" (Ministry of Family, Labour and Social Policy). According to the expert, many reforms that have been made are to encourage women to have more children. However, this is only part of the solution; in fact, most Polish experts also lift the topic of migration up as a societal and demographic problem. For instance, "Another controversy is related to the demographic problem. Poland has one of the lowest replacement rates in Europe, ie, the fertility rate is 1.3. It is pointed out that mainly young people of reproductive age emigrate, which deepens the demographic problem in our country" (expert, EU Committee member). According to this expert, the most important issue surrounding the emigration of young people from Poland is the low fertility rate. The falling birth rate is perceived as an important issue as a growing population is good for the economy. However, this particular expert continues:

'Those who could improve this situation have kids abroad, eg, in the UK. This argument, in turn, is often raised in discussions about the Polish demographic policy. It is pointed out that it is wrong because people who have migrated decide more often to have children than those that have been in the country.' (Expert, EU Committee member)

This expert first paints a picture of Poland as facing a huge demographic problem that only people of child-rearing age can solve. It should be noted that as she speaks about the Polish demographic problem, she makes no reference to the size of the Polish population at all, but rather chooses to use fertility rate numbers. She then goes on to exclude migrants as not belonging to the Polish state anymore. Rather, for this expert, Polish nationals are defined as people living in Poland. Those who migrated are othered through the idea that even though they hold the key to improving what is perceived to be the difficult demographic situation in Poland, by leaving, they choose not to do this. The reasoning as to why migrants should not belong to the Polish state anymore is given by another expert: "Polish women prefer to have children abroad because they feel safe there. But this is huge loss for Poland and for future of Poland. These children will not have Polish roots, Polish culture, and will most probably never be back, so they are lost for us" (National Advisory Committee member). This interviewee sees Polish roots as something that can be obtained solely through living in Poland and not through ancestry. Hence, outmigration from Poland is considered to be a sort of 'turning one's back on the state'. In this quote, the children of migrant families are referred to not only as lacking of Polish roots, but also as having little or no connection to Poland. Furthermore, the quote also indicates that there is a lot of attention on the future – imagining the future Poland that should be created by these very children that migrate. Hence, the emphasis is not so much on the present, but on the future of Polish nationhood, which is assumed to continue only if there are enough nuclear families to carry on traditions. Several experts stressed the importance of nuclear families, as can be seen in the following:

> 'The main problem associated with migration to other EU member states is called "Euro-orphanhood". This situation leads to multiple pathologies mainly related to family breakdown and weakening ties with their parents. It is pointed out that these children do less well in school and create behavioural problems. It is too early to indicate long-term consequences of this phenomenon, or it can be assumed that such children will also have impaired vision of the family, which may cause in the future many social problems.' (Expert, EU Committee member)

This quote from an EU Committee member illustrates very clearly the othering not only of families with one parent, but also of the children growing in these families. According to this expert, these are pathological cases that not only should be avoided, but also have a negative effect on the Polish nation as a whole. Rationality is used by the expert to motivate such a position by pointing out the problems that these children have in schools or potential behavioural issues. By using rationality to justify their position on non-nuclear families, the expert aims to point out that it is not solely their personal emotionally motivated position, but rather an impartial concern for the country. However, through this quote, everyone who is a member of a non-traditional family becomes the other.

There is a stress on the family as the centre of the nation across all interviews with Polish experts, reflecting strong traditions of social Catholicism (and its political expression in Christian democracy). These narratives expose the ways in which migration is seen as a reason for breaking family ties and as a source of social pathology. Shared cultural values provide the basis for nation-based belonging. Thus, diminished family ties challenge belonging to the nation. In this light, migration is seen as an important factor in loosening ties with nation-states:

> 'One cannot underestimate the role that the Catholic Church plays in social policy in Poland. Not only does the Church carry on direct activities, but it also affects the public debate. Churches' voice was especially strong during the discussion on the problem of euro-orphans and the impact of migration on the family. The Church criticises emigration and sees it as "chasing money", indicating that it contributes to breaking up families and its costs face mainly children.' (Expert, EU Committee member)

This quote furthermore exemplifies how Catholic values play an important role for influencing both Polish welfare policy and its idea of a good citizen and the other. The expert extenuates that the Church has criticised migrants as being motivated by their individual and solely material gains. In addition, the breaking up of 'families' shapes children's vulnerability as children left behind are perceived as being disadvantaged because they are denied the right to grow up within Polish families who reside in Poland. Through this, materialism is opposed to traditional family values, as is migration. Migrants are seen as lacking in strong values by the Church. The interpretation given by the Church of migration, as well as its consequences, translates to how migration is opposed to national values, by politicians as well as experts in social welfare. Such a tension between national and individual interests is also brought out by the next expert:

> 'Social cost related to migration is huge, they are.... Even issues of broken families, or issues related to, related to demography and so on. So, I do not think that something bad happened. But this has consequences, long-term consequences. These consequences can be negative but from individuals' [migrants'] perspective, nothing happened. Moreover, it is good that they were able to make their decisions [to migrate] by themselves, even though this is not welcomed by many, but that is how it is.' (National Advisory Committee member)

First, the issue of broken families and its relation to migration is again taken up by this expert, who also argues that even if the long-term consequences of migration were caused by individuals themselves, they should be handled by the state. Hence, there is a tension between state interests and the interests of the individuals apparent from this quote. Even though the expert does not personally criticise migrants, they refer to the fact that there is a public discourse that is casting migrants as irresponsible and not really interested in the state's concerns. However, even those migrants that do decide to return are seen as problematic, as witnessed by the next quote:

> 'This will be really difficult [the return of children from the UK] as, since ten years, they lived in the UK. Why suddenly could they be denied the right to residency? They do not have anything to do with Poland. But we hear about these sorts of problems from the UK, and this worries us. But such voices have sprung up … that these young people did not contribute to the UK's budget, so they should go back to Poland. But they do not have roots in Poland anymore.' (Government official 1)

This particular quote relates to Polish children who had been living in the UK for ten years. These children are perceived as lacking ties with Poland. This perception contradicts the experts' emphasis on the importance of families, and especially children, explained earlier. In this light, children who reside abroad for long periods of time are perceived as the other. Furthermore, adult returnees are othered too, and return migration is problematised in general. This is because returnees are perceived as a burden upon the Polish welfare state. The concern about the inclusion of returnees to the Polish welfare system was expressed by several experts as they stressed that the Polish welfare system functions not based on citizenship, but rather based on residency. Thus, people that have once decided to leave Poland should not be covered as they have freely decided to abandon their rights in Poland and hence are now the concern of some other state.

As such, the narratives on return migrants in Poland are highly connected to concerns over the demographic situation and the perception of Polish society as based on the centrality of the family unit. However, such family units can only work if smaller nuclear families stay together and take care of the maintenance of the nation. In the case of migrants, these people – so the narrative goes – have already abandoned their duties as nationals once and should therefore be treated with caution. Furthermore, they are also likely to introduce anomalies, such as broken families, which challenge the unity of the nation.

Estonia and its focus on self-sufficient individuals

What can be noticed throughout the interviews with Estonian experts is the dominating narrative of self-sufficiency that appears in subtle and less subtle ways. However, there is one crucial difference between Polish and Estonian experts, namely, the latter seemed to, on occasion, distance themselves from the discourse and even question the discourse, whereas there was more naturalisation by Polish experts. One of the examples of, on the one hand, idealising the self-sufficiency narrative while, on the other, also making it clear that it is a matter of preferences is illustrated in the following:

> 'One's view on social benefits depends on world views. Some think that developing and supporting the economy is a good way to increase people's well-being. Others think that we should borrow money from other states and pay social benefits. I support the liberal world view. I think that one should focus on the economy and then people will want to live in Estonia. I am not sure that there is a point in increasing social benefits to attract more people here. For instance, Spain has really generous social benefits after losing work for one year. People there do not want to go to work.' (EU Committee expert)

The expert clearly favours a neoliberal approach with respect to their attitudes towards social justice. She also ridiculed her opponents on several occasions during the interview by expressing the opinion that overly social-democratic views can lead to huge national debts or even people who do want to work anymore. Furthermore, she also does not see that there is much that the state can do about emigration, besides strengthening its economy. Hence, in her opinion, higher salaries would be the primary and only reason for people to consider returning. Similarly, she later expresses the opinion that migration is mostly economic. However, she is also clear that her opinion represents her personal world view and hence shows some distance from the dominant narratives.

Similar kinds of concerns about the economy and wages were also expressed by other experts:

'I think the biggest problem is low wages. People are working hard all day long and then get a ridiculously low salary for that. When it comes to benefits ... those that are already sleeping on park benches, well, they do not know how to ask and they cannot be helped. They are ignorant, they do not care. The ones who ask are receiving.' (EU Committee expert 2)

This expert also shows a very similar kind of attitude to the first one, pointing out that the state should foremost care about people who are working hard but still receive a very low salary for their work. People who are 'sleeping on park benches' are described as lacking the initiative to do anything about their life, and should not therefore be a concern for the state because they do not want to help themselves. Furthermore, a dual distinction is made between people who are either hard-working (even though struggling because of low wages) and people who are perceived as ignorant and seemingly lazy. Hence, the first category of people deserves to be helped and could be helped through an increase in their salaries, whereas the latter does not even deserve help.

As with the first expert, several other experts used more 'social' systems in other countries as negative comparisons:

'The UK has put itself into a complicated position. They have this family benefit system, which is so generous. They have a huge problem in their country with people who have no motivation to go to work. They just live out of benefits. So, their main problem is not with migrants, but locals that are unwilling to work.' (Expert from Social Ministry)

In this quote, the UK's social system is criticised because it allegedly allows people to choose not working instead of working. Work comes out as a central element in many of the interviews with Estonian experts, whereas social benefits and the importance of those is either minimised or antagonised. People relying on social benefits are considered to be either deceiving the state or just not knowing how to take care of themselves. It should be noted that in the previous quote, the expert not only criticises those using unemployment benefits, but also negatively describes a generous family benefit system that, in her opinion, decreases the motivation to work. In this quote, taking care of children is not considered work, nor is it considered reason enough not to enter the labour market as an employee. This brings out another aspect of the Estonian attitude to self-sufficiency, namely, that women who have small children are expected to work. Hence, there is no gender difference in this set of expectations to be fully employed. Furthermore, other conditions, such as disabilities, that might hinder either finding work or working are minimised:

'We are making a reform for disabled people. Most Western countries have the same system. The slogan in Netherlands is that all people who can, must work. The other slogan is that most people are capable to work. Even those that sit in the bed are capable of doing some kind of work, well unless they are in a coma.' (Expert from Social Ministry 2)

The attention here is clearly towards pushing most people into the labour market and hence decreasing the number of dependants. In this case, the state decides which people are unable to work and should rely on state help. However, even in the conditions where the state decides who can and who cannot work, there is an attitude of mistrust from one of the experts towards people who rely on social welfare: "When we had an economic crisis, we could see. When people stopped receiving unemployment benefits, so many people started receiving disability pensions. Masses ... it needs to be changed. For some reason, in certain areas, all people have disabilities and are really, really sick" (expert from Social Ministry 2). In this quote, the expert is showing suspicion with regards to the justified use of disability pensions or, in a more general respect, social benefits. She points out that it is not believable that all people receiving benefits are actually eligible for this, thus representing these people as misusing the state's support. It should be noted that the people who registered themselves for disability pensions after being unemployed for a long time are represented not as potential victims struggling to find work in their place of living, but rather as active agents who have decided to deceive the state instead of being self-sufficient and working.

In this section, we have demonstrated how the desired Estonian citizen is presented as self-sufficient and working. Hence, this creates a category of other that has come out of several quotes: the non-working, dependent citizen.

It should be noted that unlike in the Polish case, migration was not debated or questioned. This comes out from the following quote:

'Estonia regards the free movement of people as extremely vital. In the EU direction, Estonia has always said that free movement is something we support. This is the official standpoint of the country and looking at the demographics, and then we should be worried that people in the working age are going away. This is contradictory.... However, Estonia has never backed down from the position that they support the free movement.' (Expert from Social Ministry)

Official Estonian policy towards migration is hence positive and migration is presented as something beneficial for the state. The expert suggests that this policy is contradictory, indicating that the Estonian state should be more worried about the outflow of people, but also points out that there is very little discussion on the negative effects going on at the policy level.

Not only is the negative effect of migration hardly discussed, but there is an intricate relationship between Estonia's positive attitude towards migration and its ideal of self-sufficiency. In fact, such a positive view is informed by the idea that people should take care of themselves and not burden the system. Hence, emigration is seen as a way for people to be self-sufficient and to not lean on the Estonian system. Such a discourse appears, for instance, in the following quote:

'I think the UK's attitude against migration is unreasonable. I think the UK's economy has won a lot from Polish people who work there. The whole point of free mobility is that people migrate for economic reasons, that people go where they can find work. This is the whole point. Of course, then the hosting state also needs to consider that, at some point, these people might become unemployed.' (Expert from Social Ministry 2)

Sippola (2013) suggests that Estonia's official policy is that it is a duty of citizens to find ways to support themselves if the state is doing badly. Even though no expert directly represented such a view, one can see from the previous quote that the attitude towards migration is very favourable and such an attitude is well connected with the idea of self-sufficient individuals who are willing to travel to another country in order to find work. If we connect this idea to the fact that, for instance, people in Southern Estonia receiving disability pensions, potentially because they struggled to find work, were othered and used as a negative example, then we can see how migration is seen as a route to self-sufficiency. Therefore, Estonian citizens working abroad become more favourable in the eyes of the state than citizens living in Estonia but not working. This illustrates how the idea of the negative other informs the discourse and state's official policy towards migration.

Conclusion

The aim of this article was to analyse the discourses around migration othering in two states – Poland and Estonia – via the concept of the desired citizen. First, we argued that the concept of the other should be reconsidered in terms of not only being applied to 'cultural and ethnic' others, but also taking into account welfare states and the distribution of welfare. We presented this argument by showing how ethnic Russians in Estonia and Ukrainians in Poland were othered based on their ethnicity, while Estonian returnees were othered based on their ability to be self-sufficient, and Polish returnees were othered based on their economic status and ability to reproduce Polish culture and national values. Due to the strong presence of welfare states in Europe, we suggest that the idea of desired and undesired citizens motivates many welfare and social policy-related decisions at a national level. We therefore urge research to take into account welfare inclusion and exclusion when talking about the national belonging of returnees. As shown, the othering of returnees includes assumptions about the inclusion and exclusion of particular groups of individuals who are perceived as non-belonging based on the attributes and experiences that mark returnees' biographies. Consequently, individuals who do not meet assumptions about a 'good returnee'/desired citizen are othered.

Furthermore, in what constitutes our main contribution, we posit that othering in relation to welfare can help us to better understand national discourses around migration and return migration. In our case, Poland and Estonia have adopted different attitudes towards return migrants. While Estonian policy experts stressed the positive nature of migration, with migrants largely seen as successful individuals who had taken control over their lives, Polish narratives around migration were much more negative, drawing attention to the 'social costs' of migration, such as broken families. This resulted in Polish experts questioning the potential belonging of return migrants and seeing them as a burden on the welfare state, whereas Estonian experts saw return migration as mostly positive and a sign of loyalty.

We suggest that such different migration discourses might have an effect on return migration, that is, Polish returnees may be less likely to return in comparison with Estonian returnees. Of course, decisions to return are complex and include, among other factors, immigrants' experiences in the host countries; however, the discourse on returnees in countries of origin may play a role in the decision-making process as well. As mentioned earlier, national discourses around return migration are rarely discussed and even less often seen as having a potential impact on return migration. This article presents how these discourses could provide a helpful lens for understanding return migration, as well as perhaps potential migrants. In relation to the Estonian discourse of self-sufficiency, potential migrants from Estonia might view their migration in a vastly different manner than migrants from Poland, where the family plays such a huge role. More specifically, while Estonian migrants might perceive their migration as a temporary livelihood strategy, Polish migrants might be more careful around migrating, and when making a decision, be more likely to become permanent migrants. At this stage, this is naturally a hypothesis that requires further investigation; however, it nevertheless demonstrates the potential use of understanding national discourses around migration.

Note
[1] The TRANSWEL project was funded by New Opportunities for Research Funding Agency Cooperation in Europe (NORFACE).

Acknowledgments
The authors would like to thank their TRANSWEL research teams for their contributions to the data collection and stimulating discussions on discourses of belonging embedded in policy makers' narratives on returnees. We would like to thank Dr Emma Carmel and Dr James Rees for their thoughtful comments and efforts towards improving our manuscript. Above all, we owe a great debt to all the participants: civil servants, legal experts and policy stakeholders from Poland and Estonia that gave their time generously to share their expertise and experience.

References

Aidukaite, J. (2004) *The emergence of the post-socialist welfare state: The case of the Baltic states: Estonia, Latvia and Lithuania,* Stockholm: Södertörn University.

Anderson, B. (2006) *Imagined communities: Reflections on the origin and spread of nationalism,* London: Verso Books.

Anderson, B. (2013) *Us and them? The dangerous politics of immigration control,* Oxford: Oxford University Press.

Atas, N. (2018) 'The cost of becoming a neo-liberal welfare state: a cautionary case of Lithuania', *Critical Social Policy,* 38(4): 728–48.

Avato, J, Koettl, J. and Sabates-Wheeler, R. (2010) 'Social security regimes, global estimates, and good practices: the status of social protection for international migrants', *World Development,* 38(4): 455–66.

Balch, A. and Balabanova, E. (2016) 'Ethics, politics and migration: public debates on the free movement of Romanians and Bulgarians in the UK, 2006–2013', *Politics,* 36(1): 19–35.

Barker, M. (1981) *The new racism: Conservatives and the ideology of the tribe,* London: Junction Books.

Barker, M. (2001) 'Reflections on "The problems with racism"', in P. Essed and D.T. Goldberg (eds) *Race critical theories: Text and context,* Malden, MA: Blackwell Publishers.

Bocskor, Á. (2018) 'Anti-immigration discourses in Hungary during the "crisis" year: the Orbán government's "national consultation" campaign of 2015', *Sociology,* 52(3): 551–68.

Bohle, D. and Greskovits, B. (2007) 'Neoliberalism, embedded neoliberalism and neocorporatism: towards transnational capitalism in Central-Eastern Europe', *West European Politics,* 30: 443–66.

Brubaker, R. (2004) *Ethnicity without groups,* Cambridge: Harvard University Press.

Buzalka, J. (2008) *Nation and religion: The politics of commemorations in South-East Poland,* Münster: LIT Verlag.

Carmel, E. and Paul, R. (2013) 'Complex stratification: understanding European Union governance of migrant rights', *Regions and Cohesion,* 3(3): 56–85.

Carmel, E. and Sojka, B. (2018) 'Social security and the 'management' of migration', in J. Millar, *Understanding social security: Issues for policy and practice* (3rd ed.), Bristol: Policy Press.

Carmel, E., Sojka, B. and Papiez, K. (2019a) 'Beyond the rights-bearing EU mobile citizen: governing inequality and privilege in European Union social security', in A. Amelina, E. Carmel, A. Runfors and E. Scheibelhofer (eds) *Boundaries of European social citizenship*, London: Routledge.

Carmel, E., Sojka, B. and Papiez, K. (2019b) 'Inequalities, insecurities, and informalities: making sense of migrants' experiences of social security between Poland and the UK', in A. Amelina, E. Carmel, A. Runfors and E. Scheibelhofer (eds) *Boundaries of European social citizenship*, London: Routledge.

Cerami, A. (2005) *Social policy in Central and Eastern Europe: The emergence of a new European welfare regime*, Berlin: Lit.

Dustmann, C. and Görlach, J.S. (2016) 'The economics of temporary migrations', *Journal of Economic Literature*, 54(1): 98–136.

Eberts, M.W. (1998) 'The Roman Catholic Church and democracy in Poland', *Europe–Asia Studies*, 50(5): 817–42.

Ehata, R. and Seeleib-Kaiser, M. (2017) 'Benefit tourism and EU migrant citizens: real-world experiences', in J. Hudson, C. Needham and E. Heins (eds) *Social policy review 29: Analysis and debate in social policy, 2017*, Bristol: Policy Press.

Fairclough, N. (2013) *Critical discourse analysis: The critical study of language*, New York, NY: Routledge.

Ferrera, M. (2005) *The boundaries of welfare: European integration and the new spatial politics of social protection*, Oxford: Oxford University Press.

Hall, S. (1997) The spectacle of the "other" in S. Hall (ed.) *Representation: Cultural representations and signifying practices*, London and Thousand Oaks, CA: SAGE.

Holzmann, R. and Koettl, J. (2015) 'Portability of pension, health, and other social benefits: facts, concepts, and issues', *CESifo Economic Studies*, 61(2): 377–415.

Horváth, I. (2008) 'The culture of migration of rural Romanian youth', *Journal of Ethnic and Migration Studies*, 34(5): 771–86.

Kalmus, V. and Vihalemm, T. (2006) 'Distinct mental structures in transitional culture: an empirical analysis of values and identities in Estonia and Sweden', *Journal of Baltic Studies*, 37(1): 94–123.

Kuscu-Bonnenfant, I. (2012) 'Constructing the homeland: Kazakhstan's discourse and policies surrounding its ethnic return-migration policy', *Central Asian Survey*, 31(1): 31–44.

Marshall, T.H. (1963) *Citizenship and social class and other essays*, Cambridge: Cambridge University Press.

Morris, L. (2002) *Managing migration: Civic stratification and migrants' rights*, London: Routledge.

Ní Laoire, C. (2008) '"Settling back"? A biographical and life-course perspective on Ireland's recent return migration', *Irish Geography*, 41(2): 195–210.

Pennings, F. (2012) 'EU citizenship: access to social benefits in other EU member states', *International Journal of Comparative Labour Law and Industrial Relations*, 28(3): 307–34.

Perek-Białas, J. and Racław, M. (2014) 'Transformation of elderly care in Poland', in M. León (ed) *The transformation of care in European societies*, London: Palgrave Macmillan.

Petersoo, P. (2007) 'Reconsidering otherness: constructing Estonian identity', *Nations and Nationalism*, 13(1): 117–33.

Ramet, S.P. (2017) 'Controversies in the social and political engagement of the Catholic Church in Poland since 1988', in S. Ramet and I. Borowik (eds) *Religion, politics, and values in Poland*, New York, NY: Palgrave Macmillan.

Richardson, J. and Colombo, M. (2013) 'Continuity and change in anti-immigrant discourse in Italy: an analysis of the visual propaganda of the Lega Nord', *Journal of Language and Politics*, 12(2): 180–202.

Sibley, D. (1995) 'Spaces of exclusion: home, locality, nation', in D. Sibley (ed) *Geographies of exclusion*, London: Routledge.

Sippola, M. (2013) 'The awkward choices facing the Baltic worker: exit or loyalty', *Journal of Baltic Studies*, 44(4): 451–73.

Sivanandan, A. (2001) 'Poverty is the new black', *Race & Class*, 43: 1–5.

Sivanandan, A. (2006) 'Race, terror and civil society', *Race & Class*, 47: 1–8.

Taha, N., Siegmann, K.A. and Messkoub, M. (2015) 'How portable is social security for migrant workers? A review of the literature', *International Social Security Review*, 68(1): 95–118.

Triandafyllidou, A. (1998) 'National identity and the "other"', *Ethnic and Racial Studies*, 21(4): 593–612.

Van Dijk, T.A. (2018) 'Discourse and migration', in R. Zapata-Barrero and E. Yalaz (eds) *Qualitative research in European migration studies*, IMISCOE Research Series, Amsterdam: Springer.

Vihalemm, T. and Masso, A. (2003) 'Identity dynamics of Russian-speakers of Estonia in the transition period', *Journal of Baltic Studies*, 34(1): 92–116.

Wahba, J. (2015) 'Selection, selection, selection: the impact of return migration', *Journal of Population Economics*, 28(3): 535–63.

White, A. (2014) 'Double return migration: failed returns to Poland leading to settlement abroad and new transnational strategies', *International Migration*, 52: 72–84.

White, A. (2017) *Polish families and migration since EU accession*, Bristol: Policy Press.

Wieviorka, M. (2010) 'Racism in Europe: unity and diversity', in M. Martiniello and J. Rath (eds) *Selected studies in international migration and immigrant incorporation*, Amsterdam: Amsterdam University Press.

Zuba, K. (2010) 'The political strategies of the Catholic Church in Poland', *Religion, State & Society*, 38(2): 115–34.

Zubrzycki, G. (2001) '"We, the Polish nation": ethnic and civic visions of nationhood in post-communist constitutional debates', *Theory and Society*, 30(5): 629–68.

Zubrzycki, G. (2002) 'The classical opposition between civic and ethnic models of nationhood: ideology, empirical reality and social scientific analysis', *Polish Sociological Review*, 3(139): 275–95.

Żuk, P. and Żuk, P. (2018) 'Retirees without pensions and welfare: the social effects of pension privatization in Poland', *Critical Social Policy*, 38(2): 407–17.

Part II
Social policy and young people

Elke Heins

'Youth' was a prominent topic at the 2019 Social Policy Association annual conference, and the following chapters look at this broad theme from a variety of methodologies and perspectives, including youth transition studies, cultural policy and criminal justice. The widespread interest in young people is perhaps not surprising since it has been widely recognised that the 2008/09 crisis and subsequent austerity policies have had severe impacts on young people across Europe in many Social Policy fields. For instance, the spike in youth unemployment led to concerns about a 'lost generation', which, in turn, sparked a range of labour market programmes for young people. Young people are also strongly affected by more long-term labour market changes, often described as the 'gig economy', in which hyper-flexible and precarious employment forms are becoming normalised. Important intra-generational inequality trends notwithstanding, an increasing intergenerational wealth divide is manifested most clearly in housing due to the soaring property prices over the last decades mainly benefiting the 'baby boomer' generation. The increasing precarity of the youth labour market and the unaffordability of housing make it more difficult for current young adults to 'get on the property ladder', which is an important milestone for young people in liberal welfare states such as the UK.

Despite the strong reliance on the market in liberal welfare states, a tacit assumption of the UK's welfare state is that young people will be able to use their family of origin as a source of welfare while making their transition to adulthood. Indeed, the residualist nature of liberal welfare regimes pushes young people towards their family for support when transitions are 'prolonged' or 'disjointed'. Despite identifying the prominence of the family welfare source, less is known about its impact beyond the youth transition period. Sarah Weakley's comparative study in this volume uses longitudinal data from the 1970 British Cohort Study and the 1997 US National Longitudinal Survey of Youth to analyse the impact of implicit and explicit family welfare resources on young people's transition to economic independence. In both the UK and the US, the commonly used measure of parental socio-economic background was a factor that persisted and intensified as cohort members moved through a transition. Rather than inequalities reducing into adulthood, inequalities widened. The family of origin is a 'safety net' and a 'scaffold' for young people from across the income spectrum; however, greater family reliance likely exacerbates rather than reduces inequality in liberal welfare states. In the US, rather than regarding residential independence as an outcome, the ability to co-reside until 24 or the ability to move back if needed turned out to be a resource in a youth transition. Weakley found that 'early' movers have higher wages and higher odds of strong labour market attachment, which is suggestive of a 'successful' youth transition. However, these early movers had worse poverty outcomes into mid-life. Furthermore, the ability to move back into the family home (that is, 'boomerang') when needed was associated with lower poverty. This suggests not only that the ability to co-reside in this period serves as a safety net in the youth period, but also that the impact of this resource lasts well into adulthood. Trends in co-residence and labour market insecurity in the UK mirror those of the US; therefore, the US evidence can inform both future research and policy formation in the UK. The empirical evidence suggests that if social policy in the UK is interested in supporting successful youth transitions across the income spectrum, the long-lasting imbalance created by unequal family resources will need to be addressed, beginning with a restructuring of the benefit system for low-income young people alongside structural changes to the youth labour market.

Concerns for youth poverty and unemployment have also been placed further up on the agenda in Sweden. Anna Kahlmeter's contribution to this volume examines youths' labour market trajectories, with a focus on the complexity, timing and duration of labour market disadvantage for individuals with and without experience of early adulthood economic hardship, as indicated by different degrees of social assistance receipt. Utilising longitudinal Swedish register data, more than 47,000 individuals have been followed for 15 years, from the time of their residential emancipation at age 19–22 to their mid-30s. Using sequence analysis, five clusters of labour market establishment trajectories were identified. Findings from multinomial regression suggest that when early adulthood economic hardship is extensive, this is associated with elevated risks of disadvantaged labour market trajectories, such as having an insecure labour market position through large parts of the 20s or following a track of long-term labour market exclusion. On the other hand, experience of low degrees of hardship only had a weak association with disadvantaged labour market trajectories. These findings imply that social-democratic welfare states such as the Swedish one are effective in addressing low levels of financial hardship without incurring long-term disadvantages through a relatively generous benefits and social services system. However, similar to liberal welfare states, the Swedish welfare state also struggles when hardship is prolonged and the family is not available as a safety net.

Moving beyond labour market and social policy in a more narrow sense, the chapter by Katherine Tonkiss, Malgorzata Wootton and Eleni Stamou examines the articulation of notions of 'good citizenship' in the conceptualisation and operationalisation of policies targeting the cultural literacy of young people in the UK over the past decade. To do so, they analyse the findings of a systematic review of relevant policy documents published between 2007 and 2018. They argue that this policy field has been strongly shaped by the intervention of a neoliberal economic logic, with policies constructing good citizens as neoliberal subjects responsible for their own choices and capable of self-regulation to become productive contributors to the national economy with little dependence on the state. Yet, they also demonstrate that such policies have been informed by a strongly nationalist interpretation of culture, aiming to instil in young people a robust understanding of national culture as a source of binding sentiment in light of the perceived challenges associated with diverse, multicultural communities. As such, the chapter argues that cultural literacy policies have been used to promote a particular vision of the good citizen through a 'neoliberal communitarian' model of governance. This model combines the individualising logics of neoliberalism that emphasise responsibility and self-regulation with the collective focus of communitarianism on shared culture and values. These threads are deployed simultaneously to 'responsibilise' citizens in order to reduce the perceived burden that they present to the state, as well as to police nationalist parameters of inclusion and exclusion.

This section on young people concludes with a chapter by Sarah Brooks-Wilson that addresses the unintended consequences of a community youth justice sector that has been severely impacted by austerity policies and is decreasing in terms of staff, children and the wider distribution of practice. The lens of institutional geography is used to reinterpret changes in the youth justice system of England and Wales. The analysis produces new knowledge on how location, movement and ideology impact community sentence accessibility for children. Despite scant policy attention, practice locations and transport coverage operate in tandem, with one required to fill gaps left by the other in order to maintain service accessibility. Yet, in the context of persistent austerity, both services are affected by increasing service gaps and government accessibility guidance remains narrow in scope, with connections between poverty and service accessibility currently poorly acknowledged. The social policy implications are substantial given that entrenched poverty is overwhelmingly found within populations of convicted and diverted children. Overall, the contributions to this section underpin that young people have been strongly affected by policy changes in a number of welfare state areas in the context of austerity, thus providing a nice link to the following themed section.

5

The family welfare source and inequality in liberal welfare states: evidence from cohort studies

Sarah Weakley

Introduction

The family of origin, in whatever form that may take, is a key locus of support and influence in a youth transition, that is, the period between childhood and adulthood comprised of multiple status changes in employment, education and family formation domains (Settersten et al, 2005). One's family of origin shapes opportunities and ambitions, and has been conceptualised as a 'safety net' and a 'scaffold' for young people (Swartz et al, 2011). As a safety net, the family of origin provides in-kind and financial support for young people to 'fall back on' when a transition experience has been unsuccessful; as a scaffold, a family of origin provides resources for a young person to establish an independent life. In an age of economic and social precarity for young people in the Western world, the family of origin is being increasingly relied upon through the youth period and into adulthood.

However, the extent to which the family of origin must be relied upon to meet the welfare needs of young people during this period is dependent upon the organisation of the labour market and the welfare state that comprise the transition context. While many studies of youth transitions assess the changing nature of the labour market and its impacts on young people as independent actors, welfare state and family resources have been addressed less in empirical work. This gap is particularly problematic for researchers and policymakers given the emergence in current US and UK youth cohorts of longer periods of co-residence, an increase in the 'boomerang' experiences of residential (in)dependence and the prominence of intergenerational transfers. While there is some evidence of impacts on residential transitions and economic outcomes in the youth period, there is less evidence on how family resources impact outcomes in the longer term and how they might reinforce inequality.

The aim of this study is to investigate the impact of the family welfare source on a young person's long-term economic independence outcomes. The chapter first conceptualises the multidimensional outcome of interest – economic independence – and the use of the welfare mix as an organising framework. The work then briefly reviews how each of the three welfare sources impacts a young person's transition to adulthood. The methodology details the US and UK cohorts used, the longitudinal models chosen, and how family welfare is operationalised for 'implicit' and 'explicit' family welfare resources. Results from both cohorts suggest that the impacts of the family welfare source are felt long into adulthood and drive unequal outcomes between those who can and cannot access these resources during the youth period. These are issues that should be addressed by both research and policy.

Literature review: economic independence and the welfare mix

A key concept that bridges youth transitions and welfare research is 'independence', which is used here to develop the outcome of interest. Independence in youth research has traditionally been defined by the achievement of adulthood 'markers', including attaining full-time employment, moving out of the parental home, getting married and becoming a parent (Buchmann, 1989). Subsequent research rejected the rigidity of these markers for definitions of independence characterised by 'subjective feelings' consistent with Arnett's (2000) model of emerging adulthood. However, a common characteristic in both views is that independence is a status achieved in reference to the family of origin.

Liberal welfare states engage with the concept of independence quite differently, where independence is defined in reference to what it is not – 'dependence' on state resources. This conceptualisation is consistent with the organising principle of residualism, where the state aims to support only those who are deemed unable to provide for themselves via the labour market, thereby limiting 'welfare dependency' (Pierson, 1994). Therefore, independence is a status achieved in reference to the state.

Norms of youth transitions that encourage independence from the family of origin, combined with norms that encourage independence from the state, necessarily lead to contexts that value labour market success. The concept of 'economic independence' was first considered by Jones and Wallace (1992), and further qualitative research found that these ideas resonated with young people's own definitions of adulthood (Lee and Mortimer, 2009; Andrew et al, 2012). Smeeding and Phillips (2002) operationalised this concept and considered economic independence via three measures: wages from the labour market alone; income from the labour market and government assistance; and household income that includes the labour market, the state and family resources. Their work informs the three economic outcomes used in this research.

This conceptualisation of economic independence also finds coherence with a welfare state framework that can be applied to a youth transition: the welfare mix (Powell and Barrientos, 2004). Powell and Barrientos's framework was originally developed in the spirit of Esping-Andersen (1990) to compare welfare states at a macro-level on three sources of welfare: the labour market, the family and the state. In 2014, Antonucci and colleagues proposed its application to youth welfare policy and individual life courses. In their view, when applied to individual transitions, the framework can help uncover 'how the different combinations of welfare sources ... leads to different levels of decommodification and defamilialization in young people's lives' (Antonucci et al, 2014: 25). In liberal welfare states, the welfare mix favours the labour market as the primary welfare source, followed by the family and the state, and affirms the primacy of economic independence in a youth transition.

When applied to youth policy, the welfare mix also enables an investigation beyond the existing frameworks that are used to inform and assess policy interventions, which tend to focus primarily on school-to-work transitions and youth unemployment (Walther, 2006). As these frameworks do not explicitly focus on the idea of 'welfare resources', they omit discussions of the family as a key youth transition actor. To address these concerns, this research uses the welfare mix as an organising framework.

The labour market

The extent to which young people can successfully achieve economic independence with labour market returns alone has become increasingly challenging in a globalised world, even as early and steady attachment is the ascribed transition 'norm' in liberal welfare states (Walther, 2006).

One of the reasons for this challenging context is the reliance on academic qualifications in US and UK labour markets. The structure of a liberal market economy (LME) most handsomely rewards workers with 'switchable assets', who can more successfully move from one job role to another (Estevez-Abe et al, 2001) – 'assets' that are conferred primarily through academic qualifications (Iversen and Stephens, 2008). For young people with low academic qualifications – an outcome still shaped by class, despite the expansion of higher education (Shildrick, 2008) – their ability to achieve economic independence is particularly challenging (Howieson and Iannelli, 2008).

However, the flexibility and precarity of the youth labour market affects all young people. Even for those with high academic qualifications, 'stable employment biographies ... are now elusive' (Roberts, 2011: 21). Notably, flexible and precarious employment tenures are reflected in youth labour markets with higher concentrations of young people in service and retail sectors (Bell and Blanchflower, 2011), which are sectors generally comprised of a cadre of low-paid workers who work on more unstable contracts (Auer and Cazes, 2003).

Labour market flexibility for young people, particularly the rise of the 'gig economy', has been lauded as a manifestation of agency and choice that allows young people to explore career paths and more easily combine education and employment (DuBois-Reymond, 1998). However, for some groups of young people, labour market precarity may last years into the post-school period and have long-term negative impacts on economic independence. These types of 'non-standard' employment experiences are 'typified by lack of choice, control ... and [bring about] alienation and insecurity' (MacDonald and Giazitzoglu, 2019: 724). Instability and periods of youth unemployment also have knock-on impacts on individual wages in the long term (Gregg and Tominey, 2005) and, subsequently, overall household economic status.

Research continues to assert that unequal labour market outcomes in both attachment and remuneration are driven by demographic characteristics such as gender (Blau and Khan, 2017) and, particularly in the US, race[1] (Wilson, 1996). It is therefore likely that the empirical models will find variation in labour market outcomes based on these factors as main effects. However, these characteristics shape all aspects of a youth transition and will likely also moderate the impact of family welfare.

The state

Youth policy has been described by King (2016: 338) as 'social policy that addresses the needs, rights and interests of young people'. More specifically, 'youth policy' interventions tend to focus on addressing the challenges of the school-to-work transition and, in liberal welfare states, are targeted at young people deemed 'at risk' (Coles, 1995). For the 1970 British Cohort Study (BCS) cohort investigated here, who were aged 16 to 24 in 1986 to 1994, a key policy intervention was the Youth Training Scheme (YTS). YTS was a voluntary job training programme for school leavers that reached a relatively significant proportion of the national cohort; in 1988, for example, 22 per cent of school leavers in Britain participated in YTS (Bradley, 1995; Dolton et al, 2004). YTS research generally found either neutral or negative impacts on participants' wages and unemployment outcomes (reviewed in Dolton et al, 2004). Overall, this type of government investment was not found to significantly improve the lives of the 'low-achieving' target group a decade after participation.

State intervention also comes from the social security system, which is not targeted at the youth population but is a potentially notable feature of low-income young people's lives. Young people's interaction with the benefit system and their characterisation as 'deserving' of government assistance is complicated by their identity as 'semi-dependent' on their family of origin (Antonucci et al, 2014; Arundel and Ronald, 2016). This identity is reflected in government assistance policy through a 'dependency assumption' (Harris, 1989), whereby it is assumed that those under 25 will receive support from their family of origin. This assumption is illustrated by limited benefit eligibility in the US and reduced benefit eligibility in the UK, particularly for young people without children. Therefore, a relatively small proportion of young people access the benefit system in any given year, with the majority of whom being young parents.

For those who can access the benefit system, the majority do so for a short period of time or in cycles (Bane and Ellwood, 1994; Hills, 2014). Evidence on the impact of cycles of receipt for those of working age shows that low levels of conditional cash assistance from Jobseeker's Allowance (UK) and Temporary Assistance for Needy Families (US) does not increase employment prospects (Petrongolo, 2007, 2009; Manning, 2009; Ziliak, 2016), and that the subsequent wages of programme 'leavers' do not offset the loss in transfer income (Wright, 2012). There is evidence that non-conditional assistance programmes such as the Supplemental Nutrition Assistance Program (SNAP) in the US can reduce poverty for the very poor (Fox et al, 2015), serve as a lifeline for recipient families (Edin and Shaefer, 2016) and reduce income volatility (Gundersen and Ziliak, 2003). However, a spell of poverty that makes one eligible for means-tested benefits will necessarily correspond to worse economic independence outcomes.

The family

Given the challenging nature of the youth labour market and that state resources are restricted to a small group of 'at-risk' young people, the family of origin is often a primary port of call for young people in liberal welfare states. The family has been described as both a 'safety net' and a 'scaffold' (Swartz et al, 2011), with resources taking both explicit and implicit forms. Although delineated here for analytical purposes, these categories of resources are dynamic and interconnected.

Scaffolds are conceptualised as resources provided by the family of origin that enable a young person to live outside of the family home and make a 'successful' transition earlier and more permanently (Swartz et al, 2011). One's parental background and class position operate as an implicit scaffold by shaping young people's opportunity structures (Settersten et al, 2005). Social mobility research affirms that advantaged class positions (often also tied to advantaged racial positions) allow young people access to social and material resources for economic success (DiPrete and Eirich, 2006; Friedman and Laurison, 2019).

Explicit scaffolding resources from a young person's family of origin are often measured through intergenerational monetary transfers (Ermisch, 1999; Fingerman et al, 2015). Previous research has found that the gap in the amount of monetary transfers between low- and high-income families is notable, with young adults in the top quartile of the income distribution receiving average transfers more than double those of their counterparts in the bottom quartile (Schoeni and Ross, 2005). While higher-income parents can give *more* to their children in absolute terms, the relative share of parental income given to young people is similar for families in higher- and lower-income groups (Furstenberg, 2010).

Financial transfers also serve as an explicit safety net, keeping young people afloat when labour market returns are insufficient for young people with and without children (Amato et al, 2008). However, monetary transfers are not the only way that the family serves as a safety net. In-kind resources, particularly the ability for young people to stay in the family home past the normative expectation of home leaving

– either after school or after university – are an increasingly common form of family welfare resources (Roberts et al, 2016). This is illustrated by the increase in the length of co-residence and the prevalence of the 'boomerang' experiences of recent US and UK youth cohorts (Barrington and Stone, 2014; Dey and Pierret, 2014).

Research on youth transitions often views residential independence status as an outcome but measures such as the age of first move out and the incidence of moving back can be re-conceptualised as in-kind resources provided as part of the family safety net. When conceptualised as resources, this research can extend previous work, for example, which found much higher poverty rates throughout early adulthood for early home leavers in Europe (Aassve et al, 2006). Furthermore, this work can investigate how these family resources impact not just poverty, but individual labour market outcomes, as well as whether their impact differs between different demographic groups. As young people in liberal welfare states must increasingly rely on their family, these exploratory results can foreground new lines of research and policy discussions.

Methodology

This investigation aims to understand the impact of the family as a welfare source on a young person's ability to become economically independent in mid-life in the US and the UK. Given the longer time horizon of the research aim a longitudinal panel design is used, which enables inferences from cohorts to investigate 'intra-individual developmental trends' (Menard, 2004). Two cohort data sets from liberal welfare states are utilised – the 1970 BCS and the 1997 US National Longitudinal Survey of Youth (NLSY 97) – with separate analyses brought together after estimation.

The 1970 BCS is a cohort data set comprised of all young people born in one week in 1970 in the UK. Although the BCS contains data on over 17,000 respondents, there was only a subsample of 1,650 English respondents surveyed during the youth period in 1991.[2] As the youth period is the focus of this investigation, a cohort data set was synthesised using this subsample, resulting in a complete case data set of 1,131 respondents with sufficient data from ages 21, 30, 34 and 42. The number of respondents in each survey wave varied, resulting in an unbalanced panel; however, over half of the respondents had all waves and therefore a complete case analysis could occur.

The NLSY 97 is a cohort data set with 8,984 original sample members between the ages of 12 and 17 surveyed annually since 1997.

This investigation used 16 waves of data until 2013 (the ages of cohort members ranged from roughly 28 to 35), with a complete case analysis for a data set of 8,296 respondents. Although there is an age 'range' for this data set at each year, descriptive analyses found no significant differences in the variables of interest for 'younger' and 'older' cohort members, and they are therefore considered together.[3] As with the BCS, the number of respondents in each survey wave varied, resulting in an unbalanced panel.

Table 5.1 details the key features of the empirical models. Economic independence in both cases is investigated via three measures – wages, work intensity and household economic status – specified differently for each case due to data availability. Models of wages are estimated using correlated random effects models (Wooldridge, 2012), and work intensity and household economic models are estimated using ordered logistic regression models (Allison, 2009).[4] Each model was created using multiple iterations to consider collinearity, tests for stability of estimates and parsimony.

Results and analysis

This section briefly summarises the impacts of state welfare and structural drivers of labour market outcomes. The focus then turns to family welfare, where the implicit resource of parental background for both cohorts is discussed, followed by a discussion of explicit family welfare, captured here in the NLSY cohort using residential independence variables.

Although many administrative characteristics of the US and UK welfare systems differ and can be considered a 'contrast of contexts' (Skocpol and Somers, 1980), the principles of liberal welfare states are similar and life-course studies find similar transition patterns in each case. As such, this work considers the results together in the analysis.

Welfare from the state and labour market

The state

In both cases, state welfare is indicated by a single indicator that measures any means-tested benefit receipt in the year preceding the survey. This specification was especially necessary for the UK case, where benefit programmes changed notably in the survey period.[5] Overall, the reach of this resource is relatively small: 14 per cent of the UK sample were

Table 5.1: Key features of empirical models

Outcome variable specifications	Model estimated	Family welfare specifications
1970 British Cohort Study		
Waged Work: Individual Monthly Employment Income (logged)	Correlated Random Effects	Parental Income Quintile 1 (lowest) to 5 (highest)
Work Intensity: Usual weekly hours of work (ordered categories: no work = 0 to high intensity = 4)	Random Effects Ordered Logistic Regression	
Household Economic Status: Gross household income age 42 (quintiles)	Ordered Logistic Regression	
US National Longitudinal Survey of Youth 1997		
Waged Work: Individual Annual Employment Income (logged)	Correlated Random Effects	Parental Income Quintile 1 (lowest) to 5 (highest) (In Wages and Work Intensity Models)
Work Intensity: Weeks worked per year (ordered categories: none/very low = 0 to very high = 4)	Random Effects Ordered Logistic Regression	Parental History of Aid Receipt (Poverty Ratio Model)
Household Economic Status: Poverty ratio (ordered categories: 0 = above 200% Federal Poverty Line (FPL); 1 = 100–200% FPL; 2 = below 100% FPL)	Random Effects Ordered Logistic Regression	Age at Initial Move out: Before 19; 19 to 21; 21 to 24; After 24
		Moved back after initial move out

in receipt of any benefits at age 21, up to 25 per cent at age 42; in the US, 22 per cent of sample members received benefits at age 24, which plateaus into the cohort's mid-30s.

As the benefit receipt covariates compare those who do and do not receive benefits, the results are unsurprising. Rather, the inclusion of these variables is used primarily to control for this welfare source. However, the UK model speaks to and affirms previous research on YTS. YTS results in all models show that those who participated (31 per cent of the BCS sample) have 14 per cent lower wages[6] and lower odds of being in a higher household income quintile (odds ratio [OR] = 0.72) than those who did not participate (see Tables 5.2 and 5.3).

Table 5.2: Correlated Random Effects Model of Monthly Wages (ln), BCS 1970 sample

	Final Model Main Effects		Parental Income*Age	
	Coeff	t	Coeff	t
Family Welfare Vars:				
Parent Inc 1986 (Q1)				
Quintile 2	0.07	(1.49)	0.01	(0.19)
Quintile 3	0.14**	(2.76)	0.08	(1.06)
Quintile 4	0.21**	(3.04)	−0.04	(−0.39)
Quintile 5	0.34***	(4.06)	0.01	(0.06)
Missing	0.13**	(2.68)	0.06	(0.86)
Parental Inc*Age				
Q2*Age 30			0.14	(1.35)
Q3*Age 30			0.18	(1.70)
Q4*Age 30			0.44**	(3.13)
Q5*Age 30			0.41*	(2.38)
Missing*Age 30			0.16	(1.69)
Q2*Age 34			0.11	(0.98)
Q3*Age 34			0.13	(1.15)
Q4*Age 34			0.31*	(2.13)
Q5*Age 34			0.42*	(2.29)
Missing*Age 34			0.13	(1.24)
Q2*Age 42			0.02	(0.25)
Q3*Age 42			−0.03	(−0.31)
Q4*Age 42			0.31*	(2.28)
Q5*Age 42			0.55**	(3.27)
Missing*Age 42			0.004	(0.05)

(continued)

Table 5.2: Correlated Random Effects Model of Monthly Wages (ln), BCS 1970 sample (continued)

	Final Model Main Effects		Parental Income*Age	
	Coeff	t	Coeff	t
Control Vars:				
Age (Ref: 21)				
30	0.58***	(19.11)	0.42***	(4.88)
34	0.84***	(25.77)	0.71***	(7.38)
42	1.10***	(33.42)	1.06***	(12.47)
Female	−0.27***	(−8.44)	−0.27***	(−8.46)
Educ (No quals)				
CSE/NVQ 1	0.07	(0.95)	0.07	(1.00)
O level/NVQ 2	0.04	(0.59)	0.04	(0.61)
A level/NVQ 3	0.13*	(2.02)	0.14*	(2.08)
Higher Qs/NVQ 4	0.26***	(4.08)	0.26***	(4.12)
Degree+/NVQ 5	0.32***	(4.04)	0.31***	(3.97)
Region (London)				
Rest of England	−0.19**	(−2.86)	−0.19**	(−2.86)
Wales & Scotland	−0.30*	(−2.23)	−0.30*	(−2.20)
Region (mean)	*−0.01*	*(−0.16)*	*−0.01*	*(−0.20)*
Emp Status (FT)				
PT work	−0.91***	(−25.98)	−0.90***	(−25.94)
Unemployed	*−0.06*	*(−0.64)*	*−0.07*	*(−0.79)*
FT Ed	*−0.93****	*(−9.51)*	*−0.88****	*(−8.99)*
Home	*−0.18*	*(−1.64)*	*−0.16*	*(−1.48)*
Training	*−0.09*	*(−0.16)*	*−0.09*	*(−0.16)*
Sick/Disabled	*−0.28*	*(−0.87)*	*−0.29*	*(−0.91)*
Emp Stat (mean)	*−0.03*	*(−1.59)*	*−0.04*	*(−1.75)*
Married	0.05	(1.83)	0.05	(1.56)
MarStat (mean)	*0.01*	*(0.17)*	*0.02*	*(0.35)*
Young parenting	−0.03	(−0.57)	−0.03	(−0.60)
Benefit Receipt	−0.14**	(−3.05)	−0.14**	(−3.10)
Ben Recd (mean)	*−0.17**	*(−1.98)*	*−0.17*	*(−1.95)*
YTS participant	−0.15***	(−4.90)	−0.15***	(−4.81)
Constant	6.77***	(44.26)	6.84***	(42.89)
Between-Var	0.25***	(16.10)	0.26***	(16.33)
Within-Var	0.50***	(57.83)	0.50***	(57.73)
Observations	2,514		2,514	
Cases	872		872	

Notes: Displayed are the coefficients from a correlated random effects model of logged monthly wages with t statistics in parentheses.
* $p < 0.05$; ** $p < 0.01$; *** $p < 0.001$.

Table 5.3: Ordered Logistic Regression of gross household income (2012), BCS 1970 sample

	Final Model Main Effects	
	OR	t
Family Welfare Vars:		
Parental Inc 1986 (Q1)		
Quintile 2	1.28	(0.98)
Quintile 3	1.28	(0.98)
Quintile 4	3.27***	(3.59)
Quintile 5	4.03***	(3.67)
Missing	1.87**	(2.60)
Control Vars:		
HH Type (Single earner)		
Two earner household	0.60**	(−2.93)
Female	1.04	(0.31)
Educ (No quals)		
CSE/NVQ 1	1.28	(0.72)
O level/NVQ 2	0.75	(−0.94)
A level/NVQ 3	1.13	(0.40)
Higher Qs/NVQ 4	1.78	(1.85)
Degree+/NVQ 5	1.81	(1.38)
Region (London)		
Rest of England	0.71	(−1.16)
Wales and Scotland	0.45*	(−2.12)
Health (Excellent)		
Good	0.90	(−0.63)
Fair	0.64	(−1.51)
Poor	0.28***	(−3.51)
Monthly wages (ln)	1.13***	(4.68)
Emp Status 1991 (FT)		
PT work	0.68	(−1.23)
Unemployed	0.60	(−1.19)
FT Ed	1.61	(1.84)
Home	0.53	(−1.48)
Training	0.36	(−0.35)
Sick/Disabled	2.47	(0.82)
Ben Recd 1991	0.99	(−0.02)

(continued)

Table 5.3: Ordered Logistic Regression of gross household income (2012), BCS 1970 sample (continued)

	Final Model Main Effects	
	OR	t
YTS participant	0.72*	(–2.30)
cut1	0.04***	(–5.78)
cut2	0.20**	(–3.06)
cut3	1.87	(1.19)
cut4	18.65***	(5.47)
Observations	820	

Notes: Displayed are odds ratios from an ordered logistic regression of gross household income with *t* statistics in parentheses. ORs above 1 indicate higher odds of being in a higher income quintile.
* $p < 0.05$; ** $p < 0.01$; *** $p < 0.001$.

Structural drivers of labour market outcomes

The structural drivers of education, gender and race are particularly notable for youth transitions in liberal welfare states. In both cases, education covariates affirm previous research, where those with higher levels of education have higher wage outcomes, more positive work intensity outcomes and, subsequently, more positive household economic outcomes. Regarding gender, the UK models find 23 per cent lower wages on average for females, and the negative odds ratio (OR = 0.29) in the work intensity model indicates that the odds of being in a higher work intensity category are also lower for females (see Tables 5.2 and 5.4). Although the impact of gender on work intensity is not nearly as prominent in the US cohort (as shown by the odds ratio being close to 1), the wages model estimates that women in the sample have 21 per cent lower wages on average than men even when work intensity was controlled for (see Tables 5.5 and 5.6). Taken together, these two main effects suggest a systematically different experience in the labour market for females in both cases.

Finally, the impact of race on all three of the economic independence outcomes cannot be overstated for the US sample as the models find less successful economic outcomes for Black respondents when compared to their white counterparts. Black respondents have lower odds of being in a higher work intensity category (OR = 0.56), lower logged employment income on average and higher odds of being in a higher household poverty ratio group (OR = 1.76) (see Tables 5.5–5.7).

Table 5.4: Longitudinal ordered logistic regression models of work intensity, BCS 1970 sample

	Final Model Main Effects		Parental income*Age	
	OR	t	OR	t
Family Welfare Vars:				
Parental Inc 1986 (Q1)				
Quintile 2	1.43*	(2.46)	1.05	(0.14)
Quintile 3	1.10	(0.64)	0.48*	(−2.07)
Quintile 4	1.07	(0.34)	0.26**	(−2.84)
Quintile 5	0.88	(−0.59)	0.28*	(−2.16)
Missing	1.14	(0.93)	0.70	(−1.09)
Parental Inc*Age				
Quintile 2*Age 30			1.52	(0.93)
			1.60	
Quintile 3* Age 30			3.04*	(2.45)
			1.46	
Quintile 4*Age 30			5.59**	(2.60)
			1.45	
Quintile 5			3.23	(1.44)
			0.90	
Missing* Age 30			1.69	(1.25)
			1.18	
Quintile 2*Age 34			1.72	(1.23)
			1.81	
Quintile 3*Age 34			3.33**	(2.71)
			1.60	
Quintile 4*Age 34			9.68***	(3.51)
			2.52	
Quintile 5*Age 34			6.23*	(2.47)
			1.74	
Missing*Age 34			2.01	(1.69)
			1.41	
Quintile 2*Age 42			1.34	(0.66)
			1.41	
Quintile 3*Age 42			2.98*	(2.54)
			1.43	

(continued)

Table 5.4: Longitudinal ordered logistic regression models of work intensity, BCS 1970 sample (continued)

	Final Model Main Effects		Parental income*Age	
	OR	t	OR	t
Quintile 4*Age 42			7.72**	(3.25)
			2.01	
Quintile 5*Age 42			6.24**	(2.63)
			1.75	
Missing*Age 42			2.23	(1.95)
			1.56	
Control Vars:				
Age (21)				
30	2.21***	(6.37)	1.14	(0.36)
34	3.25***	(9.84)	1.44	(1.00)
42	4.43***	(11.79)	2.10*	(2.09)
Female	0.29***	(−12.58)	0.29***	(−12.47)
Educ (No quals)				
CSE/NVQ 1	1.83**	(2.72)	1.86**	(2.78)
O level/NVQ 2	1.29	(1.43)	1.29	(1.44)
A level/NVQ 3	1.58*	(2.45)	1.59*	(2.47)
Higher Q/ NVQ 4	1.53*	(2.34)	1.52*	(2.32)
Degree+/NVQ 5	1.62*	(2.05)	1.61*	(1.98)
Health (Excellent)				
Good	1.21*	(2.12)	1.20*	(1.98)
Fair	1.05	(0.33)	1.02	(0.16)
Poor	0.38***	(−3.31)	0.38***	(−3.35)
Household size	0.66***	(−10.79)	0.66***	(−11.02)
Young parenting	1.49**	(2.89)	1.50**	(2.91)
Benefit Recipient	0.30***	(−9.22)	0.30***	(−9.30)
YTS	1.06	(0.56)	1.05	(0.55)
Observations	3,269		3,269	
Cases	891		891	

Notes: Displayed are odds ratios from an ordered logistic regression of waged work intensity with *t* statistics in parentheses. Odds ratios (OR) above 1 indicate increased odds of being in a higher work intensity category. Parental income main effects in the interaction model are odds ratios for respondents at reference age 21, odds ratios in bold are those resulting from the interaction terms.
* $p < 0.05$; ** $p < 0.01$; *** $p < 0.001$.

Table 5.5: Longitudinal ordered logistic regression models of waged work intensity, NLSY 1997

	Final Model Main Effects		Parental Inc * Age		Moving out*Race	
	OR	t	OR	t	OR	t
Family Welfare Vars						
Parental Inc (Q1)						
Quintile 2	1.25***	(3.82)	1.58*	(2.38)	1.24***	(3.76)
Quintile 3	1.37***	(5.27)	1.04	(0.22)	1.36***	(5.19)
Quintile 4	1.44***	(6.02)	0.82	(−0.95)	1.44***	(6.02)
Quintile 5	1.27***	(3.83)	0.58**	(−2.58)	1.27***	(3.83)
Missing	1.21***	(3.62)	0.73	(−1.84)	1.21***	(3.58)
Parental Inc*Age						
Quintile 2*Age			0.99 1.56	(−1.17)		
Quintile 3*Age			1.01 1.05	(1.28)		
Quintile 4*Age			1.02* 0.83	(2.57)		
Quintile 5*Age			1.04*** 0.60	(3.54)		
Missing*Age			1.02** 0.74	(2.75)		
Move out (>24)						
Before 19	1.18***	(3.35)	1.18***	(3.37)	1.11	(1.56)
Between 19–21	1.25***	(4.54)	1.25***	(4.54)	1.12	(1.73)
Between 21–24	1.35***	(6.43)	1.35***	(6.41)	1.27***	(3.43)
Move Back	0.86***	(−4.54)	0.86***	(−4.54)	0.86***	(−4.52)
Move out*Race						
Before 19*Black					1.27* 1.41	(2.12)
19–21*Black					1.42** 1.59	(3.16)
21–24*Black					1.20 1.52	(1.67)
Before 19*Hisp					0.94 1.04	(−0.51)
19–21*Hisp					1.03 1.15	(0.24)
21–24*Hisp					1.04 1.32	(0.35)

(continued)

Table 5.5: Longitudinal ordered logistic regression models of waged work intensity, NLSY 1997 (continued)

	Final Model Main Effects		Parental Inc * Age		Moving out*Race	
	OR	t	OR	t	OR	t
Before 19*Mixed					0.78	(−0.48)
					0.86	
19–21*Mixed					0.86	(−0.28)
					0.96	
21–24*Mixed					0.46	(−1.41)
					0.58	
Control Vars						
Age	1.24***	(72.02)	1.22***	(31.47)	1.24***	(72.04)
Female	0.92*	(−2.43)	0.92*	(−2.42)	0.92*	(−2.47)
Race (White)						
Black	0.56***	(−13.29)	0.57***	(−13.28)	0.47***	(−8.90)
Hispanic	0.96	(−0.91)	0.96	(−0.89)	0.94	(−0.72)
Mixed Race	0.57**	(−2.99)	0.57**	(−2.98)	0.77	(−0.63)
Educ (No quals)						
GED	1.48***	(5.51)	1.47***	(5.51)	1.47***	(5.48)
HS Diploma	2.43***	(14.46)	2.43***	(14.50)	2.42***	(14.40)
AA	3.05***	(13.66)	3.05***	(13.66)	3.04***	(13.59)
Bachelor's Deg	2.82***	(15.03)	2.82***	(15.08)	2.80***	(14.92)
Masters Deg	2.86***	(12.22)	2.86***	(12.22)	2.86***	(12.24)
PhD	2.00*	(1.99)	1.99*	(1.96)	2.02*	(2.06)
Prof Degree	1.10	(0.64)	1.09	(0.58)	1.10	(0.64)
Urban (Rural)	1.18***	(5.41)	1.17***	(5.23)	1.17***	(5.37)
Unknown	0.96	(−0.76)	0.95	(−1.01)	0.96	(−0.77)
Census Reg (NE)						
North Central	1.17**	(2.95)	1.18**	(3.10)	1.17**	(2.95)
South	0.93	(−1.47)	0.93	(−1.41)	0.93	(−1.46)
West	0.88*	(−2.51)	0.87*	(−2.55)	0.87*	(−2.52)
Health (Excellent)						
Very Good	1.11***	(5.22)	1.11***	(5.14)	1.11***	(5.20)
Good	1.07**	(2.66)	1.06**	(2.62)	1.06**	(2.63)
Fair	0.88***	(−3.31)	0.89**	(−3.27)	0.88***	(−3.35)
Poor	0.41***	(−7.85)	0.41***	(−7.80)	0.41***	(−7.87)
Household Size	0.89***	(−16.44)	0.90***	(−15.95)	0.89***	(−16.46)
Young parenting	1.00	(−0.04)	1.00	(−0.18)	1.00	(−0.10)
Benefit recipient	0.63***	(−14.73)	0.63***	(−14.35)	0.63***	(−14.77)
Observations	106,365		106,365		106,365	
Cases	7,209		7,209		7,209	

Notes: Displayed are odds ratios from an ordered logistic regression of work intensity with *t* statistics in parentheses. Odds ratios (OR) above 1 indicate increased odds of being in a higher work intensity category. Odds ratios in bold are those resulting from interaction term.
* $p < 0.05$; ** $p < 0.01$; *** $p < 0.001$.

Table 5.6: Correlated random effects models of logged annual employment income, NLSY 1997

	Full Model Main Effects		Parental income*Age		Moving out*Race	
	Coeff	t	Coeff	t	Coeff	t
Family Welfare Vars:						
Parental Inc (Q1)						
Quintile 2	0.07**	(2.83)	−0.13	(−1.49)	0.07**	(2.74)
Quintile 3	0.11***	(4.26)	−0.10	(−1.19)	0.11***	(4.18)
Quintile 4	0.10***	(3.79)	−0.55***	(−6.40)	0.10***	(3.83)
Quintile 5	0.14***	(4.83)	−1.09***	(−12.48)	0.14***	(4.78)
Missing	0.11***	(4.51)	−0.34***	(−4.12)	0.11***	(4.49)
Parental Inc*Age						
Quintile 2*Age			0.01*	(2.41)		
Quintile 3*Age			0.01**	(2.58)		
Quintile 4*Age			0.03***	(8.01)		
Quintile 5*Age			0.05***	(14.90)		
Missing*Age			0.02***	(5.72)		
Moved out (>24)						
Before 19	0.19***	(8.71)	0.19***	(8.69)	0.17***	(5.71)
Between 19–21	0.19***	(9.06)	0.19***	(9.06)	0.18***	(6.11)
Between 21–24	0.12***	(5.67)	0.12***	(5.63)	0.14***	(4.45)
Move back	−0.07***	(−4.51)	−0.07***	(−4.47)	−0.06***	(−4.35)

(continued)

Table 5.6: Correlated random effects models of logged annual employment income, NLSY 1997 (continued)

	Full Model Main Effects		Parental income*Age		Moving out*Race	
	Coeff	t	Coeff	t	Coeff	t
Move Out*Race						
Before 19*Black					0.14**	(2.91)
19–21*Black					0.11*	(2.37)
21–24*Black					0.04	(0.87)
Before 19*Hisp					-0.04	(-0.78)
19–21*Hisp					-0.07	(-1.35)
21–24*Hisp					-0.12*	(-2.33)
Before 19*Mixed					0.14	(0.65)
19–21*Mixed					0.15	(0.69)
21–24*Mixed					-0.12	(-0.54)
Control Vars:						
Age	0.16***	(149.54)	0.14***	(52.34)	0.16***	(149.54)
Female	-0.24***	(-15.64)	-0.24***	(-15.63)	-0.24***	(-15.56)
Black (White)	-0.10***	(-4.93)	-0.10***	(-4.90)	-0.17***	(-4.75)
Hispanic	0.05*	(2.27)	0.05*	(2.41)	0.10**	(2.63)
Mixed Race	-0.04	(-0.56)	-0.04	(-0.53)	-0.10	(-0.58)
Educ (No quals)						
GED	0.16***	(4.95)	0.16***	(4.97)	0.16***	(4.88)

(continued)

Table 5.6: Correlated random effects models of logged annual employment income, NLSY 1997 (continued)

	Full Model Main Effects		Parental income*Age		Moving out*Race	
	Coeff	t	Coeff	t	Coeff	t
HS Diploma	0.22***	(7.61)	0.21***	(7.58)	0.21***	(7.53)
AA	0.28***	(7.53)	0.28***	(7.56)	0.28***	(7.45)
Bachelor's Deg	0.12***	(3.81)	0.12***	(3.78)	0.12***	(3.66)
Masters Deg	0.12**	(2.75)	0.12***	(2.70)	0.11**	(2.67)
PhD	-0.20	(-1.25)	-0.19	(-1.23)	-0.19	(-1.22)
Prof Deg	0.18*	(2.52)	0.19**	(2.59)	0.18*	(2.51)
Urban (Rural)	0.07***	(5.63)	0.07***	(5.34)	0.07***	(5.63)
Unknown	0.18***	(7.32)	0.17***	(7.03)	0.18***	(7.32)
Geog (mean)	-0.001	(-0.05)	0.002	(0.08)	-0.002	(-0.10)
Census Reg (NE)						
North Central	-0.12***	(-5.26)	-0.12***	(-5.26)	-0.12***	(-5.28)
South	-0.02	(-0.67)	-0.02	(-0.85)	-0.02	(-0.68)
West	0.08*	(2.36)	0.07*	(2.03)	0.08*	(2.36)
Census (mean)	-0.04**	(-3.25)	-0.04**	(-2.95)	-0.04**	(-3.26)
Work Int (V.low)						
Low work int	0.07***	(3.98)	0.08***	(4.27)	0.07***	(3.97)
Medium wk int	0.22***	(9.41)	0.22***	(9.47)	0.22***	(9.40)
High wk int	0.43***	(25.73)	0.43***	(25.85)	0.43***	(25.69)

(continued)

Table 5.6: Correlated random effects models of logged annual employment income, NLSY 1997 (continued)

	Full Model Main Effects		Parental income*Age		Moving out*Race	
	Coeff	t	Coeff	t	Coeff	t
V. high wk int	0.74***	(49.15)	0.74***	(49.08)	0.74***	(49.14)
Work int (mean)	0.18***	(19.96)	0.18***	(20.19)	0.18***	(19.84)
Household size	-0.10***	(-35.16)	-0.10***	(-34.12)	-0.10***	(-35.18)
HH size (mean)	0.09***	(11.19)	0.09***	(10.90)	0.09***	(11.06)
Married	0.20***	(16.18)	0.18***	(14.81)	0.20***	(16.19)
Mar Stat (mean)	0.09**	(2.89)	0.11***	(3.42)	0.09**	(2.95)
Young parenting	0.13***	(6.54)	0.13***	(6.44)	0.13***	(6.64)
Benefit recipient	-0.009	(-0.64)	-0.002	(-0.17)	-0.009	(-0.64)
Ben Recd (mean)	-0.73***	(-16.27)	-0.74***	(-16.42)	-0.74***	(-16.38)
Constant	4.42***	(69.00)	4.88***	(56.19)	4.44***	(67.61)
Between Var	0.48***	(77.87)	0.48***	(78.07)	0.48***	(77.73)
Within Var	0.85***	(321.35)	0.85***	(321.35)	0.85***	(321.34)
Observations	59,296		59,296		59,296	
Cases	7,037		7,037		7,037	

Notes: Displayed are coefficients from a correlated random effects model for logged monthly wages with t statistics in parentheses.

* $p < 0.05$; ** $p < 0.01$; *** $p < 0.001$.

Table 5.7: Longitudinal ordered logit models of poverty ratio, NLSY 1997

	Final Model Main Effects		PAid*Age		Moving out*Paid		Moving out*Race		Moving out*Move back	
	OR	t	OR	t	OR	t	OR	t	OR	t
Family Welfare Vars:										
Parent Aid	1.56***	(10.92)	4.71***	(7.58)	1.89***	(7.63)	1.56***	(10.94)	1.56***	(10.84)
Missing	1.26***	(3.53)	3.06***	(3.33)	1.43**	(2.92)	1.26***	(3.61)	1.25***	(3.48)
Parent Aid*Age										
P.Aid*Age			0.96***	(−5.62)						
			4.52							
P.Aid Missing*Age			0.96**	(−2.76)						
			2.94							
Move out (>24)										
Before 19	1.40***	(6.02)	1.41***	(6.09)	1.61***	(5.74)	1.86***	(7.47)	1.63***	(6.43)
19–21	1.49***	(7.09)	1.49***	(7.15)	1.91***	(7.79)	1.96***	(8.09)	1.67***	(6.83)
21–24	1.16**	(2.75)	1.17**	(2.81)	1.17	(1.86)	1.34***	(3.35)	1.24**	(3.01)
Move back	0.87***	(−3.52)	0.87***	(−3.58)	0.87***	(−3.73)	0.87***	(−3.53)	1.11	(1.23)
Move out*P.Aid										
Before 19* P.Aid					0.83	(−1.72)				
					1.34					
19–21*P.Aid					0.61***	(−4.41)				
					1.16					

(continued)

Table 5.7: Longitudinal ordered logit models of poverty ratio, NLSY 1997 (continued)

	Final Model Main Effects		PAid*Age		Moving out*Paid		Moving out*Race		Moving out*Move back	
	OR	t	OR	t	OR	t	OR	t	OR	t
21–24*P.Aid					0.97	(−0.28)				
					1.13					
Before 19*P.Aid Missing					0.66*	(−2.32)				
					1.06					
19–21*P.Aid Missing					0.84	(−0.99)				
					1.60					
21–24*P.Aid Missing					1.09	(0.48)				
					1.27					
Move out*Race										
Before 19*Black							0.52***	(−5.03)		
							0.97			
19–21*Black							0.61***	(−3.81)		
							1.19			
21–24*Black							0.79	(−1.85)		
							1.06			
Before 19*Hispanic							0.69**	(−2.92)		
							1.28			

(continued)

119

Table 5.7: Longitudinal ordered logit models of poverty ratio, NLSY 1997 (continued)

	Final Model Main Effects		PAid*Age		Moving out*Paid		Moving out*Race		Moving out*Move back	
	OR	t	OR	t	OR	t	OR	t	OR	t
19–21*Hispanic							0.60*** **1.18**	(–3.87)		
21–24*Hispanic							0.82 **1.10**	(–1.44)		
Before 19*Mixed							0.82 **1.52**	(–0.36)		
19–21*Mixed							0.52 **1.02**	(–1.13)		
21–24*Mixed							1.05 **1.41**	(0.08)		
Move out*Move Back										
Before 19*Moved back									0.70** **1.14**	(–3.20)
19–21*Moved back									0.73** **1.22**	(–2.84)
21–24*Moved back									0.79* **0.98**	(–2.10)

(continued)

Table 5.7: Longitudinal ordered logit models of poverty ratio, NLSY 1997 (continued)

	Final Model Main Effects		PAid*Age		Moving out*Paid		Moving out*Race		Moving out*Move back	
	OR	t	OR	t	OR	t	OR	t	OR	t
Control Vars:										
Age	1.08***	(16.15)	1.11***	(15.16)	1.08***	(16.13)	1.08***	(16.09)	1.08***	(16.17)
Female	0.84***	(−4.37)	0.84***	(−4.42)	0.85***	(−4.29)	0.84***	(−4.48)	0.84***	(−4.40)
Race (White)										
Black	1.76***	(11.50)	1.75***	(11.48)	1.75***	(11.41)	2.51***	(9.23)	1.76***	(11.56)
Hispanic	1.18**	(3.27)	1.18***	(3.32)	1.18**	(3.25)	1.56***	(4.82)	1.18***	(3.38)
Mixed Race	1.06	(0.33)	1.06	(0.32)	1.05	(0.28)	1.32	(0.59)	1.07	(0.37)
Educ (No quals)										
GED	0.67***	(−5.11)	0.67***	(−5.07)	0.68***	(−5.04)	0.68***	(−5.03)	0.67***	(−5.11)
HS Diploma	0.43***	(−12.18)	0.44***	(−12.09)	0.44***	(−12.05)	0.44***	(−12.05)	0.43***	(−12.17)
AA	0.35***	(−11.42)	0.35***	(−11.38)	0.35***	(−11.34)	0.35***	(−11.30)	0.35***	(−11.41)
Bachelor's Deg	0.35***	(−12.98)	0.35***	(−12.83)	0.35***	(−12.98)	0.35***	(−12.89)	0.35***	(−12.96)
Masters Deg	0.30***	(−10.53)	0.30***	(−10.44)	0.30***	(−10.51)	0.30***	(−10.56)	0.30***	(−10.53)
PhD	0.32*	(−2.24)	0.33*	(−2.23)	0.31*	(−2.27)	0.31*	(−2.27)	0.32*	(−2.26)
Prof Degree	0.37***	(−4.52)	0.38***	(−4.45)	0.37***	(−4.53)	0.37***	(−4.58)	0.37***	(−4.53)
Urban (Rural)	1.22***	(4.75)	1.21***	(4.57)	1.22***	(4.77)	1.23***	(4.81)	1.22***	(4.73)
Unknown	1.25**	(2.68)	1.24**	(2.61)	1.24**	(2.67)	1.25**	(2.70)	1.24**	(2.65)

(continued)

Table 5.7: Longitudinal ordered logit models of poverty ratio, NLSY 1997 (continued)

	Final Model Main Effects		PAid*Age		Moving out*Paid		Moving out*Race		Moving out*Move back	
	OR	t	OR	t	OR	t	OR	t	OR	t
Census Reg (NE)										
North Central	1.16*	(2.38)	1.16*	(2.41)	1.16*	(2.39)	1.16*	(2.32)	1.16*	(2.36)
South	1.25***	(3.96)	1.25***	(3.95)	1.25***	(3.92)	1.25***	(3.92)	1.25***	(3.95)
West	1.38***	(5.05)	1.38***	(5.05)	1.37***	(4.95)	1.36***	(4.88)	1.38***	(5.01)
Health (Excellent)										
Very Good	0.97	(−0.80)	0.97	(−0.88)	0.97	(−0.78)	0.97	(−0.79)	0.97	(−0.78)
Good	1.05	(1.31)	1.05	(1.28)	1.05	(1.33)	1.05	(1.35)	1.05	(1.34)
Fair	1.20***	(3.42)	1.21***	(3.48)	1.20***	(3.43)	1.20***	(3.43)	1.20***	(3.45)
Poor	1.17	(1.17)	1.19	(1.29)	1.17	(1.21)	1.18	(1.21)	1.17	(1.18)
Annual wages (ln)	0.44***	(−50.43)	0.44***	(−50.27)	0.44***	(−50.42)	0.44***	(−50.41)	0.44***	(−50.42)
Married	0.53***	(−15.03)	0.53***	(−15.23)	0.53***	(−15.05)	0.53***	(−14.99)	0.53***	(−15.07)
Young parenting	1.74***	(12.55)	1.74***	(12.55)	1.74***	(12.67)	1.73***	(12.52)	1.72***	(12.40)
Benefit recipient	2.43***	(23.90)	2.44***	(23.85)	2.44***	(23.96)	2.44***	(23.97)	2.43***	(23.90)
Observations	49,981		49,981		49,981		49,981		49,981	
Cases	6,947		6,947		6,947		6,947		6,947	

Notes: Displayed are odds ratios from an ordered logistic regression of work intensity with t statistics in parentheses. ORs above 1 indicate higher odds of being in a high poverty category. Odds ratios in bold are those resulting from interaction term.

$* p < 0.05; ** p < 0.01; *** p < 0.001.$

Family welfare

This investigation considers the family welfare source through measures of parental background in both cases – given by parental income quintile or a history of parental aid receipt – as well as measures of residential independence in the NLSY cohort.

Implicit family resources

In general, the measures of parental background impact individual employment income similarly for the BCS cohort and the NLSY cohort. Those from parental income quintiles 3 to 5 have higher average monthly wages in the UK sample (see Table 5.2) and higher average annual employment income in the US sample (see Table 5.6). The larger effect sizes for the UK cohort may be evidence that the slightly longer time horizon of this sample can show further divergence in wage outcomes with age, and suggests that parental background is not a static feature of one's life course.

To investigate whether parental background is a dynamic feature, an interaction term was modelled using parental background and age. In the UK sample, the significant and increasing interaction terms at ages 30 and older for those from quintiles 4 and 5 suggest that the difference in wages between those from the least affluent and the two most affluent parental income quintiles increases with age (see Table 5.2). Results for the US sample are similar: an interaction of parental income quintile and the continuous age variable shows that those from quintiles 2 through 5 experience larger wage growth with each half-year than those from quintile 1 (for example, interaction term Q5 = 0.05) (see Table 5.6). Together, the results show that as respondents get older, wage inequalities widen.

The work intensity models show that as a main effect, there is not a significant difference in work intensity outcomes for UK cohort members from different parental income quintiles; however, this does not hold when age dynamics are considered. The bold odds ratios in Table 5.4 suggest that as cohort members age, there is a significant difference in work intensity, with those from more affluent families having higher odds of being in a higher work intensity group.

The main effects in the US sample show significantly higher work intensity odds for all income quintiles compared to those in quintile 1 (see Table 5.5). However the parental income and age interaction shows that those from income quintiles 4 and 5 have *lower* odds of being in a high work intensity category as they age. Together with their wages results, this suggests that US cohort members from higher-income backgrounds may not have to work as much as those from lower-income backgrounds, but will receive higher labour market returns.

Explicit family resources: residential independence

More detailed NLSY data enable an investigation of residential transitions that operationalise concepts of explicit family resources (see Tables 5.5–5.7). The covariate measuring age at initial move out of the parental home was specified using four categories: an initial move out before 19 (25 per cent of the cohort); between 19 and 21 (25 per cent); between 21 and 24 (23 per cent); and 'late' movers who did not move out before age 24 (27 per cent).

The main effects models for the individual labour market outcomes (see Tables 5.5 and 5.6) indicate that those who move out earlier have higher annual employment income than late movers and have higher odds of being in a higher work intensity group (for example, for 21–24 year old movers, OR = 1.35). The largest difference in wages is between those who move out before 19 and late movers (20 per cent higher employment income for early movers), and the largest difference in work intensity odds is found between those who move out when aged 21–24 and late movers (OR = 1.35). Together, the results on these individual outcomes show an association between early home leaving and 'success' in traditional youth transition outcomes.

However, these individual results must be viewed in tandem with main effects model results for the household poverty outcome that considers welfare dependency risk. Here, those who move out earlier have between 1.2 and 1.5 times the odds of being in a higher poverty ratio group than those who do not initially leave the parental home before 24. The lower household poverty risk for late movers suggests that those who can utilise this scaffolding resource may be more adequately shielded from the challenges of being on one's own in the youth period.

The moving back measure provides a more explicit operationalisation of a safety net function. These results are unsurprisingly the inverse of the moving out results for individual outcomes, with those that move back at least once (54.5 per cent of the cohort) having lower wage trajectories and lower odds of being in a higher work intensity group (OR = 0.86) (see Tables 5.5 and 5.6). The household poverty ratio model shows more positive outcomes for those who move back, with lower odds of being in a higher poverty ratio category for those who can move back in (OR = 0.87), which further adds to evidence of this 'safety net' feature (see Table 5.7).

The impacts of moving out also differ between demographic groups. For Black cohort members on both individual outcomes, the impact of moving out earlier (before age 21) has a larger positive impact on wages (positive interaction coefficients in Table 5.6) and the odds of being in a higher work intensity group (interaction coefficients: before 19, OR = 1.27; 19–21, OR = 1.42) (see Table 5.5). The poverty ratio model (see Table 5.7) found that Black cohort members' odds of being in a high poverty group are not as negatively impacted if they move out earlier compared to White respondents (Black interaction ORs: before 19 = 0.52; 19–21 = 0.61), which is similar for Hispanic early movers (interaction ORs: before 19 = 0.69; 19–21 = 0.61). Viewed through the lens of family resource 'safety nets', these results suggest that there is a less prominent positive impact of staying in the family home through the youth period for Black and Hispanic cohort members.

Another significant interaction in the poverty ratio model investigated how moving back moderates the impact of an early or late move. Odds ratios less than 1 on the moving out and moving back interaction terms indicate that moving back into the family home moderates the negative impact of making an early move on household poverty outcomes (see Table 5.7). This suggests that the ability to move back into the family home also serves a safety net function, with negative impacts of early moves particularly high for cohort members who do not return to the family home at any point (for example, moving out main effect ORs in this interaction model: before 19 = 1.63; 19–21 = 1.67).

Finally, the poverty ratio model resulted in significantly different impacts of moving out earlier between young people from families with and without a history of benefit receipt.[7] The interaction odds ratios below 1 indicate that the impact of moving out early for families with a benefit receipt history is not as negative and therefore the gap between early and late movers is not as large (see the bold ORs in this interaction model in Table 5.7). This is not the case for young people from families without a benefit history as the significant main effect odds ratios show much higher odds of being in a high poverty ratio category for those who move out earlier. Together, these results suggest that the more positive impacts of being able to stay in the family home longer are concentrated within more advantaged families.

Summary

Key findings for both types of family welfare resources first affirm and add to what is known about the dynamic and persistent impact of family background on economic outcomes. The models then explored the impact of the in-kind resource of the family home using residential independence measures. The results from the US case suggest not only that moving out 'early' or 'late' in the youth period impacts individual and household economic outcomes differently, but that the impacts differ by race for all outcomes. The impact of one's moving out age on household poverty ratio also differ based on the family of origin's benefit receipt and if cohort members move back at least once.

Conclusion

The exploratory nature of this research has implications for future research in Social Policy and Youth Studies, and has discrete implications for both youth policy and social security policy more broadly.

Research implications

The application of the more holistic welfare mix framework allowed this study to interrogate a less empirically researched aspect of welfare: the family of origin. This explicit focus contrasts the generally implicit discussions of the family in liberal welfare policies, where the family is viewed as an assumed resource that operates relatively similarly for all young people. On the one hand, the results of this work confirm this assumption as the family of origin served a scaffolding role within and beyond the youth period, and is a safety net resource accessed by many of the respondents. Indeed, the reduced risk of long-term poverty for young people whose families are able to provide support through longer co-residence, or can offer the opportunity of a move back when needed, is explicit evidence of these resources.

On the other hand, this investigation found that family resources are not available in the same way for all young people, and that in-kind resources do not have the same positive impacts for all young people. This study found that the long-term benefits of staying in the family home are primarily concentrated for those who are already advantaged as Black and Hispanic respondents and respondents from less advantaged backgrounds do not receive the same extent of benefits from these resources. This suggests that in-kind resources are another less measured way in which families of all types support their children during precarious or chaotic transition periods, though have varying impacts. These initial results suggest that more research is needed on the nature of in-kind family resources, how families from different racial and socio-economic backgrounds negotiate the home-leaving (and home-returning) process, and why young people from different families do not seem to receive the same benefits from longer periods of co-residence. These are questions that can be addressed with both qualitative and quantitative studies in many fields.

These results also expose the contradiction of welfare state theories and policy in practice for young people, particularly in characterising liberal welfare states as contexts with little relevance of the family as a provider of welfare. Rather, the results suggest that 'independence' in one area – independence from the state – pushes young people into more dependence on their family of origin. In both countries, the trends in co-residence and 'boomerang' experiences indicate that the dependence on the family of origin will continue to be a prevalent experience in welfare states with fewer and fewer programmes of support for young people, and suggest that it might be useful to reconsider Walther's (2006) youth welfare regimes given these trends.

Finally, the limitations of this exploratory investigation regarding in-kind family welfare could be addressed by further research that considers residential transitions as drivers of outcomes. Better long-run cohort data in the UK that capture residential transitions, as well as investigations that capture multiple moves out and back, may further illuminate if the family home should be viewed unequivocally as a positive resource for young people.

Policy implications

The prevalence of family resources as a driver of economic independence outcomes and, in turn, inequality based on these resources has implications for policymakers that aim to improve outcomes for young people. The use of an organising framework of the welfare mix suggests that while it is not useful to prescribe an ideal 'mix' of resources for young people, there are ways to work within the current confines of liberal welfare state policies to assist young people who might not be able to rely on family resources to the same extent as their more advantaged peers.

The reliance on the family of origin not only has consequences for young people who wish to become independent, but also likely puts further strain on low-income families who feel obligated to provide resources to their children within and beyond the youth period. Policymakers must therefore decide who they want to support as the primary benefit unit: families who step into the role of the state in a residual system; or young people themselves. Given that the norms of youth transitions in both countries are founded on early independence, it is unlikely that states will transform to a system more common in Southern European welfare regimes, with late home leaving seen as the accepted norm. Rather, policy changes should enable young people to improve their circumstances as individual actors.

Although any policy recommendations resulting from exploratory research must be provided with wide caveats, it is still valuable to consider some changes that can improve the individual labour market experiences of young people as independent actors. In the UK, economic independence could be improved by removing different wage rates between those under and over 25 years of age, as well as by increasing apprentice wages to the minimum wage, even in their first year. Specific changes to the social security system will necessarily differ for young people with and without children, and are too numerous to detail here (for a full set of recommendations, see Weakley, 2019). However, for example, both countries can readily improve access to Working Tax Credits (in the UK) and the Earned Income Tax Credit (in the US) for low-income young workers without children. Not only does this 'make work pay' for young workers, but it has also been found to improve labour market attachment for some.

Access to affordable housing and housing assistance is perhaps the most pressing policy area for young people, and is also the area where unequal family resources are likely most explicitly expressed, as this analysis has shown. However, as a youth policy area, housing is either summarily ignored in US policy discussions, or is an area of state welfare that is continuing to be retrenched in the UK. Improving the ability for young people to access social housing, affordable housing and assistance within the ever-growing private rented sector in the UK should therefore be at the top of youth policy priorities given what this investigation uncovered about the role of unequal family resources in this sector.

Notes

[1] As the British Cohort Study (BCS) sample used in this research does not include a sufficient sample of non-white cohort members, this covariate is not included in the UK case.

2   The reason for the dearth of 1970 BCS data during the late 1980s and 1990s is related to funding, as reviewed in great detail in Helen Pearson's (2015) book *The life project*.

3   For more detail, see Weakley (2019).

4   Random effects longitudinal ordered logistic regression models are used for all of the ordinal outcomes except for BCS household income quintile, which is estimated using an ordered logistic regression model because the outcome is measured at age 42. Odds ratios (ORs) above 1 in the work intensity models indicate increased odds of being in a higher work intensity category; ORs above 1 in the BCS gross household model indicate higher odds of being in a higher income quintile; and ORs above 1 in the NLSY poverty ratio model indicate higher odds of being in a high poverty category. ORs close to 1 indicate a small difference in the outcome odds for the groups being compared.

5   In the UK case, the benefit receipt indicator is comprised of the following benefit programmes for each year: 1991 – Unemployment Benefit (UB), Supplementary Benefit/Income Support, Unemployment & Supplementary Benefit, Family Credit, Child Benefit (CB), Lone Parent Benefit, Housing Benefit (HB); 2000 – Jobseeker's Allowance (JSA), Income Support (IS), Working Families Tax Credit, CB, Council Tax Benefit, HB, Incapacity Benefit (IB); 2004 – JSA, IS, Council Tax Benefit, HB, IB, CB, Child Tax Credit, Working Tax Credit; 2012 – JSA, IS, Council Tax Benefit, HB, IB, CB, Child Tax Credit, Working Tax Credit. In the US case, the benefit receipt indicator is comprised of the same programmes for each of the survey years: Temporary Assistance for Needy Families, SNAP, SNAP–Women, Infants and Children, Supplemental Security Income, Veteran's Affairs benefits, childcare or housing assistance.

6   The percentage change in the wage models was calculated by exponentiating the coefficient, subtracting 1 and multiplying by 100.

7   The parental income quintile variable created and used in the NLSY individual models used family income in 1997 as the parental background measure, which is also used to create the poverty ratio outcome. Therefore, the history of government aid receipt was used as the measure of socio-economic status, denoted in the tables as 'Parental Aid' (P.Aid).

References

Aassve, A., Iacovou, M. and Mencarini, L. (2006) 'Youth poverty and transition to adulthood in Europe', *Demographic Research*, 15: 21–50.

Allison, P. (2009) *Fixed effects regression models*, Thousand Oaks, CA: SAGE Publications.

Amato, P.R., Landale, N.S., Havasevich-Brooks, T.C., Booth, A., Eggebeen, D.J., Schoen, R. and McHale, S.M. (2008) 'Precursors of young women's family formation pathways', *Journal of Marriage and Family*, 70: 1271–86.

Andrew, M., Eggerling-Boeck, J., Sandefur, G. and Smith, B. (2012) 'The "inner side" of the transition to adulthood: how young adults see the process of becoming an adult', in R. Macmillan (ed) *Constructing adulthood: Agency and subjectivity in adolescence and adulthood*, Stamford, CT : JAI Press Ltd, pp 225–52.

Antonucci, L., Hamilton, M. and Roberts, S. (eds) (2014) *Young people and social policy in Europe*, London: Palgrave Macmillan.

Arnett, J.J. (2000) 'Emerging adulthood: a theory of development from the late teens through the twenties', *American Psychologist*, 55: 469–80.

Arundel, R. and Ronald, R. (2016) 'Parental co-residence, shared living and emerging adulthood in Europe: semi-dependent housing across welfare regime and housing system contexts', *Journal of Youth Studies*, 19: 885–905.

Auer, P. and Cazes, S. (2003) *Employment stability in an age of flexibility. Evidence from industrialized countries*, Geneva: International Labour Organisation.

Bane, M.J. and Ellwood, D.T. (1994) *Welfare realities: From rhetoric to reform*, Cambridge, MA: Harvard University Press.

Barrington, A.L. and Stone, J.M. (2014) 'Young adults' transition to residential independence in the UK: the role of social and housing policy', in L. Antonucci, M. Hamilton and S. Roberts (eds) *Young people and social policy in Europe*, London: Palgrave Macmillan, pp 210–35.

Bell, D. and Blanchflower, D. (2011) *Youth unemployment in Europe and the United States*, Bonn: Institute of the Study of Labor.

Blau, F.D. and Kahn, L.M. (2017) 'The gender wage gap: extent, trends, and explanations', *Journal of Economic Literature*, 55: 789–865.

Bradley, S. (1995) 'The Youth Training Scheme: a critical evaluation of the literature', *International Journal of Manpower*, 16: 30–56.

Buchmann, M. (1989) *The script of life in modern society*, Chicago, IL: University of Chicago Press.

Coles, B. (1995) *Youth and social policy: Youth citizenship and young careers*, London: UCL Press.

Dey, J. and Pierret, C. (2014) 'Independence for young millennials: moving out and boomeranging back', *U.S. Bureau of Labor Statistics Monthly Labor Review*.

DiPrete, T.A. and Eirich, G.M. (2006) 'Cumulative advantage as a mechanism for inequality: a review of theoretical and empirical developments', *Annual Review of Sociology*, 32: 271–97.

Dolton, P., Galinda-Rueda, F. and Makepeace, G. (2004) 'The long term effects of government sponsored training', University of Newcastle and Centre for Economic Performance (LSE), Centre for Economic Performance (LSE), Cardiff University.

DuBois-Reymond, M. (1998) '"I don't want to commit myself yet": young people's life concepts', *Journal of Youth Studies*, 1: 63–79.

Edin, K.J. and Shaefer, H.L. (2016) *$2.00 a day: Living on almost nothing in America*, New York: Mariner Books.

Ermisch, J. (1999) 'Prices, parents, and young people's household formation', *Journal of Urban Economics*, 45: 47–71.

Esping-Andersen, G. (1990) *The three worlds of welfare capitalism*, Princeton, NJ: Princeton University Press.

Estevez-Abe, M., Iversen, T. and Soskice, D. (2001) 'Social protection and the formation of skills: a reinterpretation of the welfare state', in P. Hall and D. Soskice (eds) *Varieties of capitalism: The institutional foundations of comparative advantage*, Oxford: Oxford University Press, pp 145–84.

Fingerman, K.L., Kim, K., Davis, E.M., Furstenberg, F.F., Birditt, K.S. and Zarit, S.H. (2015) '"I'll give you the world": socioeconomic differences in parental support of adult children', *Journal of Marriage and Family*, 77: 844–65.

Fox, L., Wimer, C., Garfinkel, I., Kaushal, N. and Waldfogel, J. (2015) 'Waging war on poverty: poverty trends using a historical supplemental poverty measure', *Journal of Policy Analysis and Management*, 34: 567–92.

Friedman, S. and Laurison, D. (2019) *The class ceiling: Why it pays to be privileged*, Bristol: Policy Press.

Furstenberg, F. (2010) 'On a new schedule: transitions to adulthood and family change', *Future Child. Transitions to Adulthood*, 20: 67–88.

Gregg, P. and Tominey, E. (2005) 'The wage scar from male youth unemployment', *Labour Economics*, 12: 487–509.

Gundersen, C. and Ziliak, J.P. (2003) 'The role of food stamps in consumption stabilization', *Journal of Human Resources*, 38: 1051–79.

Harris, N.S. (1989) *Social security for young people*, Aldershot and Brookfield, VT: Avebury.

Hills, J. (2014) *Good times, bad times: the welfare myth of them and us*, Bristol: Policy Press.

Howieson, C. and Iannelli, C. (2008) 'The effects of low attainment on young people's outcomes at age 22–23 in Scotland', *British Education Research Journal*, 34: 269–90.

Iversen, T. and Stephens, J.D. (2008) 'Partisan politics, the welfare state, and three worlds of human capital formation', *Comparative Political Studies*, 41: 600–37.

Jones, G. and Wallace, C. (1992) *Youth, family and citizenship*, Buckingham: Open University Press.

King, H. (2016) 'A comparison of youth policy in England and Wales under New Labour', *Social Policy and Society*, 15: 337–50.

Lee, J.C. and Mortimer, J.T. (2009) 'Family socialization, economic self-efficacy, and the attainment of financial independence in early adulthood', *Longitudinal and Life Course Studies*, 1: 45–62.

MacDonald, R. and Giazitzoglu, A. (2019) 'Youth, enterprise and precarity: or, what is, and what is wrong with, the "gig economy"?', *Journal of Sociology*, 55: 724–40.

Manning, A. (2009) 'You can't always get what you want: the impact of the UK Jobseeker's Allowance', *Labour Economics*, 16: 239–50.

Menard, S. (2004) 'Longitudinal research', in M.S. Lewis-Beck, A. Bryman and T.F. Liao (eds) *The SAGE encyclopedia of social science research methods*, Thousand Oaks, CA: SAGE Publications.

Pearson, H. (2015) *The life project: the extraordinary story of our ordinary lives*. Berkeley, CA: Soft Skull Press.

Petrongolo, B. (2007) 'What are the long-term effects of UI? Evidence from the UK JSA reform', Discussion Paper No. 841, Centre for Economic Performance, LSE.

Petrongolo, B. (2009) 'The long-term effects of job search requirements: evidence from the UK JSA reform', *Journal of Public Economics*, 93: 1234–53.

Pierson, P. (1994) *Dismantling the welfare state? Reagan, Thatcher, and the politics of retrenchment*, Cambridge and New York, NY: Cambridge University Press.

Powell, M. and Barrientos, A. (2004) 'Welfare regimes and the welfare mix', *European Journal of Political Research*, 43: 83–105.

Roberts, J., Noden, P., West, A. and Lewis, J. (2016) 'Living with the parents: the purpose of young graduates' return to the parental home in England', *Journal of Youth Studies*, 19: 319–37.

Roberts, S. (2011) 'Beyond "NEET" and "tidy" pathways: considering the "missing middle" of youth transition studies', *Journal of Youth Studies*, 14: 21–39.

Schoeni, R. and Ross, K. (2005) 'Material assistance from families during the transition to adulthood', in R.A. Settersten Jr, F. Furstenberg and R.G. Rumbaut (eds) *On the frontier of adulthood: Theory, research, and public policy*, Chicago, IL: University of Chicago Press, pp 396–415.

Settersten, R.A., Jr, Furstenberg, F.F. and Rumbaut, R.G. (2005) *On the frontier of adulthood: Theory, research, and public policy*, Chicago, IL: University of Chicago Press.

Shildrick, T. (2008) 'Hiding out in the open: young people and social class in UK youth studies', *Youth and Policy*, 100: 209–17.

Skocpol, T. and Somers, M. (1980) 'The uses of comparative history in macrosocial inquiry', *Comparative Studies in Society and History*, 22: 174–97.

Smeeding, T.M. and Phillips, K.R. (2002) 'Cross-national differences in employment and economic sufficiency', *Annals of the American Academy of Political and Social Science*, 580: 103–33.

Swartz, T.T., Kim, M., Uno, M., Mortimer, J. and O'Brien, K.B. (2011) 'Safety nets and scaffolds: parental support in the transition to adulthood', *Journal of Marriage and Family*, 73: 414–29.

Walther, A. (2006) 'Regimes of youth transitions: choice, flexibility and security in young people's experiences across different European contexts', *Young*, 14: 119–39.

Weakley, S. (2019) 'Young people's transitions to economic independence and the role of government assistance: evidence from the US and the UK', PhD thesis, University of Edinburgh, UK.

Wilson, W.J. (1996) *When work disappears: The world of the new urban poor*, New York, NY: Knopf.

Wooldridge, J.M. (2012) *Introductory econometrics: A modern approach*, Mason, OH: South-Western Cengage Learning.

Wright, S. (2012) 'Welfare-to-work, agency and personal responsibility', *Journal of Social Policy*, 41, 309–28.

Ziliak, J. (2016) 'Temporary Assistance for Needy Families', in R. Moffitt (ed) *Economics of means-tested transfer programs in the United States* (vol I), Chicago, IL: Chicago Scholarship.

6

Economic hardship in young adulthood: a cause for concern or a matter of course while settling into the Swedish labour market?

Anna Kahlmeter

Introduction

Young adulthood is a formative phase when youths are expected to become independent by way of a gradual movement through education, family formation and establishment in the labour market. While there is a long history of interest in young people's lives, concerns for youth poverty and unemployment have been placed further up on the agenda during the past decades, perhaps due to a change in demographic trends, with an extended period between adolescence and adult roles (Arnett, 2000), and a widening gap between the young and the old in terms of living standards (Vogel and Råbäck, 2003). This study investigates the experience of economic hardship during the onset of an independent adult life, and its links to future labour market establishment trajectories.

Sweden has traditionally been characterised by relatively high levels of income equality, an encompassing welfare model (Korpi and Palme, 1998) and subsidised education at all levels (Arnesen and Lundahl, 2006). It has been categorised as a universalistic youth-to-adulthood transition regime, with a comprehensive school system and a high rate of youths having access to higher education (Walther, 2006). The educational system is oriented towards producing general, rather than vocational, skills, which has been believed to hamper the smoothness of youths' school-to-work transitions (Schröder, 2000). Moreover, looking at the youth (16–29) poverty rate, it is higher than the Organisation for Economic Co-operation and Development (OECD) average. This can partly be attributed to the fact that youths in Sweden leave the parental home earlier than in most other countries – approximately

21 years, compared to an European Union (EU) average of about 26 years (Eurostat, 2018) – making them more exposed to poverty risks (OECD, 2016).

Research on economic hardship in young adulthood has predominantly concerned poverty in terms of a relative lack of resources (for example, Ayllón, 2015) or similar indicators of low income; however, this has been found to say rather little about youths' actual living standard and future earning ability (Halleröd and Westberg, 2006). Few studies explicitly consider early adulthood economic hardship, as indicated by social assistance receipt and its links to long-term labour market trajectories. Moreover, focusing on labour market establishment as a single transition or event, rather than on sequences, does not utilise longitudinal data optimally and is likely to disguise that people move in and out of different positions. If establishment in the labour market is a discontinuous process, snapshots of single statuses in time do not provide an accurate representation, particularly in the context of the growing complexity of youth-to-adulthood transitions. These issues motivate further investigation.

The aim of this study is chiefly to contribute to an understanding of the association between the early adulthood experience of economic hardship, as indicated by different degrees of social assistance receipt, and long-term labour market establishment patterns. As part of this, the study also aims to identify typical trajectories of labour market establishment for young adults, from the time of their residential emancipation to their mid-30s. The study asks if economic hardship in early adulthood is associated with long-term disadvantage in the labour market. Utilising longitudinal Swedish register data, and using a combination of sequence analysis (Abbott and Forrest, 1986) and multinomial regression, more than 47,000 individuals are followed for 15 years, from the time of their residential emancipation at age 19–22 to their mid-30s. By studying sequences of labour market status over an extended period of time, the study puts emphasis on establishment in the labour market as a process. This is a feature largely overlooked by previous research.

Theoretical considerations and previous research

By its very nature, the experience of economic hardship is social and connects to social status through the relationship between resources, consumption and the social groups to which youths aspire to belong. Contemporary poverty theories predict that individuals with financial resources below those commanded by the average individual in society experience difficulties in participating on a par with others, which contributes to exclusion from ordinary living patterns, customs and activities (for example, Townsend, 1979). Drawing on findings from research on child poverty (for example, Masarik and Conger, 2017), scholars have put forward an argument for why experiences of economic hardship could be associated with poor outcomes. Economic hardship-induced psychological distress leads to disruptions in relationships and a feeling of uncertainty, undermining self-confidence and having a direct effect on achievement. Furthermore, lacking extra-familial sources of identity and social interaction, which education or a workplace provides, self-esteem may suffer. If the transition from financial and emotional dependence on parents to independence is the hallmark of a successful entry into adulthood, experiences of having to rely on welfare in this transition may induce feelings of inferiority and hamper success, particularly if the hardship is extensive (Elliott, 1996). Economic hardship and a problematic labour market entry may thus not just be a transitory experience, but weaken employment prospects in the long run, also termed 'scarring' (Arulampalam, 2001; Schmillen and Umkehrer, 2017).

On the other hand, young adulthood is, in essence, characterised by discontinuity and change, and economic disadvantage during this life phase may be seen as a typical nuisance and experience that many young people simply have to go through. Goffman (1963: 131) stated that, 'presumably the more allied the individual is with normals, the more he will see himself in non-stigmatic terms'. From this, it follows that what is 'normal' is contingent on context. In the context of de-standardised transitions to adulthood, where around one third of the 16–29 year olds living independently from their parents are categorised as poor (OECD, 2016), economic hardship, particularly if brief, may be perceived as a normal experience. The strain in terms of stigmatisation and harmed self-image may therefore be slight and its significance for future outcomes modest.

There is an ample body of research demonstrating a link between economic disadvantage in childhood and poor outcomes in early adulthood (Duncan et al, 1998; Berzin and De Marco, 2009), alongside a few studies finding negative social consequences of poverty spells in the overall population (for example, Mood and Jonsson, 2016). In Chapter 5 of this volume, Weakley demonstrates that welfare resources in the parental home are of significance for young people's future earnings, and that the impact of family background is amplified over time, with those from affluent families having a steeper income growth as they age. However, the literature on economic hardship in early adulthood and its links to future life chances is relatively scarce.

Concerning economic hardship as indicated by receipt of means-tested social assistance, previous studies have found this to be associated with both social background and critical life events (Lorentzen et al, 2012; Kauppinen et al, 2014). Scholars have found evidence for the generational transmission of social assistance receipt (for example, Moisio et al, 2015), though other background factors, such as parental crime, have also been found to moderate the relationship (Stenberg, 2000). Ilmakunnas (2018) found that although life-course events, such as having children, were associated with the duration of social assistance receipt, the impact of these events was also moderated by social background. Moreover, reintegration into the labour market after receiving social assistance is strongly influenced by previously attained status in terms of education and income (Hümbelin and Fritschi, 2018).

While the youth poverty rate is higher in Sweden than the OECD average, there is evidence that the experience of poverty is less persistent (Mendola et al, 2009) and not as strongly associated with future poverty risks (Ayllón, 2015) in the Scandinavian welfare context. Common to these studies is the definition of poverty as having a net equivalised household income below 60 per cent of the median income. Findings from research in a Swedish setting (Halleröd and Westberg, 2006), using both income and a deprivation index as measures of the financial situation, have indicated that youths' earnings say rather little about their actual living standard and that low income in early adulthood does not imply poor earning ability from a long-term perspective.

In contrast, scholars using other indicators of youth disadvantage have found evidence that an unsuccessful labour market entry is associated with poorer employment chances in the future (Nordström Skans, 2004; Hammer, 2007), that economic inactivity in young adulthood is associated with elevated risks of being economically inactive in adulthood (Franzén and Kassman, 2005) and that being not in employment, education or training (NEET) in early adulthood is associated with subsequent labour market risks with long-lasting implications (Bäckman and Nilsson, 2016). Schels (2013) found that while most spells of means-tested benefits are transitory, young people who received such benefits ran an elevated risk of prolonged or repeated benefits. However, there was no evidence of welfare dependency, meaning that the receipt of welfare was not *in itself* positively associated with further benefit receipt.

With reference to the preceding discussions, two hypotheses are suggested. A 'matter of course' hypothesis purports that experiences of economic hardship during young adulthood can be considered a matter of course in the development of adult roles. According to this hypothesis, we may expect a disadvantaged labour market position and a stuttering career during subsequent years but with few long-term implications for labour market opportunities. As an opposing hypothesis, it is suggested that young adulthood is a formative stage in terms of experiencing economic hardship, with links to poor establishment in the labour market. According to this 'cause for concern' hypothesis, we would expect economic hardship to be associated with unfavourable labour market trajectories, not only in the immediate aftermath, but also with long-term repercussions. Which of the two hypotheses will be empirically vindicated is of relevance for policy and practice. Support for the 'matter of course' hypothesis would suggest that the system largely works as intended for young adults and that additional efforts should rather aim at improving childhood conditions in order to prevent the reproduction of disadvantage. In contrast, evidence that economic hardship in early adulthood is, indeed, a cause for concern, net of background factors, would underscore the need for measures directed at young adults to prevent economic hardship and support a successful establishment in the labour market.

Data and method

The study utilises longitudinal Swedish full population register data from a number of national administrative registers, such as: Statistics Sweden's (SCB's) Longitudinal Integration Database for Health Insurance and Labour Market Studies (1990–2016); SCB's Geography and Domestic Residential Mobility Database (1990–2016); student registers from the National Agency for Education (1987–2016); and the Swedish National Council for Crime Prevention's data on criminal convictions (1973–2017). Information on sex, year of birth and country of birth was retrieved from the Total Population Register.

Population

The analytical sample consists of young adults aged 19–22 in 2001 who had 'left the nest' to start a household of their own during the year before, had not returned to the parental home in 2001 and were still alive and living in Sweden in 2016. Of the entire population aged 19–22 in 2001, information about type of household was missing for 1.98 per cent, whereupon they could not be included in the sample. Individuals younger than 21 who were enrolled in upper-secondary school or secondary adult education were omitted because parents' maintenance obligation remains until the youth either graduates or turns 21. Finally, 54 observations were omitted due to missing information. This adds up to a sample of 47,427 individuals who were followed over a period of 15 years until their mid-30s.

Independent variable: indicator of economic hardship

Economic hardship is operationalised as receiving means-tested social assistance the year immediately after leaving the parental home. Social assistance receipt sets a national minimum standard of living and reflects non-eligibility to, or insufficient levels of, earnings-related social insurance-type benefits. In order to be entitled to social assistance, all other means and assets need to be exhausted and the individual is also expected to actively seek work as well as partake in labour market programmes in order to enhance the prospects of becoming economically self-reliant. You have to actively apply for social assistance on a monthly basis and declare your account statements to show that there are no other means to draw on. In 2001, the estimated non-take-up rate of social assistance was 31 per cent (Matsaganis et al, 2014). Each application is individually assessed by a caseworker and the amount of assistance is assessed in relation to the national standard. This means that you can receive social assistance while working but only to the extent that the total income does not exceed the standard level; around 5 per cent of recipients work but with an insufficient income (National Board of Health and Welfare, 2019). When assessing eligibility for social assistance, all financial assets are taken into account, including financial support from parents. In that sense, receipt of social assistance reflects the coexistence of not having enough income to make ends meet while also lacking other sources of financial support. Thus, it captures the dimensions of both need and eligibility.

To get an understanding of the generosity of social assistance, it can be compared to the poverty line. While Sweden used to be one of few European countries that provided benefits above the EU's 'at risk of poverty' threshold of 60 per cent of median net income in the early 1990s, since the late 1990s, the benefit levels are below that line. For example, in 2001, the adequacy rate, defined as the level of social assistance as a percentage of the level of median income in the total population, was around 50 per cent (Kuivalainen and Nelson, 2012). The independent variable was divided into three categories: no social assistance receipt; low degree of social assistance receipt (<50 per cent of annual disposable income); and high degree of social assistance receipt (≥50 per cent of annual disposable income).

Outcome

Labour market attachment is operationalised by utilising an income maintenance model for Social Exclusion and Labour Market Attachment (SELMA) developed by Bäckman et al (2015), and was measured for the period 2002–16. The original model includes four discrete and mutually exclusive annual categories of labour market position: core labour force (CLF), insecure labour force (ILF), student and NEET. For the purposes of this study, the category 'student' was divided into the subcategories 'university student' and 'other student'. The categories are further described in Table 6.1. The SELMA model has been used as a measure of labour market attachment in numerous studies in a Nordic welfare context (for example, Jakobsen et al, 2019; Lorentzen et al, 2019) and has been subject to sensitivity analyses (Korpi et al, 2015).

Table 6.1: The SELMA model

Label	Definition
CLF	Annual labour market income[a] of at least 3.5 price base amounts (PBA[b])
ILF	Annual labour market income of between 0.5 and 3.5 PBA[c]
University student	Enrolled in university education AND labour market income below 3.5 PBA
Other student	Enrolled in other types of education, for example, adult secondary education/folk high school/vocational training, OR received student allowance, AND labour market income below 3.5 PBA
NEET	Labour market income below 0.5 PBA and not belonging to any of the categories above

Notes:
[a] Labour market income does not include unemployment benefits, student allowances or pensions. Income from parental leave, work-related social insurance benefits such as sickness benefits and family allowances are included.
[b] 3.5 PBA is roughly equivalent to an annual, full-time, low-pay income in Sweden.
[c] The category insecure labour force may include stable part-time workers, which unfortunately could not be distinguished from individuals who are in an insecure position.

Controls

The analyses include a range of pre-exposure covariates, guided by previous research. The variables controlled for are: sex (female/male); age (19–22); grades from upper-secondary school (no upper-secondary education, upper-secondary education but no grades in registers, low grades, medium grades and high grades); family type after residential emancipation (single, married or cohabiting with children, single parent); country of birth (born in Sweden, at least one parent born in Sweden; born in Sweden, both parents born outside Sweden; immigrant from Western countries; immigrant from other countries); number of criminal convictions 1994–2000 (0, 1, 2+); receipt of social assistance in 2000 (0/1); highest parental level of education (lower than three-year upper-secondary education, three-year upper-secondary education, university); parental criminal convictions (no parent, one parent, both parents convicted between 1991 and 2000); family type before residential emancipation (two-parent household, step-parent household, single-parent household, other); number of years with occurrence of social assistance before residential emancipation during 1997–99 (0–3); mean disposable income before residential emancipation during 1997–99 (equivalised by household size, four quartiles); and type of municipality of residence (metropolitan, suburban, large city, commuter municipality, sparsely populated, manufacturing, other >25,000 inhabitants, other 12,500–25,000 inhabitants, other <12,500 inhabitants). The classifications of the nine municipality categories were outlined by the Swedish Association of Local Authorities. For the variable 'parental education', the highest level of education was used for those who lived with two parents before leaving the parental home, while for those living with a single parent, the education of the co-residing parent was used.

Analytical strategy

This study employs a combination of sequence analysis and multinomial regression, and the analyses were carried out in four steps. First, the general characteristics of labour market sequences by experience of economic hardship were explored. Second, similarities between individual sequences were calculated through the Hamming distance measure, which is sensitive to differences in timing and takes the period-specific context into consideration (for a review, see Halpin, 2014).

Third, the grouping of the sequences into clusters was performed using partition around medoids (PAM) clustering. In line with recommendations, and since there is no objective measure of the appropriate cluster solution, the number of clusters was determined by visual inspection to identify analytically meaningful groups that contain a sufficient number of cases (Brzinsky-Fay, 2007). The number of clusters was deemed saturated when adding another cluster would only produce a similar version of an already-existing cluster. Each cluster was then named according to the medoid sequence. Due to computational limitations, the sequence analysis could not be employed in the full sample. Rather than restricting the analysis to a smaller sample, the sample was divided into three random subsamples. The distance calculations and the cluster analysis were performed in each subsample separately and the samples were then appended back together. Lastly, to assess the association between the early adulthood experience of economic hardship and the various labour market establishment trajectories, multinomial logistic regression analysis was employed.

The extent to which the estimates were sensitive to unobserved confounding was assessed by calculating E-values (VanderWeele and Ding, 2017) for both the adjusted association and for the limit of the confidence interval. To this end, the Karlson–Holm–Breen method (KHB) (Karlson et al, 2012) was applied to the multinomial regression, which accounts for problems related to the rescaling bias inherent in non-linear regression analysis. The E-value is defined as the strength (on the risk ratio scale) of an association that an unmeasured confounder would need to have with both the independent and the dependent variable to fully explain away the association, conditional on the covariates controlled for. A large E-value indicates that considerable unobserved confounding would be needed to explain away an estimate, while a small E-value suggests that little unobserved confounding would be needed. In the same manner, a large Confidence Interval (CI) limit implies that a large unobserved confounding would be needed to make the estimate statistically non-significant. E-values and CI limits were computed using the website provided by Mathur et al (2018).

All analyses were performed using Stata 15/SE version. Sequence analyses were performed using the SADI-package (Halpin, 2017) and the SQ-package (Brzinsky-Fay et al, 2006). For the multinomial regression analysis, the KHB package was used.

Results

Table 6.2 reports descriptive statistics for the sample by experience of economic hardship. In total, 12 per cent of the youths received

Table 6.2: Sample characteristics by degree of economic hardship in 2001 (row %)

	No social assistance	Low degree of social assistance receipt	High degree of social assistance receipt
Sex			
Male	88.5	7.8	3.7
Female	87.6	8.7	3.7
Age in 2001			
19	62.1	19.7	18.2
20	84.5	10.5	5.0
21	89.2	8.0	2.8
22	92.4	5.7	1.9
Family type after residential emancipation			
Married, or cohabiting with children	65.7	23.9	10.5
Single parent	32.3	55.5	12.2
Single	89.2	7.4	3.4
Educational attainment			
No secondary education	67.1	19.6	13.4
Secondary education, no grades in registers	81.7	13.4	4.9
Low grades	89.2	8.7	2.1
Moderate grades	95.0	4.3	0.6
High grades	97.5	2.1	0.3
Birth country			
Sweden, at least one parent born in Sweden	89.9	7.3	2.8
Sweden, no parent born in Sweden	80.0	13.0	6.9
Immigrant from Western countries[a]	71.0	18.0	11.0
Immigrant from other countries	67.8	18.1	14.1
Social assistance receipt in 2000			
No	95.0	3.9	1.1
Yes	38.1	39.6	22.3
Criminal convictions 1994–2000			
0	90.2	7.1	2.7
1	76.0	15.1	8.8
2+	61.8	20.5	17.6
Family type in 1999 before residential emancipation			
Two-parent household	93.0	5.1	1.9
Step-parent household	81.6	12.5	5.9
Family type in 1999 before residential emancipation (continued)			
Single-parent household	80.0	13.4	6.6
Other	72.8	12.8	14.4

(continued)

Table 6.2: Sample characteristics by degree of economic hardship in 2001 (row %) (continued)

	No social assistance	Low degree of social assistance receipt	High degree of social assistance receipt
Highest parental educational level			
< Three-year upper-secondary school	79.6	12.9	7.5
Three-year upper-secondary school	87.3	9.0	3.7
University	93.0	5.2	1.8
No information in registers	58.0	19.2	22.7
No. of years with social assistance before residential emancipation, 1997–99			
0	92.3	5.5	2.2
1	74.1	18.7	7.2
2	69.2	21.3	9.4
3	58.3	25.5	16.3
Mean disposable income[b] before residential emancipation, 1997–99			
First quartile	75.4	15.5	9.1
Second quartile	86.8	9.9	3.3
Third quartile	93.3	5.1	1.6
Fourth quartile	88.0	8.3	3.7
Parental criminal convictions, 1991–2000			
No parent	90.0	7.2	2.8
One parent	76.4	15.2	8.4
Both parents	60.4	19.9	19.7
Type of municipality of residence			
Metropolitan municipality	87.8	7.6	4.7
Suburban municipality	90.9	6.1	3.0
Large city	90.0	7.1	3.0
Commuter municipality	85.4	10.4	4.2
Sparsely populated municipality	82.1	13.8	4.1
Manufacturing municipality	87.9	8.9	3.2
Other >25,000 inhabitants	84.7	10.7	4.6
Other 12,500–25,000 inhabitants	84.9	10.7	4.4
Other <12,500 inhabitants	83.5	11.8	4.7
N	41,739	3,938	1,750

Notes: N = 47,427.
[a] Europe, Australia, Canada, New Zealand and the US.
[b] SEK. equivalised by household size.

means-tested social assistance in 2001. There were no substantial differences by sex, whereas the younger cohorts received assistance to a greater extent. In line with expectations, low educational attainment, criminal convictions and type of household were related to the degree of economic hardship. Parental characteristics were also of importance. Of the young people whose parents had attained a lower secondary education, more than 20 per cent received social assistance, whereas the corresponding number for youths whose parents had university education was seven per cent. Previous experience of social assistance in the family was also of importance for the risk of social assistance receipt after leaving the parental home.

Characteristics of labour market sequences

There is substantial variation in the prevalence and duration of statuses across the groups. Table 6.3 shows the average duration in each status, which is the total number of years, over the observed 15-year period, spent in one status, whether consecutively or not. The group with no economic hardship spent 11 years on average in the core labour force compared to eight and five years for the other groups. The non-hardship group also spent less time in ILF and more time as a university student. Looking at the average duration in the NEET category, those who experienced high degrees of economic hardship spent more than four years on average in the state NEET, whereas the non-hardship group spent virtually no time in this state.

At the bottom of Table 6.3, the average number of episodes in all statuses is reported, indicating the degree of volatility. Table 6.3 reveals

Table 6.3: Characteristics of labour market sequences by degree of economic hardship in 2001

Average number of years in:	No social assistance	Low degree of social assistance receipt	High degree of social assistance receipt
CLF	10.9	8.0	4.8
ILF	1.3	2.6	3.0
University student	1.7	1.1	0.6
Other student	0.7	1.5	2.1
NEET	0.6	1.8	4.5
Average number of episodes	3.8	5.3	6.0

Note: *N* = 47,427; no social assistance, *n* = 41,739; low social assistance, *n* = 3,938; high social assistance, *n* = 1,750.

that the two groups who experienced economic hardship were more volatile, with those with a high degree of hardship experiencing six episodes on average over the observed 15-year period, compared to less than four episodes for the non-hardship group.

Groups of labour market establishment sequences

Five clusters of labour market establishment sequence types were identified, which are presented in Figure 6.1, depicting the distribution of states across time and by cluster. A majority of the cases (≈52 per cent) are found in the first cluster, where the sequences are characterised by a stable position in the core labour force from the age of 19–22 to the mid-30s. The sequences in the second cluster are characterised by a relatively short period of university education, approximately corresponding to the completion of a bachelor degree (typically, three years in Sweden), followed by a stable position in the labour market. Around 25 per cent of the individuals are found in this group. The third cluster is somewhat smaller (≈11 per cent), its typical feature being a longer period in university education followed by a transition to stable employment. The fourth cluster populates around 8 per cent of the individuals and is characterised by an unstable position in the labour market during the 20s, with a transition to stable employment around age 30. The most disadvantaged labour market trajectories are found in the smallest cluster (≈5 per cent). The sequences are distinguished by a persistent NEET position throughout the observed period.

The link between economic hardship and labour market establishment trajectories

Table 6.4 reports the average marginal effects from multinomial logistic regression of low degree of assistance receipt (<50 per cent of annual disposable income) in the left column and of high degree of assistance receipt (≥50 per cent of annual disposable income) in the right column, as compared to non-recipients.

The experience of low degrees of early adulthood economic hardship is associated with a nine percentage point lower probability of following the stable employment trajectory, net of background characteristics. Looking at the crude estimates, there is a positive association with the insecure employment track and disadvantaged labour market establishment trajectory. However, these associations are weak when adjusted for confounding variables. The experience of high degree of

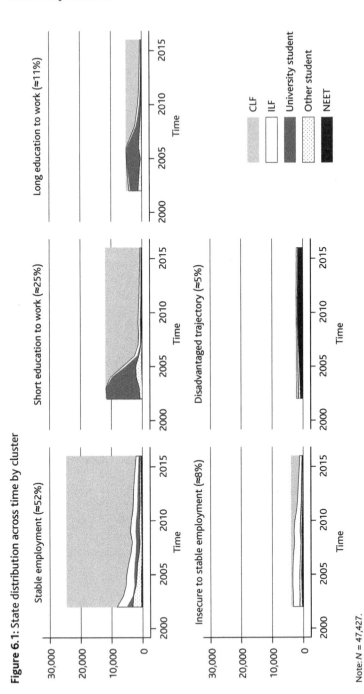

Figure 6.1: State distribution across time by cluster

Note: N = 47,427.

Table 6.4: Average marginal effects of economic hardship from multinomial logistic regression – low and high degree of social assistance receipt, compared to no receipt

		Low degree of social assistance			High degree of social assistance		
		AME	CI 95%		AME	CI 95%	
Stable employment	Crude	-0.041***	-0.057	-0.025	-0.237***	-0.258	-0.215
	Adjusted	-0.086***	-0.104	-0.068	-0.176***	-0.205	-0.147
Short education to work	Crude	-0.153***	-0.163	-0.142	-0.212***	-0.225	-0.200
	Adjusted	0.011	-0.008	0.030	0.003	-0.033	0.039
Long education to work	Crude	-0.007	-0.017	0.003	-0.051***	-0.063	-0.030
	Adjusted	0.022**	0.007	0.036	-0.003	-0.025	0.019
Insecure employment	Crude	0.125***	0.113	0.137	0.208***	0.188	0.228
	Adjusted	0.030***	0.021	0.039	0.074***	0.058	0.090
Disadvantaged trajectory	Crude	0.076***	0.067	0.085	0.292***	0.271	0.313
	Adjusted	0.023***	0.016	0.029	0.101***	0.086	0.116

Notes: $N = 47,427$; low social assistance, $n = 3,938$; high social assistance, $n = 1,750$; comparison group of non-recipients, $n = 41,739$. Adjusted models control for all variables listed under 'Data and method'. Intercept and control variables suppressed.
*** $p < 0.001$; ** $p < 0.01$; * $p < 0.05$.

economic hardship is associated with a crude difference of 24 percentage points in the probability of belonging to the stable employment cluster, 29 percentage points in the probability of a disadvantaged labour market trajectory and 21 percentage points in the probability of following the trajectory starting with insecure employment, followed by a stable position towards the end of the observed period. Adjustment for confounders reduced the crude estimates but there are still statistically significant differences ranging between seven and 18 percentage points. With respect to the educational trajectories, there are virtually no differences between either of the groups of social assistance recipients and the group of non-recipients.

Sensitivity analysis

Table 6.5 reveals that the E-values range between 1.9 and 13.0, with the association between high degrees of social assistance receipt and a disadvantaged trajectory being the most robust estimate.[1] This association has a relative risk ratio (RRR) of 6.8 (stable employment being the base outcome [see Table 6.A2 in the Appendix]). An unobserved confounder would need to be associated with both the outcome and the independent variable by a risk ratio of thirteenfold each to explain away this estimate, and by a risk ratio of elevenfold each to drive the estimates to statistical non-significance, above and beyond the observed confounders. Other estimates, for example, the association

Table 6.5: Sensitivity analyses for multinomial logit model RRR estimates

Outcome	Low degree of social assistance		High degree of social assistance	
	E-value	CI limit	E-value	CI limit
Short education to work	1.9	1.5	2.2	1.4
Long education to work	2.3	1.9	2.2	1.4
Insecure to stable employment	2.9	2.5	6.2	5.2
Disadvantaged trajectory	3.5	2.9	13.0	10.9

Notes: Base category = stable employment. N = 47,427; low social assistance, n = 3,938; high social assistance, n = 1,750; comparison group of non-recipients, n = 41,739. RRR = relative risk ratio. E-value = the strength of association (on the risk ratio scale) that an unmeasured confounder would need to have with both the exposure and outcome, conditional on the covariates controlled for, to explain away the association between the independent variable and the outcome. CI limit = the same as above but measures the strength that an unmeasured confounder would need to have to drive the association in order to be statistically non-significant

Source: VanderWeele and Ding, 2017.

between low levels of social assistance and a disadvantaged trajectory, are much less robust. In this case, an unobserved confounder would need to be associated with the outcome and the exposure by a risk ratio of 3.5 to explain away the association and of 2.9 to drive the estimates to statistical non-significance, a scenario that seems more likely.

Conclusion

The aim of this study was twofold: first, it identified and described typical labour market trajectories from young adulthood to the mid-30s; and, second, it investigated the relationship between the experience of economic hardship during the onset of an independent adult life and different labour market trajectory types. Five groups of typical labour market sequences were identified. Most young adults experience a rather swift labour market entry, with a vast majority being in the core labour force by at least the age of 25. A large group pursue education after their residential emancipation and just shy of a tenth of the youths experience a stuttering labour market position before they enter stable employment. Only a small group of youths follow a truly disadvantaged labour market trajectory. The five typical trajectories identified broadly mirror the patterns found in another Scandinavian study (Lorentzen et al, 2019).

Youths with experience of economic hardship, even when the degree of hardship was low, were found to be less likely to follow an express track to stable employment. However, this is not necessarily disadvantageous, but rather suggests that these young adults need to expand their human capital before entering the labour force. Evidently, none of the social assistance receipt groups are less likely to pursue the educational tracks and the experience of low degrees of economic hardship has no or a negligible association with disadvantaged labour market trajectories; these estimates were also least robust. This lends support to the 'matter of course' hypothesis and is in line with some previous findings (Halleröd and Westberg, 2006). Most young people in economic hardship recuperate and are fairly successful in the labour market in the long run, suggesting that the social assistance system largely works as intended and that the toll in terms of stigmatisation (Goffman, 1963) and scarring (Arulampalam, 2001) is slight from a long-term perspective. Then again, high degrees of economic hardship in early adulthood were certainly found to be an adversity that compounds the risk for following the truly disadvantaged labour market trajectory, in line with some other findings (for example, Bäckman and Nilsson, 2016; Franzén and Kassman, 2005). This finding vindicates the 'cause for concern' hypothesis and the theoretical perspective of hardship-induced distress (Elliott, 1996; Masarik and Conger, 2017) and scarring effects (Arulampalam, 2001; Schmillen and Umkehrer, 2017), with long-term persistence of labour market disadvantage linked to risks of social exclusion.

This study has the advantage of using full population longitudinal data. However, like all studies, it has some inherent limitations. For example, administrative data do not contain information on direct measures of economic hardship, such as cash margins or subjective experiences of hardship, which would certainly be relevant to capture youth disadvantage. Instead, social assistance receipt is used as an indicator. While this has many merits, it is not free of objection. For instance, not all individuals in need of, and entitled to, social assistance actually receive it (for example, Bargain et al, 2012). This implies that some individuals who are equally poor but not receiving social assistance could be in the reference group, potentially making the estimates somewhat conservative, as well as that the findings also reflect facets of social assistance receipt beyond the actual lack of financial resources.

The methods used in this study provided the opportunity to study labour market establishment as a process over an extended period of time. However, the study design also entails some obstacles. For example, the study does not account for time-varying variables over the period 2002–16, meaning that concurrent events that may impact on labour market establishment are not observed. It could be an important task for future projects to explore this further.

The take-home message from this study is that, for the most part, economic hardship in young adulthood is to be considered a matter of course in the development of adult roles and establishment in the labour market. Although leaving the parental home and establishing an independent household is a key developmental stage, in Sweden, it is not a make-or-break period. Most young people, with and without experience of early adulthood economic hardship, manage a successful labour market establishment in the long run. For example, 70 per cent of those with low levels of hardship, and nearly 40 per cent of those with high levels of hardship, were found in either the stable employment cluster or in any of the education/transition-to-work clusters. The study therefore also armours the assertion that youth labour market establishment should be analysed longitudinally and as sequences, rather than as single transitions or events, so as not to render a distorted image. However, when the hardship is extensive, even in the relatively generous Swedish welfare state, there may be cause for serious concern due to elevated risks of getting lodged in a position outside the labour market for a considerable part of adult life. In this group, young adults in need of extensive efforts to boost their chances on the labour market can be found. This points to a need for early screening by social services to identify those at risk of developing the least favourable pathways, as well as to the importance of monitoring the prevalence of extensive social assistance receipt.

Note

[1] Table 6.5 reports E-values and CI limits computed for the multinomial logistic regression and should thus be related to the relative risk ratio (RRR) estimates in Table 6.A2 in the Appendix rather than to the average marginal effects reported in Table 6.4.

References

Abbott, A. and Forrest, J. (1986) 'Optimal matching methods for historical sequences', *The Journal of Interdisciplinary History*, 16(3): 471–94.

Arnesen, A.L. and Lundahl, L. (2006) 'Still social and democratic? Inclusive education policies in the Nordic welfare states', *Scandinavian Journal of Educational Research*, 50(3) 285–300.

Arnett, J.J. (2000) 'Emerging adulthood: a theory of development from the late teens through early twenties', *American Psychologist*, 55: 469–80.

Arulampalam, W. (2001) 'Is unemployment really scarring? Effects of unemployment experiences on wages', *The Economic Journal*, 111(475): F585–F606.

Ayllón, S. (2015) 'Youth poverty, employment, and leaving the parental home in Europe', *Review of Income & Wealth*, 61(4): 651–76.

Bäckman, O. and Nilsson, A. (2016) 'Long-term consequences of being not in employment, education or training as a young adult. Stability and change in three Swedish birth cohorts', *European Societies*, 18(2): 136–57.

Bäckman, O., Jakobsen, V., Lorentzen, T., Österbacka, E. and Dahl, E. (2015) 'Early school leaving in Scandinavia: extent and labour market effects', *Journal of European Social Policy*, 25(3): 253–69.

Bargain, O., Immervoll, H. and Viitamäki, H. (2012) 'No claim, no pain. Measuring the non-take-up of social assistance using register data', *The Journal of Economic Inequality*, 10(3): 375–95.

Berzin, S.C. and De Marco, A.C. (2009) 'Understanding the impact of poverty on critical events in emerging adulthood', *Youth & Society*, 42(2): 278–300.

Brzinsky-Fay, C. (2007) 'Lost in transition? Labour market entry sequences of school leavers in Europe', *European Sociological Review*, 23(4): 209–422.

Brzinsky-Fay, C., Kohler, U. and Luniak, M. (2006) 'Sequence analysis with Stata', *Stata Journal*, 6(4): 435–60.

Duncan, G.J., Yeung, W.J., Brooks-Gunn, J. and Smith, J.R. (1998) 'How much does childhood poverty affect the life chances of children?', *American Sociological Review*, 63(3): 406–23.

Elliott, M. (1996) 'Impact of work, family, and welfare receipt on women's self-esteem in young adulthood', *Social Psychology Quarterly*, 59(1): 80–95.

Eurostat (2018) 'Bye bye parents: when do young Europeans flee the nest?', https://ec.europa.eu/eurostat/web/products-eurostat-news/-/EDN-20180515-1

Franzén, E.M. and Kassman, A. (2005) 'Longer-term labour-market consequences of economic inactivity during young adulthood: a Swedish national cohort study', *Journal of Youth Studies*, 8(4): 403–24.

Goffman, E. (1963) *Stigma: Notes on the management of spoiled identity*, Englewood Cliffs, NJ: Prentice-Hall Inc.

Halleröd, B. and Westberg, A. (2006) 'Youth problem: what's the problem? A longitudinal study of incomes and economic hardship among Swedish youth', *Acta Sociologica*, 49(1): 83–102.

Halpin, B. (2014) 'Three narratives of sequence analysis', in P. Blanchard, F. Bühlmann and J.-A. Gauthier (eds) *Advances in sequence analysis: Theory, method, applications*, Cham: Springer International Publishing, pp 75–103.

Halpin, B. (2017) 'SADI: sequence analysis tools for Stata', *The Stata Journal*, 17(3): 546–72.

Hammer, T. (2007) 'Labour market integration of unemployed youth from a life course perspective: the case of Norway', *International Journal of Social Welfare*, 16(3): 249–57.

Hümbelin, O. and Fritschi, T. (2018) 'Pathways into and out of the labor market after receiving social benefits: cumulative disadvantage or life course risk?', *The Sociological Quarterly*, 59(4): 627–54.

Ilmakunnas, I. (2018) 'Risk and vulnerability in social assistance receipt of young adults in Finland', *International Journal of Social Welfare*, 27(1): 5–16.

Jakobsen, V., Korpi, T. and Lorentzen, T. (2019) 'Immigration and integration policy and labour market attainment among immigrants to Scandinavia', *European Journal of Population*, 35(2): 305–28.

Karlson, K.B., Holm, A. and Breen, R. (2012) 'Comparing regression coefficients between same-sample nested models using logit and probit: a new method', *Sociological Methodology*, 42(1): 286–313.

Kauppinen, T.M., Angelin, A., Lorentzen, T., Bäckman, O., Salonen, T., Moisio, P. and Dahl, E. (2014) 'Social background and life-course risks as determinants of social assistance receipt among young adults in Sweden, Norway and Finland', *Journal of European Social Policy*, 24(3): 273–88.

Kohler, U., Karlson, K.B. and Holm, A. (2011) 'Comparing coefficients of nested nonlinear probability models', *Stata Journal*, 11(3): 420–38.

Korpi, T., Bäckman, O. and Minas, R. (2015) *Att möta globaliseringen: Utbildning, aktivering och social exkludering i Norden* [*Meeting globalisation: Education, activation and social exclusion in the Nordic countries*], København: Nordisk Ministerråd.

Korpi, W. and Palme, J. (1998) 'The paradox of redistribution and strategies of equality: welfare state institutions, inequality, and poverty in the Western countries', *American Sociological Review*, 63(5): 661–87.

Kuivalainen, S. and Nelson, K. (2012) 'Eroding minimum income protection in the Nordic countries? Reassessing the Nordic model of social assistance', in J. Kvist, J. Fritzell, B. Hvinden and O. Kangas (eds) *Changing social equality. The Nordic welfare model in the 21st century*, Bristol: Policy Press.

Lorentzen, T., Dahl, E. and Harsløf, I. (2012) 'Welfare risks in early adulthood: a longitudinal analysis of social assistance transitions in Norway', *International Journal of Social Welfare*, 21(4): 408–21.

Lorentzen, T., Bäckman, O., Ilmakunnas, I. and Kauppinen, T. (2019) 'Pathways to adulthood: sequences in the school-to-work transition in Finland, Norway and Sweden', *Social Indicators Research*, 141(3): 1285–305.

Masarik, A.S. and Conger, R.D. (2017) 'Stress and child development: a review of the Family Stress Model', *Current Opinion in Psychology*, 13: 85–90.

Mathur, M.B., Ding, P., Riddell, C.A. and VanderWeele, T.J. (2018) 'Web site and R package for computing E-values', *Epidemiology*, 29(5): e45–e47, https://mmathur.shinyapps.io/evalue/

Matsaganis, M., Ozdemir, E. and Ward, T. (2014) 'The coverage rate of social benefits', Research Note 9/2013, European Commission.

Mendola, D., Busetta, A. and Aassve, A. (2009) 'What keeps young adults in permanent poverty? A comparative analysis using ECHP', *Social Science Research*, 38(4): 840–57.

Moisio, P., Lorentzen, T., Bäckman, O., Angelin, A., Salonen, T. and Kauppinen, T. (2015) 'Trends in the intergenerational transmission of social assistance in the Nordic countries in the 2000s', *European Societies*, 17(1): 73–93.

Mood, C. and Jonsson, J.O. (2016) 'The social consequences of poverty: an empirical test on longitudinal data', *Social Indicators Research*, 127(2): 633–52.

National Board of Health and Welfare (Socialstyrelsen) (2019) 'Försörjningshinder och ändamål med ekonomiskt bistånd 2017. Art.no: 2019-2-5', www.socialstyrelsen.se/globalassets/sharepoint-dokument/artikelkatalog/statistik/2019-2-5.pdf

Nordström Skans, O. (2004) *Har ungdomsarbetslösheten långsiktiga effekter?*, Report 2004:13, Uppsala: Institutet för arbetsmarknadspolitisk utvärdering, www.ifau.se/globalassets/pdf/se/2004/r04-13.pdf

OECD (Organisation for Economic Co-operation and Development) (2016) *Investing in youth: Sweden*, Paris: OECD Publishing, http://dx.doi.org/10.1787/9789264267701-en

Schels, B. (2013) 'Persistence or transition: young adults and social benefits in Germany', *Journal of Youth Studies*, 16(7): 881–900.

Schmillen, A. and Umkehrer, M. (2017) 'The scars of youth: effects of early-career unemployment on future unemployment experience', *International Labour Review*, 156(3/4): 465–94.

Schröder, L. (2000) *Ungdomsarbetslösheten i ett internationellt perspektiv*, Market Policy Evaluation (IFAU) Report 2000:4, Uppsala: Institute for Labour Market Policy Evaluation (IFAU).

Stenberg, S.-Å. (2000) 'Inheritance of welfare recipiency: an intergenerational study of social assistance recipiency in postwar Sweden', *Journal of Marriage and Family*, 62(1): 228–39.

Townsend, P. (1979) *Poverty in the United Kingdom: A survey of household resources and standards of living*, Harmondsworth: Penguin Books.

VanderWeele, T.J. and Ding, P. (2017) 'Sensitivity analysis in observational research: introducing the E-value', *Annals of Internal Medicine*, 167(4): 268–74.

Vogel, J. and Råbäck, G. (2003) 'Materiell ojämlikhet i tids och internationellt perspektiv', in Statistics Sweden (ed) *Report No. 100, Välfärd och ofärd på 90-talet*, Stockholm: Statistiska centralbyrån.

Walther, A. (2006) 'Regimes of youth transitions: choice, flexibility and security in young people's experiences across different European contexts', *Young*, 14(2): 119–39.

Appendix

Table 6.A1: Sample characteristics by cluster of labour market establishment trajectory (row %)

	Stable employment	Short education to work	Long education to work	Insecure to stable employment	Disadvantaged trajectory
Degree of economic hardship 2001					
No social assistance	52.9	27.1	11.0	6.2	2.8
Low degree of social assistance	48.9	11.2	9.3	18.9	11.7
High degree of social assistance	29.0	5.2	4.9	26.9	33.9
Sex					
Male	58.5	22.3	9.0	4.8	5.4
Female	46.4	27.0	11.9	10.6	4.2
Age					
19	48.2	7.9	9.2	20.7	14.0
20	48.5	23.4	13.0	9.9	5.2
21	50.3	27.1	11.2	7.5	3.9
22	55.8	25.9	8.5	5.8	4.0
Family type after residential emancipation					
Married or cohabiting with children	54.8	6.1	6.5	23.9	8.7
Single parent	44.7	5.8	5.4	30.0	14.1
Single	51.7	25.7	10.8	7.4	4.5

(continued)

Table 6.A1: Sample characteristics by cluster of labour market establishment trajectory (row %) (continued)

	Stable employment	Short education to work	Long education to work	Insecure to stable employment	Disadvantaged trajectory
Educational attainment					
No secondary education	57.4	4.3	5.4	17.8	15.1
Secondary education, no grades in registers	59.5	19.1	7.7	10.1	3.6
Low grades	67.9	12.2	7.9	9.1	2.9
Moderate grades	52.5	29.3	12.0	4.7	1.5
High grades	29.2	50.8	16.5	2.1	1.4
Birth country					
Sweden, at least one parent born in Sweden	52.4	25.6	10.6	7.3	4.1
Sweden, no parent born in Sweden	49.4	17.6	9.6	14.3	9.0
Immigrant from Western countries[a]	48.1	22.6	8.5	11.3	9.5
Immigrant from other countries	42.7	19.1	12.2	15.9	10.2
Social assistance receipt in 2000					
No	52.2	27.3	11.0	6.5	3.1
Yes	48.5	8.5	7.4	19.2	16.4
Criminal convictions 1994–2000					
0	50.6	27.1	11.2	7.5	3.7
1	60.6	11.5	6.8	11.5	9.7
2+	55.6	7.0	5.4	13.5	18.5

(continued)

Table 6.A1: Sample characteristics by cluster of labour market establishment trajectory (row %), N=47,427 (continued)

	Stable employment	Short education to work	Long education to work	Insecure to stable employment	Disadvantaged trajectory
Family type in 1999 before residential emancipation					
Two-parent household	49.9	29.9	11.0	6.3	2.9
Step-parent household	57.0	16.1	8.9	11.6	6.4
Single-parent household	53.9	17.7	10.3	10.3	7.8
Other	40.8	12.0	11.2	17.6	18.4
Highest parental education					
< Three-year upper-secondary school	62.7	10.4	5.6	13.2	8.0
Three-year upper-secondary school	58.9	19.3	7.9	9.1	4.8
University	37.3	39.0	16.4	4.2	3.1
No information in registers	43.1	10.6	7.5	21.6	17.3
No. of years with social assistance before residential emancipation, 1997–99					
0	50.9	27.6	11.3	6.7	3.4
1	57.6	13.6	8.0	12.0	8.9
2	56.7	11.8	7.1	13.3	11.0
3	51.1	11.1	7.0	17.9	12.9
Mean disposable income[b] before residential emancipation, 1997–99					
First quartile	51.7	15.9	9.9	14.1	8.4
Second quartile	56.2	20.5	9.7	8.7	5.0
Third quartile	54.1	26.9	10.3	5.7	3.0
Fourth quartile	44.8	36.5	12.6	3.6	2.5

(continued)

Table 6.A1: Sample characteristics by cluster of labour market establishment trajectory (row %), N=47,427 (continued)

	Stable employment	Short education to work	Long education to work	Insecure to stable employment	Disadvantaged trajectory
Parental criminal convictions, 1991–2000					
No parent	51.3	26.6	11.0	7.2	4.0
One parent	55.0	15.1	8.2	13.0	8.7
Both parents	49.0	8.3	6.5	19.0	17.2
Type of municipality of residence					
Metropolitan municipality	45.0	28.0	14.9	7.1	5.1
Suburban municipality	60.4	16.4	9.8	8.2	5.2
Large city	42.4	35.5	12.1	6.1	3.9
Commuter municipality	66.6	10.0	4.8	12.1	6.4
Sparsely populated municipality	64.8	9.5	8.7	12.6	4.4
Manufacturing municipality	70.4	9.6	5.5	9.5	5.0
Other >25,000 inhabitants	59.7	17.2	8.0	9.7	5.3
Other 12,500–25,000 inhabitants	65.4	10.1	6.6	12.2	5.7
Other <12,500 inhabitants	67.1	9.5	5.0	12.8	5.6
Total	51.7	25.0	10.6	8.0	4.7
N	24,525	11,831	5,026	3,810	2,235

Notes: N = 47,427.
[a] Europe, Australia, Canada, New Zealand and the US.
[b] SEK. equivalised by household size.

Table 6.A2: Multinomial logit model, predictions (RRR) of labour market establishment trajectory

		Low degree of social assistance			High degree of social assistance		
		RRR	CI 95%		RRR	CI 95%	
Short education to work	Crude	0.341***	0.302	0.384	0.231***	0.181	0.295
	Adjusted	1.282***	1.126	1.460	1.424**	1.103	1.838
Long education to work	Crude	0.811**	0.718	0.917	0.687***	0.542	0.872
	Adjusted	1.478***	1.284	1.701	1.412**	1.093	1.824
Insecure employment	Crude	3.803***	3.439	4.204	10.259***	8.921	11.797
	Adjusted	1.744***	1.554	1.958	3.394***	2.898	3.974
Disadvantaged trajectory	Crude	4.527***	4.003	5.120	26.428***	22.959	30.423
	Adjusted	2.034***	1.761	2.350	6.765***	5.727	7.992

Notes:

Base category = stable employment. N = 47,427; low social assistance, n = 3,938; high social assistance, n = 1,750; comparison group of non-recipients, n = 41,739. Results from multinomial logistic regressions based on the KHB method (Karlson et al, 2012), and the KHB package in Stata developed by Kohler, Karlson and Holm (2011) was used. Adjusted models control for all variables listed under 'Data and method'. Intercept and control variables suppressed.

*$p < 0.05$; **$p < 0.01$; ***$p < 0.001$.

7

Cultural education and the good citizen: a systematic analysis of a neoliberal communitarian policy trend

Katherine Tonkiss, Malgorzata Wootton and Eleni Stamou

Introduction

This chapter delivers an analysis of notions of 'good citizenship' in the conceptualisation and operationalisation of policies targeting the cultural literacy of young people in the UK over the past decade, based on the findings of a systematic policy review. This review, methodological details about which are given later, included the analysis of 28 policy documents in the field of cultural literacy in the UK published since 2007. The chapter examines how, through these documents, the state defines and frames the parameters of what constitutes good citizenship in this policy field, in terms of practices, identities and values (Pykett et al, 2010; De Koning et al, 2015).

After first introducing the core concepts of good citizenship and cultural literacy that inform the chapter as a whole, the chapter provides details of the systematic review methodology and how this was deployed in this research, as well as contextual information on cultural literacy policies in the UK. It then moves into a detailed discussion of the findings of the review. Through fine-grained analysis, we show that these policies have been shaped by the intervention of a neoliberal[1] economic logic aimed at constructing young people into neoliberal subjects, and that culture has been understood in strongly nationalist terms, conceiving of the importance of nationalist sentiment in the context of perceived challenges associated with diversity.

Based on this analysis, we argue that framings of good citizenship in this policy field reflect a neoliberal communitarian model of governance. This model, which has been influential in the study of the integration of new immigrants, captures the demands placed on non-citizens to prove that they are deserving of citizenship as a 'double helix' comprised of the neoliberal responsibilisation of prospective citizens as hard-working contributors to the economy, alongside a communitarian emphasis on the need for these prospective citizens to assimilate into the national culture (Schinkel and Van Houdt, 2010; Van Houdt et al, 2011). This chapter shows that this neoliberal communitarian model shapes the policing of citizenship for existing citizens as well, suggesting the relevance of this model to understanding the policing of belonging within as well as beyond the state.

Good citizenship and cultural literacy

Parameters of inclusion and exclusion are constructed and sustained by states through a variety of formal and informal practices, and serve to produce the meaning of belonging, identifying and categorising those who are considered to be members of the in-group, defined against perceived others. These parameters do not map neatly onto the legal definition of citizen and non-citizen; rather, the parameters intersect with racialised and gendered differences to construct some citizens as belonging more than others (Yuval-Davis, 2011; Bhambra, 2015; Bosworth et al, 2018). A primary way in which states construct parameters of belonging is by invoking ideals of good citizenship that frame the ideal practices, identities and values that the citizens of the state should hold. The focus here is on *acts* of citizenship rather than status (see Isin and Nielsen, 2008), that is, the norms dictating the ways in which citizens enact their belonging to the state (Pykett et al, 2010; De Koning et al, 2015). This is particularly evident in relation to education, which has long been seen as a policy field within which states 'make' future citizens (Brooks and Holford, 2009). Formal citizenship education programmes provided in schools have emerged as a particular focus of scholarly research on this subject. Such programmes tend to focus on democratic practices and active citizenship (Bennett et al, 2009; Hartung, 2017; Hammett, 2014) but have also been utilised as a space to educate young people about multicultural realities (Brooks and Holford, 2009). In the UK, for example, following on from the recommendations of the Crick Report (Crick, 1998), perceptions that multiculturalism was undermining community cohesion and driving different communities, defined in terms of ethnic identity, to lead segregated lives (Cantle, 2001) led to the introduction of a citizenship education curriculum in schools. The aim was to find or restore a sense of 'common citizenship' and to create 'common ground between different ethnic and religious identities' (Cantle, 2001: 17) by promoting values such as respect for the rule of law.

While programmes such as these promote norms of good citizenship through formal education, wider state practices in regards to education also serve to 'discipline' the cultural context and promote it as a 'prescriptive aspect' of membership in the political community (Bhandar, 2010: 331). In this respect, learning about the development of cultural belonging and citizenship-in-practice extends well beyond the scope of citizenship education. It is these expanded practices that are the focus of the remainder of this chapter.

Although cultural literacy offers a useful terminological and analytical device for identifying and accounting for expansive cultural learning, we contest the origins of the term and seek to reframe it. Initially coined by Hirsch (1988), 'cultural literacy' refers to the ability to comprehend a cultural context and be able to participate in it. A diametrical direction to learning was put forward, advocating a focus on core knowledge and hard facts, along with the prioritisation of shared knowledge over personalised learning and skills. Stemming from the principles of essentialist education (Bagley, 1934), this framework was couched in concerns about developing collective memory, heritage and values. Politically, it has been justified through concerns with improving disadvantaged pupils' access to certain types of knowledge.

Over the last decade, there has been revived interest in cultural literacy in the UK. A focus on cultural literacy and related concerns about the universal acquisition of core knowledge has informed recent education policy reforms (Gov.uk, 2013d, 2015b) in a political context marked by declarations about the limits of multiculturalism and a concern with reinvigorating a shared sense of Britishness and shared British values. However, cultural literacy has been thoroughly critiqued in terms of both its theoretical underpinnings and its practical applications. In particular, it has been viewed as elitist, aimed at prioritising national identity and universalising Western values (Woodhouse, 1989; Schweizer, 2009). It has been criticised for relying on oversimplified, linear conceptions of teaching and learning that position learners as passive recipients of knowledge (Aronowitz and Giroux, 1985; Giroux, 2005).

Different definitions of cultural literacy can be identified in contemporary policy and research. The Cultural Literacy in Europe network (no date), for example, understands cultural literacy as an 'ability to view the social and cultural phenomena that shape our lives as being essentially readable' (see also Segal, 2014), while Maine et al

(2019) deploy a definition based on dialogic forms of interaction and collaborative co-construction. In these cases, cultural literacy goes well beyond a narrow focus on knowledge acquisition and entails knowledge, skills and broader dispositions.

In line with these approaches, we deploy 'cultural literacy' in a manner significantly removed from Hirsch's earlier definition. We adopt critical sociological perspectives on culture (Hall, 2000), considering it as a system of meaning that is fluid, contextualised, relational and dynamic. We draw on sociocultural understandings of learning (Bruner, 1996) that highlight the relational, culturally mediated and historically bounded elements of the process. Overall, we invoke a broad understanding of cultural literacy that captures the political, aesthetic and normative aspects of culture in the fullest sense.

Method

The question guiding our research into constructions of the good citizen in UK cultural literacy education policy was as follows: how has the 'good citizen' been framed in UK cultural literacy policy over the past decade? To answer this question, we conducted a systematic policy review of documents published over the past decade. This qualitative approach enabled us to identify, interrogate and analyse the content of relevant policy in detail.

A systematic search for eligible sources examining cultural literacy education – defined as formal and informal educational activities related to cultural identity, cultural practices and cultural heritage –was carried out using the Preferred Reporting Items for Systematic Reviews and Meta-Analyses (PRISMA) framework (Moher et al, 2015). The policy and legislative document repositories of the Westminster government, as well as the Scottish, Welsh and Northern Irish governments, were searched using the following search string: (Youth OR young OR child OR pupil) AND (education OR learn OR participate OR knowledge) AND (art OR dance OR drama OR film OR music OR theatre OR history OR commemoration OR museum OR galleries OR libraries OR poetry) AND (culture OR identity OR heritage OR creativity).

Searches were limited to documents published between January 2007 and June 2018.[2] In addition, manual searches of these repositories were undertaken to ensure that no relevant documents had been missed. After the removal of duplicates, 162 documents were screened against inclusion and exclusion criteria. These criteria included the date of publication, together with relevance to cultural literacy, and also restricted the data set to those documents classed as an expression of policy.[3] This included policy papers, statutory and non-statutory guidance, and legislation. A random sample of 10 per cent of all inclusion/exclusion decisions was blind-reviewed by another member of the coding team. After this initial screening process, 28 documents were deemed eligible for in-depth review.

Of the reviewed documents: 15 related to England only; eight related to Wales only; five were UK-wide; and one related to Northern Ireland only. The process did not return any results for Scotland. The lack of representation of Scottish and Northern Irish policy documents is an unfortunate result of a lack of relevant documents having been published in this time frame.[4] However, the presence of Welsh policy documents allowed for some analysis of the devolution dynamic within this policy field.

A thematic analysis of the documents was undertaken using an iterative, inductive approach to the generation of codes and themes guided by the aims and objectives of the review. To create initial codes, the coding team independently read one eligible document. Results were compared and agreed codes were developed through discussion to create a coding matrix. This process was then repeated until all documents were reviewed in-depth. A random sample of 10 per cent of each document was moderated by a second reviewer to ensure the consistency of approach.

Context: cultural literacy policy in the UK

Responsibility for policies for young people's cultural literacy in the UK involves both national and local governments. The focus of this chapter is the national tier. The devolved administrations in Scotland, Wales and Northern Ireland share these responsibilities with the Westminster government; however, the Westminster government is solely responsible for policies related to cultural literacy in England.

Learning about cultural identity, diversity and participation occurs both within and outside of classroom settings. In schools, cultural literacy is captured in traditional subjects such as history, art and music, as well as in formal citizenship education, which was introduced into school curricula at the turn of the 21st century and is focused on the exploration of a variety of social and political topics, including in relation to cultural diversity (cf Gov.uk, 2013c). Outside of the school environment, educational practices that also contribute to cultural literacy policy objectives are extensively delivered by semi-independent bodies that sit at 'arm's length' from the government and are often perceived to offer a more efficient model of governance. These bodies are sponsored by the government, for example, the Arts Council sits at arm's length from the government and is responsible for the delivery of major policy programmes, and cultural institutions such as the National Gallery and the British Museum also often sit at arm's length from the government.

The governance environment shaping the cultural literacy policy landscape has faced significant fiscal constraints due to the challenging financial context that emerged over the past decade. Following the global financial crisis in 2008, the UK experienced a period of recession, and since 2010, a programme of efficiency savings and budget cuts has been embarked upon by successive Westminster governments (Pollitt, 2010). The effect of this reduced funding is illustrated in the spending power of the Department for Digital, Culture, Media and Sport (DCMS). In 2010, the DCMS budget was cut by 25 per cent (HM Treasury, 2010) and then again in 2015 by 20 per cent (Clark, 2015). An overall budget reduction of 5.1 per cent was agreed for the 2019/20 financial year (National Audit Office, 2017).

More recently, the decision to leave the European Union (EU) ('Brexit') is set to significantly shape the policy environment for cultural literacy. In June 2016, the UK voted by 51.9 per cent to 48.1 per cent to leave the EU after a political campaign rooted firmly in anti-immigration and anti-diversity sentiment (Hobolt, 2016). The impact of Brexit on cultural literacy programmes is not fully known at the time of writing, but critical challenges for the creative industries and for educational programmes reliant on international cooperation have already been identified (DCMS Committee, 2018; Department for Education, 2018).

Neoliberal cultural education

Turning now to the findings of the analysis, there is strong evidence of a neoliberal thrust to the policy documents, which is evident in their statements about the value of learning about culture. In a minority of cases, this is conceptualised intrinsically as 'the enriching value of culture in and of itself' (Gov.uk, 2016a: 15). However, the majority of the time, the value of cultural literacy is understood instrumentally in terms of its contribution to other primary aims of government. For example, it is conceptualised in terms of the contribution that culture makes to the national economy and, therefore, the importance of investing in cultural education to build economic growth. Culture is seen to 'provide the fuel for the wider creative economy' (Gov.uk, 2018a: 13) and as an investment in the future growth of the national economy:

> The UK's future will be built at the nexus of our artistic and cultural creativity and our technical brilliance. The Centre for Economics and Business Research 2018 World Economic League Tables identify this particular blend of creativity and technology skills as the driving force behind the UK's strong economic prospects over the long term. (Gov.uk, 2018a: 4)

Many of the documents further emphasise the importance of culture to economic growth through statistical statements that serve to monetise this value. For example, the 'Culture White Paper' states that, 'In 2014, the economic contribution of museums, galleries, libraries and the arts was £5.4 billion, representing 0.3% of the total UK economy. This is up 59% (in nominal terms) since 2010' (Gov.uk, 2016a: 16). Setting the context of cultural education in such strongly economic terms means that learning about culture is then viewed through the lens of the added value that it brings to the UK economy. For example, it is noted that '[t]he creative industries ... are at the heart of the nation's competitive advantage' (Gov.uk, 2018b: 2).

Conceptualising the value of culture as economic means that the purpose of cultural education is understood as producing citizens who can contribute to this economic value, 'creating the workforce of the future in a sector that continues to help to drive forward the UK's growth agenda' (Gov.uk, 2013a: 5). Workforce creation is thus a central theme across the documents. This is expressed primarily through the language of 'skills' to be developed for use in the cultural economy. For example, the documents set out plans for programmes aimed specifically at building skills to work in the cultural sector (Gov.uk, 2016b, 2017a).

Alongside this focus on economic value is an emphasis on the benefits of cultural literacy at an individual level. Learning about culture is seen to be making a significant contribution, for example, to educational attainment, referencing research which shows that young people who participate in culture are more likely to go on to higher education. This framing is then used to underpin arguments that schools should 'promote cultural education as a means of raising the educational attainment of disadvantaged pupils' (Gov.uk, 2016a: 23).

This framing is once again grounded in an economic logic, which is particularly evident in discussions of 'talent'. Good cultural education is conceptualised as that which 'supports talent early on' (Gov.uk, 2015a) and supports 'a strong and sustainable pipeline' into the creative industries (Gov.uk, 2018b: 18).

Alongside this focus on economic growth is an emphasis on the potential impact of cultural literacy programmes on local communities. In some instances, this is expressed in relation to community cohesion, where it is framed as having value in its potential to build safe, strong and 'resilient' communities (Gov.uk, 2017b), and to 'address social isolation and foster community engagement' (Gov.uk, 2018a: 20). Yet, the economic value of this impact is again evident. Culture is seen to have value in its role in underpinning local-level regeneration, where it 'has the potential to transform communities' (Gov.uk, 2016a: 9). Under this economic logic, '[t]he development of our historic built environment' is seen as driving 'regeneration, job creation, business growth and prosperity' (Gov.uk, 2016a: 36). Cultural education, then, is contextualised with reference to the value of culture in driving regeneration to secure future local economic growth, linking this regeneration-focused understanding of value back to the perceived need for cultural literacy to build a culturally competent workforce.

There is also an emphasis in the documents on the international sphere. Primarily, this is expressed in relation to the value of cultural literacy to the ability of the UK to exert influence internationally: 'The UK is a leader in soft power. We are respected for our strong and stable democracy, our belief in individual liberty, our diversity and our freedom of expression. Our culture celebrates these values' (Gov. uk, 2016a: 42). Here, international cultural programmes are seen as a way in which to pursue liberal values. Yet, this framing also has an additional economic aspect. Cultural education programmes based in the UK are valued because they produce future citizens who will be ready to maintain and build upon the UK's international reputation and influence within the context of a globalised economy. This is expressed particularly in relation to the UK's departure from the EU, as in the following: 'The UK is a global leader in culture and creativity and, as we leave the European Union, we are committed to maintaining our position on the world stage, to driving creative innovation, and to producing talent that is recognised the world over' (Gov.uk, 2018a: 43).

The way in which cultural education is linked to Brexit is a further indication of the intervention of an economic logic into the sector. As the UK's economic future, as well as its place on the international stage, have become less certain as a result of the decision to withdraw from the EU, there are indications that the impetus to demonstrate the added value that cultural education programmes provide are becoming more important in terms of both justifying public expenditure on such programmes and framing the objectives that such programmes are designed to achieve.

Communitarian cultural education

Alongside the neoliberal thrust of the policies identified in the preceding section sits an overtly communitarian character. Within the policy documents, cultural education is understood as something that is practice-based and 'teaches children how to participate in and to create new culture for themselves', as well as something that is 'knowledge-based and teaches children about the best of what has been created and is currently being created' (Gov.uk, 2013a: 6). The documents reflect the view that the government 'should no more dictate a community's culture than we should tell people what to create or how to create it' (Gov.uk, 2016a: 13). However, it is also noted that '[k]nowledge of great works of art, great music, great literature and great plays, and of their creators, is an important part of every child's education' (Gov. uk, 2016a: 21). Indeed, many of the documents contain a cannon of British literary 'greats', including works by the Brontë sisters, Dickens, Conan Doyle and Darwin, as well as a particular emphasis on the work of Shakespeare. What emerges, then, is an institutional cannon of what counts as 'high' culture, which every young person should have knowledge of, and other forms that young people may choose to engage with based on their own preferences for creative expression.

This narrower, institutional definition of cultural education sits in tension with ambitions expressed in many of the policy documents to tackle the under-representation of particular groups of young people in cultural education activities, and generally an awareness of the barriers to young people accessing such opportunities. For example, it is noted that '[a]lthough there have been some notable improvements there remain gaps with black and minority ethnic and disabled people consistently under-represented in arts, heritage and museum engagement' (Gov.uk, 2018a: 20). Stated ambitions to tackle such under-representation focus predominantly on including young people from diverse backgrounds into the narrower, institutionalised cannon of what constitutes culture, such as classical music or ballet, rather than redefining the cannon to reflect demographic diversity.

This focus on a sense of shared culture is mirrored in relation to shared history and heritage. Activities such as visits to museums, galleries, monuments and historic sites are intended to 'celebrate our nation's rich heritage' (Gov.uk, 2018a: 8), with heritage understood in strongly national terms, as in the following: 'All young people should know about our national icons and understand the key points in our history that have shaped our national character and culture. We will support specific programmes to commemorate the events and people that make our nation what it is today' (Gov.uk, 2013a: 8). These 'national icons' include individuals such as Queen Victoria, Emily Davison and Florence Nightingale[5] (Gov.uk, 2013b), and particular emphasis is also given to commemorating the First World War. In part, this can be explained by the timing of the data collection in relation to the centenary of the First World War but it also reflects the way in which history and heritage is conceived of within cultural education with a specific narrative of British history at its centre, where the aim is to 'know and understand the history of these islands as a coherent, chronological narrative, from the earliest times to the present day: how people's lives have shaped this nation and how Britain has influenced and been influenced by the wider world' (Gov.uk, 2013b: 1).

Where the study of other cultures and histories is considered, this is primarily as a means through which to cast the British experience in international perspective, rather than for other cultures to be studied in and of themselves. For example, in England, young people study Ancient Greece in school to examine its 'influence on the western world' and then study a non-European society 'that provides contrasts with British history' (Gov.uk, 2013b: 5). The local experience of national histories, such as Anglo-Saxon and Roman cultures, is also emphasised, alongside internationally recognised world heritage sites. For example, national parks are understood to be 'the soul of Britain. They are the centre of our imagination. When people think of Britain, wherever they are, they imagine these landscapes', which 'tell the story of our nation' (Gov.uk, 2016b: 2). Returning to the institutional definition of culture identified earlier, the focus on history and heritage expressed in the documents shows that this definition is also, first and foremost, national, with learning about specifically British histories and cultures being the main priority for cultural education.

It is apparent from these findings, then, that to conceptualise cultural education is also to conceptualise the relationship between culture and particular forms of collective identity. Through statements about 'great' works of art and about national history and heritage, the analysis suggests the importance of a particular expression of British culture sitting at the heart of cultural education policy. However, this expression is distinctly different in the Welsh policy documents, where mentions of 'Britain' are far less frequent. Rather, the emphasis is specifically on Wales and Wales' place in the world as a 'unique country, with its own culture, language and government' (Welsh Government, 2008g: 5). The aim of cultural education is to 'celebrate and conserve Wales' outstanding heritage' (Welsh Government, 2008c: 11) through engagement in heritage and traditions specific to Welsh culture (Welsh Government, 2008a). Particular emphasis is placed on religion as a part of the national culture, 'allowing learners to appreciate the significance, value and impact of the rich Christian heritage and dynamic multi-faith composition of Wales past and present' (Welsh Government, 2008d: 8), contributing to a uniquely Welsh focus of policy ambitions for cultural education. While the institutional definition of culture embedded within cultural education is still understood in strongly national terms in the Welsh documents and, as such, the function of cultural education – to educate young people about *national* culture – remains the same, the expression of what counts as national is different. These multiple understandings of the national are a direct consequence of the multinational character of the UK.

A focus on shared national culture is also found in relation to an emphasis on 'fundamental British values', guidance in relation to which was introduced in 2014 and placed a duty on all schools and other providers of educational activities to promote these values as part of the wider 'Prevent' strategy that aims to stop the radicalisation that is seen to underpin the occurrence of terrorist attacks in the UK (Gov. uk, 2011). One of these values is 'mutual respect and tolerance of those with different faiths and beliefs' (Gov.uk, 2014: 5), with schools required to ensure that young people 'be encouraged to regard people of all faiths, races and cultures with respect and tolerance' (Gov.uk, 2014: 4). This emphasis is also found in the conceptualisation of citizenship education in England, where young people explore 'diverse national, regional, religious and ethnic identities in the United Kingdom and the need for mutual understanding' (Gov.uk, 2013c: 3). This emphasis on tolerance and mutual understanding can be understood in light of the emergence of these agendas from securitised concerns about radicalisation following a rise in terrorism in major English cities, as well as from a longer-standing perception that as a result of multiculturalism, these cities were becoming increasingly divided and that this was driving social exclusion (see also Cantle, 2012).

Again, there is variation here with regards to devolved contexts. In the Welsh data, greater emphasis is evident on developing Welsh young people as global citizens. For example, it is '[t]hrough engaging, practical and integrated activities' that 'children can learn more about themselves, other people and the world around them and develop an understanding of their rich cultural and religious heritage in Wales' (Welsh Government, 2008d: 12). This engagement with diverse cultures is framed both in terms of the cultural diversity to be found in Wales (Welsh Government, 2008b, 2008d) and in terms of diverse cultures around the world (Welsh Government, 2008e, 2008h, Gov.uk, 2017a). Educational providers are framed as having a 'responsibility to help students understand that their fate is inextricably linked to the lives and decisions of others around the world' (Welsh Government, 2008i: 5). The aim is to develop 'in every learner a sense of personal and cultural identity that is receptive and respectful towards others', preparing them for 'life as global citizens' (Welsh Government, 2008f: 6). However, this commitment coexists alongside the aforementioned distinctly nationalist institutional definition of Welsh heritage and culture.

For Northern Ireland, mentions of a distinctly Northern Irish collective culture are sparser than in the Welsh or British cases, with the main emphasis placed on understanding cultural differences within communities in Northern Ireland. For example, this involves 'knowing about aspects of their cultural heritage, including the diversity of cultures that contribute to Northern Ireland', at the same time as 'discussing the causes of conflict in their community, and how they feel about it' (CCEA, 2007: 95). This distinct emphasis has arisen in Northern Ireland as a country that has recently experienced significant civil conflict and, here, intercultural learning has therefore taken on a specific meaning and purpose to build understanding between communities. It is notable that in policies targeted elsewhere in the UK, sensitivity to other 'difficult pasts', including in relation to colonial legacies and enduring marginalisation, is absent.

Conclusion

These findings highlight the ways in which policy regarding the development of cultural literacy has been conceptualised in the UK over the past decade. In this final section, we discuss these findings, arguing that the functioning of cultural literacy within UK policy can best be understood with reference to a 'neoliberal communitarian' model of governance.

Neoliberal communitarianism is a model of governance which highlights that neoliberalism and communitarianism do not always exist in isolation from one another. Rather, it combines these as two seemingly contradictory threads within the same model: the individualising logics of neoliberalism, which emphasise responsibility and self-regulation (cf Clarke, 2004); alongside the collective focus of communitarianism on shared culture and values (cf Van Leeuwen, 2015). These threads exist in a 'double helix' (Schinkel and Van Houdt, 2010) through which they are deployed simultaneously to responsibilise citizens in order to reduce the perceived burden they present to the state, and to police the nationalist parameters of inclusion and exclusion in diverse contexts (Schinkel and Van Houdt; 2010; Van Houdt et al, 2011; Van Houdt and Schinkel, 2013). The focus of existing research into neoliberal communitarianism has focused, for the most part, on the integration of foreign-born future citizens through citizenship tests and other measures; however, the findings of this research suggest that this model is also shaping the way in which the cultural literacy of young UK-born people as future citizens is imagined in UK policy.

The neoliberal strand of the double helix is evident in the intervention of a neoliberal economic logic into learning about culture and belonging, and this is seen in the lengths to which the policies go in order to demonstrate the 'added value' that cultural education brings to the economy and society. This is explained in direct terms, with reference to how educational programmes can equip young people with the knowledge and skills they need to fill gaps in labour markets in creative industries, and in indirect terms, for example, with reference to boosting the health and well-being of young people and thus reducing public health-care costs, as well as in articulating a vision of culture as an individual pursuit.

It is through these mechanisms that the policies express an aim for cultural literacy to construct 'neoliberal subjects', being responsible for their own choices and capable of self-regulation to become productive contributors to the national economy with little dependence on the state. Within this responsibilising process, the risks associated with growing uncertainty are individualised and removed from state responsibility (Clarke, 2004; Clarke and Newman, 2012; Hammett, 2014). This focus on neoliberal governmentality has its roots in longer-standing trends associated with New Public Management that date back to the late 1970s, which seek to re-conceptualise the role of government as one of steering policy rather than directly managing its implementation. However, it also reflects more recent attempts to reduce the size of the state in response to financial constraints imposed on the public sector in the wake of the post-2008 recession (Skelcher et al, 2013).

In addition to this focus on neoliberal governmentality, the findings also demonstrate that UK policy conceives of learning about culture and belonging as related to specifically national expressions of culture, and it is through this framing that a communitarian form of governance is also evident from the findings. While policy discusses local, sub-national cultures to a more limited extent, the primary thrust of the focus is on the national culture, with scant mention of cultures as they exist internationally or globally. The role of cultural literacy programmes, then, is taken to be to instil in young people a strong awareness and understanding of national culture as it relates to collective, national identity – be that British, Northern Irish, Welsh or Scottish.

This nationalist conceptualisation of cultural literacy can be understood in light of British policy trends over the course of the early 21st century that have emphasised the need to strengthen national identity as a source of binding sentiment in diverse, multicultural communities. This is embodied in the language of 'British values' that began to gain political salience in the early 2000s as a result of the perceived need to strengthen the integration of diverse communities in light of the threat of home-grown terrorism and civil disorder (Crick, 1998; Cantle, 2012; Ragazzi, 2017), and that was then later articulated as 'muscular liberalism', positing that a stronger sense of national identity was needed to prevent communities from becoming isolated from society and thus – it is claimed – more vulnerable to terrorist radicalisation (Basham and Vaughan-Williams, 2013). Commentators have interpreted this as a 'backlash' against the perceived failure of multiculturalism to provide a focus of belonging in diverse societies (Vertovec and Wessendorf, 2010). In the examined period, there has been a marked policy shift away from multiculturalism and towards the strengthening of national belonging through a focus on so-called 'fundamental British values'. It is against this bedrock that we see 'neoliberal communitarian' approaches to cultural learning emerge.

References to cultural practices beyond the nation are primarily treated as 'other' cultures to be compared against 'our' culture. While, on the one hand, this could be understood as a kind of 'global orientation' (Parkeh, 2003) within cultural literacy programmes, whereby young people are encouraged to explore and examine international cultures while remaining grounded in their own national culture, on the other hand, it can also be understood with regard to the ways in which a sense of exceptionalism has long pervaded British identity. Here,

Britain is imagined as advancing liberty and justice both at home and internationally (Atkins, 2015), and this notion of British exceptionalism appears central to how the international is treated in the policy documents, with a particular focus on advancing soft power to promote core liberal values.

In conclusion, these dual strands of neoliberalism and national communitarianism found in the data suggest that cultural literacy policies promote a particular vision of good citizenship through a neoliberal communitarian model of governance. The policies function to construct the parameters of good citizenship by culturally defining the national community to which good citizens subscribe, while, at the same time, placing expectations of self-responsibility and self-regulation on these citizens in a context of neoliberalisation. This analysis mirrors closely the character of integration policies aimed at foreign-born people applying for citizenship, and, in turn, suggests the relevance of the neoliberal communitarian model to understanding the policing of belonging within as well as beyond the state.

Notes

[1] In this article, we use 'neoliberalism' to refer to policies that emphasise the deregulation of the economy, the freedom and self-dependence of the individual, and the retrenchment of the state from the lives of individuals and communities (cf Hall, 2011).

[2] The decision to analyse documents published after 1 January 2007 was made on the basis of criteria set by the wider research project in which this study was based. The date was chosen in order to capture the period within which all countries studied within the context of the project had been members of the EU.

[3] For the purposes of the review, policy was defined as an authoritative statement of a proposed course, principle or codification of government action, which typically states matters of principle and focuses on action (stating what is to be done and by whom).

[4] Had we opted for a wider time period to capture search results, we may have considered policy documents associated with a review of cultural policies undertaken in Scotland in the early years of the 21st century (see, for example, Scottish Executive, 2003). However, as noted, the parameters of the search were framed in relation to wider considerations in the research project of which this analysis formed one part; as such, it was not possible to include these earlier documents.

[5] It is notable that all of the icons listed here are women. While not the focus of this chapter, this is distinctly different to how history has been constructed in other policy documents, for example, in the Life in the UK citizenship test, where British history is presented as male-dominated (cf Brooks, 2013).

References

Aronowitz, St. and Giroux, H. (1985) *Education under siege: Conservative, liberal and radical debate over schooling*, London: Routledge and Kegan Paul.

Atkins, J. (2015) '(Re)Imaging Magna Carta: myth, metaphor and the rhetoric of Britishness', *Parliamentary Affairs*, 69(3): 603–20.

Bagley, W.C. (1934) *Education and emergent man: A theory of education with particular application to public education in the United States*, New York, NY: T. Nelson and Sons.

Basham, V.M. and Vaughan-Williams, N. (2013) 'Gender, race and border security practices: a profane reading of "muscular liberalism"', *British Journal of Politics and International Relations*, 15(4): 509–27.

Bennett, W.L., Wells, C. and Rank, A. (2009) 'Young citizens and civic learning: two paradigms of citizenship in the digital age', *Citizenship studies*, 13(2): 105–20.

Bhambra, G.K. (2015) 'Citizens and others: the constitution of citizenship through exclusion', *Alternatives*, 40(2): 102–14.

Bhandar, D. (2010) 'Cultural politics: disciplining citizenship', *Citizenship Studies*, 14(3): 331–43.

Bosworth, M., Parmar, A. and Vázquez, Y. (2018) *Race, criminal justice, and migration control: Enforcing the boundaries of belonging*, Oxford: Oxford University Press.

Brooks, R. and Holford, J.A. (2009) 'Citizenship, learning and education: themes and issues', *Citizenship Studies*, 13(2): 85–103.

Brooks, T. (2013) 'The Life in the UK test: unfit for purpose?', Durham University report, https://papers.ssrn.com/sol3/papers.cfm?abstract_id=2280329

Bruner, J.S. (1996) *The culture of education* (1st edn), Cambridge, MA: Harvard University Press.

Cantle, T. (2001) 'Community cohesion: a report of the Independent Review Team', Home Office Report, http://tedcantle.co.uk/pdf/communitycohesion%20cantlereport.pdf

Cantle, T. (2012) *Interculturalism: The new era of cohesion and diversity*, Basingstoke: Palgrave Macmillan.

CCEA (2007) 'The Northern Ireland curriculum primary', guidance, http://ccea.org.uk/sites/default/files/docs/curriculum/area_of_learning/fs_northern_ireland_curriculum_primary.pdf

Clark, N. (2015) 'Autumn statement: Department for Culture, Media and Sport's funding cut by over £1bn'. *The Independent* [online] https://www.independent.co.uk/news/uk/politics/autumn-statement-department-for-culturemedia-and-sports-funding-cut-by-over-1bn-a6749081.html.

Clarke, J. (2004) 'Dissolving the public realm? The logics and limits of neoliberalism', *Journal of Social Policy*, 33(1): 27–48.

Clarke, J. and Newman, J. (2012) 'The alchemy of austerity', *Critical Social Policy*, 32(3): 299–319.

Crick, B. (1998) *Education for citizenship and the teaching of democracy in schools*, London: Qualifications and Curriculum Authority.

Cultural Literacy in Europe (no date) 'Meeting the challenge of cultural literacy', http://cleurope.eu/

De Koning, A., Jaffe, R. and Koster, M. (2015) 'Citizenship agendas in and beyond the nation-state: (en)countering framings of the good citizen', *Citizenship Studies*, 19(2): 121–7.

Department for Education (2018) 'Erasmus in the UK if there's no Brexit deal', www.gov.uk/government/publications/erasmus-in-the-uk-if-theres-no-brexit-deal/erasmus-in-the-uk-if-theres-no-brexit-deal

DCMS (Digital, Culture, Media and Sport) Committee (2018) 'The potential impact of Brexit on the cultural industries, tourism and the digital single market', https://publications.parliament.uk/pa/cm201719/cmselect/cmcumeds/365/36502.htm

Giroux, H.A. (2005) *Border crossings – Cultural workers and the politics of education* (2nd edn), London: Routledge.

Gov.uk (2011) 'Prevent strategy 2011', policy paper, www.gov.uk/government/publications/prevent-strategy-2011

Gov.uk (2013a) 'Cultural education', policy paper, www.gov.uk/government/publications/cultural-education

Gov.uk (2013b) 'National curriculum in England: history programmes of study', guidance, www.gov.uk/government/publications/national-curriculum-in-england-history-programmes-of-study

Gov.uk (2013c) 'National curriculum in England: citizenship programmes of study', guidance, www.gov.uk/government/publications/national-curriculum-in-england-citizenship-programmes-of-study

Gov.uk (2013d) 'National curriculum in England: secondary curriculum', statutory guidance, www.gov.uk/government/publications/national-curriculum-in-england-secondary-curriculum

Gov.uk (2014) 'Promoting fundamental British values as part of SMSC in schools', guidance, www.gov.uk/government/publications/promoting-fundamental-british-values-through-smsc

Gov.uk (2015a) 'Arts and culture', policy paper, www.gov.uk/government/publications/2010-to-2015-government-policy-arts-and-culture

Gov.uk (2015b) '2010–2015 government policy: school and college qualifications and curriculum', policy paper, www.gov. uk/government/publications/2010-to-2015-government-policy-school-and-college-qualifications-and-curriculum/2010-to-2015-government-policy-school-and-college-qualifications-and-curriculum

Gov.uk (2016a) 'Culture White Paper', policy paper, www.gov.uk/government/publications/culture-white-paper

Gov.uk (2016b) 'National parks: 8 point plan for England', policy paper, www.gov.uk/government/publications/national-parks-8-point-plan-for-england-2016-to-2020

Gov.uk (2017a) 'Joint statement of the 5th meeting of the UK–China high level people to people dialogue', policy paper, www.gov.uk/government/publications/fifth-meeting-of-the-uk-china-high-level-people-to-people-dialogue-joint-statement

Gov.uk (2017b) 'Libraries shaping the future', guidance, www.gov.uk/government/collections/libraries-shaping-the-future-report-and-case-studies

Gov.uk (2018a) 'Culture is digital', policy paper, www.gov.uk/government/publications/culture-is-digital

Gov.uk (2018b) 'Creative industries sector deal', policy paper, www.gov.uk/government/publications/creative-industries-sector-deal

Hall, S. (2000) 'Who needs identity?', in P. Du Gay, J. Evans and P. Redman (eds) *Identity: A reader*, London: Sage, pp 15–30.

Hall, S. (2011) 'The neo-liberal revolution', *Cultural Studies*, 25(6): 605–728.

Hammett, D. (2014) 'Understanding the role of communication in promoting active and activist citizenship', *Geography Compass*, 8(9): 617–26.

Hartung, C. (2017) 'Global citizenship incorporated: competing responsibilities in the education of global citizens', *Discourse: Studies in the Cultural Politics of Education*, 38(1): 16–29.

Hirsch, E.D. (1988) *Culture and cultural literacy – What every American needs to know* (1st edn), New York, NY: Vintage.

HM Treasury (2010) 'Spending Review 2010'. HM Treasury [online] https://assets.publishing.service.gov.uk/government/uploads/system/uploads/attachment_data /file/203826/Spending_review_2010.pdf.

Hobolt, S.B. (2016) 'The Brexit vote: a divided nation, a divided continent', *Journal of European Public Policy*, 23(9): 1259–1277.

Isin, E.F and Nielsen, G.M. (eds) (2008) *Acts of citizenship*, London: Palgrave Macmillan.

Maine, F., Cook, V and Lähdesmäki, T. (2019) 'Reconceptualizing cultural literacy as a dialogic practice', *London Review of Education*, 17 (3): 384–393.

Moher, D., Shamseer, L., Clarke, M., Ghersi, D., Petticrew, M. Shekelle, P. and Stewart, L. (2015) 'Preferred reporting items for systematic review and meta-analysis protocols (PRISMA-P) 2015 statement', *Systematic Reviews*, 4(1).

National Audit Office (2017) A Short Guide to the Department for Digital, Culture, Media and Sport. London: National Audit Office.

Parkeh, B. (2003) 'Cosmopolitanism and global citizenship', *Review of International Studies*, 29(1): 3–17.

Pollitt, C. (2010) 'Cuts and reforms – public services as we move into a new era', *Society and Economy*, 32(1): 17–31.

Pykett, J., Saward, M. and Schaefer, A. (2010) 'Framing the good citizen', *The British Journal of Politics and International Relations*, 12(4): 523–38.

Ragazzi, F. (2017) 'Countering terrorism and radicalisation: securitising social policy?', *Critical Social Policy*, 37(2): 163–79.

Schinkel, W. and Van Houdt, F. (2010) 'The double helix of cultural assimilationism and neo-liberalism: citizenship in contemporary governmentality', *The British Journal of Sociology*, 61(4): 696–715.

Schweizer, B. (2009) 'Cultural literacy: is it time to revisit the debate?', *Thought & Action*, 25: 51–6.

Scottish Executive (2003) 'Scotland's national cultural strategy: annual report', www.webarchive.org.uk/wayback/archive/2018 0519071202mp_/http://www.gov.scot/Resource/Doc/47063/ 0017720.pdf

Segal, L. (2004) *From literature to cultural literacy*, Basingstoke: Palgrave Macmillan.

Skelcher, C., Flinders, M., Tonkiss, K. and Dommett, K. (2013) 'Public bodies reform by the UK government 2010–2015: initial findings', University of Birmingham, www.sheffield.ac.uk/polopoly_ fs/1.284208!/file/report.pdf

Van Houdt, F. and Schinkel, W. (2013) 'A genealogy of neoliberal communitarianism', *Theoretical Criminology*, 17 (4): 493-516.

Van Houdt, F., Suvarierol, S. and Schinkel, W. (2011) 'Neoliberal communitarian citizenship: current trends towards "earned citizenship" in the United Kingdom, France and the Netherlands', *International Sociology*, 26(3): 408–32.

Van Leeuwen, B. (2015) 'Communitarianism' in G. Mazzoleni (ed.), *The International Encyclopedia of Political Communication*, 2016, Hoboken, NJ: Wiley-Blackwell, pp 180-184.

Vertovec, S. and Wessendorf, S. (2010) *The multiculturalism backlash*, London: Routledge.

Welsh Government (2008a) 'Knowledge and understanding of the world', guidance, https://hwb.gov.wales/curriculum-for-wales-2008/foundation-phase/knowledge-and-understanding-of-the-world

Welsh Government (2008b) 'Moving forward – Gypsy Traveller education', guidance, https://gov.wales/sites/default/files/publications/2018-11/moving-forward-gypsy-traveller-education.pdf

Welsh Government (2008c) 'Wales, Europe and the world', guidance, https://hwb.gov.wales/storage/1a37f791-b5b7-4cb7-9b97-9f0027dd1041/wales-europe-and-the-world.pdf

Welsh Government (2008d) 'National exemplar framework for religious education', guidance, https://hwb.gov.wales/storage/87d294a8-daf2-40d3-b87b-a9cea5104e79/national-exemplar-framework-for-religious-education-for-3-to-19-year-olds.pdf

Welsh Government (2008e) 'Art and design in the national curriculum for Wales', guidance, https://hwb.gov.wales/storage/4b10c73d-a7d6-4f29-b163-c2e53bf326b0/art-and-design-in-the-national-curriculum.pdf

Welsh Government (2008f) 'Personal and social education framework for 7–19 year olds in Wales', guidance, https://hwb.gov.wales/storage/35fae761-054b-4e9b-928c-03e86b3e207f/personal-and-social-education-framework.pdf

Welsh Government (2008g) 'Education for sustainable development and global citizenship: a common understanding for schools', guidance, https://hwb.gov.wales/storage/eaf467e6-30fe-45c9-93ef-cb30f31f1c90/common-understanding-for-school.pdf

Welsh Government (2008h) 'Education for sustainable development and global citizenship: information for teacher trainees and new teachers in Wales', guidance, https://hwb.gov.wales/storage/66a188a2-144c-4584-a223-b371b40f6632/information-for-teacher-trainees-and-new-teachers.pdf

Welsh Government (2008i) 'Education for sustainable development and global citizenship', guidance, https://gov.wales/sites/default/files/publications/2018-02/education-for-sustainable-development-and-global-citizenship-in-the-further-education-sector-in-wales_0.pdf

Woodhouse, H.R. (1989) 'Critical reflections on Hirsch and cultural literacy', *Interchange*, 20(2): 80–9.

Yuval-Davis, N. (2011) *The politics of belonging: Intersectional contestations*, London: Sage.

8

How geographical and ideological proximity impact community youth justice (in)accessibility in England and Wales

Sarah Brooks-Wilson

Introduction

In England and Wales, youth justice is diminishing and diversifying, with increasingly localised delivery serving fewer convicted children in more institutional settings. Although reduced child criminalisation should be broadly celebrated (YJB, 2019d), sectoral cogence is becoming threatened by community sentence dispersal – an unintended consequence that remains opaque in policy terms. Appointment journeys are increasing in distance and complexity, with the *accessibility* policy gap remaining fractured from its higher-profile partner, *location* (YJB, 2010, 2019b; Brooks-Wilson, 2019). This chapter develops knowledge by applying the interdependent concepts of geographical and ideological proximity to youth justice for the first time, unearthing structural inequalities and system injustices in the process (D'Este et al, 2013; Rekers and Hansen, 2015; Phoenix, 2016). Community sentence completion will be evidenced as impacted by different configurations of location, ideology and accessibility, warranting urgent attention. Despite punitive treatment being ideologically outdated, recently revised case management guidance still connects appointment absence with the formal punishment of children (YJB, 2014, 2019d). Contrastingly, inclusive and flexible practice is typical of 'active' institutional types, which this chapter will align with the exonerative turn, within which 'child first' youth justice is seated (Smyth and Hattam, 2002; Haines and Case, 2015; Allars, 2018). Despite being ideologically optimal, 'active' institutional types are not universally apparent, with associated sectoral fragmentation presenting new opportunities for policy innovation, and minimum standards providing a credible solution (Bradshaw et al 2008, Padley et al, 2013; Davis et al, 2016).

This chapter develops new knowledge on youth justice accessibility, using reanalysed empirical data from a research study that took place in 2012 – a point at which austerity was starting to impact the delivery of local services. A total of 28 children and 33 practitioners were accessed in a research project containing two main case studies, with some of the most deprived neighbourhoods and highest community sentence non-completion rates in the country (DCLG, 2011; MoJ, 2012). Findings will examine three areas: how geographical and ideological proximity develop knowledge on sentence completion; problems accessing partner agencies that are not proximate; and how youth offending team (YOT) practitioners facilitate partner agency access. Implications include policy innovation through alternative 'minimum standards' approaches (Bradshaw et al 2008, Padley et al, 2013; Davis et al, 2016), with new opportunities for a malleable, accessibility safety net benefiting marginalised children who remain responsible for increasingly complicated youth justice journeys.

Background context: location and ideology

In England and Wales, children's community sentences are complex in terms of location and ideology. The Crime and Disorder Act 1998 introduced single local multi-agency YOT sites, containing diverse roles essential to children's criminogenic need and offending desistance (HM Government, 1998). Comprehensive entry-point assessments reflect YOT multi-agency expertise, with probation, social work, police, health and education secondees readily available to respond (YJB, 2014). Holistic, individualised treatment is delivered through multiple public, private and charitable organisations that process, punish and support children while encouraging them to repay harm (Burnett and Appleton, 2004). Broader social, economic, political and technological factors also shape youth justice (Yates, 2012; Haines and Case, 2018), allied services and the towns and cities that provide the backdrop. Since contemporary system inception in 1998 (HM Government, 1998), community sentences have encompassed services within *and* beyond their own multi-agency operations. For example, YOT-based staff provide support for educational (re)integration and family problems, while legal provision (such as youth courts or weekend police contact) is accessed at source. Although celebrated as holistic, this multitude of purposes and providers raises questions for a diaspora of convicted children attempting to meet compulsory attendance requirements (YJB, 2014, 2019d).

Structural inequalities and system injustices can remain poorly detected through the customary, system-oriented 'youth justice studies' lens, suggesting innovative knowledge generation to be important (Phoenix, 2016). To assess whether youth justice is cogent, it is necessary to reflect on where and how it is delivered, warranting the application of institutional geography. Addressing ideology and location, geography *in* institutions examines policies, practices and institutional norms, whereas geography *of* institutions is concerned with 'geographical patterns of social and spatial separation' (Valentine, 2001: 141; see also Manion and Flowerdew, 1982). Institutional geography provides opportunities to examine intended and unintended policy outcomes (Manion and Flowerdew, 1982), with three institutional types containing new explanatory potential (Smyth and Hattam, 2002; see also Table 8.1). The demise of the young offender and the rise of 'child first' (Haines and Case, 2015; Allars, 2018) corresponds with a shift from the punitive to the 'exonerative turn' (Brooks-Wilson, 2019: 3), though policy detail is still emerging. The shift aligns with 'active' institutional types that are inclusive, flexible and child-centred (see column 1 of Table 8.1), while also suggesting the outdatedness of 'aggressive' institutions with expectations of strict adherence to imposed requirements (Smyth and Hattam, 2002; see also column 3 of Table 8.1). Yet, the complex of youth justice purposes and providers raises questions about divergent ideological positions, and inadvertently 'passive', sectoral inconsistencies (see column 2 of Table 8.1).

Table 8.1: A typology of children's institutional disengagement

	1. Active	2. Passive	3. Aggressive
Inclusion/ exclusion	Those who do not traditionally fit are welcome	Eased out	Removal of troublemakers
Flexibility	Flexible timetabling	Inconsistent treatment	Compliance demanded
Curriculum construction	Negotiated around children's lives	Mismanaged	Hierarchical
Behaviour management	Children set the agenda	Attempts to prioritise the child are inadequate	Compliance expected

Source: Smyth and Hattam (2002: 381)

When assessing youth justice cogence, the relational concept of proximity is useful. Its connecting of geographical (locational) and ideological proximity provides new opportunities to scrutinise the interdependency of geography *of* and *in* institutions (Boschma, 2005). Close *geographical* proximity can enhance policy and practice, with increased opportunities to synthesise institutional norms through 'repeated exchanges' (Rekers and Hansen, 2015: 245) and chance encounters. Equally, close *ideological* alignment has the capacity to compensate for geographical distance (D'Este et al, 2013). Institutional proximity is particularly useful to consider as it explains how individual and group action can be constrained or enabled through the regulation of practice (Boschma, 2005). When balancing geography and ideology, 'proximity dynamics' (Boschma, 2005) emphasise the importance of optimising (rather than maximising) proximity to promote operational effectiveness (Broekel and Boschma, 2012). Excessive institutional proximity has the capacity to limit innovation and new ideas, while promoting inertia. Yet, a lack of institutional proximity can be equally problematic, with cohesion, communication and collective action potentially inhibited (Boschma, 2005). In the event of operational obstructions, a 'proximity gap' (Naudé, 2008: 2) can arise, with institutional effectiveness impeded by physical barriers (including distance, borders and transport costs) and a lack of institutional investment or demand (such as from low population density). Subsequently, questions can be raised about the need for the youth justice complex to balance youth justice geography and ideology, with close operational proximity not necessarily optimal (Smyth and Hattam, 2002; YJB, 2010, 2019b, 2019c).

Community sentence diversity and dispersal

In England and Wales, youth justice is being restructured, with proximity becoming increasingly varied. Diverse delivery is now actively endorsed at around 150 YOTs, with a departure from uniform national standards, mandatory YOT structures and managerialist performance indicators (Byrne and Brooks, 2015; YJB, 2019c). Comprehensive and cogent youth justice remains important, with it recently restated as 'vital that health, education, social care and other services form part of an integrated, multi-agency response to a child's offending' (Taylor, 2016: 3; see also HM Government, 1998). Children have been increasingly subject to maximum diversion and minimum intervention from the formal system (McAra and McVie, 2007), with community sentences falling from 64,904 to 15,635 between 2008 and 2018 (YJB, 2019b).

The subsequent reduction of YOT practitioners within this unchanging operational area suggests that staff coverage is thinning, with 19,063 YOT practitioners in 2008/09 dropping to 5,801 in 2017 (YJB, 2010, 2019a). Locally, operational divergence is increasingly apparent as some discreet YOT sites remain, while others become absorbed into larger (child- or youth-oriented) services. Practice delivery permeates some local authority settings through children's centres, with other areas merging or becoming operationally aligned with neighbours (Taylor, 2016). Although new opportunities for effectiveness are being harnessed, pockets of excellence are not indicative of overarching system cogence, with the localised effects of sectoral shrinkage still remaining unclear.

Geographical (locational) proximity is diminishing within the contemporary system, raising questions about optimal proximity and the changing relationship between location and ideology (Boschma, 2005; Broekel and Boschma, 2012). The widespread return of YOT secondees to parent organisations has resulted in a reduction of staff from children's services, probation, police, health, education, Connexions and 'other' areas, dropping from 2,745 in 2008/09 to 827 by 2017 (YJB, 2010, 2019a). Educational expertise has also fallen from 228 to 37.5 staff in the nine years since 2008/09 (YJB, 2019a), raising questions about adequate support and signposting in this priority area. Accessing parent organisations at source now makes practical sense as well-populated multi-agency YOT teams have become less justified. Yet, 'holistic' AssetPlus entry assessments and their broad sentence responses (YJB, 2014) require a wealth of specialist services that are increasingly seated beyond YOTs. YOT practitioners have a commitment to preventing child offending and reoffending, particularly by ensuring that 'services are effectively co-ordinated [and that] the number of staff with whom the child is expected to engage is manageable [while] not overloading the child with services, staff members and activities' (YJB, 2019d). Yet, alongside other economic imperatives (Yates, 2012; Haines and Case, 2018), population shrinkage has inadvertently increased accessibility requirements, with the increase in non-YOT site visits raising questions about the capacity to achieve cogent youth justice.

Significant economic constraints have raised coverage concerns for YOTs and partner agencies, with the local authority budgetary shortfall for children's social care estimated to reach £3 billion by 2024/25, for example (LGA, 2019). Health and social care funding is likely to impact children with complex needs, with rising Child and Adolescent Mental Health Service (CAMHS) assessment and treatment waiting periods providing one example of inadequate coverage. For example, South

West Yorkshire has 190 children on the waiting list for vital CAMHS support, with 53 children waiting over a year in Berkshire (Moore and Gammie, 2018). Many convicted children also struggle with mainstream education, making flexible pupil referral unit (PRU) delivery a common choice. Yet, alternative education is accessed by a minority of children and so has never been in plentiful supply. For example, in Wakefield, one PRU is available to one child at any one time within a 339-square-mile rural catchment area that has inevitable pockets of poor transport coverage (ONS, 2015; Wakefield Pupil Referral Units, 2019). Yet, questions remain about the ease of accessibility for children in different locality settings, with the dispersal and diversification of youth justice making retracted provision increasingly difficult to understand.

The built estate can only lag behind dramatic youth justice population change at a less responsive rate, giving rise to unintended (in)accessibility consequences. The custodial estate provides recent evidence, with a reduction in child custody meaning:

> a smaller youth custodial estate, but one which has been arrived at by adaptation of an existing unsatisfactory estate rather than by design. Having fewer youth custodial establishments means that on average children are now accommodated further from home, increasing journey times to and from court and undermining efforts at resettlement. (Taylor, 2016: 36)

Emerging media reports suggest 'adaptation' is not a problem exclusive to custody, with 50 per cent youth court site closures over the last nine years making children's journeys longer and more complicated (MoJ, 2016; Pidd et al, 2019). The youth justice population is overwhelmingly poor, with evidence suggesting constrained travel choices to be locally varied, while highly detrimental for youth justice sentence completion (Brooks-Wilson, 2019). Differences in population density, urbanisation and service dispersal are likely to produce distinctive (in)accessibility problems that remain opaque through the prevailing policy gap. This raises further questions about whether geographical and ideological proximity can be sufficiently rebalanced to maintain system cogence in the context of built estate 'adaptation'.

If children were not punished or disconnected from vital services when late for community sentence appointments, journey problems might be less concerning. At present, the policy gap on youth justice accessibility means that the only place journeys appear (or indicators of their lack of success) is in case management guidance for community sentence non-compliance, and two short questions on the lengthy AssetPlus entry point assessment (YJB, 2014, 2019d). At present, just three absence instances can result in sentence review, return to court and escalation, which can mean entering custody for some children (SGC, 2009). In other cases, vital service withdrawal can prolong unmet needs and offending behaviours, while impeding life quality in the long term. Yet, the punitive–exonerative paradigm shift has provided unexploited opportunities for policy innovation. Minimum standards (Bradshaw et al 2008, Padley et al, 2013; Davis et al, 2016) promote full societal participation through the identification and delivery of malleable support that accounts for local peculiarities (for further discussion, see Brooks-Wilson, 2019). This approach would address difficult-to-navigate youth justice, which remains at odds with the 'exonerative turn' (Brooks-Wilson, 2019: 3) that puts the 'child first' (Haines and Case, 2015; Allars, 2018). Consequently, policies that assume child absence culpability can be suggested as outdated, with the accompanying policy gap on accessibility rendering the problem completely opaque, despite the complex of growing structural barriers.

Methods

Youth justice geographies can reflect different interest groups, with the potential for dominant parties to inadvertently cement the social adversity of others. This makes it important to understand practice-based accounts of accessibility problems as the 'constitutive role of movement within the workings of most social institutions and social practices [focuses] on the organization of power around systems of governing mobility and immobility at various scales' (Sheller, 2018: 19). Mobilities research can unlock underexplored, diverse and socially situated experiences (Sheller and Urry, 2006; Ferguson, 2016), suggesting its relevance at the youth justice periphery. Policy-focused research is inherently political and focused on the production of knowledge for action (Bechhofer and Paterson, 2000), critiquing dominant discourses using strategic voices and end-user experiences (Holland and Blackburn, 1998). This is important because 'how mobility issues are identified, defined and presented' produces a 'socially accepted construction of reality' (Shafer, 2018: 13). In terms of position, this inductive research examines contradictions apparent when fusing theoretical knowledge on proximity with youth justice policy and practice. Although findings are not generalisable to a broader population, they uncover a new social phenomenon that remains unacknowledged in a youth justice policy context.

A qualitative research project was undertaken involving a pilot and then two case studies located in post-industrial towns – one previously permeated with coal mines and the other with cotton mills. Mining Town was larger, with 20 per cent rural land, compared with just 5 per cent in compact Mill Town (Defra, 2009). The following three questions formed part of a larger-scale research project that developed knowledge on convicted children's youth justice mobilities within an institutional geography context. Reanalysed data were used to address the following questions:

- Is the changing structure of youth justice likely to impede community sentence accessibility?
- Do movement, ideology and location interact to improve or impede community sentence accessibility?
- Do 'active' institutional types that operate within the 'exonerative turn' support cogent 'child first' youth justice?

Examination of youth justice accessibility necessitated contact with children who were not completing youth justice journeys and were experiencing economic hardship, making existing youth justice and social deprivation data pertinent to use (DCLG, 2011; MoJ, 2012). Although absence is a contributory factor for youth justice order breakdown, its exact extent is unknown, making 'breach of a court order' data the closest available proxy measure (YJB, 2019b). The two case-study locations had breach rates that were two-and-a-half times the national average, and some of the very highest in England and Wales (MoJ, 2012). The index of multiple deprivation was then used to locate participants experiencing problems found within the youth justice population, such as employment, education and health deprivation (DCLG, 2011). Adverse post-industrial effects were evident in both case-study areas, with rates of workless families with children above the national average, and around half the neighbourhoods within the fifth most deprived in the country for employment, education, skills and training. In Mill Town, health deprivation was especially significant, with nearly two thirds of neighbourhoods within the fifth most deprived in the country (ONS, 2010).

After piloting, two qualitative mixed-methods case studies were undertaken during the summer of 2012, with a total of 28 children and 33 practitioners participating in nine focus groups and 24 interviews.

Stratified sampling was used to capture the views and experiences of different practitioners working with children on the least serious community orders, through to those on the verge of custody. Child participants were accessed through practitioners, with attempts to vary gender, ethnic background and the severity of sentence. Perhaps unsurprisingly, prevailing non-attendance rates resulted in participant access barriers, and multiple no-contact research visits. Some groups are described as 'hard to reach' in research, with access and engagement barriers including social disadvantage, limited literacy and a reluctance to acknowledge status or engage with 'outsiders' (Benoit et al, 2005; Wilson and Snell, 2010; Brooks-Wilson and Snell, 2012). This research used visual methods to overcome such barriers and elevate children's voices in line with policy priorities (Horton et al, 2009; Kraftl et al, 2012; YJB, 2016). As visual methods generate different sorts of knowledge, a pilot focus group was conducted, with maps and icons eventually chosen.

Research validity was maintained through the accurate representation of different voices, with internal validity achieved through knowledge from different participant positions and previous research on children's problematic institutional journeys (Brooks-Wilson and Snell, 2012). Research dependability was achieved through interim research progress reviews, with the plain English communication of information sheets and informed consent forms supporting robust, ethical data collection (Plain English Campaign, 2009). The chaotic nature of children's lives presented a barrier for parental and carer consent, so youth justice practitioners supported the process. To protect children's safety, practitioners remained present upon request, with research inclusion precluded for those with significant mental ill health, as well as the most serious violent and sexual convictions. Each interview and focus group was recorded and transcribed, with data coded using qualitative data analysis (QDA) software. Existing knowledge informed the initial list of codes and sub-codes, such as with 'transport used: private/public/active'. Codes also emerged during the analysis, such as 'transport conflict adults' and 'confidence' (Silverman, 1993). Thematic analysis was then undertaken to arrange new empirical data into a logical structure.

Findings

These findings start by examining youth justice geographical and ideological proximity, with 'active' approaches argued to be aligned with the exonerative turn, within which 'child first' youth justice is situated (Boschma 2005, Brooks-Wilson 2019, Haines and Case, 2015, Allars 2018). Then, geographical and ideological inconsistencies will be highlighted, with evidence of difficulties accessing partner agencies. Finally, evidence will suggest that YOT practitioners facilitate partner agency access alongside the delivery of their own appointments. These findings raise questions for an increasingly diverging and dispersing sector (YJB, 2010, 2019a, 2019b; Byrne and Brooks, 2015), suggesting (in)accessibility to be increasingly problematic and in need of urgent policy attention.

Close geographical proximity and 'active' ideology support sentence completion

In terms of optimal proximity (Broekel and Boschma, 2012), this research found close geographical proximity and 'active' multi-agency practice alignment to benefit children (Smyth and Hattam, 2002):

> 'All the social work teams work within this building, so it's like – in that respect – arguably a one-stop kind of shop. So, so yeah, so many times, I'll go downstairs, and if I'm working with a young person who's in care, you know, I might walk downstairs and I might bump into him or her, and they're not here to see me, they're here to see the social worker ... when I'm working with a young person, if their life is in crisis, yeah, and in terms of engaging him or her on the, the court order, I'll share my appointments. So, if I know that by seeing the social worker or any other professional, it would benefit that young person, I would say: "Right, if you see the social worker, or you see the Connexions officer, or you see the mental health worker, as far as I'm concerned, that's an appointment with me, and it's one of your three." So, in that respect, we can be, we can be quite flexible, and even if it's not directly on the court order, if their life is in crisis, and they need that intervention of support, that's what I'll do.' (YOT practitioner, Mill Town interview 1)

This finding provides evidence of chance encounters facilitating 'child first' youth justice, with service accessibility and sentence progression facilitated (Haines and Case, 2015; Rekers and Hansen, 2015; Allars, 2018). When services were not in close geographical proximity, this research found ideological alignment to facilitate optimal proximity, providing evidence of a symbiotic relationship through shared appointments at different sites (Smyth and Hattam, 2002; D'Este et al, 2013; Rekers and Hansen, 2015):

> 'As you go in [to school] to meet [the young person], a teacher usually comes and meets you and you get to say: "How are they doing? Has there been any issues, anything we need to address in this particular session?" So, then you tailor your work around, if there's been something there, or address that first so you are seen to – then the young person knows as well because it helps them see, well, we've got a good relationship with the school, as a youth offending team. Even if it's not part of their contract as well, because we're trying to support, you know, positive roles, positive norms for them as well.' (Tier 1 YOT practitioner, Mining Town interview 4)

This research found flexible YOT timetabling to support sentence engagement and completion more broadly, with children's commitments taken into account to facilitate the inclusion of those who do not 'traditionally fit' (Smyth and Hattam, 2002): "My appointments, where I do offending behaviour and programmes, I try to make it as amenable to a young person's time – not mainly morning – 3.30 if they're in training. After five if they're at school, if they're in a job. So, I think I am quite flexible" (YOT practitioner, Mill Town interview 4). Yet, such flexibility was acknowledged as being open to misinterpretation, raising questions about excessively close ideological proximity between children and practitioners being suboptimal in the context of timetabling (Smyth and Hattam, 2002; Broekel and Boschma, 2012):

> 'Rightly or wrongly, if a young person knows were flexible, and [knows that] we'll alter [the appointment] as much as possible, if a young person missed a session, they'd probably ring up and say: "Oh, I couldn't make it, can you rearrange it?", knowing us to be flexible. So, it may be we're shooting ourselves in the foot by being really flexible!' (YOT practitioner, Mining Town interview 3)

This finding also raises questions about the ideological fragmentation of community sentences and contrasting attendance expectations within different services. This research found collaboration with non-statutory partner agencies to be crucial for the delivery of accessible youth justice. In some cases, being proximate to children's home addresses (rather than the YOT office) was most important, with the shared 'active' ideological positioning of YOTs and children's centres promoting sentence completion through 'child first' youth justice (Smyth and Hattam, 2002; Haines and Case, 2015; Allars, 2018):

> 'It's quite easy. We're lucky in Mill Town, we're scattered with community centres, Sure Start centres, community centres.... What we do is basically pick up the phone and ring the centre up and say, "Can we book a room for Wednesday for four o'clock?", and it's as straightforward as that really. Which is convenient, so were really lucky and it makes life really easy because, sometimes, years and years ago, you could usually spend an hour trying to kind of arrange a facility to meet a young person. But now we've got good resources in the community – good centres. All we do is, like I say, make a phone call, book the room.'
> (YOT manager, Mill Town interview 2)

These findings demonstrate the symbiotic relationship between geography and ideology (Boschma, 2005), with close proximity and 'active' institutional types supporting cogent youth justice. These findings will now consider proximity consistency between YOT operations and partner agencies. Implications will be raised for dispersing youth justice (YJB, 2010, 2019b), with the interdependence of accessibility and location also established.

Difficulties accessing non-YOT partner agencies

The following findings problematise the dispersal of youth justice and increasing requirements to visit partner agencies (YJB, 2010, 2019b). In particular, use of available sites raises questions about whether ideological proximity adequately compensates for built estate adaptation when maintaining accessibility (MoJ, 2016; Taylor, 2016; Pidd et al, 2019). Questions can also be raised about a wholesale shift to cogent, 'child first' youth justice being threatened by entrenched institutional norms within partner agencies (Haines and Case, 2015; Allars, 2018; YJB, 2019d). Before examining youth justice partner agencies, consideration of YOT accessibility is worthwhile. Evidence of significant YOT malleability suggests alignment with well coordinated, 'child first' youth justice (Haines and Case, 2015; Allars, 2018; YJB, 2019d): "So, if I put together YOT appointments, anything to do with education, reparation, drugs, money advice and community panels – they're all delivered, generally speaking, by staff based here. And staff who are generally very comfortable with the idea of being that bridge between – resolving the problem of transport" (YOT manager, Mining Town interview 6).

Contrastingly, this research found children's community sentence completion to be impeded by partner agency inaccessibility and attendance management strategies. In particular, increased risk of punishment and entrenchment raises questions about youth justice cogence in an increasingly dispersed system (HM Government, 1998; YJB, 2010, 2019b, 2019c, 2019d; Taylor, 2016):

> 'So, health, mental health, housing and social support – those agencies would expect the young person to be the thing that provided the elasticity, to go back to the previous conversation. There are some – police and court – police will go and get you. I mean, it generally involves the phrase "I'm arresting you for …", but they'll come and get you.' (YOT manager, Mining Town interview 6)

This finding raises questions about growing accessibility requirements for a restructuring youth justice, with ideological variance giving rise to poor sentence cohesion and a 'passive' overarching ideology (Smyth and Hattam, 2002; Boschma, 2005). In particular, this research found problems with community reparation in terms of attendance requirements and appointment locations. Reparation usually took place during weekend mornings to avoid disrupting education, resonating with 'active' institutional timetabling (Smyth and Hattam, 2002). Yet, children were required to undertake independent travel to a pre-agreed collection point, where group travel would then proceed to the main reparation site. Such accessibility arrangements raise questions about ideological confusion, with expectations of high travel dependence and independence in one journey, again giving rise to a 'passive' ideological position (Smyth and Hattam, 2002):

> 'We don't – on reparation, we don't have a policy of, you know, paying their bus fares for them to come … the ethos that we take into consideration is that they've got to

take on some responsibility for their order. They've got to get themselves to a designated place at a designated time and meet their supervisors before they go out on their reparation placements.' (Reparation coordinator, Mining Town interview 5)

Yet, in the context of accessibility, one practitioner confusingly revealed how the discretionary treatment of punctuality at a collection point could be a catalyst for formal 'non-compliance', with a significant impact on sentence completion (YJB, 2014, 2019d):

'Some of my supervisors are ex-military, ex-police. If you're not there at that time, you know, we're going – we're going without you. And it's a missed appointment, you know, so ... I'll tend to be a bit soft and I'll wait while 20 past, or I'll wait while 25 past.' (Reparation coordinator, Mining Town interview 5)

This finding evidences how strict attendance expectations resonate with 'aggressive' institutional positions, and leniency with inclusive 'active' approaches, with resulting inconsistency producing a contradictory 'passive' approach that seriously undermines children's absence culpability (Smyth and Hattam, 2002; SGC, 2009; YJB, 2014, 2019d).

Education has been identified as a 'criminogenic need' essential for desistance (Taylor, 2016). For children in this research accessing PRUs, built estate adaptation to mainstream educational sites was described as presenting accessibility *barriers* (MoJ, 2016; Taylor, 2016; Pidd et al, 2019):

'What we had before is, we had a pupil referral unit in the town centre, where young people would come to. My professional opinion thinks that worked much better [...] the biggest barrier for us is having a client who has got to catch two buses and a two-hour journey just to get to school, to be put on a three-hour timetable, and then a two-hour journey home. It's one of our biggest barriers we've got about the units.' (Education officer, Mining Town interview 7)

This finding evidences the symbiotic relationship between location and accessibility, suggesting the need to give greater attention to the latter when engaging in built estate adaptation. Complicating things further, the splitting of PRU delivery by year group meant that children with complex needs could not attend the closest, most accessible site:

'We've been told that not every PRU is going to cover both key stages – you can have one PRU that's a key stage four and one that's a key stage three.... We've got a young man who lives in [outlying village with high deprivation] that goes to a PRU seven mile away – six mile away? – wanting to go to his local one when it opens in September in [outlying village with high deprivation]. It's not going to be a key stage four PRU, so he doesn't meet the criteria to be able to go to his local PRU.' (Education officer, Mining Town interview 7)

This finding evidences how ideological distance from 'active', 'child first' YOT operations can exacerbate service accessibility when 'adapting' provision to available sites (Smyth and Hattam, 2002; D'Este et al, 2013; Haines and Case, 2015; Rekers and Hansen, 2015; MoJ, 2016; Taylor, 2016; Allars, 2018; Pidd et al, 2019). Impairing things further, the importance of education was found to justify compulsory attendance requirements, again resonating with aggressive institutional types (Smyth and Hattam, 2002):

'If attendance and behaviour in school is an issue, we put it in a young person's contract. They've to maintain an acceptable level of attendance and behaviour while in education. So that could be at school, it could be at a resource centre, or wherever. Because it's a well-known fact that young people not in education or employment are more at risk of offending.' (YOT practitioner, Mining Town interview 4)

These findings evidence the connection between (re)location and accessibility, demonstrating the need to plug the accessibility policy gap within a restructuring youth justice (YJB, 2014, 2019d). These findings will now evidence how YOT practitioners facilitate accessibility when partner agencies are not geographically or ideologically proximate (Boschma, 2005). Such help will be argued as indicative of a proximity gap through longer journey distances and a lack of local provision (Naudé, 2008), with poor sectoral communication and cohesion giving rise to suboptimal proximity (Broekel and Boschma, 2012).

YOTs facilitate partner agency access

The following findings raise questions about diminishing YOT practitioner coverage being detrimental for partner agency contact and children's community sentence completion (YJB, 2010, 2019b). Geographically dispersed caseloads and services suggest an increase in the demand for accessibility support, though a lack of specific policy detail renders growing youth justice (in)accessibility opaque (YJB, 2014, 2019d). Diverse, localised youth justice suggests children's experiences to be highly varied, presenting difficulties in establishing an overarching assessment of the problem (Byrne and Brooks, 2015; YJB, 2019c). Practitioners in this research described the timetabling of legal procedural activities (such as youth court and police station contacts) as particularly inflexible in time and space, resonating with 'aggressive' institutional types (Smyth and Hattam, 2002) and aligned with the 'punitive' rather than 'exonerative' turn. This was particularly evident when partner agencies lacked institutional proximity, with poor levels of communication, collective action and cohesion (Boschma, 2005): "If a young person's to attend the police station, it's when the police officer can see them. So, there's no negotiation on that ... and obviously court appointments – that's non-negotiable" (YOT practitioner, Mining Town interview 3).

In line with policy priorities (Taylor, 2016; YJB, 2019d), evidence in this research suggests that YOT practitioners provide vital, individualised accessibility support, with ideological polarisation presenting a 'proximity gap' that is detrimental for cogent youth justice (Naudé, 2008; Taylor, 2016; YJB, 2019d):

> 'it has to be in a police station because, obviously, they need to record the interview and things like that. Actually, as well, I helped a young person – I went with a young person as an appropriate adult for the [ID parade] service, which we don't have one in Mining Town, so we had to go to the one in [city 16 miles away] ... there isn't the facilities in Mining Town to do that, so we had to go through to [city 16 miles away] to do that. And I think there's only a couple of places in [city 16 miles away], so that one's quite restrictive in that sense.' (YOT practitioner, Mining Town interview 4)

This finding undermines notions of child absence culpability (YJB, 2014, 2019d), with a proximity gap evident through physical access barriers and a lack of local investment in services (Naudé, 2008). Evidence also suggests that YOT accessibility support extends beyond journey facilitation, with appointment negotiations also supported by YOT practitioners. The need for such support suggests pockets of suboptimal proximity within youth justice, with poor institutional cohesion and ineffective communication again apparent (Boschma, 2005):

> 'I just tried to change a bail appointment for a young person and it was obviously quite difficult. It depended on the man who was seeing them, on his shift, on the times – I couldn't just change it from one to four because the young person was doing something else. So, I suspect police appointments are quite inflexible.' (YOT practitioner, Mill Town interview 4)

Again, this finding evidences contradictory institutional types, with 'active' YOT practice facilitating access to 'aggressively' timetabled institutions (Smyth and Hattam, 2002). This research found a further proximity gap in local emergency housing provision, with accessibility barriers and poor local investment again problematic (Naudé, 2008):

> 'My last young person, he – they shipped him off to [city 16 miles away] in a bed and breakfast, and he lost that placement, so I went to [city 16 miles away] to pick him up. But I had to sit in [city 16 miles away] – ring [the emergency out-of-hours contact number] up to see if they could rehouse him somewhere, and because a lot of our bed and breakfasts that our area uses are out in [city 16 miles away or city ten miles away], I had to wait in that area until I got notification of where they'd found him a bed. So, it's a big barrier.' (YOT practitioner, Mining Town interview 3)

This evidence suggests emergency housing provision to have suboptimal proximity, with distant, poorly aligned services giving rise to poor institutional cohesion and collective action (Boschma, 2005). The prevailing proximity gap (Naudé, 2008) raises serious questions about the punitive–exonerative paradigm shift, and whether youth justice can make a wholesale transition to consider the 'child first'.

Conclusion

A reduction in the criminalisation of children represents real progress for youth justice, with maximum diversion and minimum intervention likely to improve long-term outcomes (McAra and McVie, 2007). Yet, a residual population of convicted children is likely to experience increased sentence completion problems through retracted partner agency provision and protracted accessibility requirements. If the policy gap on accessibility remains, evidence suggests that it will be a growing oversight, with restructuring youth justice increasing the distance and volume of journeys required for community sentence completion. Although the AssetPlus nods towards service access (YJB, 2014), youth justice journeys remain broadly unacknowledged in policy terms, with 'hard-to-reach' children subject to discretionary treatment before becoming detached from essential support or punished (YJB, 2014, 2019d; Brooks-Wilson, 2019). Institutional geography undermines such inequitable treatment (Smyth and Hattam, 2002), suggesting the urgent need to redirect attention towards restructuring youth justice, where accessibility problems are growing.

A broader set of factors is currently exacerbating community sentence (in)accessibility, with the shift to multiple partner agency visits limiting control over where vital contact takes place. The ideological inconsistency of children's community sentences is contributing towards poor overarching cogence, resonating with the less-than-ideal 'passive' institutional type (Smyth and Hattam, 2002). Diminishing youth justice is likely to exert little influence on entrenched ideological positions within partner agencies, with the piecemeal presence of 'active' institutional types raising questions about the feasibility of a wholesale shift to 'child first' youth justice (Haines and Case, 2015; Allars, 2018). Crucial accessibility support is becoming increasingly stretched through changes in YOT practitioner coverage, though increasing localisation means that this is not universal or well understood (YJB, 2010, 2019a). The current economic climate is compounding (in)accessibility problems further, though built estate adaptation (rather than design) provides a cost-effective solution, while being an inevitable outcome of service retraction (Yates, 2012; MoJ, 2016; Taylor, 2016; Haines and Case, 2018; Pidd et al, 2019).

These constraints inform new opportunities, with a lack of manoeuvrability directing attention to youth justice policy and practice. Plugging the policy gap on youth justice accessibility has the potential to improve long-term outcomes for children with complex needs. As such, a credible case for policy innovation can be made, with minimum standards providing a robust alternative to inequitable discretion or rigid, punitive treatment (Bradshaw et al 2008, Padley et al, 2013; Davis et al, 2016; for further discussion, see Brooks-Wilson, 2019). Ideologically, minimum standards are well aligned with 'active' institution types that complement the exonerative turn, within which 'child first' youth justice is seated (Haines and Case, 2015; Allars, 2018). Identifying an accessibility 'basket of goods' before nuancing for different localities, partner agencies and children provides the potential to support community sentence completion (for further discussion, see Brooks-Wilson, 2019). This recommendation would be further enhanced by the removal of absence as a key example of sentence 'non-compliance'. Although there are undoubtedly occasions when children choose not to attend appointments, this chapter evidences the urgent need to redirect greater attention towards a complex structural problem, and away from children with complex needs. Subsequently, the removal of discretionary three-strikes absence sanctions is also strongly recommended (YJB, 2014, 2019d).

Youth justice requires novel ideas to problematise long-standing structural inequalities and system injustices, with the punitive–exonerative paradigm shift making it pertinent to exploit opportunities that progress the 'child first' agenda (Haines and Case, 2015; Phoenix, 2016; Allars, 2018). Drawing together some final recommendations, the achievement of cogent, accessible 'child first' youth justice requires the collective consideration of location, ideology and accessibility, with an initial synthesis of ideas in this chapter suggesting the need for further research (Smyth and Hattam, 2002; Boschma, 2005; Brooks-Wilson, 2019). Poor coordination of these elements can impede accessibility, with long distances, complicated journeys and rigid attendance requirements being highly problematic, for example. Second, non-statutory key partnerships (such as with children's centres) provide legitimate opportunities for effective youth justice, warranting new connections between YOTs and diverse sectors, including transport. Such partnerships could provide new opportunities for meaningful 'child first' youth justice through, for example, the inclusion of children's strategic voice in transport planning. Importantly, findings in this research have a broader relevance beyond youth justice, raising serious questions about the sanctioning of groups with complex needs when absent from services that are difficult to access. As such, it is strongly recommended that the policy status of service accessibility is significantly elevated for hard-to-reach groups more broadly.

Funding

This work was supported by the Economic and Social Research Council (grant number ES/IO26770/1).

Acknowledgements

Particular thanks to Lisa O'Malley for supporting the development of ideas, with further thanks to Barry Goldson, Sharon Grace, Elke Heins, Simon Pemberton and James Rees for providing useful feedback on this or the underpinning research. I am grateful to all of the young people and practitioners who participated in this study. This chapter was written for Beryl Wilson who embodied 'child first'.

References

Allars, C. (2018) 'Child first, offender second, YJ Bulletin', http://youthjusticeboard.newsweaver.co.uk/yots2/1jclwv6p8jk1hm4rdqm uej?email=true&a=11&p=54280325

Bechhofer, F. and Paterson, L. (2000) *Principles of research design in the social sciences*, London: Routledge.

Benoit, C., Jansson, M., Millar, A. and Phillips, R. (2005) 'Community–academic research on hard-to-reach populations: benefits and challenges', *Qualitative Health Research*, 15(2): 263–82.

Boschma, R. (2005) 'Proximity and innovation: a critical assessment', *Regional Studies*, 39(1): 61–74.

Bradshaw, J., Middleton, S., Davis, A., Oldfield, N., Smith, N., Cusworth, L., and Williams, J. (2008) *A minimum income standard for Britain*, York: Joseph Rowntree Foundation.

Broekel, T. and Boschma, R. (2012) 'Knowledge networks in the Dutch aviation industry: the proximity paradox', *Journal of Economic Geography*, 12: 409–33.

Brooks-Wilson, S. (2019) 'Rethinking youth justice journeys: complex needs, impeded capabilities and criminalisation', *Youth Justice Journal*, https://doi.org/10.1177/1473225419893791

Brooks-Wilson, S. and Snell, C. (2012) '"Hard to reach" or "accessible when approached"? Exploring the feasibility and value of sustainable development discussions with marginalized pupil groups', *Children, Youth and Environments*, 22(2): 1–24.

Burnett, R. and Appleton, C. (2004) 'Joined up services to tackle youth crime: a case study in England', *British Journal of Criminology*, 44(1): 34–5.

Byrne, B. and Brooks, K. (2015) *Post-YOT youth justice*, London: Howard League for Penal Reform.

Davis, A., Hill, K., Hirsch, D. and Padley, M. (2016) *A minimum income standard for the UK in 2016*, York: Joseph Rowntree Foundation.

DCLG (Department for Communities and Local Government) (2011) *Indices of deprivation 2010*, London: Department for Communities and Local Government, https://www.gov.uk/government/statistics/english-indices-of-deprivation-2010

Defra (Department for Environment, Food and Rural Affairs) (2009) *Rural urban classification*, London: Department for Environment, Food and Rural Affairs.

D'Este, P., Guy, F. and Iammarino, S. (2013) 'Shaping the formation of university–industry research collaborations: what type of proximity does really matter?', *Journal of Economic Geography*, 13(4): 537–58.

Ferguson, H. (2016) 'Researching social work practice close up: using ethnographic and mobile methods to understand encounters between social workers, children and families', *British Journal of Social Work*, 46: 153–68.

Haines, K. and Case, S. (2015) *Positive youth justice: Children first, offenders second*, Bristol: Policy Press.

Haines, K. and Case, S. (2018) 'The future of youth justice', *Youth Justice*, 18(2): 131–48.

HM Government (1998) *Crime and Disorder Act 1998*, London: HM Government.

Holland, J. and Blackburn, J. (1998) *Whose voice? Participatory research and policy change*, London: Intermediate Technology Publications.

Horton, J., Kraftl, P., Woodcock, A., Newman, M., Kinross, M., Adey, P. and Den Besten, O. (2009) *Involving pupils in school design: A guide for schools*, Coventry: Arts and Humanities Research Council, University of Leicester, University of Northampton, Keele University and Coventry University.

Kraftl, P., Horton, J. and Tucker, F. (2012) *Critical geographies of childhood and youth: Contemporary policy and practice*, Bristol: Policy Press.

LGA (Local Government Association) (2019) 'Explaining variation in spending – children's services', www.local.gov.uk/sites/default/files/documents/Explaining%20Variation%20in%20Spending%20-%20Children%27s%20Services%2C%20Full%20Report_0.pdf

Manion, T. and Flowerdew, R. (1982) 'Introduction: institutional approaches in geography', in R. Flowerdew (ed) *Institutions and geographical patterns*, London: Croom Helm.

McAra, L. and McVie, S. (2007) 'Youth justice? The impact of system contact on patterns of desistance from offending', *European Journal of Criminology*, 4(3): 315–45.

MoJ (Ministry of Justice) (2012) 'Offences resulting in a disposal regionally 2009–10', freedom of information request, 13 February, London: Ministry of Justice.

MoJ (2016) 'Court closures announcement', www.magistrates-association.org.uk/news/court-closures-announcement

Moore, A. and Gammie, J. (2018) *Revealed: Hundreds of children wait more than a year for specialist help*, London: Health Service Journal, www.hsj.co.uk/quality-and-performance/revealed-hundreds-of-children-wait-more-than-a-year-for-specialist-help/7023232.article

Naudé, W. (2008) 'Geography, transport and Africa's proximity gap', *Journal of Transport Geography*, 17: 1–9.

ONS (Office for National Statistics) (2010) 'Neighbourhood statistics', www.neighbourhood.statistics.gov.uk/dissemination/LeadAreaSearch.do?a=7&r=1&i=1001&m=0&s=1267887517622&enc=1&areaSearchText=&areaSearchType=140&extendedList=true&searchAreas=Search

ONS (2015) 'Population density tables', www.ons.gov.uk/peoplepopulationandcommunity/populationandmigration/populationestimates/datasets/populationdensitytables

Padley, M., Bevan, M.A., Hirsch, D. and Tunstall, B. (2013) *Minimum acceptable place standards*, Loughborough and York: Centre for Research in Social Policy, Loughborough University and Centre for Housing Policy, University of York.

Phoenix, J. (2016) 'Against youth justice and youth governance, for youth penalty', *British Journal of Criminology*, 56: 123–40.

Pidd, H., Parveen, N., Wolfe-Robinson, M. and Halliday, J. (2019) 'Youth court system in "chaos" says children's commissioner', www.theguardian.com/society/2019/nov/03/youth-court-system-in-chaos-says-childrens-commissioner

Plain English Campaign (2009) *How to write in plain English*, New Mills: Plain English Campaign.

Rekers, J. and Hansen, T. (2015) 'Interdisciplinary research and geography: Overcoming barriers through proximity', *Science and Public Policy*, 42: 242–54.

SGC (Sentencing Guidelines Council) (2009) *Overarching principles – Sentencing youths*, London: Sentencing Guidelines Council.

Shafer, J. (2018) 'Mobilization – a new concept in analysing transport system dynamics, or how security and mobility are melded to trigger change', *Applied Mobilities*, https://doi.org/10.1080/23800127.2018.1488201

Sheller, M. (2018) 'Theorising mobility justice', *Tempo Social*, 30(2): 17–34.

Sheller, M. and Urry, J. (2006) 'The new mobilities paradigm', *Environment and Planning*, 38: 207–26.

Silverman, D. (ed) (1993) *Qualitative research: Theory, method and practice*, London: Sage.

Smyth, J. and Hattam, R. (2002) 'Early school leaving and the cultural geography of British high schools', *British Educational Research Journal*, 28(3): 375–97.

Taylor, C. (2016) *Youth justice review: Final report*, London: Youth Justice Board.

Valentine, G. (2001) *Social geographies: Space and society*, Harlow: Pearson.

Wakefield Pupil Referral Units (2019) 'Wakefield pupil referral units', www.wakefieldprus.co.uk/

Wilson, S.J. and Snell C. (2010) '"Bad for the penguins … because they need ice and that to live on": an exploratory study into the environmental views, concerns and knowledge of socially disadvantaged young people', *Journal of Youth Studies*, 13(2): 151–67.

Yates, J. (2012) 'What prospects youth justice? Children in trouble in the age of austerity', *Social Policy and Administration*, 46(4): 432–47.

YJB (Youth Justice Board) (2010) 'Youth justice annual statistics: 2008 to 2009, workload tables 08-09, Appendix A resource tables', www.gov.uk/government/statistics/youth-justice-annual-statistics-2008-2009

YJB (2014) 'AssetPlus model document', https://assets.publishing.service.gov.uk/government/uploads/system/uploads/attachment_data/file/364092/AssetPlus_Model_Document_1_1_October_2014.pdf

YJB (2016) *Participation strategy: Giving young people a voice in youth justice*, London: Youth Justice Board.

YJB (2019a) 'Youth justice statistics: 2017–2018, youth justice statistics additional annexes, annex F – resources in YOTs', www.gov.uk/government/statistics/youth-justice-statistics-2017-to-2018

YJB (2019b) 'Youth justice statistics: 2017–2018 supplementary tables ch5 sentencing of children', www.gov.uk/government/statistics/youth-justice-statistics-2017-to-2018

YJB (2019c) 'Standards for children in the youth justice system 2019', https://assets.publishing.service.gov.uk/government/uploads/system/uploads/attachment_data/file/780504/Standards_for_children_in_youth_justice_services_2019.doc.pdf

YJB (2019d) 'Financial accounts', https://assets.publishing.service. gov.uk/government/uploads/system/uploads/attachment_data/ file/820763/YJB_Annual_Report_and_Accounts_2018-19_pages_ web.pdf

Part III
Austerity

Marco Pomati

The economic downturn of the late 2000s and early 2010s, now known as the Great Recession, led to a major fall in economic output that, combined with state support for the financial sector and fiscal stimuli, increased government debt and deficits around the world. This global financial crisis was followed in countries like the UK by a period of austerity, advocated on the grounds that government needed a period of fiscal consolidation. The theme of austerity has been at the forefront of most Social Policy conferences and publications but the impact of austerity on most aspects of life in the UK has been so great that it led to the damning report by the United Nations Rapporteur Professor Philip Alston and revived epidemiological interest in the effects of economic policies of austerity on suicides, morbidity and life expectancy (Karanikolos et al, 2013). Part III of the volume provides a critical review of some of the key policies implemented as part of this period of austerity and the implications that they have had on some of the most vulnerable sections of the population.

Over the past ten years, the government has deliberately chosen to make working-age benefits substantially lower through policies such as changes in social security indexation from retail prices to consumer prices, the benefit cap, the bedroom tax, the two-child limit and caps to local housing allowances. The Institute for Fiscal Studies estimates that social security cuts led to social security expenditure levels in 2019/20 that were £39 billion lower than they would have been without these cuts (Crawford and Zaranko, 2019). This was combined with an increase in benefit sanctions and the disruptive rollout of Universal Credit. In Chapter 9, Donald Hirsch explores the evolution of the level of benefits entitlement of different UK families and whether these are enough to meet minimum needs. Hirsch uses the Minimum Income Standard, a family-specific budget derived by iterative group discussions between people from a wide range of socio-economic backgrounds, supplemented by selective inputs from nutrition, domestic and transportation experts. The result of these discussions is a set of costed baskets of material and social needs required to reach a minimum acceptable standard of living, which can then be compared to income safety nets provided by the government. Hirsch finds that since 2010, safety net benefits have declined but pensioners' entitlements are much closer to what they need (just over 90 per cent). This ties into the widespread perception that pensioners have been protected from the worst effects of austerity. On average, families with children get slightly over half and singles without children only a third. Hirsch shows that for a single person aged over 35 living in a rented one-bedroom flat on means-tested Jobseeker's Allowance, once utility bills have been paid, it is now a financial struggle to maintain a reasonable diet, let alone a decent life. Hirsch concludes that although the UK's safety net benefits have never maintained a systematic link with need, they have recently become less adequate and more arbitrary. He provides a strong case for strengthening the link between basic household needs and government safety net benefits.

In the UK, austerity has not been limited to the provision of social security. Most government departmental budgets were cut and there was a clear shift in responsibility from central to local government, which also had its budgets slashed. The cuts to local government have also resulted in a marked decrease in the provision of key services, which is an issue explored by Emma Davidson in Chapter 10. Davidson finds that libraries can be important spaces for support workers to meet clients, as well as for those with fewer resources to access computers, books or simply a safe communal space outside of their home. Future lack of investment in universal public services may perpetuate and further widen the inequalities in access to these resources.

Chapter 11 on the challenges of exiting homelessness by Christina Carmichael documents how increases in benefit sanctioning and conditionality, combined with cuts to homelessness services over the last ten years, have resulted in overwhelmed practitioners increasingly forced to focus on crisis management, while little or no resources are left to invest in prevention and helping users to transition out of homelessness. Carmichael's interviews with homeless service users and practitioners suggest that contrary to the prevailing narrative of welfare dependency, insufficient funding has impaired transitions into work.

Following the sectoral focus of the chapters by Hirsch, Davidson and Carmichael on the effect of austerity on social security provision, libraries and homelessness services, respectively, Chapter 12 by Crossley links these and other aspects of austerity in one overall narrative, which, according to Crossley, has led to an increasingly fragmented and disparate economy and geography of welfare. He also questions the use of new information technology (IT) systems and the related expansion of cybernetic relations to register, administer, manage and target some of the most vulnerable members of society. He argues that these virtual systems emerge as a way of dealing with cases that need physical and in-depth contact in the context of austerity budgets rather than a tested way of pooling information to save lives. Crossley's argument suggests that they can also be a way to exclude service users from decision-making about their entitlement and ultimately their lives, reconfiguring the power relations between the public and the state.

The future of austerity remains unclear. Politicians across the political spectrum have signalled that they want to distance themselves from austerity and most manifestos before the 2019 general election included some commitments to increases in government spending. Boris Johnson, the current Prime Minister and leader of the Conservative Party, shared anecdotes about his informal opposition to austerity at the beginning of the 2010s (Forsyth and Balls, 2019); however, so far, there are no clear signs of a commitment to reversing the cuts explored in this issue. Although Brexit will most likely continue to dominate the political arena for some time, the Social Policy community has the opportunity to provide a large body of evidence and reflections on the effects of austerity over the last ten years, and to offer clear policy recommendations for the future.

References

Crawford, R. and Zaranko, B. (2019) *Tax revenues and spending on social security benefits and public services since the crisis*, London: Institute for Fiscal Studies. https://www.ifs.org.uk/uploads/BN261-Tax-revenues-and-spending-on-social-security-benefits-and-public-services-since-the-crisis.pdf

Forsyth, J. and Balls, K. (2019) '"Austerity was not the way forward": an interview with Boris Johnson', *The Spectator*, 30 November, www.spectator.co.uk/2019/11/austerity-was-not-the-way-forward-an-interview-with-boris-johnson/

Karanikolos, M., Mladovsky, P., Cylus, J., Thomson, S., Basu, S., Stuckler, D., Mackenbach, J.P. and McKee, M. (2013) 'Financial crisis, austerity, and health in Europe', *The Lancet*, 381(9874): 1323–31.

After a decade of austerity, does the UK have an income safety net worth its name?

Donald Hirsch

Introduction

The term 'safety net', applied to minimum incomes, is seductively reassuring. It expresses a principle that no matter what their circumstances, the state will ensure that citizens will receive an income enabling them to survive, at least at a subsistence level. Structurally, the UK's social security system provides such a safety net for all its citizens: some variant of Income Support (IS) is available to all categories of working-age adults, and Pension Credit (PC) to those above state pension age, to guarantee a minimum level of income to those without other resources. Moreover, the system was designed to provide a given level of disposable income – after covering expenses that vary across households, including rent, local taxes and the cost of disability, all of which are covered in separate benefits based on individual circumstances.

In practice, there are three big problems with this system: the lack of any empirical link between support levels and need; the inconsistent treatment of different groups; and the exclusion of particular households or groups from a basic level of support. As argued later, each of these problems has always existed but all are getting worse, and the third is being applied in new forms.

First, what counts as a 'safety net' has no systematic relationship with what it actually costs to live, whether at a subsistence or other level. While the present rates originated from some notional calculation of subsistence after the Second World War (Bradshaw, 2013), today, any relationship with contemporary minimum needs is theoretical. Even to the extent that the rates have been politically regarded as being just enough to live on, recent real-terms cuts in working-age benefits have made this assumption invalid. The argument that 'at least in the UK you are guaranteed enough for some form of subsistence' does not hold if there is nothing to stop means-tested support from falling well below a subsistence level.

Second, while entitlements under the system originally related to some assumptions (however faulty) about household needs, the relationship of entitlements to needs has more recently become increasingly compromised. Since the 1990s, some more 'deserving' groups have seen their entitlements rise faster than others', so that a child, a working-age adult and a pensioner have entitlements today whose respective levels vary dramatically relative to their needs. Moreover, throughout the 2010s, a growing range of claimants have not even been able to access the level of disposable income implied by standard entitlements rates. The capping of benefits according to households' circumstances, including the number of children and the level of their housing costs, has greatly weakened the relationship between safety-net income and levels of need.

A third flaw relates to 'holes' in the safety net, which have always existed but are growing in size and number. Households can spend periods without income, or having to rely on income much lower than promised by the system, if they fail to meet conditionality rules, for example, or the administration of the system fails to provide income in a timely way. Universal Credit systematically creates the latter situation as new claimants spend time waiting for payment (Foley, 2017; National Audit Office, 2018). Emergency hardship payments have been cut back and are not always available. Conditionality has always existed but has been imposed in a more draconian way. These and other changes since 2010 that cause people to be left without support were summed up by Perry et al (2015).

Much attention has rightly been given to the worst situations, where people find that they have no safety net at all due to payment delays or sanctions (Dwyer, 2018; National Audit Office, 2018). Among the growing number of visitors to food banks, the single most cited driving force is having problems with receiving their benefits. Not surprisingly, it is when people find themselves without money for a period that they are most likely to resort to food banks. However, even among those facing the desperate situation of not having enough food, another widely cited factor is that benefits are simply too low to make ends meet: most food-bank managers now cite this as a high or very high impact factor affecting food bank users (Sosenko et al, 2019). This chapter's focus is on the changes that austerity has brought to safety-net entitlements themselves. Among those not being sanctioned and whose benefits are delivered in a timely manner, to what extent are they protecting households against severe poverty and hardship?

The level of basic entitlements

Origins of safety-net levels and changes over time

William Beveridge's (1942) report on the future of social security recommended setting National Assistance entitlements at rates compatible with fulfilling minimal dietary and other physical requirements, informed by a pre-war Ministry of Labour survey based on the expenditure of working-class households. Slightly adapted in the National Assistance Act 1948, this formed the benchmark for the means-tested safety net that later transformed into Supplementary Benefit and then IS (Bradshaw, 2013). Annual increments in their levels were subsequently based on political decisions and, at various times, pegged to earnings or prices, rather than any new assessment of need. Thus, today, levels of safety-net income guarantees have no meaningful empirical grounding in the actual cost of subsistence or a minimum living standard.

At a stretch, it could be asserted that, in one sense, safety-net benefits have come to *represent* a subsistence level: an official view of what the poorest groups should live on, uprated annually at least in line with living costs. However, if this view ever had any validity, this has been fatally undermined by the breaking of the inflation link: if benefits are deemed to be just enough to live on and then decline in real value, they must logically become too little to live on. In 2012, the link between inflation and working-age benefit uprating was abandoned, replaced, first, by three years of fixed-rate 1 per cent increases and then by a four-year freeze (Osborne, 2012, 2015). Between April 2012 and April 2019, benefits thus rose 3 per cent in total, while the Consumer Prices Index (CPI) rose by a cumulative 13 per cent. If IS/Jobseekers Allowance (JSA) rates were assumed to exactly provide subsistence in 2012, they therefore fell 10 per cent short of doing so by 2019.

Changing relativities: comparing children, working-age and pensioner entitlements

If the minimum incomes supported by benefit entitlements provided just enough for 'minimum needs', we might expect the relative

213

amounts given to different demographic groups to remain similar over time. However, over the past 20 years, these relativities have changed dramatically. Under the New Labour government, safety-net benefits for children and for pensioners rose significantly faster than inflation, in particular, through the Child Tax Credit (CTC) and PC, while adult safety-net benefits (notably, IS/JSA) had inflation-only upratings. This was driven by stated government objectives of ending child and pensioner poverty, with no equivalent for tackling working-age poverty (Joyce and Sibieta, 2013). Since 2010, PC has continued to rise, while both IS/JSA and CTC have fallen, in real terms. This has resulted in a dramatic change in the relative entitlements of different groups, as illustrated in Figure 9.1.

One comparison made in Figure 9.1 is between minimum benefits received by an adult without children and the amount allocated per child. The latter is calculated as the average for the first two children, and includes 'family' benefits triggered by having any children. In 1997, the amount per child was under half the amount per adult; by 2010, it was similar amounts for each, triggered by rising support for children and stagnating support for adults. Over the same period, the safety-net benefit rate for a pensioner rose from about a third above that of a working-age adult to around double the rate. Since the onset of austerity, pensioner benefits have risen in real terms while both working-age adults and children have seen a fall, further widening the gap between pensioner and other benefits.

Changing relativities: the safety net compared to earnings

If the safety net is supposed to protect households against the loss of earnings and other entitlements, one way of considering its adequacy over the long term is to compare it to average earnings levels. While means-tested benefits are not the same as insurance benefits protecting workers against the loss of earnings, their level relative to what people can earn is an indicator of how far society is willing to go in protecting people against misfortune. Rising earnings are one indicator of growing prosperity, and benefits relative to earnings help determine the relative incomes of the poorest members of society, and hence relative deprivation. In short, they show how much we are willing to see the poorest fall behind.

The simplest indicator of safety net benefits relative to earnings is a comparison of the weekly single rate of IS or its predecessors of Supplementary Benefit and National Assistance with average weekly

Figure 9.1: Changes in weekly minimum income entitlements since 1997 (in 2019 prices)

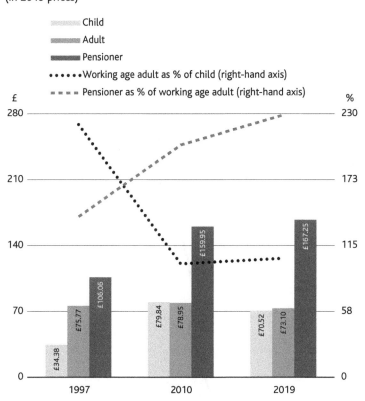

Notes: Benefits for a 'child' calculated as difference between entitlements of a couple with two children aged under 11 and a couple without children, divided by two. Since benefits for the first child are greater than for subsequent children, per-child benefits are somewhat higher than shown for a single-child family and lower for a family with three or more children; also, 1997 entitlements are £12.10 a week higher (2019 prices) for children over 11. However, the broad pattern illustrated by this graph applies to all family types. Working-age adult is IS/JSA for a single person. Pensioner is IS/PC minimum guarantee, single rate.

Sources: Author calculations from Institute for Fiscal Studies (2019), ONS (2019) and CPI data

earnings. This shows what minimum income a single person is guaranteed if they have no income from work compared to what they would earn as an average worker. An advantage of this indicator is that it can be shown in consistent form over a very long period, and Figure 9.2 does so over the past half-century.

Figure 9.2 shows that since the late 1970s, there has been a dramatic and almost continuous decline in the basic level of minimum benefits for

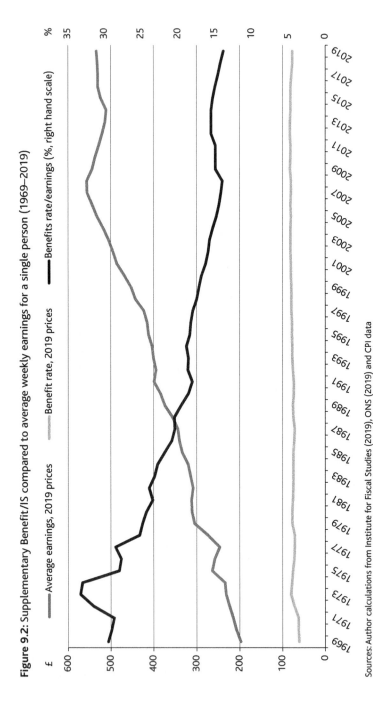

Figure 9.2: Supplementary Benefit/IS compared to average weekly earnings for a single person (1969–2019)

Sources: Author calculations from Institute for Fiscal Studies (2019), ONS (2019) and CPI data

a single person relative to average earnings. Before that time, the benefit level had been between a quarter and a third of earnings, whereas it is now only a seventh. The clear-cut cause of this decline is that benefits were mainly pegged to prices but earnings rose substantially in real terms. Up until the late 1990s, this relative decline affected pensioner and children's benefits as well as working-age adult rates, though pensioners and children have since risen substantially in real terms, as shown in Figure 9.1. One interesting aspect of Figure 9.2 is that there have only been two periods since 1980 when single adults' benefits have slightly improved relative to earnings: during the recessions of the early 1990s and the late 2000s, when earnings were falling in real terms but benefits were still being uprated by inflation. A significant effect of the latter case is that during 2010–12, inflation was relatively high at a time when earnings were stagnating, and the effect was for benefit rates to be better insulated than pay against the effect of recession. This trend was used by the Chancellor of the Exchequer, George Osborne to recast the notion of 'fairness' and justify a restriction of benefit increases to below inflation, declaring in his 2012 *Autumn Statement*:

> We have to acknowledge that over the last five years those on out of work benefits have seen their incomes rise twice as fast as those in work. With pay restraint in businesses and government, average earnings have risen by around 10% since 2007. Out of work benefits have gone up by around 20%. That's not fair to working people who pay the taxes that fund them. Those working in the public services, who have seen their basic pay frozen, will now see it rise by an average of 1%. A similar approach of a 1% rise should apply to those in receipt of benefits. That's fair and it will ensure that we have a welfare system that Britain can afford. (Osborne, 2012)

This statement was of great significance because it justified breaking the rule, for the first time since the Second World War, that benefits should rise at least in line with prices. After 2012, three years of 1 per cent rises in most working-age benefits were followed by four years of zero increases. In introducing this change, the Chancellor correctly asserted that people on benefits had been shielded from the real-term falls seen by working-age people during a recession; however, he conveniently ignored that over the long term, the former had become far worse off relative to the latter. Thus, by 2019, the relative value of the safety net had returned to its all-time low.

Changing relativities: entitlements compared to the Minimum Income Standard

Comparing the safety-net benefits to average earnings, like a comparison to average household incomes, gives a broad picture of the extent of protection relative to current norms. However, it does not show whether recipients can meet their needs in the context of contemporary society. Since 2008, the Minimum Income Standard (MIS) has produced more direct benchmarks showing the income needed for a social minimum. MIS set out to operationalise Townsend's (1979) concept that in order to escape poverty, you need to be able to participate in society and have what is considered essential according to contemporary norms. The MIS method comprises detailed deliberations among groups of members of the public to identify the content of budgets sufficient to allow different household types to reach a minimum, defined in terms of both meeting material needs and having the opportunities and choices required to participate in society. These budgets are costed to show how much households require to reach a minimum acceptable standard of living (Hirsch, 2019; Davis et al, 2017).

Figure 9.3 shows how safety-net incomes have fared against this standard. It confirms that the adequacy of the safety net varies greatly from one group to the next, with pensioners getting approximately what they need, families with children getting slightly over half and a single person without children getting only a third. Figure 9.3 also shows how benefits have declined against this adequacy benchmark for all groups.

For pensioners, a slight deterioration in minimum benefit adequacy may seem surprising given that their main safety net benefit (PC) has risen with earnings or CPI inflation, whichever is greatest. However, minimum pensioner costs overall have risen faster than CPI, partly because some items such as domestic fuel that figure prominently in pensioner budgets have high inflation rates, and partly because certain specifications set by members of the public in the MIS research have increased, for example, because of a growing emphasis on pensioners being able to participate fully in society. However, pensioners' minimum needs remain mainly covered by minimum benefits, and are largely stable in these terms. In contrast, for working-age adults with and without children, an already-inadequate package has declined substantially since 2010. In particular, over the past nine years, the adequacy of income support for a single person has declined from an already-austere situation of getting less than half to now getting

Figure 9.3: Safety net benefits relative to a MIS (2010–19)

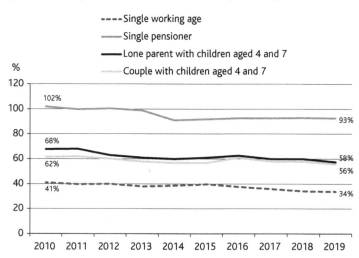

Notes: Comparison based on budgets net of rent, childcare and council tax. Income does not include benefits associated with those items. However, the fact that since 2013, Council Tax Support does not fully cover council tax is taken into account by subtracting the typical shortfall from safety-net benefit income.

Source: MIS database

only one third of what they need. Most of this has occurred because benefits have risen more slowly than costs, and been frozen since 2016. A further factor taken into account in Figure 9.3 is that since 2013, all working-age applicants have had to contribute to the cost of council tax an amount that is not fully reimbursed through Council Tax Support, which therefore systematically reduces disposable income.

Breaking the link between entitlement and need

Up to here, safety-net benefits have been reported as if they are paid according to a consistent schedule based on the amounts assigned to the different types of individuals who live in a 'benefit unit' (single, couple or family with dependent children), each of whom has a standard entitlement. However, increasingly, benefits do not provide a disposable income based on these amounts, either because basic benefits are restricted or because housing-related benefits do not pay for the full amount incurred in rent, and the shortfall needs to be made up from basic benefits.

Four particular cases of this are:

- The benefit cap, which restricts the total level of benefits that any one family can receive, currently to £442 a week in London and £385 outside London. This measure 'punishes' families for having multiple children or high housing costs, or both, by greatly restricting the support available to cover the costs that these circumstances generate. Moreover, when the cap's arbitrary level was reduced in 2016 from its original level of £500, its reach extended to hit more or less all families of five or more, and some four-person families (such as a couple with two children) who face private sector rents (Hirsch, 2015). Thus, it is no longer just families with exceptional circumstances whose benefits are being curtailed by the cap.
- The 'two child limit', under which the calculation of means-tested benefits stops taking account of third or subsequent children born after April 2017. Since 29 per cent of all children, and 42 per cent of children in non-working families, have at least two siblings (author calculation from the Family Resources Survey), this will have extremely wide-ranging effects – even were it to have some behavioural effect by deterring people from having additional children. Like the benefit cap, this policy will result in larger families falling much further short of meeting their needs on benefits, though it is being introduced more slowly, so some existing three-child families will remain unaffected until the early 2030s under present rules. For many families affected, the benefit cap will become less significant as the two-child limit will cause benefits to fall below the cap. Conversely, even those larger families unaffected by the two-child limit because they were created before 2017 are likely to be hit by the benefit cap.
- For social tenants, the 'bedroom tax' rule that deducts Housing Benefit (HB) for those considered to be 'underoccupying' their homes. The deductions are 14 per cent of rent for one 'spare' bedroom and 25 per cent for two or more. To avoid this deduction, families may need to be highly adaptable in their living arrangements, and persuade their landlords to make this possible. For example, a family with a boy and a girl would need to occupy a two-bedroom home until the oldest child turns ten, and then move to a three-bedroom property; yet, in practice, social housing transfers are highly contingent on availability. Those unable to avoid the bedroom tax must cover their rent from sources other than HB.

- For private tenants, caps to the Local Housing Allowance (LHA), the limit to the rent levels that can be reimbursed through HB. Originally set at levels sensitive to local rent levels, the levels of the allowance have been detached from market rents since 2012 and have been frozen since 2015. This means that anyone living in a home with a rent at the limit of eligibility in 2012, which has since risen at an average rate, now has to find 7 per cent of that rent from general benefits outside London, and 10 per cent in London (author calculation based on the Office for National Statistics [ONS] rent index). More usually, it has increased an existing shortfall: even before the LHA freeze, the assumption that the state would usually cover the rent for non-working households renting privately was out of date, with most having to contribute out of their basic benefits. The Resolution Foundation estimates that, on average, HB now covers just 55 per cent of the housing costs of non-working, private renting 'millennial' families (born 1981–2000) at age 25; the equivalent figure for 'generation X' families (born 1966–80) at the same age was 77 per cent (Judge and Tomlinson, 2018).

Each of these measures in some sense penalises a household that has not 'behaved' in a prescribed way, either in terms of how many children they have or what steps they take to limit their housing costs. Such penalties depart from the principle of basing benefits on needs, and take no account of how much control households have in practice over costs such as rent. Together, they help create a safety net that varies greatly in its adequacy according to the individual circumstances of households.

Figure 9.4 illustrates this by showing how claimants are typically affected by the aforementioned measures, in terms of what proportion of minimum income is provided by benefits. It is worth recalling that even without the four restrictions to benefits shown here, the adequacy of benefits has been deteriorating, as shown in Figure 9.3: in 2010, they typically provided almost two thirds of minimum requirements for families with children, and the trend has been for this to decline to not much more than half. The first section of Figure 9.4 shows that for those currently hit by the benefit cap, this already falls to below half, and for those hit by the two-child policy, it falls further. Reductions in adequacy due to the bedroom tax and the LHA freeze are less steep, yet still significant, and add to the extent to which benefits fall short of meeting needs. For a single person without children, shown here because they are particularly likely to be renting in the private sector, the LHA freeze brings benefits below a third of required disposable income.

Figure 9.4: Policy effects on the percentage of MIS covered by the safety net (2019)

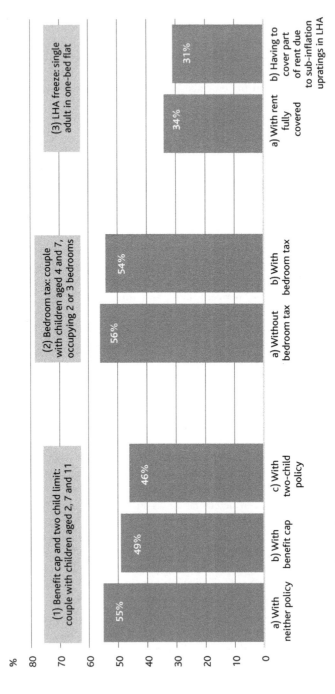

Source: Author calculations from MIS data

The safety net and subsistence: an illustration

The preceding analysis has shown that the UK's 'safety-net' benefits, which have never maintained a systematic link with subsistence, have recently become both less adequate and more arbitrary in terms of enabling claimants to make ends meet at some basic level. It is clear that they leave many people well short of what the public considers necessary as a minimum. However, how low have they become in relation to subsistence?

A more tangible way to consider this question than the percentages presented earlier is to take the example of a single person, aged over 35, living in a rented one-bedroom flat, on means-tested JSA. Using the last case in Figure 9.4, where recent sub-inflation increases in LHA have necessitated a contribution to rent out of basic benefits, and also where a contribution has to be made to help cover council tax, this person's £72.10 a week headline benefit entitlement translates into £64.25 disposable income (all figures for 2019). After subtracting the utility bills estimated for this case in the MIS research (water, gas and electricity), this reduces to £44 in their pocket, compared to over £180 that is needed, after bills, for a minimum standard of living. This remaining £44 is lower even than the £49.64 allocated just to food in the MIS single person's budget. Around £5 of this is allocated to occasionally eating out; even if this is excluded, the food budget is just above the single person's £44 total spending money after bills. Therefore, in this case, disposable income on benefits is not even enough to meet a food budget, let alone the wide range of other things that you need to buy. Many of these are not optional, even in relation to nutrition: you need to spend money on transport just to get to the shops to buy the food, on clothing to look presentable when you get there and on household goods that allow you to sit down, cook and eat what you have bought. In other words, the safety-net income for a single person is too low even to fund a reasonable diet, let alone a decent life.

Conclusion

This chapter has shown how the 'safety net' originally designed to prevent people in the UK from being left without the means of subsistence is no longer providing any systematic form of protection. The most that can be said is that all groups have some entitlement to safety-net income, rather than to zero, though sanctions and waiting periods can nevertheless leave some people without income for significant amounts of time.

One aspect of this disintegration of the safety net is that there is no 'floor' below which its level cannot fall. The fact that benefits can be arbitrarily frozen during periods of inflation destroys any notion that they support some living standard, even one of subsistence. In the worst cases, benefit rates are now not even sufficient to maintain a reasonable diet, regardless of how frugal other areas of spending become.

The other aspect of disintegration is the detachment of entitlement from need in a range of individual circumstances related to family size and to housing. A wide range of claimants have their normal entitlements affected by the benefit cap, the two-child limit, the 'bedroom tax', the LHA freeze or a combination of these. Such restrictions are not just exceptions, but becoming the 'new norm'. Two of these policies in particular have increasing 'bite' over time: the LHA limits on rents eligible for benefits as rising rent levels are not matched by rises in these limits; and the benefit cap, which has been lowered and will increasingly affect not just larger families, but those with as few as two children at its present rate. It is possible to envisage a future where a lifting of the freeze on benefit rates but not on the benefit cap means that a growing number of families continue to have their benefits frozen at the level of the cap while their costs rise with inflation.

Far from affecting only a few selected groups, this detachment of entitlement from need could actually end up impacting the majority of families requiring safety-net benefits. As well as the four in ten children in non-working families who have at least two siblings, and are therefore likely to be impacted by the two-child limit and/or the benefit cap, over a quarter (27 per cent) live in private rented accommodation and are thus vulnerable to the effect of LHA limits, which are increasingly out of line with rents. The majority of children in non-working families (58 per cent) are affected by at least one of these two characteristics – a large family or a private tenancy (author calculations from the Family Resources Survey). Behavioural responses (having fewer children and moving to cheaper accommodation) could potentially reduce these proportions. Whether or not this occurs in the future, these figures suggest that standard safety-net incomes are being restricted for most claimants based on current living patterns. This is a gloomy picture that will not be resolved by only piecemeal reforms such as abolishing individual policies like the two-child limit. A safety net worth its name would need to create a new, systematic relationship between basic household needs and the delivery of an income guarantee. For pensioners, PC combined with the new, more adequate, single-tier pension comes close to achieving this. For working-age households unable to support themselves by their own means, the present system comes nowhere near providing an adequate system of protection.

References

Beveridge, W. (1942), *Social Insurance and Allied Services*, Cmd 6404, London: HMSO. Bradshaw, J. (2013) *Jonathan Bradshaw, selected writings 1972–2011*, York: University of York.

Davis, A., Hirsch, D. and Padley, M. (2017) 'The minimum income standard as a benchmark of a "participatory social minimum"', *Journal of Poverty and Social Justice* 26(1): 19–34.

Dwyer, P. (2018) 'Punitive and ineffective: benefit sanctions within social security', *Journal of Social Security Law* 25(3): 142–57.

Foley, B. (2017) *Delivering on Universal Credit*, London: Citizens Advice.

Hirsch, D. (2015) *The cost of a child in 2015*, London: Child Poverty Action Group.

Hirsch, D. (2019) *A minimum income for the United Kingdom in 2019*, York: Joseph Rowntree Foundation.

Institute for Fiscal Studies (2019) 'Fiscal facts', www.ifs.org.uk/tools_ and_resources/fiscal_facts

Joyce, R. and Sibieta, L. (2013) *Labour's record on poverty and inequality*, London: Institute for Fiscal Studies.

Judge, L. and Tomlinson, D. (2018) *Home improvements*, London: Resolution Foundation and Intergenerational Commission.

National Audit Office (2018) 'Rolling out Universal Credit', London: National Audit Office.

ONS (Office for National Statistics) (2019) 'Average weekly earnings', www.ons.gov.uk/employmentandlabourmarket/peopleinwork/ earningsandworkinghours/datasets/averageweeklyearnings

Osborne, G. (2012) *Autumn statement*, London: HM Treasury, www. gov.uk/government/speeches/autumn-statement-2012-chancellors-statement

Osborne, G. (2015) *Summer budget speech*, London: HM Treasury.

Perry, J., Purcell, L. and Cooper, N. (2015) *Restoring faith in the safety net*, London: Church Action on Poverty.

Sosenko, F., Littlewood, M., Bramley, G., Fitzpatrick, S., Blenkinsopp, J. and Wood, J. (2019) *The state of hunger, year 1 main report*, London: Trussell Trust.

Townsend, P. (1979) *Poverty in the United Kingdom*, London: Penguin.

10

A new page? The public
library in austerity

Emma Davidson

Introduction

> Too often when countries undertake major consolidations ...
> it is the poorest – those who had least to do with the
> cause of the economic misfortunes – who are hit hardest.
> Perhaps that has been a mistake that our country has made
> in the past. This Coalition Government will be different.
> (Osborne, 2010: 51)

Following the 2008/09 recession, the Conservative–Liberal Democrat
Coalition government committed to significant reductions in public
expenditure relative to the economy. This policy of fiscal consolidation
set out cuts of £83 billion to be delivered by 2015, amounting to 14 per
cent of all public spending. The aspiration was to reduce the gross
domestic product (GDP) budget deficit from 11 per cent to 1 per cent
and 'secure' Britain's economic stability (HM Treasury, 2010). Fiscal
consolidation has been sustained by the Conservative governments that
followed, as exemplified by successive cuts to local government spending
powers (Hastings et al, 2015a; Gray and Barford, 2018; National Audit
Office, 2018). Estimates suggest that the most severe reductions have
taken place in English councils, with spending cuts thought to be as
high as a quarter (24 per cent) between 2009/10 and 2016/17. This
is double that of Scotland and Wales (11.5 per cent and 12 per cent,
respectively), where the autonomy provided by devolution is thought to
have 'buffered' councils from the deepest cuts (Gray and Barford, 2018).

Despite variation across jurisdictions, local government across Britain
remains under pressure, even more so due to a respective growth in
demand for key services. According to the National Audit Office
(2018), this has forced local authorities to prioritise service areas

where they have significant statutory responsibilities, such as adult and children's social care. A recent report (Amin-Smith and Phillips, 2019) estimated that spending on adult social care services in England was cut by 5 per cent between 2009/10 to 2017/18, while acute children's social care services increased by 10 per cent over the same period. This can be contrasted to the massive reductions in spending on other areas: children's and youth centres were down by over 60 per cent; planning/ development and housing was cut by a half; while cultural and leisure services were reduced by 40 per cent. A similar pattern of spending cuts was observed elsewhere (Besemer and Bramley, 2012; Hastings et al, 2015a; Gray and Barford, 2018). The 2015 Spending Review and 2017 Budget brought councils some respite by introducing extra funding to relieve pressure in adult social care and a levelling off of the rate of reductions (National Audit Office, 2018). Yet, commentators remain concerned that funding available to councils will become increasingly inadequate, with services at risk of reduction or disappearance, and local communities facing increased responsibility for local service delivery (Levitas, 2012; Lowndes and McCaughie, 2013).

This chapter engages with these concerns, using the case of the public library as an example of how austerity measures are impacting on public services. Despite their statutory protection, libraries have endured seismic shifts in provision, with budget cuts contributing to limited opening hours, reduced staff and, in many cases, closures (Grant, 2016; CIPFA, 2019; Mackay, 2019; Merson, 2019). Austerity measures have also stimulated radical changes to delivery models, including: the co-location of traditionally distinct services within single buildings or campuses; the wholesale transfer of library services to charitable trusts or community-managed services; and the increased reliance on volunteers. To understand the scale and impact of these changes, this chapter combines national published public library statistics with data from qualitative interviews based in Scotland. While no claims to comprehensiveness are made in relation to the qualitative data, the aim is to contribute to a growing body of evidence on the challenges facing public libraries, the strategies being used in response and the effects of these changes on everyday lives (Rooney-Browne, 2009; Child and Goulding, 2012; Goulding, 2013; Pautz and Poulter, 2014; Casselden et al, 2019; Corble, 2019; Hitchen, 2019). The chapter argues that like cuts to public services overall, the impacts of cuts to public libraries are concentrated on the most marginalised people and the most marginalised places. It is shown that while public libraries are utilising a range of approaches to 'weather the storm' (Lowndes and McCaughie, 2013), including a greater reliance on volunteers and shared services, resilience to reductions in public expenditure has its limits, both in terms of staff morale and service capacity. It is concluded that while choking public spending has enacted new, and in some cases improved, organisational practices, sustained 'chipping away' will have a deleterious effect on the most vulnerable communities. At a community level, these effects are multiplied when budgetary cuts are extended to other universal services, whether youth services, leisure or refuse collection.

A fair deal for all?

The claim made by central government to justify austerity was that spending cuts would be spread evenly across all sectors of society. The 2010 Spending Review, which gave the mandate for fiscal consolidation, described the approach as a 'new vision for a fairer Britain' (HM Treasury, 2010). This new vision argued that the existing system of support had failed the poorest members of British society, trapping them in a cycle of welfare dependency. Cuts to welfare would deliver greater opportunities for social mobility and enable a greater proportion to be spent on services for the poorest children. A similar narrative is present in George Osborne's 2015 Budget speech, where he maintained that the government was 'continuing to devote a greater share of state support to the most vulnerable' (Osborne, 2015).

Despite the inevitability within government discourse of us 'being in it together', a mounting body of academic and policy research tells us that this is not a policy implemented with fairness in mind (Duffy, 2013) and that the cuts have, in fact, fallen hardest on particular places, services and parts of the population (Hastings et al, 2015b; Gray and Barford, 2018). Neil Amin-Smith and David Phillips's (2019) recent work, for instance, concluded that cuts have been far larger for councils serving more deprived communities. Drawing on data for England only, they found that cuts averaged around 31 per cent for the most deprived fifth of council areas, compared to 17 per cent for the least deprived fifth of council areas. This is a pattern that reflects the fact that affluent areas with higher property and land values have more opportunities to generate alternative revenue streams compared to deprived areas more dependent on government funding (National Audit Office, 2018: para 1.8). The National Audit Office (2018: 4) has also reported a majority of local authorities with social care responsibilities drawing on financial reserves, while reports of bankruptcy and the need to cut services to a 'core offer' have mounted in recent years (Chakelian, 2018). In their interrogation of local authority budgets across Britain between 2010 and 2017, Mia Gray and Anna Barford (2018) also found a relationship between grant dependence and cuts in service spending. The most severe cuts to local spending were generally associated with areas that they describe as 'multiple deprivation', which is a pattern clearest in England, where all 46 councils that cut spending by 30 per cent or more fit this categorisation. The North was hit with the most severe cuts to local spending, followed closely by parts of London. The research also shows a large part of Southern England, primarily around the 'home counties', with low levels of reliance on central government and only relatively minor local service cuts.

Since the use of council services varies by socio-economic group, reductions in spending also have an inequitable effect on different income groups. Annette Hastings and colleagues (2015a) found that 'pro-poor services' (such as housing and homelessness, social work, and social care services) had been protected from cuts in relative terms. Despite this, their research revealed significant pressure, as demonstrated by overstretched staff, rising unmet needs and a growing unwillingness for services to take responsibility (Hastings et al, 2015a: 104). Their conclusion was that the cumulative impact of even small savings was more detrimental to poorer people, while better-off service users were able to navigate the consequences of austerity (for example, by driving to a service no longer available in their locality). This reminds us that all cuts to services are experienced in the context of the wider costs of recession (Lowndes and McCaughie, 2013).

Austerity localism

The 'fair for all' rhetoric on spending cuts has also been framed alongside a commitment to greater independence for local authorities and the communities within them. Echoing David Cameron's (now-abandoned) 'Big Society', this manifestation of localism has been conceptualised in political discourse by the transfer of power to local authorities, increased competition within public service provision and the 'empowerment' of communities through social action (Clayton et al, 2016; see also Dagdeviren et al, 2019). David Featherstone and colleagues (2012) framed this as 'austerity localism', whereby responsibility for delivering local services, and managing budgets, is devolved from central to local government, while successive spending cuts are legitimised through the continued promise of local autonomy and community empowerment.

Responsibility to tackle social inequalities is deflected onto councils and other local bodies, while the state remains unaccountable. Featherstone et al (2012: 179) state that this has the potential for 'pernicious consequences' since it promotes a form of localism that fails to recognise, and work to address, the 'inequalities that exist within and between places'.

This levelling out of inequality is apparent in the conceptualisation of community empowerment within austerity localism. The notion of 'local people' and 'local communities' not only assumes consensus and homogeneity in how individuals want their community to be developed, but also treats everyone as equal in terms of their capacity to be involved in these (Featherstone et al, 2012: 178). For Ruth Levitas (2012: 331), the reality is that social, economic and cultural resources are unequally distributed, which disadvantages more deprived localities. This is illustrated in research by Lindsay Findlay-King and colleagues (2018), who examined the asset transfer of leisure services. Here, the discourse of 'community empowerment' was frequently used to reframe budget cuts in a more progressive light. The consequence was that community groups supporting the service were rarely 'empowered' in decision-making or in developing the service. Moreover, engagement privileged volunteer groups with high social capital and those in 'stable' communities (Findlay-King et al, 2018: 166). Hastings et al (2015a) similarly found that the capacity within disadvantaged communities to support localism was limited due to a lack of resources and support for capacity-building. This is not to say that localism cannot be effective, but rather that there is an unevenly distributed capacity to take on more responsibility between more and less disadvantaged neighbourhoods.

Austerity localism is also linked to the concept of 'resilience', that is, the ability to draw on one's own resources to 'bounce back' against adversity. The most important aspect of resilience is the capacity not only to keep going, but also to learn, adapt and change (Shaw, 2012). For local government, institutional resilience is the ability not only to 'weather the storm' (Lowndes and McCaughie, 2013), but also to deploy austerity as a tool to enable innovative and creative approaches to practice and delivery. Austerity has undoubtedly provoked institutional change, with budget cuts being the impetus for change such as asset transfer, community management and innovation in practice. However, as Vivien Lowndes and Kerry McCaughie (2013) point out, while local government is exhibiting agency and resourcefulness, this cannot shift the hard reality of a budget deficit. Rather than a progressive transformation, they argue that these processes are better described as 'institutional bricolage' to 'weather the storm'. Hastings et al (2015b: 617) agree: sustained budget cuts will not result in a progressive rolling back of the state; rather, if sustained, cuts will eventually destabilise creative adaptations and undermine public services.

Public libraries in austerity

> [the public library is] a canary in the coal mine for what is happening across the local government sector. (Rob Whiteman, chief executive officer of the Chartered Institute of Public Finance and Accountability [CIPFA], quoted in Cain, 2018)

Cultural services are one of the areas of local government funding where spending has been significantly reduced across Britain. Included in this category are public libraries, and they have suffered as a result. According to annual data collected by CIPFA (2009, 2019), spending is estimated to have dropped by 30 per cent in the period from March 2008 to March 2018, from £1,059 million to £741 million. The number of public libraries has also been affected, with a reduction of almost 800 services open for more than ten hours a week between 2008 and 2018. This represents a fifth (18 per cent) of all public libraries. Mobile services, which are widely regarded as having a significant impact on tackling social isolation and loneliness, have faced even larger cuts, with the number of services falling from 555 in 2008 to only 191 in 2018, equivalent to two thirds (66 per cent) of services. While care must be taken when interpreting CIPFA figures as a national data set, particularly given the level of missing data at a local authority level (O'Bryan, 2018), it remains likely that these figures will underestimate the full rate of decline. It is known that further services are under review, and additional reductions (through either reduced opening hours or closures) in many areas appear imminent.[1]

What is notable from the available data is the marked variation in service provision *across* the nations, with Scotland exhibiting the lowest rate of decline and Wales the greatest (15 per cent compared to 28 per cent). Similar differences are identified across the English regions, with the highest decline reported in the West Midlands and North-West. In line with Gray and Barford's (2018) analysis of local government cuts, it is in the East and South-East of England that reductions to services were below average (see Table 10.1).

Table 10.1: Number of public libraries open more than ten hours per week (2008–18)

Area	2008	2013	2018	Number change	% change
East Midlands	344	317	300	−44	−13%
Eastern	302	292	273	−29	−10%
Greater London	388	356	340	−48	−12%
North-East	225	208	196	−29	−13%
North-West	480	430	372	−108	−23%
South-East	555	537	499	−56	−10%
South-West	351	327	303	−48	−14%
West Midlands	411	339	309	−102	−25%
Yorkshire and The Humber	413	363	359	−54	−13%
England[a]	3,469	3,181	2,853	−616	−18%
Wales	338	307	244	−94	−28%
Scotland	604	581	521	−83	−15%
GB total	4,411	4,069	3,618	−793	−18%

Note [a] English total based on regional data from 149 authorities, of which 34 provided partial data. Where data were unavailable, the most reliable figure was used to provide an estimate.

Source: CIPFA Public Library Statistics (2009–19)

Closer analysis shows that, *numerically*, the reduction in services is concentrated in a small number of local authorities: 25 of the 201 of those providing data accounted for over 40 per cent of the drop in services open for more than ten hours. These local authorities vary considerably, with the biggest 'losers' including Birmingham, Lancashire, Rhondda Cyon Taff, Hampshire, Flintshire, Cumbria, Nottinghamshire and Fife. Of course, a large numerical variation can only be meaningfully when understood in context. Experientially, the reduction of public libraries in Birmingham from 51 to 18 will be subjectively different than, say, the Island community of Orkney where libraries were reduced from four to two. Looking instead at the percentage reduction in service provision, there were 19 local authorities who reduced libraries by more than 35 per cent. Seven of these were in the North of England, four were in Wales, three were in Greater London and two were in the West Midlands. Three were in Scotland, of which two were in very rural island locations (Shetland and Orkney). Notably, none were in the East, South-East or South-West of England. Meanwhile, some of the greatest losses were in authorities with long-standing areas of deprivation, including Brent, Barking and Dagenham, Wakefield, and Newcastle-upon-Tyne.

Press and local media coverage can give a useful insight into how library closures are framed and responded to. Local press reports for all 19 local authorities who reduced libraries by more than 35 per cent were examined. In 17 cases, the closure of local libraries was reported as being a consequence of budget cuts or financial pressure across the local authority. In Flintshire, where libraries were cut by more than half, the council reported having already made cuts of £79 million over the last decade, which included youth clubs, homeless accommodation and school music lessons, in addition to the loss of over half of its libraries (Flintshire County Council, 2018). Similarly, in the Metropolitan Borough of Bury in Greater Manchester, the council closed nine of its 13 libraries in response to what was described as 'huge pressure to save money, particularly due to the rising costs of social care' (Wilkinson, 2017). Stoke-on-Trent, which also lost half its libraries, has been faced with the need to make massive savings while improving failures in statutory services. As well as hundreds of jobs being cut, the council is exploring further controversial cost cutting, including cuts to grass cutting, street cleaning and Christmas lights (Corrigan, 2019).

Public libraries and austerity localism

The extent of closures and cuts to service provision offers strong evidence that public libraries are part of the 'collateral damage' (Davies, 2012: 357) of forcing down and 'hollowing out' (Robertson and McMenemy, 2018) public services that provide preventive and universal support to the most marginalised people and places. Yet, political discourse has also presented closures and reduced services as a pragmatic decision to focus on a smaller, more sustainable, number of libraries. For instance, Cumbria, in the North-West of England, reported the reduction in libraries as a realistic, practical way to make the service stronger and more resilient in the face of the changing needs and demands of customers (Arts Council England, 2017: 12). Likewise, Brent Libraries is one of several library services championing 'fewer but better' library buildings. As part of its contentious 'Libraries Transformation Project' (O'Bryan, 2018: 22), half of the libraries in the borough were closed, enabling an enhanced service to be concentrated on the best-located libraries. Elsewhere, the 'fewer but better' approach has been associated with the 'community hub' model, where investment is made into a single service providing integrated social and health services previously delivered from multiple spaces (for example, in East Ayrshire and Fife). Meanwhile, others have sought acquiescence from campaigners by promoting community alternatives, such as Bolton's 'book drop-off points', and the possibility of community-managed services in the future (for example, in Wakefield).

Indeed, a significant part of the rhetoric surrounding library closures has focused on responsibilising individuals and communities in the future of their library service, and this is reflected in the growth in volunteers. The national published data by CIPFA show a 34 per cent increase in the number of volunteers, alongside a respective decline of 31 per cent of total staff, largely accounted for by voluntary redundancy. Professional librarians have faced an even greater drop, with total professional staff reducing by over a half (52 per cent) since the start of the recession (see Table 10.2). These data suggest that public libraries are relying on volunteers not only to support services, but to keep them open (Robertson and McMenemy, 2018: 96).

The rhetoric of austerity localism emphasises the increased autonomy of local services, and greater responsiveness to local needs. Yet, the transformation in library services suggests that the primary motivation for volunteers is as a means to 'plug gaps' left by retreating public provision (Findlay-King et al, 2018: 158). Volunteers can act as the 'social glue' for the community (Goulding, 2006), but for them to be effective, they must be well resourced and managed. As shown by Casselden et al (2015), if absent, this can result in mistrust between front-line staff and volunteers, especially when volunteers replace paid staff in specialist roles. Other work points to the variation in capacity of volunteers across different areas, which is a finding noted by Forkert (2016: 22), who found that residents in the deprived area of Lewisham had little free time and were unable to provide the expertise and reliability of trained librarians.

In addition to the growth in volunteers, many local authorities have sought to outsource library services to non-profit organisations independent from the local authority, community-run libraries

Table 10.2: Number of staff and volunteers (2008–18)

Staff and volunteers	2007/08	2012/13	2017/18	% change
Total staff (full-time equivalent)	25,769	20,302	15,483	–31%
Total professional staff	5,297.9	3,550.7	2,340.1	–52%
Total volunteers	15,008	33,808	51,394	34%
Number of volunteer hours	544,755*	1,103,623	1,780,843	38%

Note: *Data only available for 2008/09.

supported by the local authority or independent community libraries run outside the statutory network (Department for Culture, Media and Sport, 2018). Across all these models, there are significant financial benefits, for example, through lower rates and taxes, the ability to raise funding from alternative sources, and savings gained by merging services into single buildings (for example, library and leisure centres) (Goulding, 2013). Although, as noted earlier, CIPFA figures are not fully comprehensive, they can provide a broad indication of this transformation in delivery models. Data from 163 local authorities on the type of libraries provided in the locality were collected in March 2018. Of the 3,185 libraries for which there were data, 25 per cent were operated through an alternative delivery model. The majority of these (15 per cent) were categorised as 'commissioned community co-produced libraries', typically trusts or arm's-length companies; 6 per cent were independent libraries and 5 per cent were managed by the community. From the data available, commissioned and community-managed libraries were fairly spread across Britain, though a fairly large proportion (32 per cent) of commissioned libraries are operating in Scotland. The independent libraries were notably all based in fairly affluent authorities (Devon, Hampshire, Nottinghamshire, Shropshire, Suffolk), where residents arguably have the social and economic capacity to support the service.

The final point before moving on is the promise that austerity localism can generate creativity. Forkert (2016: 11) has questioned this notion of what she calls 'austere creativity', that is 'the resourcefulness and ingenuity of citizens to adapt and "problem solve" in the face of cuts'. In Lewisham, where her research was based, library closures were met with significant protest from local people but, in the end, many took the pragmatic view that it was best to keep the libraries open with volunteers than to lose them altogether. Once in the hands of volunteers, Forkert (2016: 26) found little evidence of 'anything challenging or oppositional' within the service, leading her to question how the new organisation was representing the multifaceted needs of the community that it was meant to represent. In her discussion of alternative delivery models, Goudling (2013) has raised similar questions. Within commissioned services, public libraries are unable to raise a surplus. This financial position, she argues, can result in commissioned services focusing on profitable parts of the business, such as cafe or events, with an accompanying 'mission drift' away from the library as a resource that reflects the needs of the local community.

Everyday austerity in the library

Data and methods

The final part of this chapter examines data from ongoing research funded by the Leverhulme Trust on the role and value of public libraries in austere times (see also Davidson, 2019). The research has used qualitative case studies to investigate the everyday social worlds and interactions in libraries, with a particular focus on groups less able, excluded or disenfranchised from local processes of participation. The case studies, all based in Scotland, are mobilising a range of practical methods to answer the research questions, including observations, participation in activities run in library spaces and in-depth interviews and group discussions with staff, library users and non-users.

The data presented here are drawn from interviews conducted in 2018/19 across seven different Scottish local authorities, and include discussions with 36 library staff members, seven professionals from other sectors (including youth workers, community workers and third sector organisations) and 50 local residents. The names of and background information on the local authorities, as well as the staff and members of the public, have been removed to maintain the anonymity of participants.

The research sites were purposively selected to gain insight into the contextual factors shaping public libraries. As well as socio-economic variation across areas, the sample deliberately included public libraries with different management structures and physical characteristics (for instance, a trust, community hubs, co-located provision and branch libraries).

Interviews with professionals were steered by a semi-structured topic guide that focused on respondents' understanding of: the role and purpose of public libraries; the experiences of working in, for or with public libraries; the views on library users and reasons for non-use; and the 'value' of public libraries and how such value can be evidenced. Care was taken to include professionals from a range of positions and seniority, as well as non-library services, so as to generate rich insight and knowledge on the role of public libraries at a local level.

Engagement with local residents was varied in approach, with the primary aim again being to collate a diverse range of perspectives on public libraries. Interviews with library users were undertaken in public libraries, with recruitment either at the point of library visit or during researcher participation in a library activity (such as a book group). To explore non-use and address gaps in under-represented groups (such as young parents and young people), recruitment also took place in venues outside the library, including shops, community centres, youth clubs and playgroups. As with the professionals, discussions with residents focused on their experiences of using (or not using) the public library, as well as their views on its role and value in the local area and society more generally. Overall, the approach was conversational in style to allow residents' own experiences to guide the interview. Nonetheless, all interviews sought to explore key themes, including views on 'community' and 'public spaces', as well as the impact of austerity on themselves, public services and their neighbourhood.

Findings

It was noted earlier that the cuts being made to library services are experienced in the wider context of the recession (Lowndes and McCaughie, 2013). A large proportion of library users interviewed, especially those visiting to use the computers, described how they were managing the consequences of welfare reform and cuts to local services. Indeed, it was remarkable how quickly an initial conversation about their use of the public library turned to anxieties about work, housing and family finances:

> 'My partner is out of work, but he is starting a new job. He gets whatever he can. But I'm worried, we are worried about getting moved onto Universal Credit, and about feeding the family. This summer has been hard with no school meals, and I'm cooking with cans from the food bank.' (Andrea, infrequent library user – only visits with her children)

> 'I'm here all the time. I'm trying, I'm trying. I really am, but there is so much poverty and just not enough jobs.' (Bill, regular library user – computers only)

The libraries visited during the research were all engaged in delivering essential services at a local level. The most obvious example of this was in relation to the free computer and Wi-Fi services, now a requirement to access many digitised public services, such as universal job search, benefit applications and housing lists. For those without a computer at home, this meant that the public library had become an essential local resource:

'I've not been a library user, but I don't have a PC at home. I come in here to check my universal job search and I'm waiting for news on Universal Credit. I'm finding the whole thing very stressful. Me and my husband don't have any idea what the impact will be on our money.' (Jane, regular library user – computers only)

The significance of the library service was even greater in instances where other local services, such as job clubs and employability services, had been closed or their opening hours reduced. In these instances, the 'rolling back of the state' described by Dagdeviren et al (2019) had created gaps in local provision that libraries were being expected to fill.

Book borrowing, footfall, attendance at events and the use of services such as computers are all measureable indicators of the value of public libraries. However, the social value of public libraries is often intangible, subjective and frustratingly challenging to measure (Jaeger et al, 2013). Throughout the research, there was constant evidence of libraries acting as 'social infrastructure' (Klinenberg, 2018). They were places where people are allowed, even encouraged, to congregate; as such, they encourage interaction and the formation of civic engagement. As discussed elsewhere (Given and Leckie, 2003; Aabø and Audunson, 2012), the research found multiple instances of the library as an example of a 'third space', that is, a space for recurring interaction, both loose and more formal, and the possibility of connections with other individuals and the spaces we live in. One such example related to the number of support workers using the library. Libraries were regarded by support workers not only as a safe space to meet clients, but also as somewhere to promote independent living skills, for example, by supporting clients to talk to staff, to have responsibility for recalling their pin number and to learn to access the computers. In one local authority, a support worker highlighted that the library was even more essential due to the closure of day centres:

'there will be no place for people to come today. That is why these community spaces are so important, if they aren't there, where do these people go? They end up hanging out on the street, getting influenced by bad people.

There is nowhere for them to be part of the community.'
(Johnny, support worker)

There were also numerous examples of lonely and socially isolated individuals visiting the library as part of their everyday routine. For elderly people, in particular, visits often involved reading the newspapers or browsing the bookshelves. While interactions with staff and other visitors were often fairly minimal, for example, entailing a short conversation, the library visit provided essential social contact:

'I come in every day to read the papers. I have done it for years, ever since my wife died. I don't get the books; I just sit for a few hours and have a read. I just want the library to stay the same, I don't know what I would do if it changed.' (Andrew, regular library user)

'I don't like to be in the house, so the library is so important to me; it is what keeps me going. I don't really see anyone else.' (Kath, regular library user)

In relation to this type of activity, one library staff member said "that is what the library is for, that is how it is helping folk". Indeed, most were eager to look at ways to demonstrate the wider health and social well-being benefits of public libraries. The difficulty was in how best to 'sell' this to either a board of directors or local councillors when it does not come with a clear financial value. Correspondingly, several library staff pointed to the lack of value given to their own specialist skills in creating a vital public space: "I find it really quite sad that we don't actually seem to be valued as librarians, we're just managers of different kinds. You could be anybody and I think we're going to lose quite a lot of [voice trails off]" (Betty, library manager).

While opinion was split over the necessity for a public library to be run by a professional librarian, there was broad agreement that staff running a library service have specialist skills, and that these skills are distinct from those required to run a community centre, leisure centre or local council office. These same concerns emerged in discussions about volunteers. Although the use of volunteers has not grown so rapidly in Scotland as in England and Wales, several library staff noted that the need to 'fill gaps' in services meant that volunteers were frequently assigned wide role activities, which library staff consider the most interesting part of their job. It was also noted that while volunteering was a benefit to the sustainability of the service, it was difficult and costly to manage: "There's still a cost attached to using volunteers, as much as it's sort of this ideal situation, you've still got someone to manage that. That comes back to capacity, that's a cost, and if someone's [a volunteer is] doing that, what are we not doing?" (Fred, library staff).

In a number of locations, what was striking was the shift towards a culture of managerialism and an associated focus on measurable targets and outputs. Although not unique to local authorities that had moved into a trust, in such cases, there was a more obvious emphasis on branding, the notion of 'the customer' and the drive for consistency across the service. In these instances, the autonomy among library staff to sustain a contextualised local service was limited by the objectives of the trust:

> 'It [the transfer to the trust] was all about the money, about the tax. Not about the services. So, although I don't think it isn't getting worse, I worry about the direction, the leadership and where that is going in relation to the core library aims.' (Julie, library staff)

> 'Before we were down to the trust, we saw the library as being this universal trusted space, but that's changed because we have to have a more commercial way of thinking.' (Bobby, library staff)

Although specific concerns were voiced in relation to services moving to a trust, there was also some agreement that pressures would have been greater had they remained as part of the local authority. What was clear from the research was that regardless of the delivery model, all services were facing and feeling the pressure of reductions to budgets. As well as staff cuts, this has meant that libraries cannot do everything that they want to do. Services must prioritise where they focus. While, in some cases, this has involved local communities through surveys, there was little by way of community empowerment through involvement in decision-making or service delivery.

Conclusion

> 'What it boils down to is: we need more money.' (Library staff)

In order to grasp the varied influence of local context on national policy, this chapter has combined methodological approaches. It began by interrogating national data published by CIPFA on public libraries, with the particular aim of gaining insight into local variability in national patterns of continuity and change. The findings helpfully remind us that policy processes do not affect change in localities in a homogeneous way; rather, different places exhibit important variations in how public library estates are funded, delivered and experienced. While analysis at this level can identify possible explanatory factors for cuts in spending (such as grant dependence), a more nuanced investigation can extend this understanding. How, for example, do contextual factors interact to shape outcomes and how are these outcomes experienced by individuals, institutions and communities? Exploratory qualitative investigation can be utilised to generate insight into such questions by providing rich, in-depth evidence on the factors that serve to create and entrench inequalities 'within and between places' (Featherstone et al, 2012: 179). Considering multiple sources of qualitative data – whether library staff, other professionals or local residents – provides a deeper understanding of how different people give meaning to the same social phenomenon.

The current state of the contemporary public library cannot solely be attributed to austerity. The rise of the digital age and the associated shift in user needs and demands have changed our relationship to books and informal education. Wider processes of modernisation and individualisation have also globalised the concept of community and how we use and value public spaces. It is perhaps these aspects of social change that have legitimised such huge changes being made to the library sector. This chapter has shown that since the start of the recession, the number of public libraries in Britain has reduced significantly, as has the number of staff within them. Volunteers are increasingly being relied upon to provide core services, and delivery models independent from the local authority are becoming more popular. Austerity has undoubtedly played a key role in forcing these changes, most obviously as a consequence of reductions to local government budgets and the consequential need to make cuts to local services. At a national level, there is recognition that the gradual but steady 'chipping away' at the public library estate is unlikely to be reversed.

Since the use of council services varies by socio-economic group, reductions in spending also have an inequitable effect on different income groups. Annette Hastings and colleagues (2015a) found that 'pro-poor services' (such as housing and homelessness, social work, and social care services) had been protected from cuts in relative terms. Despite this, their research revealed significant pressure, as demonstrated by overstretched staff, rising unmet needs and a growing unwillingness for services to take responsibility (Hastings et al, 2015a: 104). Their conclusion was that the cumulative impact of even small savings was more detrimental to poorer people, while better-off service users were able to navigate the consequences of austerity (for example, by driving to a service no longer available in their locality). This reminds us that all cuts to services are experienced in the context of the wider costs of recession (Lowndes and McCaughie, 2013). A further key consequence of the efforts to protect 'pro-poor services' has been that universal services like public libraries have been hit by much more significant cuts to spending. Kirsten Besemer and Glen Bramley (2012) argue that this distribution of cuts has been justified by the misaligned perception that universal services are only valued by more affluent parts of the population, and are therefore dispensable. While protecting core statutory services may seem logical in a financial crisis, this rationale fails to recognise that cuts to universal services are likely to be counterproductive in the longer term (Besemer and Bramley, 2012). Universal services like public libraries, sports and culture are, of course, valued across the social spectrum. More significantly, their critical preventive role will likely be affected by cuts to services.

Unquestionably, these processes are having severe consequences on the public library sector and the communities that depend on them. Yet, it is critical that we recognise these changes as reflective of the wider state withdrawal from the public realm. The decision-making processes that result in closures to libraries are the same as those that result in: funding being removed from youth clubs; post offices being closed; school football pitches being privatised; and investment being made in student flats instead of affordable housing for local people. Austerity localism has been conceptualised as a progressive response by the state: rolling back state intervention and transferring power to local government will benefit local communities; increased competition in public service provision will create efficiencies; while social action will empower local people.

For such aspirations to be enacted, the public realm must be thought of as much more than just public space. Franco Bianchini and Hermann Schwengel (1991: 229) described the public realm as the 'sphere of social relations going beyond our own circle of friendships, and of family and professional relations'. They argue that the public realm is 'bound up with the ideas of expanding one's mental horizons, of experiment, adventure, discovery, surprise' (Bianchini and Schwengel, 1991: 229). For this image of the public sphere to be realised, there must be financial investment; yet, the political attractiveness of austerity localism has been in enabling the retraction of state investment in public services. As this chapter has shown, cuts have disproportionately impacted the most deprived areas. The CIPFA data presented suggest that the same processes are taking place in the library sector. What is also clear from the qualitative data is that despite what we might hope, for the most marginalised individuals, the public library is not a space where broadening mental horizons is necessarily a priority. They are places in which individuals get the services they require to navigate the worst effects of everyday life in a deprived community. That might be access to a computer, a book for a child or a place 'just to be'.

British policy on public libraries recognises the ways in which they support and engage in the public realm, describing them as being at the heart of the neighbourhoods they serve, and well placed to connect, unite and build vibrant communities (see, for example, Sieghart, 2014; Scottish Library and Information Council, 2015; Welsh Government, 2017). However, the reality being faced is that in many local authorities, budgets are being slashed and the sustainability of library estates is being subjected to scrutiny, especially in the face of rising pressure from social care. In the short term, it seems likely that the reliance on volunteers across the sector will continue, as will the emergence of new delivery models. The most concerning issue is that disinvestment in community libraries (and other universal public services) will perpetuate inequalities that already exist in disadvantaged areas, while more affluent areas will continue to use their own resources to navigate closures, or successfully campaign against them.

This chapter has demonstrated the important role that qualitative research can play in helping to give meaning to national statistics and the local variability therein. National statistics can provide an indication of patterns of social change and of further areas for in-depth analysis. Moving forward, attention must be given to the development of openly available and reliable statistics on public libraries at a national and local authority level. Currently, the data collected by CIPFA are the primary source of information regarding long-term trends for public libraries. However, the data in their raw form are only available commercially and problems have been identified in reporting, especially in terms of missing data (O'Bryan, 2018). These are not issues unique to public libraries. Reporting at a national level is also limited for other similarly affected services, such as youth work. As reported in this chapter, there is burgeoning evidence of the inequitable impact of austerity measures. Future research must continue to report on these processes as a new Conservative government begins its new term. Utilising national and local administrative data sources is critical, as is investigating the possibilities of combining multiple qualitative data sets from different studies (Davidson et al, 2018). Together, these approaches can help us to continue to develop a nuanced and contextualised understanding of austerity's continued effect on our nations, our neighbourhoods and our personal lives.

Note

[1] For current data on proposed changes to services, see: www. publiclibrariesnews.com/

References

Aabø, S. and Audunson, R. (2012) 'Use of library space and the library as place', *Library & Information Science Research*, 34: 138–49.

Amin-Smith, N. and Phillips, D. (2019) *English council funding: What's happened and what's next?*, IFS Briefing Note BN250, London: The Institute for Fiscal Studies.

Arts Council England (2017) *Libraries as community hubs: Case studies and learning. A report for Arts Council England*, London: Renaisi.

Besemer, K. and Bramley, G. (2012) 'Local services under siege: attitudes to public services in a time of austerity', Working Paper Analysis Series No. 2, Poverty and Social Exclusion, funded by the ESRC.

Bianchini, F. and Schwengel, H. (1991) 'Re-imagining the city', in J. Corner and S. Harvey (eds) *Enterprise and heritage: Crosscurrents of national culture*, London: Routledge.

Cain, S. (2018) 'Nearly 130 public libraries closed across Britain in the last year', *The Guardian*, 7 December.

Casselden, B., Pickard, A.J. and Mcleod, J. (2015) 'The challenges facing public libraries in the Big Society: the role of volunteers, and the issues that surround their use in England', *Journal of Librarianship and Information Science*, 47: 187–203.

Casselden, B., Pickard, A., Walton, G. and Mcleod, J. (2019) 'Keeping the doors open in an age of austerity? Qualitative analysis of stakeholder views on volunteers in public libraries', *Journal of Librarianship and Information Science*, 51: 869–83.

Chakelian, A. (2018) 'Why are councils collapsing?', *New Statesman*, 12 September.

Child, R. and Goulding, A. (2012) 'Public libraries in the recession: the librarian's axiom', *Library Review*, 61: 641–63.

CIPFA (Chartered Institute of Public Finance and Accountancy) (2009) *Public library statistics 2008/09 estimates and 2007/08 actuals PDF*, London: Chartered Institute of Public Finance and Accountancy.

CIPFA (2019) *Public library statistics 2018/19 estimates and 2017/18 actuals PDF*, London: Chartered Institute of Public Finance and Accountancy.

Clayton, J., Donovan, C. and Merchant, J. (2016) 'Distancing and limited resourcefulness: third sector service provision under austerity localism in the north east of England', *Urban Studies*, 53: 723–40.

Corble, A.R. (2019) *The death and life of English public libraries: Infrastructural practices and value in a time of crisis*, London: Goldsmiths, University of London.

Corrigan, P. (2019) 'Approved! Stoke-on-Trent City Council will cut 200 jobs and £5.5 million of services', *StokeonTrentLive*, 17 October.

Dagdeviren, H., Donoghue, M. and Wearmouth, A. (2019) 'When rhetoric does not translate to reality: hardship, empowerment and the third sector in austerity localism', *The Sociological Review*, 67: 143–60.

Davidson, E. (2019) 'The voices of Scottish librarians: continuity and change', *Scottish Affairs*, 29(4): 395–413.

Davidson, E., Edwards, R., Jamieson, L. and Weller, S. (2018) 'Big data, qualitative style: a breadth-and-depth method for working with large amounts of secondary qualitative data', *Quality & Quantity*, 53(1): 363–76.

Davies, S. (2012) 'The public library in the UK's Big Society', *Prometheus*, 30: 353–8.

Department for Culture, Media and Sport (2018) *Definitions for types of libraries in the extended basic dataset*, London: DCMS.

Duffy, S. (2013) *A fair society? How the cuts target disabled people*, London: The Centre for Welfare Reform on behalf of Campaign for a Fair Society.

Featherstone, D., Ince, A., Mackinnon, D., Strauss, K. and Cumbers, A. (2012) 'Progressive localism and the construction of political alternatives', *Transactions of the Institute of British Geographers*, 37: 177–82.

Findlay-King, L., Nichols, G., Forbes, D. and Macfadyen, G. (2018) 'Localism and the Big Society: the asset transfer of leisure centres and libraries – fighting closures or empowering communities?', *Leisure Studies*, 37(2): 158–70.

Flintshire County Council (2018) 'Budget position 2018/19 and beyond', www.flintshire.gov.uk

Forkert, K. (2016) 'Austere creativity and volunteer-run public services: the case of Lewisham's libraries', *New Formations*, 87: 11–28.

Given, L.M. and Leckie, G.J. (2003) '"Sweeping" the library: mapping the social activity space of the public library. A version of this article was presented at the Library Research Seminar II: Partners and Connections, Research and Practice, held at College Park, Maryland, November 2001', *Library & Information Science Research*, 25: 365–85.

Goulding, A. (2006) *Public libraries in the 21st Century: Defining services and debating the future*, London: Ashgate Publishing Company.

Goulding, A. (2013) 'The Big Society and English public libraries: where are we now?', *New Library World*, 114: 478–93.

Grant, A. (2016) 'Libraries in capital could face closures as £6.4m cuts announced', *Edinburgh Evening News*, 23 November.

Gray, M. and Barford, A. (2018) 'The depths of the cuts: the uneven geography of local government austerity', *Cambridge Journal of Regions, Economy and Society*, 11: 541–63.

Hastings, A., Bailey, N., Bramley, G., Gannon, M. and Watkins, D. (2015a) *The cost of the cuts: The impact on local government and poorer communities*, York: Joseph Rowntree Foundation.

Hastings, A., Bailey, N., Gannon, M., Bramley, G. and Watkins, D. (2015b) 'Coping with the cuts? The management of the worst financial settlement in living memory', *Local Government Studies*, 41: 601–21.

Hitchen, E. (2019) 'The affective life of austerity: uncanny atmospheres and paranoid temporalities', *Social & Cultural Geography*, DOI: 10.1080/14649365.2019.1574884.

HM Treasury (2010) *Spending Review 2010*, Norwich: The Stationery Office.

Jaeger, P.T., Gorham, U., Bertot, J.C. and Sarin, L.C. (2013) 'Democracy, neutrality, and value demonstration in the age of austerity', *The Library Quarterly*, 83: 368–82.

Klinenberg, E. (2018) *Palaces for the people: How to build a more equal and united society*, London: The Bodley Head.

Levitas, R. (2012) 'The just's umbrella: austerity and the Big Society in Coalition policy and beyond', *Critical Social Policy*, 32: 320–42.

Lowndes, V. and McCaughie, K. (2013) 'Weathering the perfect storm? Austerity and institutional resilience in local government', *Policy & Politics*, 41: 533–49.

Mackay, D. (2019) 'Library group urges Moray Council not to axe facilities in next round of budget cuts', *The Press and Journal*, 30 July.

Merson, A. (2019) 'We won't shut Aberdeen libraries – council co-leader rules out "draconian step" in budget cuts', *Evening Express*, 4 March.

National Audit Office (2018) *Financial sustainability of local authorities*, London: NAO.

O'Bryan, J. (2018) *Analysing data: CIPFA statistics and the future of England's libraries*, London: DCMS.

Osborne, G. (2010) 'June Budget report statement to the House of Commons'. UK Parliament Electoral Commission Committee, available at: https://publications.parliament.uk/pa/cm201011/cmhansrd/cm100622/debtext/100622-0004.htm#10062245000001 [accessed 26.02.20].

Osborne, G. (2015) 'Chancellor George Osborne's summer Budget 2015 speech', HM Treasury.

Pautz, H. and Poulter, A. (2014) 'Public libraries in the "age of austerity": income generation and public library ethos', *Library and Information Research*, 38: 20–36.

Robertson, C. and McMenemy, D. (2018) 'The hollowing out of children's public library services in England from 2010 to 2016', *Journal of Librarianship and Information Science*, 52(1): 91–105.

Rooney-Browne, C. (2009) 'Rising to the challenge: a look at the role of public libraries in times of recession', *Library Review*, 58: 341–52.

Scottish Library and Information Council (2015) *Ambition and opportunity: A strategy for public libraries in Scotland 2015–2020*, Glasgow: Scottish Library and Information Council, Carnegie UK Trust, COSLA and Scottish Government.

Shaw, K. (2012) 'The rise of the resilient local authority?', *Local Government Studies*, 38: 281–300.

Sieghart, W. (2014) *Independent library report for England*, London: Department for Culture, Media and Sport.

Welsh Government (2017) *Connected and ambitious libraries: The sixth quality framework of Welsh public library standards 2017–2020*, Cardiff: Llywodraeth Cymru.

Wilkinson, D. (2017) 'The closing date for these 10 libraries has been revealed as more than two-thirds of town's branches shut down', *Manchester Evening News*, 7 June.

11

No way home: the challenges of exiting homelessness in austere times

Christina Carmichael

Introduction

In 2010, and in the wake of a global financial crisis, the Conservative-led Coalition government implemented an unprecedented drive of austerity measures. This included radical reforms to housing and welfare policies, as well as indirect cuts via a drastic reduction to local government budgets (Levitas, 2012). That the UK austerity programme has been presented by the government both as a 'necessary evil' in a time of economic hardship and as something that 'we are all in together' (Cameron, 2010) has served to mask the highly uneven manner in which it has translated, and continues to translate, into people's everyday lives (Hitchen, 2016; Strong, 2018). Thus, for researchers seeking to fully understand the implications of austerity, emphasis must be placed on examining the lived experiences of those bearing the brunt of the cuts to public services.

Drawing on interviews with single homeless people and practitioners living and working in homelessness accommodation projects, this chapter explores the ways in which austerity manifests at the 'street level' for a particularly poor and marginalised population. While existing research has assessed the impact of recent housing and welfare reforms on those at risk of or transitioning into homelessness and those sleeping rough (Fitzpatrick et al, 2016; Johnsen et al, 2016; Wilson and Barton, 2019), this chapter offers additional insight by placing focus on the implications of austerity for transitions out of homelessness. The data presented in this chapter reveal the ways in which austerity-driven policies are actively hindering service users' efforts to move beyond homelessness and leaving them increasingly susceptible to longer-term cycles of instability.

Policy context

Since 2010, significant upward trends have been recorded across all forms of homelessness. The number of statutory homelessness acceptances, that is, households to whom the local authority have a duty to secure accommodation, stood at 56,600 in 2017/18. While a small reduction on the previous year, this is an overall increase of 42 per cent since 2009/10 (Fitzpatrick et al, 2019). However, this represents only the tip of an increasingly large iceberg. Latest figures indicate a significant rise between 2009/10 and 2017/18 in instances of rough sleeping (165 per cent) and sofa surfing (26 per cent) (Fitzpatrick et al, 2019). While figures show that the number of people residing in homelessness accommodation projects has actually dropped by 20 per cent during this period, this is a reflection of reduced capacity as a result of funding losses, rather than reduced demand (Fitzpatrick et al, 2019).

Non-statutory services for single homeless people – those that sit outside of the legislative remit – are primarily delivered by the voluntary sector. The majority of voluntary sector services rely, at least partially, on statutory funding previously administered through the ring-fenced Supporting People stream. In 2009, the ring fence was removed, and by 2011, Supporting People had been subsumed into the Formula Grant. As a result, local authorities are no longer required to allocate a set amount of funds to housing and homelessness-related provision, and may prioritise as they see fit (Homeless Link, 2013). Between 2008/09 and 2017/18, funding for single homelessness via the Formula Grant reduced by 50 per cent, representing an approximate shortfall in spending of £5 billion during that period (Thunder and Rose, 2019). Given the breadth of cuts to local government under austerity, it is unsurprising that provision for single homelessness has suffered to this extent.

Crucially, this period has also seen extensive cuts to the 'floating' (community-based) services that provide a broad range of support aimed at preventing entries and re-entries into homelessness. The severity of cuts to specialist forms of floating support is of particular concern, with St Mungo's (2018) reporting drastic budget reductions across support for mental ill health (44 per cent), substance use (41 per cent) and ex-offenders (88 per cent) between 2014 and 2018. Despite the fact that homelessness prevention has been a central feature in successive governments' agendas, preventive strategies are being increasingly undermined by austerity-driven cuts: where local authorities are forced to choose between funding prevention services and 'crisis management', the latter inevitably prevails (Thunder and Rose, 2019). While new legislation in the form of the Homelessness Reduction Act 2017 increases the statutory rights of homeless people to access assistance and accommodation, without an increase in local government budget and resource levels, its potential impact is arguably limited. Indeed, early indications suggest that a significant proportion of local authorities are failing to implement their new statutory duties (see New Government Network, 2019).

For those attempting to exit homelessness, austerity reforms to housing and welfare have been particularly impactful. On housing, successive Coalition and Conservative governments have continued to prioritise the owner-occupied and private rental markets over the building of social housing, despite lengthy waiting lists for the latter (Hodkinson and Robbins, 2013; Tunstall, 2015). Between 2009/10 and 2012/13, expenditure on housing development (primarily the building of social housing) fell by 44 per cent or £4.8 billion in real terms, representing one of the biggest percentage cuts to a government budget under austerity (Tunstall, 2015: 29). Through amendments made to the Localism Act 2011, social housing has essentially been rebranded as a temporary and conditional tenure, to which access is heavily restricted (Hodkinson and Robbins, 2013). Local authorities now have the right to: (1) exclude people from housing registers based on specific histories and/or behaviours; (2) offer time-limited tenancies; and (3) discharge their duty to statutorily homeless persons via private rented tenancies (Stephens and Stephenson, 2016). The scarcity of social housing, coupled with the low priority of single homeless people on housing registers, has resulted in private rented sector (PRS) accommodation becoming a major destination for those attempting to avoid or exit homelessness (Homeless Link, 2018). This is despite long-standing concerns around the accessibility and suitability of PRS accommodation for those with complex support needs. Indeed, conversely, the end of an assured shorthold tenancy in the private sector has been noted as the primary cause for becoming homeless in the UK in recent years (Fitzpatrick et al, 2019).

Welfare reforms with particular relevance to single homelessness include the replacement of legacy benefits with a single payment via Universal Credit, caps to Local Housing Allowance and the intensification of sanctioning and conditionality in accessing out-of-work benefits (Jobseekers Allowance and Employment and Support Allowance) (Watts et al, 2014; Patrick, 2015; Reeve, 2017; Fitzpatrick et al, 2019). Taken together, these pose significant barriers for those wishing to exit homelessness and secure longer-term stability. Existing research indicates that benefit sanctions are being disproportionately administered to homeless people unable to meet conditionality requirements as a result of their circumstances (Reeve, 2017), while the delays associated with Universal Credit payments have been shown to leave single people at an increased risk of accruing rent arrears (Fitzpatrick et al, 2019).

Cultures of 'worklessness and dependency'?

The austerity programme has been accompanied by a government rhetoric in which poverty is defined in wholly individual and behavioural terms, and the structural components of unemployment, welfare dependency, housing precarity and homelessness are either overlooked or actively denied. While it is by no means new to blame those in poverty for their circumstances, behavioural explanations gained significant traction during the Coalition and Conservative administrations, and are increasingly visible in policy and public discourses (Pemberton et al, 2016; Shildrick et al, 2016).

Here, the post-war consensus around the welfare state has been challenged by a hegemonic culture that presents it as the 'anti-thesis of self-reliance, responsibility and independence' (Reeve, 2017: 67–8) – the most unassailable and 'commonsensical' of societal values. The apparent existence of a 'culture of entrenched worklessness and dependency' (Duncan Smith, 2012) is attributed to an overly 'generous' (Osborne, 2013) welfare state that fails to 'incentivise' employment. Those in receipt of benefits are frequently vilified and placed in contrast with the 'hard-working majority' in what Patrick (2015: 24) has referred to as a 'contemporary reworking of longstanding distinctions between "undeserving" and "deserving" populations'. This is well evidenced if we look to speeches made my members of the Coalition cabinet:

> Large numbers sitting on out of work benefits [go] unchallenged, many unwilling or unable to take advantage of the job opportunities being created.... It is a system set around the minority. An exemption here, an addition there, all designed around the needs of the most dysfunctional and disadvantaged few. (Duncan Smith, 2012)

> For too long, we've had a system where people who did the right thing – who get up in the morning and work

hard – felt penalised for it, while people who did the wrong
thing got rewarded for it. (Osborne, 2013)

By choosing to frame welfare in this way, the government effectively
created a backdrop against which harsh cuts to public services and
increasingly conditional access to welfare were legitimised and even
celebrated. That the existence of social housing exacerbates rather
than alleviates poverty has also been a central line of argument within
this rhetoric and provides a rationale for the restrictions to access
described earlier: 'Social housing, once a support for families working
hard to give their children something better, has too often become a
place of intergenerational worklessness, hopelessness and dependency'
(Duncan Smith, 2011).

In the same vein, Conservative Members of Parliament (MPs) have
repeatedly denied the connections between austerity measures and
rising homelessness figures, and explained away the government's
responsibility by focusing on individual pathology and behaviour.
When presented with evidence of the impacts of welfare reform on
homelessness, Housing Minister James Brokenshire responded that he
'didn't see it in those terms' and instead attributed blame to substance
use and family breakdown (*The Guardian*, 2018).

Current debates in homelessness service provision

Before moving on, and in order to situate the empirical material detailed
in the following, it is important to provide some brief context as regards
provision for single homelessness in the UK. Overall, the empirical
evidence base for 'what works' in supporting successful homelessness
exits, achieving longer-term stability and preventing homelessness
re-entries is relatively well established. Indeed, existing research has
consistently pointed to the importance of: (1) access to affordable,
secure and permanent accommodation; (2) financial security and access
to/the maintenance of paid employment; and (3) positive health and
well-being, including support for mental ill health and substance misuse
(for example, Pleace and Bretherton, 2017; Downie et al, 2018).

In the UK context, non-statutory services for single homeless people
largely adhere to a linear model of provision. Essentially, services are
structured in a way that homeless people may 'progress' through
multiple stages, from more to less intensive services, and eventually
into independent living, though service users may, in practice, skip
steps depending on the level of need (Buckingham, 2010; Homeless

Link, 2015, 2018). Specific time limits are normally attached to stays at each 'stage' – usually between three months and two years, though sometimes less – with these being a prerequisite for services to receive statutory funding. The rationale for such an approach is rooted in a 'treatment first' philosophy, which argues that for homeless people to manage housing in the long term, it is necessary to first address their additional support needs (mental ill health, substance misuse, offending behaviours and so on) and that progress should be conditional on that basis. The appropriateness of this sort of approach has increasingly been called into question, with specific concerns around the lack of service user choice and control, as well as the implications that longer-term stays in hostels/supporting housing may have for service user well-being (Johnsen and Teixeira, 2010; Blood et al, 2018). In light of this, and while still in the relatively early stages of implementation, Housing First models have emerged as an alternative and potentially more successful way of supporting single homeless people. Effectively 'skipping' the transitional stages described earlier, this approach involves placing homeless people directly into permanent independent tenancies, private or social, with access to ongoing support – either from internal support workers or from specialist services where needed (Johnsen and Teixeira, 2010; Blood et al, 2018). While a number of Housing First pilots have appeared in recent years, this model remains in its infancy in the UK context (Blood et al, 2018).

Research design

This chapter draws on a series of interviews conducted with homeless service users and practitioners to explore how austerity is translating into the 'street-level' realities of homelessness. A total of 40 semi-structured interviews took place between June 2017 and 2018, with a sample comprising nine practitioners working in local authority housing departments, 14 practitioners working in voluntary sector homelessness organisations and 17 single homeless people ('service users'), though the primary focus of this chapter will be on the narratives of the voluntary sector and service user interviewees. Data were collected and analysed in accordance with a constructivist grounded theory (CGT) framework (Charmaz, 2014). CGT is an inductive, iterative and theory-building approach to qualitative research, which was chosen to ensure that participants' experiences and priorities remained central throughout the research process. Interviews followed a semi-structured format and were audio-recorded and transcribed verbatim. Full ethical clearance was received from the researcher's university prior to the commencement of the study and pseudonyms are used throughout.

Service user interviewees (15 male; two female) were recruited at non-specialist homelessness accommodation projects in East Anglia and Greater London, with initial contact made via a gatekeeper figure (usually a service manager or key worker). The vast majority of interviewees were living in these services – either a hostel or supported housing project – at the point of interview. Two interviewees had recently moved into independent tenancies but had remained in contact with their former service. Direct causes of homelessness varied among the service users but most had been experiencing homelessness for a significant period of time at the point of interview and presented with some form of additional support need. In the majority of cases, interviewees' experiences of homelessness had included a period or multiple periods of rough sleeping prior to entering services. A smaller minority had moved directly into services, either from sofa surfing or following a discharge from hospital. The voluntary sector practitioner sample comprised practitioners working in hostels, supported housing projects and day-centre/advice services. Eight were front-line support staff, while six worked in back-office or management roles. All but one of the services were at least partially reliant on statutory funding via their local authority, and all had seen some form of reduction to that funding since 2010.

Rhetoric versus reality: barriers to 'independence'

Interviewees' accounts point to the extensive challenges that single homeless people face in their attempts to move away from homelessness. Austerity-driven policies are shown to have worsened structural barriers to moving on, and placed the components necessary for longer-term stability out of reach. There is a paradox, then, between rhetoric and reality (Patrick, 2015): government discourses tell us of the importance of moving away from cultures of 'dependence' and 'worklessness', yet the picture that emerged here was one of a system 'backing up', and a population of homeless people 'stuck' in services. Notably, while the chaotic nature of 'first-stage' hostels did highlight specific concerns for service user well-being, the barriers to moving on identified by interviewees were generally consistent across hostel and supported housing contexts.

Voluntary sector practitioners repeatedly spoke of a marked increase in complex support needs among those presenting to non-specialist accommodation projects, with the service user population characterised as more 'entrenched', 'demanding' and 'critical' than in years previous. This was usually attributed to the stripping back of preventive and specialist services, particularly around mental health, as well as the removal of a 'safety net' that had previously protected the most vulnerable members of society from absolute homelessness:

> 'It's as if they removed a layer without putting anything in the place to catch people that may fall through the net, so we become the go-to guys, and it seems as if we're having people who have very serious and enduring mental health issues who are having to live in a homeless hostel and that's not fair ... we've had more safeguarding issues raised in this hostel this year than I've ever seen in its entirety because we're having very vulnerable people in here.' (Bella, manager, hostel)

Subsequent efforts to (re-)engage service users with specialist mental health and substance use services were often arduous. Specific barriers included a lack of suitable provision in local areas, lengthy waiting times, higher thresholds and conditionality clauses around access. Instances of exclusion from services based on a dual diagnosis (combined mental ill health and substance misuse) were particularly common, and resulted in service users being bounced between various providers, with minimal intervention. In the absence of specialist support and in contending with the service environment itself (Johnsen and Teixeira, 2010), service users' well-being often worsened during their time in services. Where primary support and health-related needs were going unmanaged, steps towards longer-term goals (housing, education, employment) were effectively forced onto the back burner:

> 'The [mental health service] waiting list is so long, so my clients they're just waiting and waiting and waiting, and they just get more poorly to be honest.' (Sophie, front-line practitioner, supported housing)

> 'I came in here in a bit of a state.... I was quite shocked at how long it took to get a script ... they need to script people pretty much straight away, not put them through months and months ... because as soon as you got the Methadone, and as soon as that started working properly ...

I sort of started putting things in place.' (Liam, service user, supported housing)

Where service users were in a position to think about moving on, the majority faced difficulties in gaining access to accommodation, with barriers to both social housing and the PRS regularly noted. While they remained the favoured destination for service users, social housing tenancies were depicted as increasingly out of the reach of single homeless people. As per the Localism Act 2011, the right of local authorities to reject applicants based on histories of antisocial and offending behaviour, rent arrears, and/or substance misuse effectively excluded the majority of service users from the bidding process entirely (Rowe and Wagstaff, 2017). Where conditions for access to the housing register were set out by local authorities, these were generally deemed implausible within the confines of the service environment:

> '[The local authority] want our clients to pretty much bend over backwards before they will give them a low banding. You're talking 12 months paying off any debts ... six to 12 months engaging with substance misuse, six to 12 months of no offending. For some of our guys, that's never gonna happen and part of the reason is because they are stuck in an environment like this.' (Zara, front-line practitioner, hostel)

That private rented tenancies represent a viable alternative for moving on was heavily disputed by both practitioners and service users. High rental costs, a lack of accommodation at the rate of Local Housing Allowance and the need for upfront cash payments were all recognised to be significant barriers to the private sector (Rowe and Wagstaff, 2017). Even in cases where properties were affordable to service users, landlords were often unwilling to rent to homeless people, welfare recipients and ex-offenders (Fitzpatrick et al, 2018). Given that the private rental market is, at least at the cheapest end, highly oversubscribed and competitive, service users often felt themselves to be at the bottom of a very long list (Homeless Link, 2018):

> 'They've put the rent up, not many landlords now will take people if you're on Housing Benefit ... and if you've got to wait eight weeks for the council to pay your rent and stuff, who's gonna give you a place with no money for eight weeks?' (Nick, service user, hostel)

'I've seen five people in eight years go into private rented ...
private landlords will not take people on Housing Benefit ...
even if they would take Housing Benefit long term, which
they won't ... with our guys, private landlords don't want
to take them, there's a stigma attached.' (Rosie, manager,
supported housing)

Crucially, the rollout of Universal Credit was viewed as further reducing
access to the private sector. This was noted in relation to not only well-
documented delays and underpayments, but also landlords' aversion to
relying on payment from the tenant rather than the local authority as
previous (Reeve et al, 2016).

Notably, while service users were generally keen to exit homelessness
services, they also showed deep concern over the prospect of moving
into private rented accommodation. Steve presented with minimal
support needs and spoke of his support workers' intentions to try and
move him on imminently. However, he was seemingly overwhelmed
about the financial burdens that this would entail:

'I don't know whether I'm going to [move on] just yet; I
need to find something that can be feasible, like I can afford
all the bills, and at the minute, it's posing quite hard to find,
so I could be here for an extra few months.... It's not even
just the rent ... most places want the first month's deposit
and then a month's rent, and then all the admin fees ...
how the hell am I going to afford that?' (Steve, service user,
supported housing)

The hesitancy that Steve and others expressed must be situated
alongside their trajectories into and through homelessness. A significant
proportion of service users interviewed had previously been evicted
from a private rented or social tenancy, while others had experienced
attempts at moving on – normally to undesirable areas and without
support – that ultimately broke down. As such, it is unsurprising that
they wish to avoid falling into the same cycle repeatedly.

As earlier, secure employment has been identified as a crucial
component in exiting homelessness in the long term. The majority of
service users expressed that (re-)entering the paid employment market
was a key objective for them, and many were taking active steps to
find work at the time of the interview. This was often of particular
priority given the challenges faced in maintaining access to regular

Jobseekers Allowance/Universal Credit payments (Reeve, 2017). However, service users generally felt that they were overlooked in the employment market. Regular complaints included a lack of (funded) training and education opportunities, minimal job prospects for those with criminal records, and sanctioning procedures and hostility at JobCentre Plus:

> 'I've got a criminal record; it's hard, I want to get a job, but it's hard for me to find a job ... employers don't even look at you.' (Nick, service user, hostel)

> 'The way people go through like CVs, if you haven't got the education, if you haven't got the qualifications, those applications, your application just goes in the bin.' (Liam, service user, supported housing)

Where service users had accessed work, this tended to be on a low-paid zero-hours or temporary basis and did not offer the level of financial security to allow for moving on. As a result of Housing Benefit rules, accepting work also regularly resulted in a rise in rental costs within hostels/supported housing projects, thus increasing the likelihood of eviction. That being in work was often actually more precarious than remaining on unemployment benefits was a particular source of frustration. Here, the need for something akin to a 'grace period', whereby service users could work and reside in a hostel for a set period, or whereby those in employment could more easily access housing, was regularly emphasised:

> 'If they [local authorities] want more successes ... people are saying "I'd rather be working and out there and have money in my own pocket" ... but then they've then got a massive rent to pay at [hostel] ... so places need to have some sort of subsidy on it.' (Liam, service user, supported housing)

> 'We're gonna end up getting him in arrears with his rent because he's not earning absolutely loads ... Housing Benefit can't calculate what he's entitled to 'cause one week he might work 24 hours but the next week he might work 16 hours, every time he puts in a wage slip his Housing Benefit gets stopped.... [He's] got no chance of maintaining employment.' (Leanne, front-line practitioner, hostel)

Overall, interviewees' accounts serve as a counter to dominant government rhetoric (Patrick, 2015). While billed as incentivising moves away from 'worklessness' and 'welfare dependency', the austerity programme (paradoxically) seems to be doing the opposite and pushing those in homelessness services further away from housing and employment markets. As elsewhere, there was little evidence to suggest a 'culture of worklessness' or that benefits represented a preferred 'lifestyle choice' for service users. Instead, the emotional and practical burden of accessing and surviving on welfare benefits was a consistent theme (Shildrick et al, 2012; Patrick, 2015). These accounts are also indicative of the need for ongoing and practical support for those attempting to access, or maintain, employment during (and beyond) their transitions out of homelessness.

What is also apparent is here is that public perceptions of homeless people often exacerbated the service users' efforts to move on further (for instance, in trying to access a PRS tenancy or in applying for work). This is not divorced from, but rather created and reinforced by, the political contexts described here. The way in which the government chooses to frame homelessness, welfare dependency, poverty and so on inevitably filters into public attitudes and responses (Pemberton et al, 2016).

Stuck in the system

In the absence of appropriate housing options, and in responding to increasingly complex needs, practitioners reported difficulties in adhering to designated time frames for moving on. Services designed specifically to address short-term needs were often becoming longer-term options by default, raising major concerns for the well-being of both those in services and those left on the streets for longer:

> 'The whole system is backing up. If we're not moving people on, [night shelters] aren't moving people on, so the people on the streets can't get in.' (Martin, manager, supported housing)

> 'The turnaround should be around one to three months.... I've known somebody to stay in a direct access service for over two years.' (Leanne, front-line practitioner, hostel)

From the practitioner perspective, this standstill had resulted in a general sense of despondency and hopelessness across the service user population. Increases in antisocial and criminal behaviour, abandonment from services, and relapses into substance misuse were contextualised and rationalised alongside a lack of opportunity for moving on:

'Ten years ago, the sector was better at picking people up and addressing their problems quickly across a range of agencies.... If you have to wait for services, then that downward spiral for people will continue ... and they are going to slip into antisocial behaviour.' (Charles, manager, hostel)

'The more setbacks they get, eventually they get very despondent, which I think anybody would.... If all you're wanting to do is just fix the problems in your life and every step of the way you're just hitting your head on a wall ... it can be quite damaging to the mental health to be honest.' (Zara, front-line practitioner, hostel)

For Scott, who was living in a supported housing project, actively using opiates and struggling to access substance-based support, this sense of hopelessness was particularly pronounced. In the face of multiple barriers and little sense of what he should 'do next', he seemed to have become fairly resigned to his situation. At points within the interview, for example, he began to question the value of tackling his substance use entirely:

'I look at people who do have scripts ... and I kind of think, "Yeah, that would be great" ... but I'd still be tied to getting up and having to go out and get something anyway, which is the same as what I'm doing anyway.... It seems quite difficult to say to myself ... "Things will be better tomorrow." I get impatient and I'm not sure how optimistic I am about the future or what I see for myself.' (Scott, service user, supported housing)

Interview data also pointed to a significant rise in cases of revolving-door homelessness, whereby service users re-enter into services after a period of maintaining independent accommodation. In one direct access hostel, for example, it was reported that the number of service users who had been through the service at least once before increased from 18 in 2010 to 75 in 2017. In the absence of specialist support, practitioners felt that service users were often being moved on without fully resolving their underlying issues (mental ill health, substance use), and that this placed them at risk of essentially repeating the cycle. Service user accounts reinforced this issue further: several had experienced homelessness on multiple occasions and alluded to facing problems in maintaining independent tenancies without ongoing support. Here, the impact of the cuts to floating and prevention-oriented support was particularly apparent:

> 'I'm always ending up, you know, in hostels, I always go back. I felt so stressed and depressed.... I felt closed in and claustrophobic, that's why I left [my accommodation] and why I became homeless.' (Ellie, service user, supported housing)

> 'I was half living in the house ... which was, er, gradually deteriorating.... I couldn't afford to, the boiler had broken, everything just piled on top ... everything was a fight.... I wanted to get out.' (Scott, service user, supported housing)

Difficulties in breaking cycles of service 'dependency' among single homeless people are by no means new. Rather, they have been a long-standing concern of practitioners and policymakers, as well as a central critique of linear-style (treatment first) service provision for some time (Johnsen and Teixeria, 2010). What these data indicate is that the risk of getting stuck in an 'institutional loop' (Benjaminsen and Knutagård, 2016: 58) seems to be starker in the current climate, particularly where the services that work to prevent homelessness re-entries are increasingly being decommissioned.

Services under strain

Interviews also highlighted that voluntary sector services and practitioners were being placed under significant strain as they attempted to reconcile the demands of an increasingly challenging and despondent client group with the realities of austerity-led policy and provision. As a result of cuts to funding and staffing levels, many practitioners described changes to the nature of their work. Here, their focus had transferred from broader forms of support and engagement to the management of 'crises', with a reduction in one-on-one time with service users being a particularly common complaint. Given the hostility often experienced by service users in the broader service context described earlier, the fact that practitioners may no longer have the capacity to help them navigate this system is certainly a cause for major concern:

> 'You can be dealing with an overdose, and somebody kicking off, and somebody wanting to make a phone call and people coming through the front door.... With some of our complex needs clients, [we] used to be able to drive them to mental health appointments, stay with them at [local drug service] to make sure they get on a script, sit with them through a mental health assessment.... Can't do that anymore, we have to cut back on all our expenses ... [we're] restricted to the hostel at all times.' (Leanne, front-line practitioner, hostel)

Despite few of the front-line staff working in homelessness accommodation projects receiving specialist training (Reeve et al, 2018), responding to high-level support needs seemed to be an increasingly central part of their work. Practitioners often expressed that they felt ill-equipped to respond to mental health and substance-related issues but were unable to access support from external providers, as Zara notes:

> 'We recently had somebody who binges alcohol trying to cut the vein artery in his leg with glass ... we could not get him engaged with mental health, we're not specifically trained in mental health, we're not specifically trained in drug use or any of these things, yet it felt like "Oh, he's there with you, you deal with it" ... it was just so frustrating ... just to watch him going through all that ... but not being able to get that help for him.' (Zara, front-line practitioner, hostel)

While a source of frustration, instances of 'passing the buck' were generally framed as a consequence of extensive cuts rather than individual or organisation fault. Zara, for example, went on to say that:

> 'With the cuts going right across the board, it's just been hit at every angle and the only people that are suffering from that is these guys ... mental health services, they're totally understaffed.' (Zara, front-line practitioner, hostel)

Overall, there was a sense that practitioners' beliefs about what 'good practice' looked like, generally described in terms of intensive, holistic and person-centred support involving multiple agencies, were being challenged by the political and organisational contexts in which they are now operating. Such challenges were a great source of distress, particularly given the deep commitment and connectedness that practitioners expressed towards their work and client group. Indeed, many spoke of the emotional toll that their work entailed, raising significant concerns around the potential for burnout and low rates of retention:

> 'The reason why I came into this job is to help and support our clients to get access to services, and I'm just watching them get pulled away ... and that means the staff team struggles. I find that hard now, it's making my job more difficult.' (Bella, manager, hostel)

> 'People would get a shock if they came into homelessness services now and found out how difficult it really is.... I lie in bed at two o'clock in the morning worrying.' (Rachel, front-line worker, hostel)

These findings echo broader concerns raised in the literature around the pressures being placed on voluntary sector services as the state 'rolls back' (Milbourne and Cushman, 2015; Jones et al, 2016; Daly, 2018). While the resilient and innovative nature of the voluntary sector is often emphasised, it is also important to recognise how sensitive it is to the austerity context in which it is operating, particularly in terms of the well-being of front-line practitioners (Daly, 2018).

Conclusion

Set against the backdrop of almost a decade of austerity, this chapter has explored the lived realities of single homeless people and those who work to support them as they navigate the challenging and complex task of exiting homelessness in the long term. Through a harmful combination of welfare and housing reforms, cuts to homelessness services via local government, and significant strains on the health and social care sectors, the data evidence the ways in which the austerity programme has inhibited rather than 'incentivised' departures from dependency and worklessness (Patrick, 2015). That voluntary sector homelessness services and practitioners are increasingly under strain as they come to terms with the realities of austerity policies and provision is also recognised. The concluding argument of this chapter, then, is that it is important for policymakers to resist penalising single homeless people who struggle to move out of services in an expected manner, and instead recognise the deep personal challenges and the increasing number of structural and societal barriers that hinder their efforts.

In austere times, the focus of policy and provision often (understandably) centres on 'crisis management'. However, the consequence of this is both a decline in the preventive function of services and local authorities (Thunder and Rose, 2019), and a masking of the challenges faced by the 'hidden' population residing in homelessness services. In responding to the growing number of people facing homelessness, priority must be refocused on prevention, and for those already in services, attention must be turned to building longer-term resettlement strategies and improving access to broader and more responsive forms of support.

Given that the newly elected government is keen to suggest that they are 'turning the page' on austerity (BBC, 2019), it will be important to see what comes next and what may be recouped and reconstructed in the aftermath. While the economic rationale for austerity is seemingly weakened, and increased spending has been promised, there are two key areas that will require scrutiny moving forward. The first is whether economic uncertainty around national growth and Brexit will mean that such spending actually materialises in reality; the second is whether ideological choices mean that (single) homelessness remains a lesser priority when compared with health, education or social care for the elderly. If so, the prospects for a major shift in policy responses towards homelessness seem remote.

Not for the first time, questions are also raised around the appropriateness of linear service models for single homeless people. As has been argued elsewhere (Johnsen and Teixeira, 2010), service users – and particularly those with complex support needs – have been shown here to be at increasing risk of getting 'stuck' in endless cycles of homelessness and instability. Thus, the growing recognition of the value of the Housing First model is certainly warranted. However, an important caveat to this is that access to suitable housing must always be accompanied by proper mechanisms through which broader sources of support may be routinely accessed. The impacts of the austerity programme, not only on the homeless sector itself, but also on broader health and social care provision, must be taken fully into account in ongoing responses to homelessness. A valuable avenue for future research, then, would be to examine the effects of austerity on a wider range of services than is discussed here, and to explicitly consider the implications that these hold for those at risk of, or facing, homelessness.

While the localised scale of this study leaves substantial room for the further examination of the issues raised here, it does serve to highlight the contribution that 'street-level' accounts can offer. In listening to homeless people and practitioners (and others who are feeling the brunt of policy reform), we gain a far more nuanced view of the lived realities of austerity than is recognised in dominant discourses. With this understanding, we are well placed to contest and counter the austerity rhetoric, and thus lay a foundation for more appropriate policy responses in the future (Hitchen, 2016; Garthwaite, 2016; Rose and McAuley, 2019). As Sarah, a service user in supported housing stated: "Start listening to the homeless. Ask, listen to the people that are actually living it, that's what they should do, they should listen to us, let our lives be heard and done something with."

References

BBC (British Broadcasting Corporation) (2019) 'Chancellor Sajid Javid declares end of austerity', 4 September, www.bbc.co.uk/news/business-49577250

Benjaminsen, L. and Knutagård, M. (2016) 'Homelessness research and policy development: examples from the Nordic countries', *European Journal of Homelessness*, 10(3): 45–66.

Blood, I., Goldup, M., Peters, L. and Dulson, S. (2018) *Implementing Housing First across England, Scotland and Wales*, London: Crisis and Homeless Link.

Buckingham, H. (2010) 'Capturing diversity: a typology of third sector organisations' responses to contracting based on empirical evidence from homelessness services', TSRC Working Paper 41.

Cameron, D. (2010) 'Prime Minister's speech on the economy', 7 June, www.gov.uk/government/speeches/prime-ministers-speech-on-the-economy

Charmaz, K. (2014) *Constructing grounded theory: A practical guide through qualitative analysis* (2nd edn), London: Sage.

Daly, A. (2018) 'Embodied austerity: narratives of early austerity from a homelessness and resettlement service', *Ethics and Social Welfare*, 12(1): 65–77.

Downie, M., Gousy, H., Basran, J., Jacob, R., Rowe, S., Hancock, C., Albanese, F., Pritchard, R., Nightingale, K. and Davies, T. (2018) *Everybody in: How to end homelessness in Great Britain*, London: Crisis.

Duncan Smith, I. (2011) 'Speech to the Conservative Party conference', 3 October, www.politics.co.uk/comment-analysis/2011/10/03/iain-duncan-smith-speech-in-full

Duncan Smith, I. (2012) 'Reforming welfare, transforming lives', 25 October, www.gov.uk/government/speeches/reforming-welfare-transforming-lives

Fitzpatrick, S., Pawson, H., Bramley, G., Wilcox, S. and Watts, B. (2016) *The homelessness monitor: England 2016*, London: Crisis.

Fitzpatrick, S., Pawson, H., Bramley, G., Wilcox, S., Watts, B. and Wood, J. (2018) *The homelessness monitor: England 2018*, London: Crisis.

Fitzpatrick, S., Pawson, H., Bramley, G., Wilcox, S., Watts, B. and Wood, J. (2019) *The homelessness monitor: England 2019*, London: Crisis.

Garthwaite, K. (2016) 'Stigma, shame and "people like us": an ethnographic study of foodbank use in the UK', *Journal of Poverty and Social Justice*, 24(3): 277–89.

Hitchen, E. (2016) 'Living and feeling the austere', *New Formations*, 87: 102–18.

Hodkinson, S. and Robbins, G. (2013) 'The return of class war conservatism? Housing under the UK Coalition Government', *Critical Social Policy*, 33(1): 57–77.

Homeless Link (2013) *Who is supporting people now? Experiences of local authority commissioning after Supporting People*, London: Homeless Link.

Homeless Link (2015) *Moving on from homelessness: How services support people to move on*, London: Homeless Link.

Homeless Link (2018) *Support for single homeless people in England: Annual review 2018*, London: Homeless Link.

Johnsen, S. and Teixeira, L. (2010) *Staircases, elevators and cycles of change: 'Housing First' and other housing models for homeless people with complex support needs*, London: Crisis.

Johnsen, S., Watts, B. and Fitzpatrick, S. (2016) *First wave findings: Homelessness. Welfare conditionality study briefing paper*, York: University of York.

Jones, G., Meegan, R., Kennett, P. and Croft, J. (2016) 'The uneven impact of austerity on the voluntary and community sector: A tale of two cities', *Urban Studies*, 53(10): 2064–80.

Levitas, R. (2012) 'The just's umbrella: austerity and the Big Society in Coalition policy and beyond', *Critical Social Policy*, 32(3): 320–42.

Milbourne, L. and Cushman, M. (2015) 'Complying, transforming or resisting in the new austerity? Realigning social welfare and independent action among English voluntary organisations', *Journal of Social Policy*, 44(3): 463–85.

New Government Network (2019) 'NGLN leadership index, April 2019', www.nlgn.org.uk/public/wp-content/uploads/Leadership-Index_April-2019.pdf

Osborne, G. (2013) 'George Osborne welfare speech in full', 2 April, www.politics.co.uk/comment-analysis/2013/04/02/george-osborne-welfare-speech-in-full

Patrick, R. (2015) 'Rhetoric and reality: exploring lived experiences of welfare reform under the Coalition', in L. Foster, A. Brunton, C. Deeming and T. Haux (eds) *In defence of welfare 2*, Bristol: Social Policy Association, pp 24–7.

Pemberton, S., Fahmy, E., Sutton, E. and Bell, K. (2016) 'Navigating the stigmatised identities of poverty in austere times: resisting and responding to narratives of personal failure', *Critical Social Policy*, 36(1): 21–37.

Pleace, N. and Bretherton, J. (2017) *Crisis skylight: Final report of the University of York evaluation*, London: Crisis.

Reeve, K. (2017) 'Welfare conditionality, benefit sanctions and homelessness in the UK: ending the "something for nothing culture" or punishing the poor?', *Journal of Poverty and Social Justice*, 25(1): 65–78.

Reeve, K., Cole, I., Batty, B., Foden, M., Green, S. and Pattison, B. (2016) *Home: No less will do: Homeless people's access to the private rented sector*, Sheffield: Sheffield Hallam University and Crisis.

Reeve, K., McCarthy, L., Pattinson, B., Parr, S., Batty, E., Maye-Banbury, A., Bashir, N, and Dayson, C. (2018) *The mental health needs of Nottingham's homeless population: an exploratory research study: Project Report*. Sheffield: Centre for Regional Economic and Social Research.

Rose, W. and McAuley, C. (2019) 'Poverty and its impact on parenting in the UK: re-defining the critical nature of the relationship through examining lived experiences in times of austerity', *Children and Youth Services Review*, 97: 131–41.

Rowe, S. and Wagstaff, T. (2017) *Moving on: Improving access to housing for single homeless people in England*, London: Crisis.

Shildrick, T., MacDonald, R., Furlong, A., Roden, J. and Crow, R. (2012) *Are cultures of worklessness passed down the generations?*, York: JRF.

Shildrick, T., MacDonald, R. and Furlong, A. (2016) 'Not single spies but in battalions: a critical, sociological engagement with the idea of so-called "Troubled Families"', *The Sociological Review*, 64(4): 821–36.

Stephens, M. and Stephenson, A. (2016) 'Housing policy in the austerity age and beyond', in M. Fenger, J. Hudson and C. Needham (eds) *Analysis and debate in Social Policy 2016: Social policy review 28*, Bristol: Policy Press, pp 63–85.

St Mungo's (2018) *Home for good: The role of floating support services in ending rough sleeping*, London: St Mungo's.

Strong, S. (2018) 'Food banks, actually existing austerity and the localisation of responsibility', *Geoforum*, https://doi.org/10.1016/j.geoforum.2018.09.025

The Guardian (2018) 'Rise in homelessness not result of our policies, says Housing Secretary', 18 December, www.theguardian.com/politics/2018/dec/18/rising-homelessness-is-not-due-to-tory-policies-says-james-brokenshire

Thunder, J. and Rose, C. (2019) *Local authority spending on homelessness: Understanding recent trends and their impact*, Stanmore: WPI Economics.

Tunstall, R. (2015) *The coalition's record on housing: Policy, spending and outcomes 2010–2015*. London: Centre for Analysis of Social Exclusion.

Watts, B., Fitzpatrick, S., Bramley, G. and Watkins, D. (2014) *Welfare sanctions and conditionality in the UK*, York: Joseph Rowntree Foundation.

Wilson, W. and Barton, C. (2019) *Briefing paper number 02007: rough sleeping (England)*, London: House of Commons Library.

12

'Everywhere and nowhere': interventions and services under austerity

Stephen Crossley

Introduction

> In order to truly understand the power of the state in its full
> specificity, i.e., the particular symbolic efficacy it wields, one
> must ... integrate into one and the same explanatory model
> intellectual traditions customarily perceived as incompatible.
> It is necessary, first, to overcome the opposition between a
> physicalist vision of the social world that conceives of social
> relations as relations of physical force and a 'cybernetic'
> or semiological vision which portrays them as relations
> of symbolic force, as relations of meaning or relations of
> communication. The most brutal relations of force are
> always simultaneously symbolic relations. (Bourdieu et al,
> 1994: 12)

In the lead-up to the 2010 general election, various aspects and activities
of the welfare state were used to justify the need for a period of austerity
and some belt tightening by the government. A picture was painted
of an expensive and overly bureaucratic central government, with too
many middle-managers making decisions about communities that
they were too removed from. It was accused of providing services to
those who did not really need them or, conversely, were becoming
too dependent on them. The political arguments for austerity thus
'moved uncomfortably between the "economic necessity" claim and a
more moral and social vocabulary of responsibility and interdependence'
(Clarke and Newman, 2012: 303).

The programme of austerity was also largely justified because of the
alleged unsustainable cost of 'handouts' to groups such as 'shirkers',

271

'troubled families' and 'benefits cheats'. These groups were then set against more honourable and deserving groups like 'hardworking families' and 'taxpayers'. It is therefore unsurprising that different research studies have exposed the deleterious effects on some of the most disadvantaged groups in society (Beatty and Fothergill, 2016). One investigation into the use of benefit sanctions in the UK highlighted that they are inefficient, cause great suffering and are unjust, and also noted 'the persistent, insensitive, uncaring and relentless harassment by the DWP [Department for Work and Pensions] of those who fail to meet the requirements of conditionality in social security' (Adler, 2018: 150). In his statement about the poverty and hardship that he witnessed on his visit to the UK, the UN Special Rapporteur on Extreme Poverty and Human Rights, Philip Alston (2018: 18), remarked that 'The costs of austerity have fallen disproportionately upon the poor, women, racial and ethnic minorities, children, single parents, and people with disabilities. The changes to taxes and benefits since 2010 have been highly regressive, and the policies have taken the highest toll on those least able to bear it.' The intense focus on and targeting of these groups has not always been visible. Alston also noted the emergence of a 'digital welfare state' in the UK and raised concerns about the increasing use of online services and decisions based, in part, on algorithms.

This chapter examines some of the contradictions and tensions within this restructuring, and how they affect the delivery of local services and the experience of service users. In doing so, it draws on the work of Pierre Bourdieu and Loic Wacquant. Bourdieu (2014: 4) argued that states have the 'monopoly of legitimate physical and symbolic violence' and also highlighted the struggles that take place throughout the bureaucratic field (Bourdieu et al, 1994). In an article on 'Rethinking the state' he, along with Wacquant and Farage, argued that in order to fully understand the state, it is necessary to be cognisant of its physical presence and force, as well as the symbolic power that it is able to wield (Bourdieu et al, 1994). Wacquant has been a robust and incisive critic of the tendency of neoliberal programmes to 'punish the poor' (as was Bourdieu in his later writings) and while the focus of much of his work has been on the US, his work has been used in social policy discussions and analyses in the UK in recent years (Garrett, 2015; Crossley, 2016a; Cummins, 2018; Flint and Powell, 2019). Wacquant (2010: 214) has argued for a 'thick' sociological understanding of neoliberalism which recognises that the 'fiercely interventionist' activity of the neoliberal state, usually directed at the most marginalised and oppressed groups, is 'not a deviation from neoliberalism but one of its constituent ingredients'.

The chapter begins with a brief overview of some of the physical and symbolic restructuring that has taken place, and is continuing, under austerity. The attention then shifts to focus on the impacts on the delivery of local services, primarily on those services that are targeted at marginalised groups and communities. This section notes the adjustments in the relations between the state and some of its most disadvantaged citizens, from an emphasis on being intensive and 'up close', to one that is more distant, less visible and yet still pervasive, and back again. The chapter concludes with a brief summary of the changing relations and who benefits the most from them.

Austerity: restructuring relations and redefining perimeters

> Brick by brick, edifice by edifice, we are slowly dismantling the big-state structures we inherited from the last government. (Cameron, 2012a)

Academic researchers have written about 'the violence of austerity' (Cooper and Whyte, 2017) and 'why austerity kills' (Stuckler and Basu, 2013). This section examines some of the 'brutal relations of force' (Bourdieu et al, 1994: 12) in both physical and symbolic relations between the state and its citizens that have occurred under austerity. While austerity is sometimes presented and discussed as the withdrawal of the state, or a reduction in many of its welfare functions, a closer look reveals significant restructuring in the activities of the state, both physically and symbolically.

One of the most obvious examples of the simultaneous changes to physical and symbolic relations in the early stages of the austerity project was the shift from regionalism to localism (Shaw and Robinson, 2012). The regional architecture of the Labour governments was removed and replaced with the rhetoric of localism and a range of new local initiatives. Regional government offices were abolished and not replaced with any local infrastructure, and regional development agencies were scrapped, replaced with local enterprise partnerships and a new Regional Growth Fund. In health policy, ten strategic health authorities in England, which mirrored, with one exception, the government office regions, were abolished in 2013 as part of the Health and Social Care Act and replaced with 211 clinical commissioning groups. The responsibility for public health was transferred from the

National Health Service (NHS) to local authorities. This switch was accompanied by the creation of new health and well-being boards and local Healthwatch organisations supporting patient and service user involvement in health and social care services in each local authority area. Other localist initiatives included the requirement of the 12 largest cities outside London to hold referenda on having elected mayors, and the imposition of police and crime commissioners on police forces across England.

These changes were justified, in part, by portraying the regional tier as 'unwieldy, interfering, and more concerned with fussy structures than actual job creation' (Kelly, 2011, cited in Shaw and Robinson, 2012: 233). One former civil servant argued that it was not what had been done about regional offices, but how it had been done, noting a 'highly vitriolic press statement announcing the closure' (Cooper, 2011) from the then Communities Secretary Eric Pickles. In the press release, Pickles (2010) stated: 'Let me be clear: The Government Offices are not voices of the region in Whitehall. They have become agents of Whitehall to intervene and interfere in localities, and are a fundamental part of the "command and control" apparatus of England's over-centralised state.'

In place of the 'command and control' apparatus, which was being dismantled, the Coalition government expected, if not exhorted, local communities and third sector organisations to pick up the slack and support those cast adrift by the state's retrenchment. In came the rhetoric of localism, devolution and empowerment, and the concept of the Big Society. Rowan Williams, who was the Archbishop of Canterbury at the time, suggested that the concept of the 'Big Society' was 'designed to conceal a deeply damaging withdrawal of the state from its responsibilities to the most vulnerable' (Helm and Coman, 2012; for a critique of the Big Society, see also Ishkanian and Szreter, 2012). However, Cameron (2015) attempted to portray his vision as being about a 'smarter state', rather than necessarily a smaller one. He argued that the government had 'reduced the size of the civil service, made better use of government property, bought smarter and spread the use of technology' before professing that 'the next 5 years will be about going further' (Cameron, 2015).

Unfortunately for the groups tasked with stepping into the breach, there were also changes to the funding relations between central government and local authorities, as well as between the government and citizens more directly. The National Audit Office (NAO, 2018: 4) highlighted that between 2010/11 and 2017/18, local authorities had experienced cuts of nearly 50 per cent in the funding they received from central government. The NAO (2018: 5) also argued that 'changes in funding arrangements and new pressures on demand have created both new opportunities and further pressures for the sector'. However, in contrast to the rhetoric of localism and devolution, the NAO also noted that 'conditions attached to central government funding risk creating a centralised local authority financial system where the scope for local discretion is being eroded' (Kara, 2019). These cuts also affected voluntary sector organisations, many of whom rely on government funding for a large proportion of their income.

Financial support to individuals was also cut in myriad ways. Beatty and Fothergill (2016: 3) estimated that the post-2015 welfare reforms would take 'the cumulative loss [within the benefits system] since 2010 to £27bn a year – equivalent to £690 a year for every adult of working age'. The Local Government Association (LGA, 2018: 1) noted that 573,000 fewer households received tax support in October 2017 in comparison to four years earlier. Government statistics (DWP, 2019) note that, as at May 2019, around 320,000 working-age Housing Benefit (HB) recipients had seen a reduction in the amount of HB they received each week as a result of the Spare Room Subsidy scheme, also known as the 'bedroom tax'. The average reduction was £15.41 per week. A 'benefit cap' was introduced, limiting the amount of financial support that any single household could receive, and to 'put a stop to the most outrageous cases [of] families getting £80, £90, £100,000 a year to live in homes that most people who pay the taxes towards those benefits could not possibly afford' (Cameron, 2012b).

These cuts have had severe consequences for many of the people affected by them. Numerous researchers and campaign groups have chronicled the devastation experienced by people living on low incomes. Stuckler et al (2017: 20) note that programmes of austerity in Europe and the UK 'impacted most on those already vulnerable, such as those with precarious employment or housing, or with existing health problems [and] was associated with worsening mental health and, as a consequence, increasing suicides'. Infant mortality is rising in England and Wales, especially among disadvantaged groups (Taylor-Robinson et al, 2019), with poverty and a shortage of midwives cited as possible explanations (Campbell, 2018). Furthermore, life expectancy among adults in England and Wales has fallen (Pike, 2019). The Institute and Faculty for Actuaries (2018) argued that this was 'a trend rather than a blip'.

These policies formed part of the 'ideological reworking' (Clarke and Newman, 2012: 300) of the financial crisis of 2007/08, which saw the crisis shift from being a financial services problem to a public spending one. Scapegoats were required and the recipients of welfare and public services were blamed for a bloated and perverse welfare state that incentivised inactivity over 'doing the right thing' and finding work. In 2010, shortly after becoming Prime Minister, David Cameron told *The Times* that 'There is no way of dealing with an 11 per cent budget deficit just by hitting either the rich or the welfare scrounger' (Watson, 2010). Politicians of all colours railed against the 'something for nothing' culture, with Rachel Reeves, the then shadow Work and Pensions Secretary, telling *The Guardian* in 2015 that Labour was 'not the party of people on benefits' (Gentleman, 2015). Fears were stoked about households where 'three generations had never worked' and where 'cultures of worklessness' were passed down from generation to generation (Shildrick et al, 2012); 'poverty porn' programmes were made about people being 'On benefits and proud'; and George Osborne (2012) lamented people 'sleeping off a life on benefits' while others got up early and 'went to work'. 'Troubled families' were blamed for the riots that took place in 2011 and were accused of costing 'the taxpayer' £9 billion a year (Cameron, 2011).

Categories and labels such as 'the welfare scrounger' and 'troubled families' are examples of the symbolic power that the state and others have in creating groups or classes of people and bringing them to life in the eyes of the public, and have importance in political struggles: 'The categories of perception, the schemata of classification, that is, essentially, the words, the names which construct social reality as much as they express it, are the stake par excellence of political struggle, which is a struggle to impose the legitimate principle of vision and division' (Bourdieu, 1989: 20–1). Such labels and the wider discourses surrounding them and other 'social problems' have been used as a justification by successive governments to change not only the way in which the state operates, becoming more 'fiercely interventionist' (Wacquant, 2010: 214), but also where it operates. In Wacquant's (2010: 217, emphases added) words, the neoliberal form of governance has arisen 'from *struggles over and within the bureaucratic field*, aiming to redefine the perimeter, missions, priorities, and modalities of action of public authorities with respect to definite problem territories and categories'. The next section examines the redefining of some of these perimeters and modalities of action in more detail.

Physical relations and algorithmic relations

> Buildings stabilize social life. They give structure to social institutions, durability to social networks, persistence to behaviour patterns. (Gieryn, 2002: 35)

> We are witnessing the gradual disappearance of the post-war British welfare state behind a webpage and an algorithm. In its place, a digital welfare state is emerging. (Alston, 2018)

Austerity measures had a profound impact on local services, the places where they were delivered and the people who relied on them. Neighbourhood buildings such as libraries, community centres, youth clubs and children's centres were forced to close, 'rebrand', reduce their opening hours and/or target their services at certain groups.

Research carried out in 2018 suggested that more than 1,000 registered children's centres may have closed between 2009 and 2017, while also warning of 'evidence of a further wave of large scale closures in the pipeline as a "tipping point" is reached' (Smith et al, 2018: 4). Many of these closures took place in a relatively small number of areas and were carried out in less deprived areas. Smith et al (2018: 4) note that 'the proportion of centres in the 30 per cent most disadvantaged areas remained constant from 2009 to 2017 at just over 50'. However, these headline numbers tell only part of the story of the restructuring, as the authors point out:

> Numbers are important – particularly if your local centre closes. But equally important are the services offered. More centres operate on a part-time basis only and the number of services has fallen. While most centres still offer open access services to families of all backgrounds, these have been reduced, restricted to fewer centres or to fewer sessions.... There was a greater focus on more limited services targeted at referred families, with less open access and different services distributed across centres in the same authority. (Smith et al, 2018: 4)

Research carried out in 2018 by the Chartered Institute for Public Finance and Accountancy suggested that over 570 libraries have closed since 2012 as a result of austerity measures and cuts to library funding (Onwuemezi, 2017; Page, 2018). The research also highlights the increasing role played by volunteers in keeping some remaining libraries open. This, of course, was the aim of the Big Society initiative that emerged in the lead-up to the 2010 general election: public services would be replaced or delivered by volunteers or voluntary sector organisations.

The uneven impacts of, for example, welfare reforms (Beatty and Fothergill, 2016), cuts to local government funding (Innes and Tetlow, 2015) and public health allocations present barriers to some groups who may wish to get involved with volunteering. Not everyone possesses the various forms of capital required to take on the running of public services such as libraries, museums or youth groups. Changes within the benefits system, such as increased conditionality for some benefits, changes to eligibility criteria and the threat of sanctions for mistakes or non-compliance, meant that for some groups, such as lone parents with school-aged children and unemployed people, volunteering became a less attractive and accessible option.

In addition to these issues, the rolling out of changing roles for both public sector and voluntary sector organisations at a time of cuts did not always go smoothly. In an examination of 'austerity localism' in the North-East of England, Clayton et al (2016: 736) argue that although cuts to local government presented a 'potentially enhanced role for the third sector, this does not necessarily coincide with a progressive form of local revitalisation in this marginalised region'. In an example of the 'struggles' that take place within the bureaucratic field, they suggest that 'austerity localism' 'cumulatively worked to sever relationships and trust, creating forms of disconnect between those in power and those who feel on the receiving end of damaging decisions' (Clayton et al, 2016: 737). In a research project examining experiences of austerity in a disadvantaged neighbourhood in the West Midlands, Jones et al (2019: 9) used remarkably similar language to describe the impact of a stalled regeneration programme that acted as 'a visual reminder' of the 'perceived neglect by the local authority, engendering distrust and a sense of being forgotten and demeaned by those in power'.

In an examination of 'the cost of the cuts' in the relatively early stages of the coalition government, Hastings et al (2015) discussed the impact of austerity measures on service users, front-line staff, the voluntary sector and impoverished groups and places. They highlighted that the cuts increased pressure on local voluntary sector organisations and on poorer communities, even when local authorities attempted to protect 'pro-poor' services. Council officers involved in the research expressed concern that 'vulnerable clients could become less visible in the cases where services were withdrawn from neighbourhoods and it became harder for these groups to contact the council' (Hastings et al, 2015: 107). Furthermore, the researchers argued that the 'cumulative impact' of numerous small changes to service delivery (such as opening times, the location of services, changes to eligibility criteria, the introduction of charges and so on) was to 'narrow the social realm of children and families' (Hastings et al, 2015: 106). In a more extreme example of the potential cumulative impact of austerity measures, *The Guardian* covered the story of a Cambridgeshire resident who had to walk 24 miles to the nearest jobcentre to sign on because he could not afford the £7 bus fare (Tickle, 2019).

At the same time that many universally accessible public buildings were closing or seeing their opening hours reduced, the government was attempting to expand its targeted reach into the private spheres of some of the most disadvantaged groups in society. Two family programmes that received central government funding from the Coalition and Conservative governments involved home visits and 'intensive' levels of support for marginalised families: the Troubled Families Programme (TFP), which then Prime Minister David Cameron (2016) called 'perhaps the most intensive form of state intervention there is'; and the Family Nurse Programme, which is structured around regular home visits and 'a highly personalised intervention' (FNP, 2019).

The TFP was based on a model of family intervention that put the relationship between a single worker and 'troubled families' at the heart of its approach. Workers were purported to be dedicated to the families they worked with, being willing and able to 'walk in their shoes', and were presented as the antidote to the alleged impersonal and uncaring nature of social work practice, which was characterised as 'assessing the hell out of them [families]' (House of Commons Public Accounts Committee, 2014: 21) but not able to effect any lasting change. Louise Casey, the civil servant in charge of the programme in its first phase, stated that the TFP 'starts with what's happening in the families' (House of Commons Public Accounts Committee, 2014: 46) and works backwards from that, and also argued that 'All of what we do [in the TFP] turns on something very simple: the relationship between the worker and the family' (Casey, quoted in Aitkenhead, 2013).

Other policy areas throw up more evidence of increasing incursions into the lives of marginalised groups. David Webster, a research fellow at Glasgow University, noted in 2015 that the number of people looking for work who had received benefits sanctions exceeded the number of people who received fines through the magistrates and sheriff courts, and were treated 'much worse than those fined in the courts' (Webster,

2015). Many of the incursions affect children and young people, as well as their families. The most recent set of government statistics highlight that the numbers of children taken into care in England has increased for ten consecutive years, and are at their highest level on record, at 75,420 (Department for Education, 2019). Recent research undertaken by social work academics shows that there is a social gradient in child welfare interventions: as deprivation increases, so does a child's chance of being engaged with children's services in some way. This social gradient was found in every local authority and was described as a 'systematic, structural relationship', in much the same way that there are social gradients in health and educational inequalities. The researchers argued that these findings could not be explained as a 'postcode lottery' and were, instead, evidence of 'child welfare inequalities': 'unequal chances, experiences and outcomes of child welfare that are systematically associated with social advantage/disadvantage' (Bywaters et al, 2014: 1). Jones et al (2019: 10) highlight how the 'bedroom tax' impacted on the sleeping arrangements of families as, under the policy, the age at which children could share a bedroom regardless of their gender was increased to ten.

However, this intensification in activity is not necessarily uniform and, in any case, the rhetoric of policy documents does not always match the reality of policy implementation. In the TFP, the strong relationship between the family worker and the families that they were purportedly working with was not as strong or as 'intensive' as it appeared on paper. In the first phase of the programme, many 'troubled families' were 'turned around' despite never having met or engaged with a worker on the programme (Bawden, 2015). In evaluation documents covering both phases of the programme, significant numbers of the families on the programme could not recall the name of the worker who was expected to be 'dedicated' to them and could be found 'standing alongside them' (DCLG, 2012: 18). Workers on the programme have also highlighted the sizeable administrative burden that accompanied the programme, which prevented them from spending more time with the families (Crossley, 2017: 124).

As part of a research project examining social work practices in two local authority areas, Disney et al (2019) note how the changing territories of the state sometimes mean that not all children and families are subject to the same intensive monitoring and supervision. One social worker involved with the research articulated how 'the expansion of the area covered by their teams impacted upon their ability to practice effectively' (Disney et al, 2019: 45), particularly with regard to multi-agency meetings or supervision meetings on the other side of the city. Another social worker discusses a particularly problematic journey that they 'hate' and remarks that 'isn't it funny the children that are further away we don't think about as much?' (Disney et al, 2019: 45–6). In a discussion of the 'unbounded office' the authors present examples of social workers working beyond their usual workplace and over their work hours, often at home in the evenings and weekends. Cameron's vision of a 'smarter state' is difficult to reconcile with the stories of social workers starting to write up case notes 'every Friday from 8 o'clock [PM] until whatever time in the morning' (Disney et al, 2019: 43) because of their workload, or the family support worker who did not have a work-enabled tablet and so was unable to work remotely – though the authors note that 'this did not eliminate the emotional pressures of their work seeping into their home environment' (Disney et al, 2019: 43).

In some areas, there is evidence of Cameron's desire to 'go further' in the use of technology, often at the expense of physical encounters and interactions. In the early stages of the TFP, there was a strong rhetorical focus on family workers getting beyond 'the front door' of the family home in order to work with them intensively and effect change within the household (Crossley, 2016b). However, as time has gone on, the discourse around the TFP has changed. There is less emphasis on the troubles of the families themselves, and more on the 'service transformation' that is accompanying the programme, and the potential of data and digital information in identifying 'troubled families' earlier. A number of posts on the government's 'troubled families' blog page[1] highlight the importance of data to the ongoing TFP. One post by the West Sussex TFP coordinator begins by stating that 'Delivering an effective service to customers with complex needs is necessarily a data-driven enterprise', while another by Manchester City Council paints a typically dystopian and deterministic picture of a family struggling to pay the bills, for whom things 'quickly spiral out of control and before you know it, the teachers are concerned, Children's Services are knocking on your door, and everything has just gone from bad to worse with no hope in sight'. The answer, thankfully, is already with us:

> So what can be done? How can we intervene early and prevent this inevitable roller-coaster? This is where data sharing, and the new public service delivery data sharing power proposed by the Digital Economy Bill, comes in; and if we add a dose of 21st century technology, we can save lives and deliver excellent value for money to the taxpayer.

Families are more likely to be accessed via a 'virtual front door' than through their own physical front door. A guest post on the blog page by Nesta extolling the benefits of algorithmic tools in children's social care tells the tale of 'Molly', a social worker who works as 'part of the "Front Door team"', fielding calls from concerned citizens about children's welfare'. In 2019, the government's Digital Marketplace website contained details of a local authority who were seeking a supplier who could 're-design, build and test a system to manage the digital front door for the Family Support Service, including the underpinning data management system to meet multiple statutory requirements'. The expansion of these online, or cybernetic, relations is usually in response to the inability of local authorities to maintain or develop physical relations with their residents as a result of austerity policies.

Bristol City Council provides a good example of some of these shifting forms of relations. In 2014, an internal 'troubled families' update included a quote from a male key worker who was proud of his hands-on approach to family work:

> When mum was finding it hard to manage her mental health I would often have to leave a whole morning or afternoon to visit as it has sometimes taken over an hour of banging on the door to get in to the house. Persistence has got me in the door even on bad days.

In 2019, as part of a series of articles in *The Guardian* about the increasing use of algorithmic tools in the delivery of welfare services, a case study of Bristol noted that officers could now 'download an individual's digital "vulnerability profile" including percentage scores denoting the likelihood of a range of other harms' (Booth, 2019a). These profiles included 7,000 children, which highlights the expansion of surveillance that is possible via a digital welfare state. *The Guardian* series included an article on how algorithmic welfare decisions 'punish the poor' (Pilkington, 2019) in numerous different countries across the globe, echoing Wacquant's conclusions in relation to wider neoliberal interventions. In an article on the UK, it was reported that the DWP 'has hired nearly 1,000 new IT [information technology] staff in the past 18 months and has increased spending to about £8m a year on a specialist "intelligent automation garage" where computer scientists are developing over 100 welfare robots, deep learning and intelligent automation for use in the welfare system' (Booth, 2019b). The DWP was also reported to be 'testing artificial intelligence to judge the likelihood that citizens' claims about their childcare and housing costs are true when they apply for benefits' (Booth, 2019b), while another article highlighted the number of local authorities using predictive analytics and algorithmic decision-making, despite concerns about their reliability (Marsh, 2019). The spread of this technology and the speed at which it is being put to use appears to be primarily in one direction. In discussing the introduction of Universal Credit as a 'digital by default' benefit, Alston (2018: 7) wondered why 'some of the most vulnerable and those with poor digital literacy had to go first in what amounts to a nationwide digital experiment', noting the large numbers of marginalised groups that do not use or have access to the internet at home or have difficulties filling out online application forms.

Alston (2018: 8–9) argued that it was libraries that were 'on the frontline of helping the digitally excluded and digitally illiterate who wish to claim their right to Universal Credit', and reported that around a third of new Universal Credit claims failed in the application process and never reached the payment stage. Alston (2018: 9) remarked that he was 'unaware of any effort by DWP to estimate the number of people who do not even attempt to apply due to digital exclusion'.

The benefits – for want of a better word – of new digital technologies appear to be accruing primarily to the government. State agencies are investing heavily in the cybernetic oversight of marginalised populations while those same populations struggle to keep pace with the technological prowess expected of them to claim the benefits that they are entitled to or access the services that are purported to be there to support them. Nearly 1,000 IT staff are hired while citizens are forced to rely on services under intense pressure and often staffed, in part at least, by volunteers. Of course, it is not an 'either/or' situation in terms of how the state engages and interacts with disadvantaged groups. Engagement – or non-engagement – with online processes has real-life consequences, as witnessed by the potential for people looking for work to be sanctioned if they do not record 35 hours of job-seeking activity on their online Universal Jobmatch account. Information collected from professionals on home visits, during multi-agency meetings and brief encounters on the street becomes data that can then be shared, analysed and used to help 'predict' the need for future and potentially earlier interventions. Thereby, so the cycle of interventions continues, with an increasing focus on the most 'at-risk' groups, while other groups see less and less of the state as it retreats from its traditional spaces and its functions are increasingly carried out by a new cadre of cybernetic civil servants.

Conclusion

> The state is not an apparatus oriented to the common
> good, it is an apparatus of constraint, of maintenance of
> public order but to the benefit of the dominant. (Bourdieu,
> 2014: 5)

Austerity has led to an increasingly fragmented and disparate economy and geography of welfare. These changes have affected people's ability to access services, leaving some of them isolated and excluded from activities that they previously enjoyed. Decisions on how local public services can support or 'intervene' in some locations and with certain groups can be influenced by algorithms designed by global IT companies, when once discretion would be exercised primarily by local workers such as neighbourhood police officers, patch-based social workers or youth workers, for example. Citizens are increasingly likely to engage with the state online as opposed to in the physical world, despite many of them not having the appropriate forms of capital to do so.

The programme of austerity does not, then, relate solely to a reduction in the amount of funding afforded to public services. If it did, then a case could just about be made that austerity might be 'over', as claimed by Theresa May when she was Prime Minister (Inman, 2018). In Bourdieusian terms, it seeks to fundamentally alter the relations between different agents in the bureaucratic field, changing the nature and the location of everyday struggles between citizens and the welfare state, and 'upgrading' the forms of capital that are required to successfully negotiate digital resources and services. These altered relations are most keenly felt by some of the most marginalised and already disadvantaged groups. Increased targeting of these groups for physical interventions can lead to the increased risk of cybernetic or algorithmic targeting, and vice versa, highlighting the simultaneous nature of the physical and symbolic forces that Bourdieu articulated in the quote at the start of this chapter.

A Bourdieusian analysis can help to shed light on the 'For whose benefit?' question that Patrick (2017) asked of some of the early welfare reforms of the Coalition government, and what types of capital are required to access and benefit from services at the current time. Future research could explore how the changing nature of the bureaucratic field affects the practices and day-to-day work of street-level bureaucrats. The extent and long-term consequences of austerity on the workers tasked with implementing it also requires further examination, along with how this process changes their relations with citizens and service users. The extent and reach of private sector companies' involvement with local service provision, both in terms of work directly with members of the public and in back-office functions, should also be mapped. Changes to the fabric of the state may be nothing new, but that does not mean that contemporary developments represent more of the same. We would do well to examine these spatial shifts more closely.

Note
¹ See: https://troubledfamilies.blog.gov.uk/

References
Adler, M. (2018) *Cruel, inhuman or degrading treatment?*, Basingstoke: Palgrave.
Aitkenhead, D. (2013) 'Troubled Families head Louise Casey: "What's missing is love"', *The Guardian*, 29 November, www.theguardian. com/society/2013/nov/29/troubled-families-louise-casey-whats-missing-love
Alston, P. (2018) 'Statement on visit to the United Kingdom', 16 November, www.ohchr.org/Documents/Issues/Poverty/EOM_GB_16Nov2018.pdf
Bawden, A. (2015) 'Is the success of the government's troubled families scheme too good to be true?', *The Guardian*, 11 November 2015. www.theguardian.com/society/2015/nov/11/troubled-family-programme-government-success-council-figures
Beatty, C. and Fothergill, S. (2016) 'The uneven impact of welfare reform: the financial losses to places and people', CRESR, Sheffield Hallam University, www4.shu.ac.uk/research/cresr/sites/shu.ac.uk/files/welfare-reform-2016.pdf
Booth, R. (2019a) 'How Bristol assesses citizens' risk of harm – using an algorithm', *The Guardian*, 15 October, www.theguardian.com/uk-news/2019/oct/15/bristol-algorithm-assess-citizens-risk-harm-guide-frontline-staff
Booth, R. (2019b) 'Benefits system automation could plunge claimants deeper into poverty', *The Guardian*, 14 October, www.theguardian.com/technology/2019/oct/14/fears-rise-in-benefits-system-automation-could-plunge-claimants-deeper-into-poverty
Bourdieu, P. (1989) 'Social space and symbolic power', *Sociological Theory*, 7(1): 14–25.
Bourdieu, P. (2014) *On the state*, Cambridge: Polity Press.

Bourdieu, P., Wacquant, L. and Farage, S. (1994) 'Rethinking the state: genesis and structure of the bureaucratic field', *Sociological Theory*, 12(1): 1–18.

Bywaters, P., Brady, G., Sparks, T. and Bos, E. (2014) 'Deprivation and inequalities in children's services', Research Briefing Paper 1, www. coventry.ac.uk/globalassets/media/global/05-research-section-assets/ research/surge/projects/mapping-child-services---research-briefing-paper-1.pdf

Cameron, D. (2011) 'Troubled families speech', 15 December, www. gov.uk/government/speeches/troubled-families-speech

Cameron, D. (2012a) 'Brick by brick, we're tearing down the big state', *Daily Telegraph*, 28 March, www.telegraph.co.uk/news/politics/ david-cameron/9171481/Brick-by-brick-were-tearing-down-the-big-state.html

Cameron, D. (2012b) 'Welfare speech', 25 June, www.gov.uk/ government/speeches/welfare-speech

Cameron, D. (2015) 'Prime Minister: my vision for a smarter state', 11 September, www.gov.uk/government/speeches/prime-minister-my-vision-for-a-smarter-state

Cameron, D. (2016) 'Prime Minister's speech on life chances', 11 January, www.gov.uk/government/speeches/prime-ministers-speech-on-life-chances

Campbell, D. (2018) 'Concern at rising infant mortality rate in England and Wales', *The Guardian*, 15 March, www.theguardian. com/society/2018/mar/15/concern-at-rising-infant-mortality-rate-in-england-and-wales

Clarke, J. and Newman, J. (2012) 'The alchemy of austerity', *Critical Social Policy*, 32(3): 299–319.

Clayton, J., Donovan, C. and Merchant, J. (2016) 'Distancing and limited resourcefulness: third sector service provision under austerity localism in the North East of England', *Urban Studies*, 53(4): 723–40.

Cooper, H. (2011) 'Tiers shed as regional government offices disappear', *The Guardian*, 29 March, www.theguardian.com/society/2011/ mar/29/regional-government-disappears-1500-jobs-lost

Cooper, V. and Whyte, D. (2017) *The violence of austerity*, London: Pluto Press.

Crossley, S. (2016a) '"Realising the (troubled family)", "crafting the neoliberal state"', *Families, Relationship and Societies*, 5(2): 263–79.

Crossley, S. (2016b) 'From the desk to the front-room? The changing spaces of street-level encounters with the state under austerity', *People, Policy and Place*, 10(3): 193–206.

Crossley, S. (2017) '"Making trouble": a Bourdieusian analysis of the UK government's Troubled Families programme', PhD thesis, http://etheses.dur.ac.uk/12271/

Cummins, I. (2018) *Poverty, inequality and social work: The impact of neoliberalism and austerity politics on welfare provision*, Bristol: Policy Press.

DCLG (Department for Communities and Local Government) (2012) *Working with troubled families*, London: DCLG.

Department for Education (2019) 'Children looked after in England including adoption: 2017 to 2018', www.gov.uk/government/collections/statistics-looked-after-children#history

Disney, T., Warwick, L., Ferguson, H., Leigh, J., Singh Cooner, T., Beddoe, L., Jones, P. and Osborne, T. (2019) '"Isn't it funny the children that are further away we don't think about as much?": using GPS to explore the mobilities and geographies of social work and child protection practice', *Children and Youth Services Review*, 100: 39–49.

DWP (Department for Work and Pensions) (2019) 'Benefits statistical summary, August 2019', www.gov.uk/government/publications/dwp-benefits-statistics-august-2019/dwp-benefits-statistical-summary-august-2019

Flint, J. and Powell, R. (2019) *Class, Ethnicity and State in the Polarized Metropolis: Putting Wacquant to work*, Basingstoke: Palgrave.

FNP (Family Nurse Programme) (2019) 'The programme: theories that underpin the programme', https://fnp.nhs.uk/about-us/the-programme/

Garrett, P.M. (2015) '"Introducing Michael Gove to Loïc Wacquant": why social work needs critical sociology', *British Journal of Social Work*, 46(4): 873–89.

Gentleman, A. (2015) 'Labour vows to reduce reliance on food banks if it comes to power', *The Guardian*, 17 March, www.theguardian.com/society/2015/mar/17/labour-vows-to-reduce-reliance-on-food-banks-if-it-comes-to-power?CMP=aff_1432&utm_content=The+Independent&awc=5795_1571745624_eab557a2ac467cf4808cc6816ffc6f6a

Gieryn, T.F. (2002) 'What buildings do', *Theory and Society*, 31(1): 35–74.

Hastings, A., Bailey, N., Bramley, G., Gannon, M. and Watkins, D. (2015) *The cost of the cuts: The impact on local government and poorer communities*, York: Joseph Rowntree Foundation.

Helm, T. and Coman, J. (2012) 'Rowan Williams pours scorn on David Cameron's "big society"', *The Guardian*, 24 June, www.theguardian.com/uk/2012/jun/23/rowan-williams-big-society-cameron

House of Commons Public Accounts Committee (2014) *Programmes to help families facing multiple challenges: Fifty-first report of session 2013–14*, London: The Stationery Office.

Inman, P. (2018) 'Is austerity really over? Theresa May's promise lacks key details', *The Guardian*, 4 October, www.theguardian.com/politics/2018/oct/04/is-austerity-really-over-theresa-mays-promise-lacks-key-details

Innes, D. and Tetlow, G. (2015) *Central cuts, local decision-making: Changes in local government spending and revenues in England, 2009–10 to 2014–15*, IFS Briefing Note BN166, London: Institute for Fiscal Studies.

Institute and Faculty for Actuaries (2018) 'CMI Mortality Projections Model CMI_2018 briefing note', www.actuaries.org.uk/system/files/field/document/CMI%20WP119%20v01%202019-03-07%20-%20CMI%20Mortality%20Projections%20Model%20CMI_2018%20Briefing%20Note.pdf

Ishkanian, A. and Szreter, S. (2012) *The Big Society debate: A new agenda for social welfare?*, Cheltenham, Edward Elgar.

Jones, D., Lowe, P. and West, K. (2019) 'Austerity in a disadvantaged West Midlands neighbourhood: everyday experiences of families and family support professionals', *Critical Social Policy*, https://journals.sagepub.com/doi/full/10.1177/0261018319840923

Kara, A. (2019) 'Local government in 2019: a pivotal year', NAO blog, www.nao.org.uk/naoblog/local-government-in-2019/

Kelly, R. (2011) *What's left for the North East? An essay*, Newcastle: Durham Book Festival/New Writing North.

LGA (Local Government Association) (2018) 'Local government funding: moving the conversation on', www.local.gov.uk/sites/default/files/documents/5.40_01_Finance%20publication_WEB_0.pdf

Marsh, S. (2019) 'One in three councils using algorithms to make welfare decisions', *The Guardian*, 15 October, www.theguardian.com/society/2019/oct/15/councils-using-algorithms-make-welfare-decisions-benefits

NAO (National Audit Office) (2018) *Financial sustainability of local authorities 2018*, London: NAO, www.nao.org.uk/wp-content/uploads/2018/03/Financial-sustainabilty-of-local-authorites-2018.pdf

Onwuemezi, N. (2017) 'Latest CIPFA figures reveal "catastrophic" scale of library closures', 8 December, www.thebookseller.com/news/cipfa-library-figures-687596

Osborne, G. (2012) 'Speech to the Conservative Party conference', 8 October, www.newstatesman.com/blogs/politics/2012/10/george-osbornes-speech-conservative-conference-full-text

Page, B. (2018) 'Latest CIPFA stats reveal yet more library closures and book loan falls', 7 December, www.thebookseller.com/news/cipfa-records-yet-more-library-closures-and-book-loan-falls-911061

Patrick, R. (2017) *For whose benefit? The everyday realities of welfare reform*, Bristol: Policy Press.

Pickles, E. (2010) 'Pickles outlines plans to abolish regional government', 22 July, www.gov.uk/government/news/pickles-outlines-plans-to-abolish-regional-government

Pike, H. (2019) 'Life expectancy in England and Wales has fallen by six months', *British Medical Journal*, 364: l1123, www.bmj.com/content/364/bmj.l1123

Pilkington, E. (2019) 'Digital dystopia: how algorithms punish the poor', *The Guardian*, 14 October, www.theguardian.com/technology/2019/oct/14/automating-poverty-algorithms-punish-poor

Shaw, K. and Robinson, F. (2012) 'From "regionalism" to "localism": opportunities and challenges for North East England', *Local Economy: The Journal of the Local Economy Policy Unit*, 27(3): 232–50.

Shildrick, T., Macdonald, R., Furlong, A., Roden, J. and Crow, R. (2012) *Are cultures of worklessness passed down the generations?*, York: JRF.

Smith, G., Sylva, K., Smith, T., Simmons, P. and Omonigho, A. (2018) *Stop start: Survival, decline or closure? Children's centres in England, 2018*, London: Sutton Trust, https://www.suttontrust.com/our-research/sure-start-childrens-centres-england/

Stuckler, D. and Basu, S. (2013) *The body economic: Why austerity kills: Recessions, budget battles, and the politics of life and death*, New York, NY: Basic Books.

Stuckler, D., Reeves, A., Loopstra, R., Karanikolos, M. and McKee, M. (2017) 'Austerity and health: the impact in the UK and Europe', *European Journal of Public Health*, 27 (Supp 4): 18–21.

Taylor-Robinson, D., Lai, E.T.C., Wickham, S., Rose, T., Norman, P., Bambra, C., Whitehead, M. and Barr, B. (2019) 'Assessing the impact of rising child poverty on the unprecedented rise in infant mortality in England, 2000–2017: time trend analysis', *BMJ Open*, 9: e029424, https://bmjopen.bmj.com/content/9/10/e029424

Tickle, L. (2019) 'Need to sign on? You'll have to walk 24 miles to the jobcentre', *The Guardian*, 7 January, www.theguardian.com/uk-news/2019/jan/07/need-to-sign-on-youll-have-to-walk-24-miles-to-jobcentre

Wacquant, L. (2010) 'Crafting the neoliberal state: workfare, prisonfare, and social insecurity', *Sociological Forum*, 25(2): 197–220.

Watson, R. (2010) 'Public sector will bear the brunt of cuts, says Cameron', *The Times*, 19 June, www.thetimes.co.uk/article/public-sector-will-bear-the-brunt-of-cuts-says-cameron-gwh8xbjdb82

Webster, D. (2015) 'Benefit sanctions: Britain's secret penal system', Centre for Crime and Justice Studies, www.crimeandjustice.org.uk/resources/benefit-sanctions-britains-secret-penal-system

Index

Note: page numbers in *italic* type refer to figures; those in **bold** type refer to tables.

A

academic qualifications, and the labour market 100
accessibility issues, community youth justice in England and Wales 183, 184, 188–89, 190, 194–95, 196–97, 198, 200, 201
Achiume, T. 5–6, 7
'active' institutional approach, community youth justice in England and Wales 183–84, 185, **185**, 191–94, 195, 196, 197, 200, 201
Adler, M. 272
affordable housing 128
'aggressive' institutional approach, community youth justice in England and Wales 185, **185**, 196, 198, 199
Alexander, Claire 2, 5
Ali, Nasreen 2–3, 25–50
Alston, Philip 5, 207, 272, 277, 283
Amin-Smith, Neil 229
Andall-Stanberry, M. 38–39
Anderson, B. 55–56
anti-discrimination legislation 25
anti-racism policies 11, 54
  in higher education 39
anti-terrorism strategies 172, 176
Antonucci, L. 99
Arnett, J.J. 98
Arts Council 168
asylum seekers 12
  see also migration
'austere creativity' 236
austerity 176, 207–9, 227–28, 229–30, 243, 249, 271–73, 277, 284–85
  and community youth justice in England and Wales 95–96, 184
  and homelessness 208, 249–66

and libraries 208, 228–29, 232–45, **233**, **235**
  physical and algorithmic relations 277–83
  racially disparate impact of 6, 7
  restructuring of government relations 273–76
  and welfare provision in the UK 212–13
austerity localism 230–32, 243–44, 278
  and libraries 234–36, **235**

B

'baby boomer' generation 93
Bäckman, O. 141
Bakkar, N. 63
BAME (black and minority ethnic) academics:
  absence of in Social Policy 1
  higher education inequalities 7
  Social Policy higher education 2, 27, 28, 29, 30, 32, 40–41
BAME (black and minority ethnic) groups:
  BAME deficits 10, 18
  criminal justice system 8
  housing inequalities 7–8
  labour market inequalities 6–7, 8, 52
  poverty rates 6, 7
  racially disparate impact of austerity policies on 6, 7
  school exclusions 8
  under-representation of in cultural engagement 171
BAME (black and minority ethnic) researchers 26
BAME (black and minority ethnic) students:
  higher education inequalities 7, 9

Social Policy higher education 2, 27, 28, 29–32, **31**, *32*, **34**, 42–43, 46–47
  admissions, retention and achievement 33, *35*, 35–40, *37*
  unsatisfactory experiences of higher education 36, 37–39
Bangladeshi groups:
  housing inequalities 7
  labour market inequalities 6
Bangladeshi students, and higher education 33
Banting, K. 14
Barford, Anna 230
Barker, M. 71
Barking and Dagenham; libraries and austerity 233
Barrientos, A. 99
BCS (British Cohort Study) 1970 93, 101, 103, **105**, **106–7**, **108–9**, **110–11**, 123
'bedroom tax' (Spare Room Subsidy) 207, 220, 221, *222*, 224, 275, 280
benefit cap 207, 212, 220, 221, *222*, 224
benefit sanctions 207, 212, 223, 251, 252, 259, 272, 278, 279
  and homelessness 208
benefits *see* welfare provision
Berkshire; CAMHS (Child and Adolescent Mental Health Services) 188
BES (British Election Studies) 15
Besemer, Kirsten 243
Beveridge, William 17, 213
Bhambra, G. 17
Bianchini, Franco 243–44
'Big Society' 230, 274, 278
biological racism; British-Asian Muslim Macken young women in Sunderland study 58, 61
Birmingham; libraries and austerity 233
BIS (Department of Business, Innovation and Skills) 33, 35
#BlackLivesMatter 1
black people; prison population 8
Black Power movement 9
Black-African groups:
  criminal justice system 8
  higher education inequalities 7
  housing inequalities 8
  labour market inequalities 6
Black-Caribbean groups:
  criminal justice system 8

higher education inequalities 7
housing inequalities 8
labour market inequalities 6
Black-Caribbean students, and higher education 33, 36
Bolton; libraries and austerity 235
'boomeranging' 94, 103, 127
Bourdieu, Pierre 271, 272, 273, 276, 284
Bowler, Rick 3, 51–70
Bowyer, G. 6–7
Bramley, Glen 243
Brent; libraries and austerity 233, 234
Brexit 209
  and cultural education 168, 170–71
  and homelessness 265
  and racial hate crime 52, 64
Bristol City Council; troubled families programme 282
British Asian Muslims 3
  see also British-Asian Muslim Macken young women in Sunderland study
British Cohort Study (BCS) 1970 93, 101, 103, **105**, **106–7**, **108–9**, **110–11**, 123
British Election Studies (BES) 15
British exceptionalism 176–77
British Journal of Social Work 26
British Museum 168
British National Party 52
British Social Attitudes (BSA) Survey 15
British Sociological Association 47
British-Asian Muslim Macken young women in Sunderland study 3, 51, 52, 56–57, 63–65
  contextual and conceptual landscapes 53–56
  solutions to failed monocultural landscapes 62–63
  study findings 57–58
  cultural awareness of local landscapes 60–62
  cultural ignorance and racism 58–60
Britishness:
  monocultural white imaginary of 3
  and race 53, 54
Brokenshire, James 253
Brooks-Wilson, Sarah 95–96, 183–206
BSA (British Social Attitudes) Survey 15

Bury, Greater Manchester; libraries and austerity 234
Bywaters, P. 280

C

Cabinet Office; 'Race disparity audit' 6, 7–8
Cameron, David 230, 249, 273, 274, 276, 279, 281
CAMHS (Child and Adolescent Mental Health Services) 187–88
Cantle, T. 164–65
Carmichael, Christina 208, 249–69
Carmichael, Stokely (Kwame Ture) 9–10
Casey, Louise 279
Casselden, B. 235
Catholic Church, in Poland 75, 76, 79, 80
'cause for concern' hypothesis of economic hardship in young adulthood 139, 152
Cerami, A. 75
CGT (constructivist grounded theory) 254
#CharitySoWhite 1
Chartered Institute of Public Finance and Accountability (CIPFA) 232, 235, 236, 242, 277–78
Child and Adolescent Mental Health Services (CAMHS) 187–88
'child first' youth justice 183, 185, 191–92, 194, 195, 197, 199, 200, 201
child poverty 137
Child Tax Credits (CTC) 214
children in care 280
children's benefits 214, *215*, 217, 218, *219*
children's centres 187, 277
Chinese students, and higher education 33
Chowdry, H. 36
CIPFA (Chartered Institute of Public Finance and Accountability) 232, 235, 236, 242, 277–78
city mayors 274
Clark, J. 271
classism 71
Clayton, J. 278
clinical commissioning groups 273
Coalition (Conservative -Liberal Democrat) government 227, 249, 251, 252, 274, 279, 284

see also austerity
Cohen, S. 17
Cole, Bankole 2–3, 25–50
Coman, J. 274
communitarian cultural education in the UK 95, 171–74, 175
see also cultural education in the UK; 'neoliberal communitarian' model of governance
communities:
and austerity localism 231
and culture 170
community sentences *see* community youth justice, England and Wales
community youth justice, England and Wales 95–96, 183–84, 200–201
    accessibility issues 183, 184, 188–89, 190, 194–95, 196–97, 198, 200, 201
    'active' institutional approach 183–84, 185, **185**, 191–94, 195, 196, 197, 200, 201
    'aggressive' institutional approach 185, **185**, 196, 198, 199
    'child first' youth justice 183, 185, 191–92, 194, 195, 197, 199, 200, 201
    community sentence diversity and dispersal 186–89
    context 184–86, **185**
    custodial estate 188
    economic constraints on 187–88, 200
    educational services 187–88, 196–97
    geographical proximity 183, 184, 185, 187, 192–94
    ideological proximity 183, 184, 185
    institutional geography 185, 200
    location issues 183
    partner agencies 184, 194–97, 198–99, 201
    'passive' institutional approach 185, **185**, 195–96, 200
    study findings 191–99
    study methods 189–91
    YOTs (youth offending teams) 184, 186, 187, 192–94, 197, 198–99, 200
conditionality in welfare provision 212, 251, 252, 272, 278
    and homelessness 208
conference content and race in Social Policy 2, 27, 44, **46**

Conservative governments 251,
252–53, 279
see also austerity; Coalition
(Conservative -Liberal Democrat)
government
constructivist grounded theory
(CGT) 254
Consumer Price Index (CPI) 213
Convention for Refugees, 1951 12
co-residence of young people in
family home 94, 102–3, 124–25,
126, 127
Council Tax Support 219
CPI (Consumer Price Index) 213
Craig, Gary 1, 2–3, 25–50
SPA The missing dimension report
1–2, 5, 8–9
creativity, and austerity 236
Crenshaw, K. 11
Crick, Bernard 14
Crick Report 164
Crime and Disorder Act 1998 184
Crossley, Stephen 208–9, 271–90
CRT (Critical Race Theory) 10, 11
CSP (Critical Social Policy) 26, 44, **45**
CTC (Child Tax Credits) 214
cultural awareness of local landscapes;
British-Asian Muslim Macken
young women in Sunderland
study 60–62
cultural education in the UK 95,
163–66
communitarian 171–74, 175
'fundamental British values'
173–74, 176
neoliberal 95, 168–71, 175
'neoliberal communitarian' model
of governance 163–64, 174–77
policy context 167–68
study method 166–67
cultural ignorance and racism;
British-Asian Muslim Macken
young women in Sunderland
study 58–60
Cultural Literacy in Europe network
165
cultural racism; British-Asian Muslim
Macken young women in
Sunderland study 58, 59–60, 61
cultural services, and austerity 232
culture, economic value of 169
Cumbria; libraries and austerity 233,
234
curriculum content and race in Social
Policy 2, 27, 40

D

Dagdeviren, H. 239
Davidson, Emma 208, 227–48
DCMS (Department for Digital,
Culture, Media and Sport) 168
deep diversity 14
Delgado, R. 10–11
demographic crisis, in Poland 77–78,
81–82
Department for Digital, Culture,
Media and Sport (DCMS) 168
Department of Business, Innovation
and Skills (BIS) 33, 35
Department of Work and Pensions
(DWP) 282–83
devolution, and welfare provision
1616
Devon; libraries and austerity 236
Digital Marketplace website 282
digital welfare system see IT
(information technology)
disability welfare provision, Estonia
84
Disney, T. 280–81
diversity:
and solidarity 13–15
super-diverse spaces 52
tolerance and respect for 173–74
DNA records 8
dress, and cultural racism; British-
Asian Muslim Macken young
women in Sunderland study 58,
59–60, 61
'dual exclusion' 64
Duncan Smith, I. 252, 253
DWP (Department of Work and
Pensions) 282–83

E

Earned Income Tax Credits (US) 128
East Ayrshire; libraries and austerity
234
Eastern region of England; libraries
and austerity 232, 233, **233**
Economic and Social Research
Council (ESRC) 26
economic growth, and culture 169
economic hardship in young
adulthood see Sweden; young
people's labour market trajectories
education:
and community youth justice in
England and Wales 187–88,
196–97

policy reforms 165
PRUs (pupil referral units) 188,
 196–97
see also higher education
EHRC (Equality and Human Rights
 Commission) 6, 7
Eliot, T.S. 12
emergency hardship payments 212
employment:
flexible/precarious 93, 100
and homelessness 258–59
Employment and Support Allowance
 251
England:
children in care 280
cultural literacy education 167
infant mortality rates 275
libraries and austerity 232, 233,
 233, 234, 236
life expectancy 275
local government and austerity 227,
 228, 229–30
see also community youth justice,
 England and Wales
Equality Act 2010 53, 54
Equality and Human Rights
 Commission (EHRC) 6, 7
Equality Challenge Unit 7
Esping-Andersen, G. 17, 99
ESRC (Economic and Social
 Research Council) 26
Estonia:
ethnic Russians in 73
neoliberalism in 75, 76, 82
return migration and welfare state
 3–4, 75, 76, 77, 82–86, 87
self-sufficiency in 75, 76, 82–86
Ethnic and Racial Studies 44
EU (European Union); social security
 portability policies 3, 71, 74,
 76–77
Evans, G. 15
everyday racism 11, 54, 60–61
ex-offenders, and homelessness 250,
 257

F
families:
Family Nurse Programme 279
importance of in Poland's welfare
 system 79–82
TFP (Troubled Families
 Programme) 276, 279, 280, 281

family welfare support for young
 people 93–94, 97–98, 99, 102–3,
 106–7, 110–11, 112–13, 114–18,
 138–39
explicit resources; residential
 independence 124–25
implicit resources 123–24
moving back into family home 94,
 102–3, 124–25, 126, 127
policy implications 127–28
and race 109, **112–13, 114–17,**
 118–22, 126
research implications 126–27
as a safety net 97, 102, 124–25, 126
as a scaffold 97, 102, 124, 126
UK 93, 94
US 94
Farage, S. 272
Far-Right political activity,
 Sunderland 52
Featherstone, David 230–31, 242
fertility rate, Poland 78
Fife; libraries and austerity 233, 234
Findlay-King, Lindsay 231
First World War, and cultural
 education 172
Flintshire; libraries and austerity 233,
 234
food banks 212
Forkert, K. 235, 236
'fundamental British values' 173–74,
 176

G
gender, and labour market inequality
 100
general election, UK, 2010 271
general election, UK, 2019 16
geographical proximity, and
 community youth justice in
 England and Wales 183, 184, 185,
 187, 192–94
Geography and Domestic Residential
 Mobility Database (1990–2016),
 SCB (Statistics Sweden) 139
Germany, Turkish immigrants 73
Giazitzoglu, A. 100
Gieryn, T.F. 277
'gig economy' 93, 100
global financial crisis 2008 207, 276
impact on cultural organisations
 168
public sector finance cuts 176
see also austerity; Great Recession

globalisation, and welfare provision 1616
Goffman, E. 137
Goldberg, T.G. 11
'good citizenship,' and cultural education in the UK 95, 163–66
communitarian cultural education 171–74, 175
'fundamental British values' 173–74, 176
'neoliberal communitarian' model of governance 163–64, 174–77
neoliberal cultural education 168–71, 175
policy context 167–68
study method 166–67
Goodhart, David 2, 13–14, 15
Gordon, P. 13
Goudling, A. 236
Gray, Mia 230
Great Recession 207
see also global financial crisis 2008
Grosfoguel, R. 16, 17
Gruenwald, D. 55

H

Hall, S. 15, 54, 58
Hamilton, Charles 9–10
Hampshire; libraries and austerity 233, 236
Harper, S.R. 37–38
Harries, B. 53, 54
Harris, N. 14
Hastings, Annette 230, 231, 232, 242–43, 278–79
hate crime:
and the Brexit referendum 64
racist 52, 61
HB (Housing Benefit) 220, 258, 259
LHA (Local Housing Allowance) limits 207, 221, 222, 224, 251, 257
Health and Social Care Act 2013 273
health policy 273–74
Healthwatch organisations 274
HEIDI Plus (Higher Education Interactive Dash Board Information) 30
Heins, Elke 93–96
Helm, T. 274
heritage, and cultural education 172–73
HESA (Higher Education Statistics Agency) datasets 27, 30, 31

higher education:
curriculum content and race in Social Policy 2, 27, 40
decolonisation of curricula 1, 8
gender inequalities 7, 40
racial inequalities 7, 8, 9
Russell group universities 7, 35, 43, 47
variation in wage benefits between universities and degree subjects 36
see also race, and Social Policy higher education
Higher Education Interactive Dash Board Information (HEIDI Plus) 30
Higher Education Statistics Agency (HESA) datasets 27, 30, 31
Hirsch, Donald 165, 166, 207–8, 211–25
history:
and cultural education 172–73
Race, ethnicity & equality in UK History: A report and resource for change. RHS (Royal Historical Society) 1, 5, 9, 47
Holmes, C. 17
Home Office, hostile environment policies 12, 13, 51, 54
homelessness, and austerity 208, 249, 264–66
barriers to 'independence' 255–60
being stuck in the system 260–62
current debates in service provision 253–54
Housing First model 254, 265
non-statutory services 253–54
policy context 250–52
research design 254–55
services under strain 262–64
'treatment first' model 254
voluntary sector services 250, 262–64, 264–65
'worklessness and dependency' cultures 252–53
Homelessness Reduction Act 2017 251
Horváth, I. 74
hostile environment policies 12, 13, 51, 54
housing:
and homelessness 251
price rises 93
and young people 128

see also affordable housing; PRS (private rented sector); social housing
Housing Benefit *see* HB (Housing Benefit)
Housing First model of homelessness assistance 254, 265

I

ideological proximity, and community youth justice in England and Wales 183, 184, 185
Ilmakunnas, I. 138
immigration:
   and cultural education in the UK 163–64
   hostile environment policies 12, 13, 51, 54
   Income Support (IS) 211, 213, 214, *216*
Indian students, and higher education 33
infant mortality rates 275
information technology *see* IT (information technology)
Institute and Faculty for Actuaries 275
Institute for Fiscal Studies 207
institutional canon of UK 171
institutional geography, and community youth justice in England and Wales 185, 200
institutional racism:
   London Metropolitan Police Service 9, 10
   in the welfare system 17
intergenerational monetary transfers 102
intergenerational wealth divide 93
internal others 73
international affairs, and culture 170–71
Irving, Z. 40
IS (Income Support) 211, 213, 214, *216*
Islamophobia 3, 55, 61
IT (information technology):
   and access to welfare services 209, 238–39, 272, 277, 282–83
   and TFP (Troubled Families Programme) 281–82

J

Jobseeker's Allowance (JSA) 101, 208, 213, 214, 251, 259
Johnson, Boris 209
Jones, D. 278, 280
Jones, G. 99
Joseph Rowntree Foundation 7
journal content and race in Social Policy 1, 2, 26, 44, **45**, 46
Journal of Migration Studies 44
JSA (Jobseeker's Allowance) 101, 208, 213, 214, 251, 259
JSP (Journal of Social Policy) 44, **45**

K

Kahlmeter, Anna 94–95, 135–62
Kalmus, V. 75
Khan, Sara 52
King, H. 101
Kymlicka, W. 14

L

Labour governments 214
   and regionalism 273
labour market:
   gender inequality 100
   racial and ethnic inequalities 6–7, 100
   and young people 97, 99–100, **106–7**, 109, **110–11**, **112–13**, **114–17**, **118–22**
   see also Sweden; young people's labour market trajectories
Lancashire; libraries and austerity 233
Lawrence, Stephen 9, 10
Leverhulme Trust 237
Levitas, Ruth 231
Lewisham; libraries and austerity 235, 236
LHA (Local Housing Allowance) limits 207, 221, *222*, 224, 251, 257
Liberty 51
libraries, and austerity 208, 228–29, 232–34, **233**, 241–45, 277–78, 283
   austerity localism 234–36, **235**, 243–44
   co-location with other services 228, 229
   health and well-being benefits of libraries 239–40
   managerialism 241

study method and findings 237–41
support workers' use of 239–40
transfer to charitable trust/
community management 228,
235–36
volunteers 228, 229, 235, **235**,
240–41, 242, 244, 278
life expectancy 275
literary canon of UK 171
local government:
and austerity 208, 227–28, 229–30,
242–43, 274–75, 277–78
and homelessness 250–51
institutional resilience 231–32
public health responsibilities 274
Local Housing Allowance (LHA)
limits 207, 221, *222*, 224, 251,
257
Localism Act 2011 251, 257
localism, shift to from regionalism
273–74
location, of youth justice services *see*
community youth justice, England
and Wales
London:
libraries and austerity 233
local government and austerity 230
London Metropolitan Police Service,
institutional racism in 9, 10
Longitudinal Integration Database
for Health Insurance and Labour
Market Studies (1990–2016), SCB
(Statistics Sweden) 139
Lowndes, Vivien 231–32

M

MacDonald, R. 100
MacPherson Report 9, 10
Maine, F. 165–66
managerialism, and libraries 241
Manchester 53
Manchester City Council, TFP
(Troubled Families Programme)
281
Marshall, T.H. 73
'matter of course' hypothesis of
economic hardship in young
adulthood 139, 151, 152
May, Theresa 51, 284
mayors, elected 274
McCaughie, Kerry 231–32
Meer, Nasar 2, 5–23
mental ill health, and homelessness
250, 256, 263

#MeToo 1
migration:
and everyday bordering 12–13
and hostile environment policies
12, 13
'othering' of migrants 3–4, 71,
72–73, 86
and welfare tourism 74
MIS (Minimum Income Standard)
207–8, 218–19, *219*
'Mobile Welfare in a Transnational
Europe: An Analysis of Portability
Regimes of Social Security
Rights' (TRANSWEL) research
project 76
monocultural failed spaces 52
Sunderland 53, 56, 62–63
monocultural landscapes *see* British-
Asian Muslim Macken young
women in Sunderland study
multiculturalism 164, 165, 172, 176
multiple others 73
Murji, K. 9, 18
'muscular liberalism' 176
Muslims:
Islamophobia 3, 55
Muslim identity 55
prison population 8
see also British-Asian Muslim
Macken young women in
Sunderland study
Myes, J. 15

N

National Agency for Education data
(Sweden), 1987–2016 139
National Assistance 214
National Assistance Act 1948 213
National Audit Office 227–28,
229–30, 274–75
National Crime Intelligence DNA
Database 8
National Education Opportunity
Network 33
National Gallery 168
National Health Service (NHS) 274
'national icons' 172
National Longitudinal Survey of
Youth, US, 1997 93, 103–4, **105**,
112–13, **114–17**, **118–22**, 123–26
national parks 172
National Union on Students 9
nation-states, and othering 72–73

NEET (young people not in
employment, education or
training) 138
'neoliberal communitarian' model of
governance 95, 163–64, 174–77
see also cultural education in the
UK
neoliberal cultural education in the
UK 95, 168–71, 175
see also cultural education in the
UK
neoliberalism 272–73, 282
New Labour *see* Labour governments
'new progressive's dilemma' in Social
Policy 14–15, 16
New Public Management 175
new racism 71
Newcastle-upon-Tyne 233
Newman, J. 271
NHS (National Health Service) 274
North of England; local government
and austerity 230
North-East of England 278
Northern Ireland; cultural literacy
education 167, 174, 176
North-West of England; libraries and
austerity 232, **233**, 234
Nottinghamshire; libraries and
austerity 233, 236

O

OECD (Organisation for Economic
Cooperation and Development),
youth poverty data 135, 138
online activism 1
Open University 36
Orkney; libraries and austerity 233
Osborne, George 217, 229, 252–53,
276
'othering':
British-Asian Muslim Macken
young women in Sunderland
study 62
internal others 73
multiple others 73

P

Pakistani groups:
housing inequalities 7
labour market inequalities 6
Pakistani students, and higher
education 33
Parekh, B. 14–15

partner agencies, and community
youth justice in England and
Wales 184, 194–97, 198–99, 201
'passive' institutional approach,
community youth justice in
England and Wales 185, **185**,
195–96, 200
Patrick, R. 43–44, 252–53, 284
Paul, K. 53
PC (Pension Credit) 211, 214, 218
pensioners' benefits 208, 211, 214,
215, 217, 218, *219*, 224
Perry, J. 212
Petersoo, P. 73
Phillips, Coretta 2
Phillips, David 229
Phillips, K.R. 99
Pickles, Eric 274
place-conscious education 55
Poland:
demographic crisis 77–78, 81–82
importance of families in welfare
system 79–82
influence of Catholic Church in
75, 76, 79, 80
return migration and welfare state
3–4, 75–76, 77–82, 86–87
Ukrainians in 86
police and crime commissioners 274
Policy and Politics 26
Pomati, Marco 207–9
portability of rights to welfare
provision 3, 71, 74, 76–77
see also return migration
poverty:
'poverty porn' 276
theories of 136–37
Powell, M. 99
'Prevent' strategy 172
PRISMA (Preferred Reporting Items
for Systematic Reviews and Meta-
Analyses) framework 166
prison population, racial inequalities
in 8
private rented sector *see* PRS (private
rented sector)
'progressive's dilemma' 2, 13–14,
15, 18
'pro-poor' services, and austerity
230, 242–43
PRS (private rented sector) 128
and homelessness 251, 257–58
LHA (Local Housing Allowance)
limits 207, 221, *222*, 224, 251,
257

PRUs (pupil referral units) 188,
196–97
psychological distress, and economic
hardship 137, 152
public health policies 273–74
public libraries *see* libraries
public realm 243–44
pupil referral units (PRUs) 188,
196–97

Q

Quality Assurance Agency 43, 44

R

race:
and family welfare support for
young people 109, **112–13,**
114–17, 118–22, 126
and higher education 7, 8, 9
and labour market inequality 100
and Social Policy 1–4, 5–9, 18,
25–26
everyday bordering 2, 12–13, 18
institutional racism 2, 5, 9–11, 18
provenance and revision 16–18
and 'solidarities' 2, 13–15, 18
SPA's profile in relation to 'race'
2–3, 43–44, **45–46,** 46
'whiteness' of Social Policy 41–42
and Social Policy higher education
2, 25–26, 46–47
BAME (black and minority
ethnic) academics 2, 27, 28, 29,
30, 32, 40–41
BAME (black and minority
ethnic) students 2, 27, 28,
29–33, **31,** *32,* **34,** *35,* 35–40,
37, 42–43, 46–47
curricula 2, 27, 40
experts' views 27, 41–43
literature review 32–33, *34, 35,*
35–41, *37*
published data 30–32, **31**
study overview 27
survey **28,** 28–31
teaching and learning
environment 32, 37–40
see also racial and ethnic
inequalities; racism
'Race disparity audit,' Cabinet Office
6, 7–8
Race Relations Act 1968 10
racial and ethnic inequalities:
austerity policies 6

higher education 7
housing 7–8
labour market 6–7
poverty 6
racial hate crime 61
and Brexit 52, 64
racism 3, 53, 54
British-Asian Muslim Macken
young women in Sunderland
study 58–60, 60–61, 64
institutional racism 2, 5, 9–11, 18
social desensitisation to 11
in 1960s Britain 53
Razak, Amina 3, 51–70
Rees, James 1–4
Reeve, K. 252
Reeves, Rachel 276
refugees 12
see also migration
regeneration, and culture 170
Regional Growth Fund 273
regionalism, shift to localism 273–74
religious hate crimes 59, 60–61
'resilience' 231–32
Resolution Foundation 221
responsibility, and cultural literacy
policies in the UK 95
return migration 72, 74
Estonia 3–4, 75, 76, 77, 82–86, 87
'othering' of migrants in 3–4, 72
Poland 3–4, 75–76, 77–82, 86–87
Rhodes Must Fall 1
Rhondda Cyon Taff; libraries and
austerity 233
RHS (Royal Historical Society); *Race,
ethnicity & equality in UK History:
A report and resource for change* 1,
5, 9, 47
Rollock, N. 7
rough sleeping 250, 255
see also homelessness, and austerity
Royal Historical Society *see* RHS
(Royal Historical Society)
Runnymede Trust 13, 35
Rushton, P. 52
Russell group universities 7, 35, 43,
47

S

Saar, Maarja 3–4, 71–91
safe spaces 55–56
British-Asian Muslim Macken
young women in Sunderland
study 56

'safety net' welfare provision in the UK *see* welfare provision
scarring, and economic hardship 137, 151, 152
SCB (Statistics Sweden):
Geography and Domestic Residential Mobility Database (1990–2016) 139
Longitudinal Integration Database for Health Insurance and Labour Market Studies (1990–2016) 139
Schels, B. 138
Schwengel, Hermann 243–44
Scotland:
cultural literacy education 167, 176
libraries and austerity 228–29, 232, 233, **233**, 234, 236, 237–41
local government and austerity 227
self-esteem, and economic hardship 137
self-regulation, and cultural literacy policies in the UK 95
SELMA (Social Exclusion and Labour Market Attachment) model 141, **141**
Senior, N. 33, 37
Shafer, J. 189
Sheller, M. 189
Shropshire; libraries and austerity 236
Sibley, D. 65n1
Sippola, M. 85
skin colour, and biological racism; British-Asian Muslim Macken young women in Sunderland study 58, 61
Smeeding, T.M. 99
Smith, G. 277
Smith, M. 15
'smokescreens' 11
SNAP (Supplemental Nutrition Assistance Program), US 102
Social Administration Association 25
social care services, and local government funding cuts 228
social citizenship 73
Social Exclusion and Labour Market Attachment (SELMA) model 141, **141**
social housing 128
and homelessness 251, 257
racial inequalities in 7–8
social media, and online activism 1
Social Policy and Administration 26
Social Policy and Society (SPS) 44, **45**

Social Policy Association *see* SPA (Social Policy Association)
Social policy Review (SPR) 26, 44, **45**
social rights 73–74
social welfare provision *see* welfare provision
social work practices 280–81
socialist movements, race and class solidarity in 15
Sociology, racial inequality in 5
sofa surfing 250, 255
see also homelessness, and austerity
Sojka, Bozena 3–4, 71–91
'solidarities,' and Social Policy 13–15
South of England; local government and austerity 230
South West Yorkshire; CAMHS (Child and Adolescent Mental Health Services) 187–88
South-East of England; libraries and austerity 232, 233, **233**
South-West of England; libraries and austerity 233, **233**
Soviet Union 75
SPA (Social Policy Association) 1–2, 25
BAME action plan 4
conferences 2, 27, 44, **46**, 93
The missing dimension report 1–2, 5, 8–9
profile in relation to 'race' 2–3, 43–44, **45–46**, 46–47
publications 27, 44
'Race, Racism and Social Policy' conference, 2019 6
REF2021 (Research Excellence Framework 2021) 1
see also race, and Social Policy
higher education
Spare Room Subsidy ('bedroom tax') 207, 220, 221, *222*, 224, 275, 280
Spending Review 2010 229
SPR (Social policy review) 26, 44, **45**
SPS (Social Policy and Society) 44, **45**
St Mungo's 250
Stamou, Eleni 95, 163–82
St-Arnaud, S. 15
Statistics Sweden *see* SCB (Statistics Sweden)
statutory homelessness 250
see also homelessness, and austerity
Stevenson, J. 39
stigma, and economic hardship 137, 151

Stoke-on-Trent; libraries and austerity 234
strategic health authorities 273
Stuckler, D. 275
substance abuse, and homelessness 250, 256, 261, 263
Suffolk; libraries and austerity 236
Sunderland:
  social and political context 52
  see also British-Asian Muslim Macken young women in Sunderland study
super-diverse spaces 52
Supplemental Nutrition Assistance Program (SNAP), US 102
Supplementary Benefit 213, 214, *216*
Supporting People 250
Sweden:
  education system 135
  young people's labour market trajectories 94–95, 135–36, 151–53
    Appendix **158–62**
    data and methodology 139–43, **141**
    labour market establishment sequences **146**, 146–47, *148*, **149**, 150
    sensitivity analysis **150**, 150–51
    study results 143, **144–45**, **146**, 146–47, *148*, **149**, **150**, 150–51
    theory and previous research 136–39
  youth poverty rate 135, 138
Swedish National Council for Crime Prevention data, 1973–2017 139

T

Taha, N. 71
Temporary Assistance for Needy Families (US) 101
terrorism 172, 176
TFP (Troubled Families Programme) 276, 279, 280, 281
Titmuss, Richard 17
Tonkiss, Katherine 95, 163–82
Total Population Register, Sweden 139
Townsend, P. 218
Trades Union Congress 6

TRANSWEL ('Mobile Welfare in a Transnational Europe: An Analysis of Portability Regimes of Social Security Rights') research project 76
'treatment first' model of homelessness assistance 254
Triandafyllidou, A. 73
Troubled Families Programme (TFP) 276, 279, 280, 281
two-child limit on welfare benefits 207, 220, 221, *222*, 224

U

UCAS (Universities and Colleges Admissions Service) datasets 27, 30, 31, 35
unemployment:
  racial inequalities in 6
  and young people 93
United Nations (UN) Special Rapporteur on Contemporary Forms of Racism, Racial Discrimination, Xenophobia and Related Intolerance 5–6
United Nations (UN) Special Rapporteur on Extreme Poverty and Human Rights 5, 7, 207, 272
Universal Credit 207, 212, 238–39, 251, 258, 259, 283
universities:
  decolonisation of curricula 1, 8
  Russell group universities 7, 35, 43, 47
  see also higher education
Universities and Colleges Admissions Service (UCAS) datasets 27, 30, 31, 35
Universities UK 9
University of Bedfordshire 30
University of East London 36
University of Oxford 1

V

Vihalemm, T. 75
Virdee, S. 15
voluntary sector:
  and austerity 274, 275, 278
  and homelessness 250, 262–64, 264–65
volunteering:
  and libraries 228, 229, 235, **235**, 240–41, 242, 244, 278
  and welfare benefit reforms 278

W

Wacquant, Loic 272–73, 276, 282
Wakefield:
libraries and austerity 233
PRUs (pupil referral units) 188
Wales:
cultural literacy education 167,
173, 174, 176
infant mortality rates 275
libraries and austerity 232, 233,
233, 234
life expectancy 275
local government and austerity 227
see also community youth justice,
England and Wales
Wallace, C. 99
Walther, A. 127
Weakley, Sarah 93–94, 97–133,
137–38
Webster, David 279
welfare benefits *see* CTC (Child
Tax Credits); Employment and
Support Allowance; HB (Housing
Benefit); IS (Income Support);
JSA (Jobseeker's Allowance);
PC (Pension Credit); Universal
Credit; welfare provision;
Working Tax Credits
'welfare chauvinism' 13
welfare mix, and young people 99
welfare provision 17, 73–74, 83, 84,
93, 128, 207
cuts in 207, 228, 229–30, 238
Estonia 3–4, 75, 76, 77, 82–86, 87
generation transmission of 138
and homelessness 251–52
impact on volunteering 278
and IT (information technology)
209, 238–39, 272, 277, 282–83
and migration 12–13, 71–72,
72–74
return migration 3–4, 71, 72,
76–87
Poland 3–4, 75–76, 77–82, 86–87
portability of rights to 3, 71, 74,
76–77
and race 13, 17
'safety net' provision in the UK
207–8, 211–13, 223–25
basic entitlement levels 213–15,
215, *216*, 217–19, *219*
'bedroom tax' (Spare Room
Subsidy) 207, 220, 221, *222*,
224

benefit cap 207, 212, 220, 221,
222, 224
benefit sanctions 207, 212, 223,
251, 252, 259, 272, 278, 279
breaking of link with inflation/
prices 213, 217
breaking the entitlement/need
link 219–21, **222**
children's benefits 214, *215*, 217,
218, *219*
conditionality 212, 251, 252,
272, 278
LHA (Local Housing Allowance)
limits 207, 221, *222*, 224, 251,
257
MIS (Minimum Income Standard)
207–8, 218–19, *219*
pensioners' benefits 208, 214,
215, 217, 218, *219*, 224
two-child limit 207, 220, 221,
222, 224
working age benefits 207,
211–12, 214, *215*, 217, 218–19,
219, 224–25
Southern European policies 128
and young people 93, 94, 97, 99,
101–2, 104, 106, **106–7**, **108–9**,
128
welfare states *see* welfare provision
welfare tourism 74
West Midlands, England 278
libraries and austerity 232, 233,
233
West Sussex; TFP (Troubled Families
Programme) 281
Whiteman, Rob 232
whiteness 10
and British identity 53
of Social Policy 41–42
Why is My Curriculum White? 1, 8
Williams, F. 5, 8, 17
Williams, Rowan 274
'Windrush generation' 12, 13
Wootton, Malgorzata 95, 163–82
working age benefits 207, 211–12,
214, *215*, 217, 218–19, *219*,
224–25
Working Tax Credits 128
world heritage sites 172

X

xeno-racism 59, 72

Y

YAV (Young Asian Voices) youth project, Sunderland *see* British-Asian Muslim Macken young women in Sunderland study
YOTs (youth offending teams) 184, 186, 187, 192–94, 197, 198–99, 200
  see also community youth justice, England and Wales
young BAME (black and minority ethnic) groups:
  unemployment 6
  see also British-Asian Muslim Macken young women in Sunderland study
Young, P. 40
young people:
  and housing 128
  impact of austerity policies on 93
  and the labour market 93
  labour market trajectories in Sweden 94–95, 135–36, 151–53
    Appendix **158–62**
    data and methodology 139–43, **141**
    study results 143, **144–45, 146,** 146–47, *148,* **149, 150,** 150–51
    theory and previous research 136–39
  see also community youth justice, England and Wales; family welfare support for young people; youth transitions

young women *see* British-Asian Muslim Macken young women in Sunderland study
youth justice, England and Wales *see* community youth justice, England and Wales
youth offending teams (YOTs) 184, 186, 187, 192–94, 197, 198–99, 200
  see also community youth justice, England and Wales
youth transitions:
  economic independence and the welfare mix 98–103
  family welfare support 93–94, 97–98, 99, 102–3, **106–7, 110–11, 112–13, 114–18,** 123–28, 138–39
  and the labour market 97, 99–100, **106–7,** 109, **110–11, 112–13, 114–17, 118–22**
  policy implications 127–28
  and race 109, **112–13, 114–17, 118–22,** 126
  research implications 126–27
  study methodology 103–4, **105**
  and welfare provision 94, 97, 99, 101–2, 104, 106, **106–7, 108–9**
  see also young people, labour market trajectories in Sweden
YTS (Youth Training Scheme), UK 101, 106

Z

'zones of freedom' 55–56
Zubrzycki, G. 76